Mastering Concurrency Programming with Java 8

Master the principles and techniques of multithreaded programming with the Java 8 Concurrency API

Javier Fernández González

BIRMINGHAM - MUMBAI

Mastering Concurrency Programming with Java 8

Copyright © 2016 Packt Publishing

All rights reserved. No part of this book may be reproduced, stored in a retrieval system, or transmitted in any form or by any means, without the prior written permission of the publisher, except in the case of brief quotations embedded in critical articles or reviews.

Every effort has been made in the preparation of this book to ensure the accuracy of the information presented. However, the information contained in this book is sold without warranty, either express or implied. Neither the authors, nor Packt Publishing, and its dealers and distributors will be held liable for any damages caused or alleged to be caused directly or indirectly by this book.

Packt Publishing has endeavored to provide trademark information about all of the companies and products mentioned in this book by the appropriate use of capitals. However, Packt Publishing cannot guarantee the accuracy of this information.

First published: February 2016

Production reference: 1220216

Published by Packt Publishing Ltd.
Livery Place
35 Livery Street
Birmingham B3 2PB, UK.

ISBN 978-1-78588-612-6

www.packtpub.com

Credits

Author
Javier Fernández González

Reviewers
Antonio Gomes Rodrigues
Bradley Symons
Tagir Valeev

Commissioning Editor
Dipika Gaonkar

Acquisition Editor
Tushar Gupta

Content Development Editor
Shali Deeraj

Technical Editor
Gaurav Suri

Copy Editor
Dipti Mankame

Project Coordinator
Kinjal Bari

Proofreaders
Safis Editing

Indexers
Priya Sane

Graphics
Kirk D'Penha

Production Coordinator
Shantanu N. Zagade

Cover Work
Shantanu N. Zagade

About the Author

Javier Fernández González is a software architect with almost 15 years' experience with Java technologies. He has worked as a teacher, researcher, programmer, analyst, writer, and now as an architect in all types of projects related to Java, especially J2EE. As a teacher, he has taught over 1,000 hours of training in basic Java, J2EE, and Struts framework. As a researcher, he has worked in the field of information retrieval, developing applications in order to process large amounts of data in Java and has been a part of several journal articles and conference presentations as a coauthor. In recent years, he has worked on developing J2EE web applications for various clients from different sectors (public administration, insurance, healthcare, transportation, and so on). Currently, he is working as a software architect at Capgemini, which includes developing and maintaining applications for an insurance company. Also, he is the author of the book *Java 7 Concurrency Cookbook, Packt Publishing*.

> To Nuria, Paula, and Pelayo, for your infinite love and patience.

About the Reviewers

Antonio Gomes Rodrigues has worked with high-traffic websites, traders applications, Cloud applications, and so on. He has experience of working with many performance tools, such as JProfiler, Yourkit, VisualVM, Dynatrace, AppDynamics, Introscope, NewRelic, JMeter, LoadRunner, and so on. To put in place, he has worked on performance strategies, load testing, training, troubleshooting, and so on. He shares his knowledge in his French blog (http://arodrigues.developpez.com/), conferences, and book reviews.

> I would like to thank my wife Aurélie for her support and my child Timothée.

Bradley Symons graduated with a BSc (Hons) degree in Computer Science and has gained the Oracle Java Professional Programmer certification. His current occupation is as a Java server-side developer, but he has previously worked with a variety of languages, including Ruby and Python. With over a decade of coding experience, he has worked for a variety of business sectors, including AI, Finance, Travel, and Entertainment. He is highly interested in Spring, AOP, and concurrency. Currently, he is learning Cuba among other recent developments within the Java world. He is well-regarded as an avid follower of coding best practices, refactoring patterns, and TDD. He personally expresses his admiration for the technical contributions from the legendary Martin Fowler.

> I would like to thank Jim Combes, my old team lead, for offering me the role as a Java Developer and allowing my enthusiastic interest in Java to grow and develop over the years.

Tagir Valeev, PhD, is a research assistant in A.P. Ershov Institute of Informatics Systems, Novosibirsk, Russia, and a lead developer in Development Group Ltd., Novosibirsk, Russia. He is a Java programming professional, a contributor to the FindBugs project (Java static analysis tool), and the author of the StreamEx project, which enhances the Java 8 Stream API. He is also officially an OpenJDK author, contributing enhancements and bug fixes in Stream API implementation. He answered many questions on StackOverflow related to Stream API and Java concurrency.

> Big thanks to my wife Ekaterina and my son Artyom, for support and patience which helped me so much to finish the reviewing.

www.PacktPub.com

eBooks, discount offers, and more

Did you know that Packt offers eBook versions of every book published, with PDF and ePub files available? You can upgrade to the eBook version at www.PacktPub.com and as a print book customer, you are entitled to a discount on the eBook copy. Get in touch with us at customercare@packtpub.com for more details.

At www.PacktPub.com, you can also read a collection of free technical articles, sign up for a range of free newsletters and receive exclusive discounts and offers on Packt books and eBooks.

https://www2.packtpub.com/books/subscription/packtlib

Do you need instant solutions to your IT questions? PacktLib is Packt's online digital book library. Here, you can search, access, and read Packt's entire library of books.

Why subscribe?

- Fully searchable across every book published by Packt
- Copy and paste, print, and bookmark content
- On demand and accessible via a web browser

Table of Contents

Preface	**xi**
Chapter 1: The First Step – Concurrency Design Principles	**1**
Basic concurrency concepts	**1**
Concurrency versus parallelism	2
Synchronization	2
Immutable object	3
Atomic operations and variables	4
Shared memory versus message passing	4
Possible problems in concurrent applications	**4**
Data race	4
Deadlock	5
Livelock	6
Resource starvation	6
Priority inversion	7
A methodology to design concurrent algorithms	**7**
The starting point – a sequential version of the algorithm	7
Step 1 – analysis	8
Step 2 – design	8
Step 3 – implementation	9
Step 4 – testing	9
Step 5 – tuning	9
Conclusion	11
Java concurrency API	**12**
Basic concurrency classes	12
Synchronization mechanisms	12
Executors	13
The Fork/Join framework	14

  Parallel streams   14
  Concurrent data structures   15
 Concurrency design patterns   **15**
  Signaling   16
  Rendezvous   16
  Mutex   17
  Multiplex   17
  Barrier   18
  Double-checked locking   18
  Read-write lock   19
  Thread pool   20
  Thread local storage   20
 The Java memory model   **20**
 Tips and tricks to design concurrent algorithms   **21**
  Identify the correct independent tasks   22
  Implement concurrency at the highest possible level   22
  Take scalability into account   23
  Use thread-safe APIs   23
  Never assume an execution order   24
  Prefer local thread variables over static and shared when possible   24
  Find the more easily parallelizable version of the algorithm   25
  Using immutable objects when possible   25
  Avoiding deadlocks by ordering the locks   26
  Using atomic variables instead of synchronization   27
  Holding locks for as short a time as possible   28
  Taking precautions using lazy initialization   29
  Avoiding the use of blocking operations inside a critical section   29
 Summary   **30**
Chapter 2: Managing Lots of Threads – Executors   **31**
 An introduction to executors   **31**
  Basic characteristics of executors   32
  Basic components of the executor framework   33
 First example – the k-nearest neighbors algorithm   **33**
  K-nearest neighbors – serial version   34
  K-nearest neighbors – a fine-grained concurrent version   36
  K-nearest neighbors – a coarse-grained concurrent version   40
  Comparing the solutions   42

The second example – concurrency in a client/server environment	**44**
Client/server – serial version	45
The DAO part	45
The command part	45
The server part	47
Client/server – parallel version	48
The server part	49
The command part	53
Extra components of the concurrent server	53
Comparing the two solutions	**61**
Other methods of interest	**63**
Summary	**64**
Chapter 3: Getting the Maximum from Executors	**67**
Advanced characteristics of executors	**67**
Cancellation of tasks	68
Scheduling the execution of tasks	68
Overriding the executor methods	69
Changing some initialization parameters	69
The first example – an advanced server application	**70**
The ServerExecutor class	71
The statistics object	71
The rejected task controller	72
The executor tasks	73
The executor	74
The command classes	77
The ConcurrentCommand class	77
Concrete commands	79
The server part	81
The ConcurrentServer class	81
The RequestTask class	85
The client part	88
The second example – executing periodic tasks	**89**
The common parts	90
The basic reader	92
The advanced reader	96
Additional information about executors	**100**
Summary	**101**

Chapter 4: Getting Data from the Tasks – The Callable and Future Interfaces — **103**

Introducing the Callable and Future interfaces — **103**
- The Callable interface — 104
- The Future interface — 104

First example – a best-matching algorithm for words — **105**
- The common classes — 106
  - A best-matching algorithm – the serial version — 107
    - The BestMatchingSerialCalculation class — 107
    - The BestMachingSerialMain class — 108
  - A best-matching algorithm – the first concurrent version — 109
    - The BestMatchingBasicTask class — 110
    - The BestMatchingBasicConcurrentCalculation class — 111
  - A best-matching algorithm – the second concurrent version — 114
  - The word exists algorithm – a serial version — 115
    - The ExistSerialCalculation class — 116
    - The ExistSerialMain class — 116
  - The word exists algorithm – the concurrent version — 117
    - The ExistBasicTasks class — 117
    - The ExistBasicConcurrentCalculation class — 119
    - The ExistBasicConcurrentMain class — 120
  - Comparing the solutions — 120
    - Best-matching algorithms — 120
    - Exist algorithms — 122

The second example – creating an inverted index for a collection of documents — **123**
- Common classes — 124
  - The Document class — 124
  - The DocumentParser class — 124
- The serial version — 125
- The first concurrent version – a task per document — 127
  - The IndexingTask class — 128
  - The InvertedIndexTask class — 129
  - The ConcurrentIndexing class — 130
- The second concurrent version – multiple documents per task — 133
  - The MultipleIndexingTask class — 133
  - The MultipleInvertedIndexTask class — 134
  - The MultipleConcurrentIndexing class — 135
- Comparing the solutions — 136
- Other methods of interest — 137

Summary — **138**

Chapter 5: Running Tasks Divided into Phases – The Phaser Class — 141
An introduction to the Phaser class — 142
Registration and deregistration of participants — 142
Synchronizing phase changes — 143
Other functionalities — 143
First example – a keyword extraction algorithm — 144
Common classes — 146
- The Word class — 146
- The Keyword class — 147
- The Document class — 148
- The DocumentParser class — 149

The serial version — 150
The concurrent version — 154
- The KeywordExtractionTask class — 154
- The ConcurrentKeywordExtraction class — 159

Comparing the two solutions — 161
The second example – a genetic algorithm — 162
Common classes — 164
- The Individual class — 164
- The GeneticOperators class — 165

The serial version — 166
- The SerialGeneticAlgorithm class — 167
- The SerialMain class — 168

The concurrent version — 169
- The SharedData class — 170
- The GeneticPhaser class — 171
- The ConcurrentGeneticTask class — 172
- The ConcurrentGeneticAlgorithm class — 175
- The ConcurrentMain class — 176

Comparing the two solutions — 177
- The Lau15 dataset — 177
- The Kn57 dataset — 177
- Conclusions — 178

Summary — 178

Chapter 6: Optimizing Divide and Conquer Solutions – The Fork/Join Framework — 181
An introduction to the Fork/Join framework — 182
Basic characteristics of the Fork/Join framework — 183
Limitations of the Fork/Join framework — 184
Components of the Fork/Join framework — 184

- **The first example – the k-means clustering algorithm** — 185
  - The common classes — 187
    - The VocabularyLoader class — 188
    - The Word, Document, and DocumentLoader classes — 188
    - The DistanceMeasurer class — 190
    - The DocumentCluster class — 191
  - The serial version — 192
    - The SerialKMeans class — 192
  - The concurrent version — 195
    - Two tasks for the Fork/Join framework – AssignmentTask and UpdateTask — 196
    - The ConcurrentKMeans class — 199
    - The ConcurrentMain class — 201
  - Comparing the solutions — 201
- **The second example – a data filtering algorithm** — 203
  - Common parts — 203
  - The serial version — 204
    - The SerialSearch class — 204
    - The SerialMain class — 205
  - The concurrent version — 207
    - The TaskManager class — 207
    - The IndividualTask class — 209
    - The ListTask class — 211
    - The ConcurrentSearch class — 213
    - The ConcurrentMain class — 214
  - Comparing the two versions — 214
- **The third example – the merge sort algorithm** — 215
  - Shared classes — 216
  - The serial version — 216
    - The SerialMergeSort class — 217
    - The SerialMetaData class — 219
  - The concurrent version — 220
    - The MergeSortTask class — 220
    - The ConcurrentMergeSort class — 222
    - The ConcurrentMetaData class — 223
  - Comparing the two versions — 223
- **Other methods of the Fork/Join framework** — 224
- **Summary** — 224

Chapter 7: Processing Massive Datasets with Parallel Streams – The Map and Reduce Model — 227

- **An introduction to streams** — 227
  - Basic characteristics of streams — 228
  - Sections of a stream — 229
    - Sources of a stream — 229
    - Intermediate operations — 231
    - Terminal operations — 232

MapReduce versus MapCollect	232
The first example – a numerical summarization application	**233**
The concurrent version	234
The ConcurrentDataLoader class	234
The ConcurrentStatistics class	235
The ConcurrentMain class	243
The serial version	245
Comparing the two versions	245
The second example – an information retrieval search tool	**246**
An introduction to the reduction operation	247
The first approach – full document query	249
The basicMapper() method	250
The Token class	251
The QueryResult class	252
The second approach – reduced document query	253
The limitedMapper() method	253
The third approach – generating an HTML file with the results	254
The ContentMapper class	256
The fourth approach – preloading the inverted index	257
The ConcurrentFileLoader class	258
The fifth approach – using our own executor	259
Getting data from the inverted index – the ConcurrentData class	260
Getting the number of words in a file	260
Getting the average tfxidf value in a file	261
Getting the maximum and minimum tfxidf values in the index	262
The ConcurrentMain class	263
The serial version	264
Comparing the solutions	265
Summary	**269**
Chapter 8: Processing Massive Datasets with Parallel Streams – The Map and Collect Model	**271**
Using streams to collect data	**271**
The collect() method	272
The first example – searching data without an index	**274**
Basic classes	275
The Product class	275
The Review class	276
The ProductLoader class	276
The first approach – basic search	277
The ConcurrentStringAccumulator class	279
The second approach – advanced search	280
The ConcurrentObjectAccumulator class	282

A serial implementation of the example	283
Comparing the implementations	283
The second example – a recommendation system	**284**
Common classes	284
The ProductReview class	285
The ProductRecommendation class	285
The recommendation system – the main class	285
The ConcurrentLoaderAccumulator class	289
The serial version	290
Comparing the two versions	290
The third example – common contacts in a social network	**291**
Base classes	293
The Person class	293
The PersonPair class	293
The DataLoader class	293
The concurrent version	294
The CommonPersonMapper class	294
The ConcurrentSocialNetwork class	295
The ConcurrentMain class	299
The serial version	300
Comparing the two versions	300
Summary	**301**

Chapter 9: Diving into Concurrent Data Structures and Synchronization Utilities — 303

Concurrent data structures	**304**
Blocking and non-blocking data structures	304
Interfaces	305
Classes	308
Using the new features	310
First example with ConcurrentHashMap	310
Another example with ConcurrentHashMap	315
An example with the ConcurrentLinkedDeque class	316
Atomic variables	320
Synchronization mechanisms	**321**
The CommonTask class	322
The Lock interface	323
The Semaphore class	325
The CountDownLatch class	326
The CyclicBarrier class	328
The CompletableFuture class	330
Using the CompletableFuture class	332
Summary	**340**

Chapter 10: Integration of Fragments and Implementation of Alternatives — 341

Big-block synchronization mechanisms — 342
An example of a document clustering application — 342
- The four systems of k-means clustering — 343
  - The Reader system — 343
  - The Indexer system — 345
  - The Mapper system — 347
  - The Clustering system — 348
- The main class of the document clustering application — 349
- Testing our document clustering application — 352

Implementation of alternatives with concurrent programming — 354
- The k-nearest neighbors' algorithm — 354
- Building an inverted index of a collection of documents — 355
- A best-matching algorithm for words — 355
- A genetic algorithm — 356
- A keyword extraction algorithm — 357
- A k-means clustering algorithm — 357
- A filtering data algorithm — 358
- Searching an inverted index — 358
- A numeric summarization algorithm — 359
- A search algorithm without indexing — 359
- A recommendation system using the Map and Collect model — 360

Summary — 360

Chapter 11: Testing and Monitoring Concurrent Applications — 361

Monitoring concurrency objects — 362
- Monitoring a thread — 362
- Monitoring a lock — 364
- Monitoring an executor — 366
- Monitoring the Fork/Join framework — 368
- Monitoring a Phaser — 370
- Monitoring a stream — 371

Monitoring concurrency applications — 372
- The Overview tab — 374
- The Monitor tab — 375
- The Threads tab — 376
- The Sampler tab — 378
- The Profiler tab — 379

Testing concurrency applications — 380
- Testing concurrent applications with MultithreadedTC — 380

Testing concurrent applications with Java Pathfinder	385
Installing Java Pathfinder	385
Running Java Pathfinder	387
Summary	**392**
Index	**393**

Preface

Nowadays, computer systems (and other related systems, such as tablets or smartphones) allow you to do several tasks simultaneously. This can be possible because they have concurrent operating systems that control several tasks at the same time. You can also have one application that executes several tasks (read a file, show a message, or read data over a network) if you work with the concurrency API of your favorite programming language. Java includes a very powerful concurrency API that allows you to implement any kind of concurrency application with little effort. This API increases the features provided to programmers in every version. Now, in Java 8, it has included the stream API and new methods and classes to facilitate the implementation of concurrent applications. This book covers the most important elements of the Java concurrency API, showing you how to use them in real-world applications. These elements are as follows:

- The executor framework, to control the execution of lots of task
- The Phaser class, to execute tasks that can be divided into phases
- The Fork/Join framework, to execute the tasks that solve a problem using the divide and conquer technique
- The stream API, to process big sources of data
- Concurrent data structures, to store the data in concurrent applications
- Synchronization mechanisms, to organize concurrent tasks

However, it includes much more: a methodology to design concurrency applications, design patterns, tips and tricks to implement good concurrency applications, and tools and techniques to test concurrency applications.

What this book covers

Chapter 1, The First Step – Concurrency Design Principles, will teach you the design principles of concurrency applications. They will also learn the possible problems of concurrency applications and a methodology to design them followed by some design patterns, tips, and tricks.

Chapter 2, Managing Lots of Threads – Executors, will teach you the basic principles of the executor framework. This framework allows you to work with lots of threads without creating or managing them. You will implement the k-nearest neighbors algorithm and a basic client/server application.

Chapter 3, Getting the Maximum from Executors, will teach you some advanced characteristics of executors, including cancelation and scheduling of tasks to execute a task after a delay or every certain period of time. You will implement an advanced client/server application and a news reader.

Chapter 4, Getting Data from the Tasks – The Callable and Future Interfaces, will teach you how to work in an executor with tasks that return a result using the Callable and Future interfaces. You will implement a best-matching algorithm and an application to build an inverted index.

Chapter 5, Running Tasks Divided into Phases – The Phaser class, will teach you how to use the Phaser class to execute tasks that can be divided into phases in a concurrent way. You will implement a keyword extraction algorithm and a genetic algorithm.

Chapter 6, Optimizing Divide and Conquer Solutions – The Fork/Join Framework, will teach you how to use a special kind of executor optimized by those problems that can be resolved using the divide and conquer technique: the Fork/Join framework and its work-stealing algorithm. You will implement the k-means clustering algorithm, a data filtering algorithm, and the merge-sort algorithm.

Chapter 7, Processing Massive Datasets with Parallel Streams – The Map and Reduce Model, will teach you how to work with streams to process big datasets. In this chapter, you will learn how to implement map and reduce applications using the stream API and much more functions of streams. You will implement a numerical summarization algorithm and an information retrieval search tool.

Chapter 8, Processing Massive Datasets with Parallel Streams – The Map and Collect Model, will teach you how to use the collect() method of the stream API to perform a mutable reduction of a stream of data into a different data structure, including the predefined collectors defined in the Collectors class. You will implement a tool to search data without indexing, a recommendation system, and an algorithm to calculate the list of common contacts of two persons in a social network.

Chapter 9, Diving into Concurrent Data Structures and Synchronization Utilities, will teach you how to work with the most important concurrent data structures (data structures that can be used in concurrent applications without causing data race conditions) and all the synchronization mechanisms included in the Java concurrency API to organize the execution of tasks.

Chapter 10, Integration of Fragments and Implementation of Alternatives, will teach you how to implement a big application made by fragments of concurrent applications with their own concurrency techniques using shared memory or message passing. You will also learn different implementation alternatives to the examples presented in the book.

Chapter 11, Testing and Monitoring Concurrent Applications, teaches you how to obtain information about the status of some of the Java concurrency API elements (thread, lock, executor, and so on). You will also learn how to monitor a concurrent application using the Java VisualVM application and how to test concurrent applications with the MultithreadedTC library and the Java Pathfinder application.

What you need for this book

To follow this book, you need basic knowledge of the Java programming language. A basic knowledge of concurrency concepts is welcome too.

Who this book is for

If you are a Java developer who knows the basic principles of concurrent programming but you want to get an expert knowledge of the Java concurrency API to develop optimized applications that takes advantage of all the hardware resources of computers, then this book is for you.

Conventions

In this book, you will find a number of text styles that distinguish between different kinds of information. Here are some examples of these styles and an explanation of their meaning.

Code words in text, database table names, folder names, filenames, file extensions, pathnames, dummy URLs, user input, and Twitter handles are shown as follows: "The `Product` class stores the information about a product."

A block of code is set as follows:

```
if (problem.size() > DEFAULT_SIZE) {
    divideTasks();
    executeTask();
    taskResults=joinTasksResult();
    return taskResults;
} else {
    taskResults=solveBasicProblem();
    return taskResults;
}
```

New terms and important words are shown in bold. Words that you see on the screen, for example, in menus or dialog boxes, appear in the text like this: "Leave the default value and click on the **Next** button."

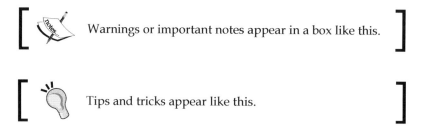

> Warnings or important notes appear in a box like this.

> Tips and tricks appear like this.

Reader feedback

Feedback from our readers is always welcome. Let us know what you think about this book—what you liked or disliked. Reader feedback is important for us as it helps us develop titles that you will really get the most out of.

To send us general feedback, simply e-mail `feedback@packtpub.com`, and mention the book's title in the subject of your message.

If there is a topic that you have expertise in and you are interested in either writing or contributing to a book, see our author guide at `www.packtpub.com/authors`.

Customer support

Now that you are the proud owner of a Packt book, we have a number of things to help you to get the most from your purchase.

Downloading the example code

You can download the example code files from your account at http://www.packtpub.com for all the Packt Publishing books you have purchased. If you purchased this book elsewhere, you can visit http://www.packtpub.com/support and register to have the files e-mailed directly to you.

You can download the code files by following these steps:

1. Log in or register to our website using your e-mail address and password.
2. Hover the mouse pointer on the **SUPPORT** tab at the top.
3. Click on **Code Downloads & Errata**.
4. Enter the name of the book in the **Search** box.
5. Select the book for which you're looking to download the code files.
6. Choose from the drop-down menu where you purchased this book from.
7. Click on **Code Download**.

Once the file is downloaded, please make sure that you unzip or extract the folder using the latest version of:

- WinRAR / 7-Zip for Windows
- Zipeg / iZip / UnRarX for Mac
- 7-Zip / PeaZip for Linux

Errata

Although we have taken every care to ensure the accuracy of our content, mistakes do happen. If you find a mistake in one of our books—maybe a mistake in the text or the code—we would be grateful if you could report this to us. By doing so, you can save other readers from frustration and help us improve subsequent versions of this book. If you find any errata, please report them by visiting http://www.packtpub.com/submit-errata, selecting your book, clicking on the **Errata Submission Form** link, and entering the details of your errata. Once your errata are verified, your submission will be accepted and the errata will be uploaded to our website or added to any list of existing errata under the Errata section of that title.

To view the previously submitted errata, go to https://www.packtpub.com/books/content/support and enter the name of the book in the search field. The required information will appear under the **Errata** section.

Piracy

Piracy of copyrighted material on the Internet is an ongoing problem across all media. At Packt, we take the protection of our copyright and licenses very seriously. If you come across any illegal copies of our works in any form on the Internet, please provide us with the location address or website name immediately so that we can pursue a remedy.

Please contact us at copyright@packtpub.com with a link to the suspected pirated material.

We appreciate your help in protecting our authors and our ability to bring you valuable content.

eBooks, discount offers, and more

Did you know that Packt offers eBook versions of every book published, with PDF and ePub files available? You can upgrade to the eBook version at www.PacktPub.com and as a print book customer, you are entitled to a discount on the eBook copy. Get in touch with us at customercare@packtpub.com for more details.

At www.PacktPub.com, you can also read a collection of free technical articles, sign up for a range of free newsletters, and receive exclusive discounts and offers on Packt books and eBooks.

Questions

If you have a problem with any aspect of this book, you can contact us at questions@packtpub.com, and we will do our best to address the problem.

The First Step – Concurrency Design Principles

Users of computer systems are always looking for better performance for their systems. They want to get higher quality videos, better video games, and faster network speed. Some years ago, processors gave better performance to users by increasing their speed. But now, processors don't increase their speed. Instead of this, they add more cores so that the operating system can execute more than one task at a time. This is named **concurrency**. Concurrent programming includes all the tools and techniques to have multiple tasks or processes running at the same time in a computer, communicating and synchronizing between them without data loss or inconsistency. In this chapter, we will cover the following topics:

- Basic concurrency concepts
- Possible problems in concurrent applications
- A methodology to design concurrent algorithms
- The Java concurrency API
- The Java memory model
- Concurrency design patterns
- Tips and tricks to design concurrency algorithms

Basic concurrency concepts

First of all, let's present the basic concepts of concurrency. You must understand these concepts to follow the rest of the book.

Concurrency versus parallelism

Concurrency and parallelism are very similar concepts. Different authors give different definitions to these concepts. The most accepted definition talks about concurrency when you have more than one task in a single processor with a single core and the operating system's task scheduler quickly switches from one task to another, so it seems that all the tasks run simultaneously. The same definition talks about parallelism when you have more than one task that run simultaneously at the same time, in a different computer, processor, or core inside a processor.

Another definition talks about concurrency when you have more than one task (different tasks) running simultaneously on your system. One more definition discusses parallelism when you have different instances of the same task running simultaneously over different parts of a dataset.

The last definition that we include talks about parallelism when you have more than one task that runs simultaneously in your system and talks about concurrency to explain the different techniques and mechanisms programmers have to synchronize with the tasks and their access to shared resources.

As you can see, both concepts are very similar and this similarity has increased with the development of multicore processors.

Synchronization

In concurrency, we can define **synchronization** as the coordination of two or more tasks to get the desired results. We have two kinds of synchronization:

- **Control synchronization**: When, for example, one task depends on the end of another task, the second task can't start before the first has finished
- **Data access synchronization**: When two or more tasks have access to a shared variable and only one of the tasks can access the variable at any given time

A concept closely related to synchronization is **critical section**. A critical section is a piece of code that can be only executed by a task at any given time because of its access to a shared resource. **Mutual exclusion** is the mechanism used to guarantee this requirement and can be implemented by different ways.

Keep in mind that synchronization helps you avoid some errors you can have with concurrent tasks (they will be described later in this chapter), but it introduces some overhead to your algorithm. You have to calculate very carefully the number of tasks, which can be performed independently without intercommunication in your parallel algorithm. It's the **granularity** of your concurrent algorithm. If you have a **coarse-grained granularity** (big tasks with low intercommunication), the overhead due to synchronization will be low. However, maybe you won't benefit all the cores of your system. If you have a **fine-grained granularity** (small tasks with high intercommunication), the overhead due to synchronization will be high and maybe the throughput of your algorithm won't be good.

There are different mechanisms to get synchronization in a concurrent system. The most popular mechanisms from a theoretical point of view are:

- **Semaphore**: A semaphore is a mechanism that can be used to control the access to one or more units of a resource. It has a variable that stores the number of resources that can be used and two atomic operations to manage the value of the variable. A **mutex** (short for **mutual exclusion**) is a special kind of semaphore that can take only two values (*resource is free* and *resource is busy*), and only the process that sets the mutex to *busy* can release it.
- **Monitor**: A monitor is a mechanism to get mutual exclusion over a shared resource. It has a mutex, a condition variable, and two operations to wait for the condition and to signal the condition. Once you signal the condition, only one of the tasks that are waiting for it continues with its execution.

The last concept related to synchronization you're going to learn in this chapter is **thread safety**. A piece of code (or a method or an object) is **thread-safe** if all the users of shared data are protected by synchronization mechanisms, a nonblocking **compare-and-swap** (CAS) primitive or data is immutable, so you can use that code in a concurrent application without any problem.

Immutable object

An **immutable object** is an object with a very special characteristic. You can't modify its visible state (the value of its attributes) after its initialization. If you want to modify an immutable object, you have to create a new one.

Its main advantage is that it is thread-safe. You can use it in concurrent applications without any problem.

An example of an immutable object is the `String` class in Java. When you assign a new value to a `String` object, you are creating a new string.

Atomic operations and variables

An **atomic operation** is a kind of operation that appears to occur instantaneously to the rest of the tasks of the program. In a concurrent application, you can implement an atomic operation with a critical section to the whole operation using a synchronization mechanism.

An **atomic variable** is a kind of variable with atomic operations to set and get its value. You can implement an atomic variable using a synchronization mechanism or in a lock-free manner using CAS, which doesn't need any synchronization.

Shared memory versus message passing

Tasks can use two different methods to communicate with each other. The first one is **shared memory,** and normally it is used when the tasks are running in the same computer. The tasks use the same memory area where they write and read values. To avoid problems, the access to this shared memory has to be in a critical section protected by a synchronization mechanism.

The other synchronization mechanism is **message passing** and normally is used when the tasks are running in different computers. When a task needs to communicate with another, it sends a message that follows a predefined protocol. This communication can be synchronous if the sender is blocked waiting for a response or asynchronous if the sender continues with their execution after sending the message.

Possible problems in concurrent applications

Programming a concurrent application is not an easy job. If you incorrectly use the synchronization mechanisms, you can have different problems with the tasks in your application. In this section, we describe some of these problems.

Data race

You can have a **data race** (also named **race condition**) in your application when you have two or more tasks writing a shared variable outside a critical section—that's to say, without using any synchronization mechanisms.

Under these circumstances, the final result of your application may depend on the order of execution of the tasks. Look at the following example:

```
package com.packt.java.concurrency;

public class Account {

  private float balance;

  public void modify (float difference) {

    float value=this.balance;
    this.balance=value+difference;
  }

}
```

Imagine that two different tasks execute the `modify()` method in the same `Account` object. Depending on the order of execution of the sentences in the tasks, the final result can vary. Suppose that the initial balance is 1000 and the two tasks call the `modify()` method with 1000 as a parameter. The final result should be 3000, but if both tasks execute the first sentence at the same time and then the second sentence at the same time, the final result will be 2000. As you can see, the `modify()` method is not atomic and the `Account` class is not thread-safe.

Deadlock

There is a **deadlock** in your concurrent application when there are two or more tasks waiting for a shared resource that must be free from the other, so none of them will get the resources they need and will be blocked indefinitely. It happens when four conditions happen simultaneously in the system. They are **Coffman's conditions**, which are as follows:

- **Mutual exclusion**: The resources involved in the deadlock must be nonshareable. Only one task can use the resource at a time.
- **Hold and wait condition**: A task has the mutual exclusion for a resource and it's requesting the mutual exclusion for another resource. While it's waiting, it doesn't release any resources.
- **No pre-emption**: The resources can only be released by the tasks that hold them.
- **Circular wait**: There is a circular waiting where Task 1 is waiting for a resource that is being held by Task 2, which is waiting for a resource being held by Task 3, and so on until we have Task *n* that is waiting for a resource being held by Task 1.

There exist some mechanisms that you can use to avoid deadlocks:

- **Ignore them**: This is the most commonly used mechanism. You suppose that a deadlock will never occur on your system, and if it occurs, you can see the consequences of stopping your application and having to re-execute it.
- **Detection**: The system has a special task that analyzes the state of the system to detect if a deadlock has occurred. If it detects a deadlock, it can take action to remedy the problem. For example, finishing one task or forcing the liberation of a resource.
- **Prevention**: If you want to prevent deadlocks in your system, you have to prevent one or more of Coffman's conditions.
- **Avoidance**: Deadlocks can be avoided if you have information about the resources that are used by a task before it begins its execution. When a task wants to start its execution, you can analyze the resources that are free in the system and the resources that the task needs to decide that it can start its execution or not.

Livelock

A **livelock** occurs when you have two tasks in your systems that are always changing their states due to the actions of the other. Consequently, they are in a loop of state changes and unable to continue.

For example, you have two tasks—Task 1 and Task 2—and both need two resources: Resource 1 and Resource 2. Suppose that Task 1 has a lock on Resource 1, and Task 2 has a lock on Resource 2. As they are unable to gain access to the resource they need, they free their resources and begin the cycle again. This situation can continue indefinitely, so the tasks will never end their execution.

Resource starvation

Resource starvation occurs when you have a task in your system that never gets a resource that it needs to continue with its execution. When there is more than one task waiting for a resource and the resource is released, the system has to choose the next task that can use it. If your system has not got a good algorithm, it can have threads that are waiting for a long time for the resource.

Fairness is the solution to this problem. All the tasks that are waiting for a resource must have the resource in a given period of time. An option is to implement an algorithm that takes into account the time that a task has been waiting for a resource when it chooses the next task that will hold a resource. However, fair implementation of locks requires additional overhead, which may lower your program throughput.

Priority inversion

Priority inversion occurs when a low-priority task holds a resource that is needed by a high-priority task, so the low-priority task finishes its execution before the high-priority task.

A methodology to design concurrent algorithms

In this section, we're going to propose a five-step methodology to get a concurrent version of a sequential algorithm. It's based on the one presented by Intel in their *Threading Methodology: Principles and Practices* document.

The starting point – a sequential version of the algorithm

Our starting point to implement a concurrent algorithm will be a sequential version of it. Of course, we can design a concurrent algorithm from scratch, but I think that a sequential version of the algorithm will give us two advantages:

- We can use the sequential algorithm to test if our concurrent algorithm generates correct results. Both algorithms must generate the same output when they receive the same input, so we can detect some problems in the concurrent version, such as data races or similar conditions.

- We can measure the throughput of both algorithms to see if the use of concurrency gives us a real improvement in the response time or in the amount of data the algorithm can process in a time.

Step 1 – analysis

In this step, we are going to analyze the sequential version of the algorithm to look for the parts of its code that can be executed in a parallel way. We should pay special attention to those parts that are executed most of the time or that execute more code because, by implementing a concurrent version of those parts, we're going to get a greater performance improvement.

Good candidates for this process are loops where one step is independent of the other steps or portions of code that are independent of other parts of the code (for example, an algorithm to initialize an application that opens the connections with the database, loads the configuration files, initialize some objects. All the previous tasks are independent of each other).

Step 2 – design

Once you know what parts of the code you are going to parallelize, you have to decide how to do that parallelization.

The changes in the code will affect two main parts of the application:

- The structure of the code
- The organization of the data structures

You can take two different approaches to accomplish this task:

- **Task decomposition**: You do task decomposition when you split the code in two or more independent tasks that can be executed at once. Maybe some of these tasks have to be executed in a given order or have to wait at the same point. You must use synchronization mechanisms to get this behavior.
- **Data decomposition**: You do data decomposition when you have multiple instances of the same task that work with a subset of the dataset. This dataset will be a shared resource, so if the tasks need to modify the data you have to protect access to it by implementing a critical section.

Another important point to keep in mind is the granularity of your solution. The objective of implementing a parallel version of an algorithm is to achieve improved performance, so you should use all the available processors or cores. On the other hand, when you use a synchronization mechanism, you introduce some extra instructions that must be executed. If you split the algorithm into a lot of small tasks (fine-grained granularity), the extra code introduced by the synchronization can provoke performance degradation. If you split the algorithm into fewer tasks than cores (coarse-grained granularity), you are not taking advantage of all the resources. Also, you must take into account the work every thread must do, especially if you implement a fine-grained granularity. If you have a task longer than the rest, that task will determine the execution time of the application. You have to find the equilibrium between these two points.

Step 3 – implementation

The next step is to implement the parallel algorithm using a programming language and, if it's necessary, a thread library. In the examples of this book, you are going to use Java to implement all the algorithms.

Step 4 – testing

After finishing the implementation, you have to test the parallel algorithm. If you have a sequential version of the algorithm, you can compare the results of both algorithms to verify that your parallel implementation is correct.

Testing and debugging a parallel implementation are difficult tasks because the order of execution of the different tasks of the application is not guaranteed. In *Chapter 11, Testing and Monitoring Concurrent Applications*, you will learn tips, tricks, and tools to do these tasks efficiently.

Step 5 – tuning

The last step is to compare the throughput of the parallel and the sequential algorithms. If the results are not as expected, you must review the algorithm, looking for the cause of the bad performance of the parallel algorithm.

You can also test different parameters of the algorithm (for example, granularity or number of tasks) to find the best configuration.

There are different metrics to measure the possible performance improvement you can obtain parallelizing an algorithm. The three most popular metrics are:

- **Speedup**: This is a metric for relative performance improvement between the parallel and the sequential versions of the algorithm:

$$Speedup = \frac{T_{sequential}}{T_{concurrent}}$$

  Here, $T_{sequential}$ is the execution time of the sequential version of the algorithm and $T_{concurrent}$ is the execution time of the parallel version.

- **Amdahl's law**: This is used to calculate the maximum expected improvement obtained with the parallelization of an algorithm:

$$Speedup \leq \frac{1}{(1-P) + \frac{P}{N}}$$

  Here, P is the percentage of code that can be parallelized and N is the number of cores of the computer where you're going to execute the algorithm.

  For example, if you can parallelize 75% of the code and you have four cores, the maximum speedup will be given by the following formula:

$$Speedup \leq \frac{1}{(1-0.75) + \left(\frac{0.75}{4}\right)} \leq \frac{1}{0.44} \leq 2.29$$

- **Gustafson-Barsis' law**: Amdahl's law has a limitation. It supposes that you have the same input dataset when you increase the number of cores, but normally, when you have more cores, you want to process more data. Gustafson law proposes that when you have more cores available, bigger problems can be solved in the same time using the following formula:

$$Speedup = N - (1-P)*(N-1)$$

  Here, N is the number of cores and P is the percentage of parallelizable code.

If we use the same example as before, the scaled speedup calculated by the Gustafson law is:

$$Speedup = 4 - 0.25 * (3) = 3.25$$

Conclusion

In this section, you learned some important issues you have to take into account when you want to parallelize a sequential algorithm.

First of all, not every algorithm can be parallelized. For example, if you have to execute a loop where the result of an iteration depends on the result of the previous iteration, you can't parallelize that loop. Recurrent algorithms are another example of algorithms that can be parallelized for a similar reason.

Another important thing you have to keep in mind is that the sequential version of an algorithm with better performance can be a bad starting point to parallelize it. If you start parallelizing an algorithm and you find yourself in trouble because you don't easily find independent portions of the code, you have to look for other versions of the algorithm and verify that the version can be parallelized in an easier way.

Finally, when you implement a concurrent application (from scratch or based on a sequential algorithm), you must take into account the following points:

- **Efficiency**: The parallel algorithm must end in less time than the sequential algorithm. The first goal of parallelizing an algorithm is that its running time is less than the sequential one, or it can process more data in the same time.
- **Simplicity**: When you implement an algorithm (parallel or not), you must keep it as simple as possible. It will be easier to implement, test, debug, and maintain, and it will have fewer errors.
- **Portability**: Your parallel algorithm should be executed on different platforms with minimal changes. As in this book you will use Java, this point will be very easy. With Java, you can execute your programs in every operating system without any change (if you implement the program as you must).
- **Scalability**: What happens to your algorithm if you increase the number of cores? As mentioned before, you should use all the available cores, so your algorithm should be ready to take advantage of all available resources.

Java concurrency API

The Java programming language has a very rich concurrency API. It contains classes to manage the basic elements of concurrency, such as `Thread`, `Lock`, and `Semaphore`, and classes that implement very high-level synchronization mechanisms, such as the **executor framework** or the new parallel `Stream` API.

In this section, we will cover the basic classes that form the concurrency API.

Basic concurrency classes

The basic classes of the Java concurrency API are:

- The `Thread` class: This class represents all the threads that execute a concurrent Java application
- The `Runnable` interface: This is another way to create concurrent applications in Java
- The `ThreadLocal` class: This is a class to store variables locally to a thread
- The `ThreadFactory` interface: This is the base of the Factory design pattern that you can use to create customized threads

Synchronization mechanisms

The Java concurrency API includes different synchronization mechanisms that allow you to:

- Define a critical section to access a shared resource
- Synchronize different tasks in a common point

The following mechanisms are considered to be the most important synchronization mechanisms:

- The `synchronized` keyword: The `synchronized` keyword allows you to define a critical section in a block of code or in an entire method.
- The `Lock` interface: `Lock` provides a more flexible synchronization operation than the `synchronized` keyword. There are different kinds of Locks: `ReentrantLock`, to implement a Lock that can be associated with a condition; `ReentrantReadWriteLock`, which separates read and write operations; and `StampedLock`, a new feature of Java 8 that includes three modes for controlling read/write access.

- The `Semaphore` class: The class that implements the classical semaphore to implement synchronization. Java supports binary and general semaphores.
- The `CountDownLatch` class: A class that allows a task to wait for the finalization of multiple operations.
- The `CyclicBarrier` class: A class that allows the synchronization of multiple threads in a common point.
- The `Phaser` class: A class that allows you to control the execution of tasks divided into phases. None of the tasks advance to the next phase until all of the tasks have finished the current phase.

Executors

The executor framework is a mechanism that allows you to separate thread creation and management for the implementation of concurrent tasks. You don't have to worry about the creation and management of threads, only about creating tasks and sending them to the executor. The main classes involved in this framework are:

- The `Executor` and `ExecutorService` interface: They include methods common to all executors.
- `ThreadPoolExecutor`: This is a class that allows you to get an executor with a pool of threads and optionally define a maximum number of parallel tasks
- `ScheduledThreadPoolExecutor`: This is a special kind of executor to allow you to execute tasks after a delay or periodically
- `Executors`: This is a class that facilitates the creation of executors
- The `Callable` interface: This is an alternative to the *Runnable* interface—a separate task that can return a value
- The `Future` interface: This is an interface that includes the methods to obtain the value returned by a `Callable` interface and to control its status

The Fork/Join framework

The **Fork/Join framework** defines a special kind of executor specialized in the resolution of problems with the divide and conquer technique. It includes a mechanism to optimize the execution of the concurrent tasks that solve these kinds of problems. Fork/Join is specially tailored for fine-grained parallelism as it has a very low overhead in order to place the new tasks into the queue and take queued tasks for execution. The main classes and interfaces involved in this framework are:

- `ForkJoinPool`: This is a class that implements the executor that is going to run the tasks
- `ForkJoinTask`: This is a task that can be executed in the `ForkJoinPool` class
- `ForkJoinWorkerThread`: This is a thread that is going to execute tasks in the `ForkJoinPool` class

Parallel streams

Streams and **Lambda expressions** are maybe the two most important new features of the Java 8 version. Streams have been added as a method in the `Collection` interface and other data sources and allow processing all elements of a data structure, generating new structures, filtering data and implementing algorithms using the map and reduce technique.

A special kind of stream is a parallel stream which realizes its operations in a parallel way. The most important elements involved in the use of parallel streams are:

- The `Stream` interface: This is an interface that defines all the operations that you can perform on a stream.
- `Optional`: This is a container object that may or may not contain a non-null value.
- `Collectors`: This is a class that implements reduction operations that can be used as part of a stream sequence of operations.
- Lambda expressions: Streams has been thought to work with Lambda expressions. Most stream methods accept a lambda expression as a parameter. This allows you to implement a more compact version of the operations.

Concurrent data structures

Normal data structures of the Java API (`ArrayList`, `Hashtable`, and so on) are not ready to work in a concurrent application unless you use an external synchronization mechanism. If you use it, you will be adding a lot of extra computing time to your application. If you don't use it, it's probable that you will have race conditions in your application. If you modify them from several threads and a race condition occurs, you may experience various exceptions thrown (such as, `ConcurrentModificationException` and `ArrayIndexOutOfBoundsException`), there may be silent data loss or your program may even stuck in an endless loop.

The Java concurrency API includes a lot of data structures that can be used in concurrent applications without risk. We can classify them in two groups:

- **Blocking data structures**: These include methods that block the calling task when, for example, the data structure is empty and you want to get a value.
- **Non-blocking data structures:** If the operation can be made immediately, it won't block the calling tasks. Otherwise, it returns the `null` value or throws an exception.

These are some of the data structures:

- `ConcurrentLinkedDeque`: This is a non-blocking list
- `ConcurrentLinkedQueue`: This is a non-blocking queue
- `LinkedBlockingDeque`: This is a blocking list
- `LinkedBlockingQueue`: This is a blocking queue
- `PriorityBlockingQueue`: This is a blocking queue that orders its elements based on its priority
- `ConcurrentSkipListMap`: This is a non-blocking navigable map
- `ConcurrentHashMap`: This is a non-blocking hash map
- `AtomicBoolean`, `AtomicInteger`, `AtomicLong`, and `AtomicReference`: These are atomic implementations of the basic Java data types

Concurrency design patterns

In software engineering, a **design pattern** is a solution to a common problem. This solution has been used many times, and it has proved to be an optimal solution to the problem. You can use them to avoid 'reinventing the wheel' every time you have to solve one of these problems. **Singleton** or **Factory** are the examples of common design patterns used in almost every application.

Concurrency also has its own design patterns. In this section, we describe some of the most useful concurrency design patterns and their implementation in the Java language.

Signaling

This design pattern explains how to implement the situation where a task has to notify an event to another task. The easiest way to implement this pattern is with a semaphore or a mutex, using the `ReentrantLock` or `Semaphore` classes of the Java language or even the `wait()` and `notify()` methods included in the `Object` class.

See the following example:

```
public void task1() {
  section1();
  commonObject.notify();
}

public void task2() {
  commonObject.wait();
  section2();
}
```

Under these circumstances, the `section2()` method will always be executed after the `section1()` method.

Rendezvous

This design pattern is a generalization of the **Signaling** pattern. In this case, the first task waits for an event of the second task and the second task waits for an event of the first task. The solution is similar to that of Signaling, but in this case you must use two objects instead of one.

See the following example:

```
public void task1() {
  section1_1();
  commonObject1.notify();
  commonObject2.wait();
  section1_2();
}
public void task2() {
  section2_1();
  commonObject2.notify();
  commonObject1.wait();
  section2_2();
}
```

Under these circumstances, `section2_2()` always will be executed after `section1_1()` and `section1_2()` after `section2_1()`, take into account that, if you put the call to the `wait()` method before the call to the `notify()` method, you will have a deadlock.

Mutex

A mutex is a mechanism that you can use to implement a critical section ensuring mutual exclusion. That is to say, only one task can execute the portion of code protected by the mutex at one time. In Java, you can implement a critical section using the `synchronized` keyword (that allows you to protect a portion of code or a full method), the `ReentrantLock` class, or the `Semaphore` class.

Look at the following example:

```
public void task() {
  preCriticalSection();
  lockObject.lock() // The critical section begins
  criticalSection();
  lockObject.unlock(); // The critical section ends
  postCriticalSection();
}
```

Multiplex

The **Multiplex design pattern** is a generalization of the mutex. In this case, a determined number of tasks can execute the critical section at once. It is useful, for example, when you have multiple copies of a resource. The easiest way to implement this design pattern in Java is using the `Semaphore` class initialized to the number of tasks that can execute the critical section at once.

Look at the following example:

```
public void task() {
  preCriticalSection();
  semaphoreObject.acquire();
  criticalSection();
  semaphoreObject.release();
  postCriticalSection();
}
```

Barrier

This design pattern explains how to implement the situation where you need to synchronize some tasks at a common point. None of the tasks can continue with their execution until all the tasks have arrived at the synchronization point. The Java concurrency API provides the `CyclicBarrier` class, which is an implementation of this design pattern.

Look at the following example:

```
public void task() {
  preSyncPoint();
  barrierObject.await();
  postSyncPoint();
}
```

Double-checked locking

This design pattern provides a solution to the problem that occurs when you acquire a lock and then check for a condition. If the condition is false, you have had the overhead of acquiring the lock ideally. An example of this situation is the lazy initialization of objects. If you have a class implementing the `Singleton` design pattern, you may have some code like this:

```
public class Singleton{
  private static Singleton reference;
  private static final Lock lock=new ReentrantLock();
  public static Singleton getReference() {
    lock.lock();
    try {
        if (reference==null) {
           reference=new Object();
        }
    } finally {
        lock.unlock();
    }
    return reference;
  }
}
```

A possible solution can be to include the lock inside the conditions:

```
public class Singleton{
  private Object reference;
  private Lock lock=new ReentrantLock();
  public Object getReference() {
    if (reference==null) {
       lock.lock();
```

```
      try {
          if (reference == null) {
             reference=new Object();
          }
      } finally {
          lock.unlock();
      }
    }
    return reference;
  }
}
```

This solution still has problems. If two tasks check the condition at once, you will create two objects. The best solution to this problem doesn't use any explicit synchronization mechanism:

```
public class Singleton {

  private static class LazySingleton {
    private static final Singleton INSTANCE = new Singleton();
  }

  public static Singleton getSingleton() {
    return LazySingleton.INSTANCE;
  }

}
```

Read-write lock

When you protect access to a shared variable with a lock, only one task can access that variable, independently of the operation you are going to perform on it. Sometimes, you will have variables that you modify a few times but read many times. In this circumstance, a lock provides poor performance because all the read operations can be made concurrently without any problem. To solve this problem, there exists the read-write lock design pattern. This pattern defines a special kind of lock with two internal locks: one for read operations and the other for write operations. The behavior of this lock is as follows:

- If one task is doing a read operation and another task wants to do another read operation, it can do it
- If one task is doing a read operation and another task wants to do a write operation, it's blocked until all the readers finish
- If one task is doing a write operation and another task wants to do an operation (read or write), it's blocked until the writer finishes

The Java concurrency API includes the class `ReentrantReadWriteLock` that implements this design pattern. If you want to implement this pattern from scratch, you have to be very careful with the priority between read-tasks and write-tasks. If too many read-tasks exist, write-tasks can be waiting too long.

Thread pool

This design pattern tries to remove the overhead introduced by creating a thread for the task you want to execute. It's formed by a set of threads and a queue of tasks you want to execute. The set of threads usually has a fixed size. When a thread approaches the execution of a task, it doesn't finish its execution; it looks for another task in the queue. If there is another task, it executes it. If not, the thread waits until a task is inserted in the queue, but it's not destroyed.

The Java concurrency API includes some classes that implement the `ExecutorService` interface, which internally uses a pool of threads.

Thread local storage

This design pattern defines how to use global or static variables locally to tasks. When you have a static attribute in a class, all the objects of a class access the same occurrences of the attribute. If you use thread local storage, each thread accesses a different instance of the variable.

The Java concurrency API includes the `ThreadLocal` class to implement this design pattern.

The Java memory model

When you execute a concurrent application in a computer with several cores or processors, you can have a problem with memory caches. They are very useful to increment the performance of the application, but they can cause data inconsistency. When a task modifies the value of a variable, it's modified in the cache, but it's not modified in the main memory immediately. If another task reads the value of that variable before it's updated in the main memory, it will read the old value of the variable.

Other problems that may exist with concurrent applications are the optimizations introduced by the compilers and code optimizer. Sometimes, they reorder the instructions to get a better performance. In sequential applications, this doesn't cause any problems, but in concurrent applications it can provoke unexpected results.

To solve problems such as this, programming languages introduced memory models. A memory model describes how individual tasks interact with each other through memory and when changes made by one task will be visible to another. It also defines what optimizations of code are allowed and under what circumstances.

There are different memory models. Some of them are very strict (all of the tasks always have access to the same values) and others are less stringent (only some instructions update the values in the main memory). The memory model must be known by the compiler and optimizer developers, and it's transparent to the rest of the programmers.

Java was the first programming language that defined its memory model. The original memory model defined in the JVM had some issues, and it was redefined in Java 5. That memory model is the same in Java 8. It's defined in JSR 133. Basically, the Java Memory Model defines the following:

- It defines the behavior of the volatile, synchronized, and final keywords.
- It ensures that a properly synchronized concurrent program runs correctly on all architectures.
- It creates a partial ordering of the **volatile read**, **volatile write**, **lock**, and **unlock** instructions denominated as **happens-before**. Task synchronization helps us establish the happens-before relations too. If one action happens-before another, then the first is visible to and ordered before the second.
- When a task acquires a monitor, the memory cache is invalidated.
- When a task releases a monitor, the cache data is flushed into the main memory.
- It's transparent for Java programmers.

The main objective of the Java memory model is that the properly written concurrent application will behave correctly on every **Java Virtual Machine (JVM)** regardless of operating system, CPU architecture, and the number of CPUs and cores.

Tips and tricks to design concurrent algorithms

In this section, we have compiled some tips and tricks you have to keep in mind to design good concurrent applications.

Identify the correct independent tasks

You can only execute concurrent tasks that are independent of each other. If you have two or more tasks with an order dependency between them, maybe you have no interest in trying to execute them concurrently and including a synchronization mechanism to guarantee the execution order. The tasks will execute in a sequential way, and you will have to overcome the synchronization mechanism. A different situation is when you have a task with some prerequisites, but these prerequisites are independent of each other. In this case, you can execute the prerequisites concurrently and then use a synchronization class to control the execution of the task after completion of all the prerequisites.

Another situation where you can't use concurrency is when you have a loop, and all the steps use data generated in the step before or there is some status information that goes from one step to the next step.

Implement concurrency at the highest possible level

Rich threading APIs, as the Java concurrency API, offer you different classes to implement concurrency in your applications. In the case of Java, you can control the creation and synchronization of threads using the `Thread` or `Lock` classes, but it also offers you high-level concurrency objects, such as executors or the Fork/Join framework that allows you to execute concurrent tasks. This high-level mechanism offers you the following benefits:

- You don't have to worry about the creation and management of threads. You only create tasks and send them for execution. The Java concurrency API controls the creation and management of threads for you.
- They are optimized to give better performance than using threads directly. For example, they use a pool of threads to reuse them and avoid thread creation for every task. You can implement these mechanisms from scratch, but it will take you a lot of time, and it will be a complex task.
- They include advanced features that make the API more powerful. For example, with executors in Java, you can execute tasks that return a result in the form of a `Future` object. Again, you can implement these mechanisms from scratch, but it's not advisable.
- Your application will be migrated easier from one operating system to another, and it will be more scalable.

- Your application might become faster in the future Java versions. Java developers constantly improve the internals, and JVM optimizations will be likely more tailored for JDK APIs.

In summary, for performance and development time reasons, analyze the high-level mechanisms your thread API offers you before implementing your concurrent algorithm.

Take scalability into account

One of the main objectives when you implement a concurrent algorithm is to take advantage of all the resources of your computer, especially the number of processors or cores. But this number may change over time. Hardware is constantly evolving and its cost becomes lower each year.

When you design a concurrent algorithm using data decomposition, don't presuppose the number of cores or processors that your application will execute on. Get the information about the system dynamically (for example, in Java you can get it with the method `Runtime.getRuntime().availableProcessors()`) and make your algorithm use that information to calculate the number of tasks it's going to execute. This process will have an overhead over the execution time of your algorithm, but your algorithm will be more scalable.

If you design a concurrent algorithm using task decomposition, the situation can be more difficult. You depend on the number of independent tasks you have in the algorithm and forcing a bigger number of tasks will increment the overhead introduced by synchronization mechanisms, and the global performance of the application can be even worse. Analyze in detail the algorithm to determine whether you can have a dynamic number of tasks or not.

Use thread-safe APIs

If you need to use a Java library in a concurrent application, read its documentation first to know if it's thread-safe or not. If it's thread-safe, you can use it in your application without any problem. If it's not, you have the following two options:

- If a thread-safe alternative exists, you should use it
- If a thread-safe alternative doesn't exist, you should add the necessary synchronization to avoid all possible problematic situations, especially data race conditions

For example, if you need a List in a concurrent application, you should not use the `ArrayList` class if you are going to update it from several threads because it's not thread-safe. In this case, you can use a thread-safe class such as `ConcurrentLinkedDeque`, `CopyOnWriteArrayList`, or `LinkedBlockingDeque`. If the class you want to use is not thread-safe, first you must look for a thread-safe alternative. Probably, it will be more optimized to work with concurrency that any alternative that you can implement.

Never assume an execution order

The execution of tasks in a concurrent application when you don't use any synchronization mechanism is nondeterministic. The order in which the tasks are executed and the time each task is in execution before the processor moves on to another task is determined by the scheduler of the operating system. It doesn't care if you observe that the execution order is the same in a number of executions. The next one could be different.

The result of this assumption used to be a data race problem. The final result of your algorithm depends on the execution order of the tasks. Sometimes, the result can be right, but at other times it can be wrong. It can be very difficult to detect the cause of data race conditions, so you must be careful not to forget all the necessary synchronization elements.

Prefer local thread variables over static and shared when possible

Thread local variables are a special kind of variable. Every task will have an independent value for this variable, so you don't need any synchronization mechanism to protect access to this variable.

This can sound a little strange. Every object has its own copy of the attributes of the class, so why do we need the thread local variables? Consider this situation. You create a `Runnable` task, and you want to execute multiple instances of that task. You can create a `Runnable` object for each thread you want to execute, but another option is to create a `Runnable` object and use that object to create all the threads. In the last case, all the threads will have access to the same copy of the attributes of the class except if you use the `ThreadLocal` class. The `ThreadLocal` class guarantees you that every thread will access its own instance of the variable without the use of a Lock, a semaphore, or a similar class.

Another situation when you can take advantage of Thread local variables is with static attributes. All instances of a class share the static attributes, but you declare them with the `ThreadLocal` class. In this case, every thread will have access to its own copy.

Another option you have is to use something like `ConcurrentHashMap<Thread, MyType>` and use it like `var.get(Thread.currentThread())` or `var.put(Thread.currentThread(), newValue)`. Usually, this approach is significantly slower than `ThreadLocal` because of possible contention (`ThreadLocal` has no contention at all). It has an advantage though: you can clear the map completely and the value will disappear for every thread; thus, sometimes it's useful to use such an approach.

Find the more easily parallelizable version of the algorithm

We can define an algorithm as a sequence of steps to solve a problem. There are different ways to solve the same problem. Some are faster, some use fewer resources, and others fit better with special characteristics of the input data. For example, if you want to order a set of numbers, you can use one of the multiple sorting algorithms that have been implemented.

In a previous section of this chapter, we recommended you use a sequential algorithm as the starting point to implement a concurrent algorithm. There are two main advantages to this approach:

- You can easily test the correctness of the results of your parallel algorithm
- You can measure the improvement in performance obtained with the use of concurrency

But not every algorithm can be parallelized, at least not so easily. You might think that the best starting point could be the sequential algorithm with the best performance solving the problem you want to parallelize, but this can be a wrong assumption. You should look for an algorithm than can be easily parallelized. Then, you can compare the concurrent algorithm with the sequential one with the best performance to see which offers the best throughput.

Using immutable objects when possible

One of the main problems you can have in a concurrent application is a data race condition. As we explained before, this happens when two or more tasks modify the data stored in a shared variable and access to that variable is not implemented inside a critical section.

For example, when you work with an object-oriented language such as Java, you implement your application as a collection of objects. Each object has a number of attributes and some methods to read and change the values of the attributes. If some tasks share an object and call to a method to change a value of an attribute of that object and that method is not protected by a synchronization mechanism, you probably will have data inconsistency problems.

There are special kinds of object named immutable objects. Their main characteristic is that you can't modify any attributes after initialization. If you want to modify the value of an attribute, you must create another object. The `String` class in Java is the best example of immutable objects. When you use an operator (for example, = or +=) that we might think changes the value of a String, you are really creating a new object.

The use of immutable objects in a concurrent application has two very important advantages:

- You don't need any synchronization mechanism to protect the methods of these classes. If two tasks want to modify the same object, they will create new objects, so it will never occur that two tasks modify the same object at a time.
- You won't have any data inconsistency problems, as a conclusion of the first point.

There is a drawback with immutable objects. If you create too many objects, this may affect the throughput and memory use of the application. If you have a simple object without internal data structures, it's usually not a problem to make it immutable. However, making immutable complex objects that incorporate collections of other objects usually leads to serious performance problems.

Avoiding deadlocks by ordering the locks

One of the best mechanisms to avoid a deadlock situation in a concurrent application is to force tasks to get shared resources always in the same order. An easy way to do this is to assign a number to every resource. When a task needs more than one resource, it has to request them in order.

For example, if you have two tasks, T1 and T2, and both need two resources, R1 and R2, you can force both to request first the R1 resource and then the R2 resource. You will never have a deadlock.

On the other hand, if T1 first requests R1 and then R2 and T2 first requests R2 and then R1, you can have a deadlock.

For example, a bad use of this tip is as follows. You have two tasks that need to get two `Lock` objects. They try to get the locks in different order:

```
public void operation1() {
  lock1.lock();
  lock2.lock();
  ….
}
public void operation2() {
  lock2.lock();
  lock1.lock();
  …..
}
```

It's possible that `operation1()` executes its first sentence and `operation2()` its first sentence too, so they will be waiting for the other `Lock` and you will have a deadlock.

You can avoid this simply by getting the locks in the same order. If you change `operation2()`, you will never have a deadlock as follows:

```
public void operation2() {
  lock1.lock();
  lock2.lock();
  …..
}
```

Using atomic variables instead of synchronization

When you have to share data between two or more tasks, you have to use a synchronization mechanism to protect the access to that data and avoid any data inconsistency problems.

Under some circumstances, you can use the `volatile` keyword and not use a synchronization mechanism. If only one of the tasks modifies the data and the rest of the tasks read it, you can use the volatile keyword without any synchronization or data inconsistency problem. In other scenarios, you need to use a lock, the synchronized keyword, or any other synchronization method.

In Java 5, the concurrency API included a new kind of variable called atomic variables. These variables are classes that support atomic operations on single variables. They include a method, denominated by `compareAndSet(oldValue, newValue)`, that includes a mechanism to detect if assigning to the new value to the variable is done in one step. If the value of the variable is equal to `oldValue`, it changes it to `newValue` and returns true. Otherwise, it returns `false`. There are more methods that work in a similar way, such as `getAndIncrement()` or `getAndDecrement()`. These methods are also atomic.

This solution is lock-free; that is to say, it doesn't use locks or any synchronization mechanism, so its performance is better than any synchronized solution.

The most important atomic variables that you can use in Java are:

- `AtomicInteger`
- `AtomicLong`
- `AtomicReference`
- `AtomicBoolean`
- `LongAdder`
- `DoubleAdder`

Holding locks for as short a time as possible

Locks, as with any other synchronization mechanism, allow you to define a critical section that only one task can execute at a time. While a task is executing the critical section, the other tasks that want to execute it are blocked and have to wait for the liberation of the critical section. The application is working in a sequential way.

You have to pay special attention to the instructions you include in your critical sections because you can degrade the performance of your application without realizing it. You must make your critical section as small as possible, and it must include only the instructions that work on shared data with other tasks, so the time that the application is executing in a sequential way will be minimal.

Avoid executing inside the critical section the code you don't control. For example, you are writing a library that accepts a user-defined `Callable`, which you need to launch sometimes. You don't know what exactly will be in that `Callable`. Maybe it blocks input/output, acquires some locks, calls other methods of your library, or just works for a very long time. Thus, whenever possible, try to execute it when your library does not hold any locks. If it's impossible for your algorithm, specify this behavior in your library documentation and possibly specify the limitations to the user-supplied code (for example, it should not take any locks). A good example of such documentation can be found in the `compute()` method of the `ConcurrentHashMap` class.

Taking precautions using lazy initialization

Lazy initialization is a mechanism that delays object creation until the object is used in the application for the first time. Its main advantage is it minimizes the use of memory because you only create the objects that are really needed, but it can be a problem in concurrent applications.

If you have a method that initializes an object and this method is called by two different tasks at once, you can initialize two different objects. This, for example, can be a problem with singleton classes because you only want to create one object of these classes.

A elegant solution to this problem has been implemented, as the Initialization-on-demand holder idiom (https://en.wikipedia.org/wiki/Initialization-on-demand_holder_idiom).

Avoiding the use of blocking operations inside a critical section

Blocking operations are those operations that block the task that calls them until an event occurs. For example, when you read data from a file or write data to the console, the task that calls these operations must wait until they finish.

If you include one of these operations into a critical section, you are degrading the performance of your application because none of the tasks that want to execute that critical section can execute it. The one that is inside the critical section is waiting for the finalization of an I/O operation, and the others are waiting for the critical section.

Unless it is imperative, don't include blocking operations inside a critical section.

Summary

Concurrent programming includes all the necessary tools and techniques to have multiple tasks or process running at the same time in a computer, communicating and synchronizing between them without data loss or inconsistency.

We started this chapter by introducing the basic concepts of concurrency. You must know and understand terms such as concurrency, parallelism, and synchronization to fully understand the examples of this book. However, concurrency can generate some problems, such as data race conditions, deadlocks, livelocks, and others. You must also know the potential problems of a concurrent application. It will help you identify and solve these problems.

We also explained a simple methodology of five steps introduced by Intel to convert a sequential algorithm into a concurrent one and showed you some concurrency design patterns implemented in the Java language and some tips to take into account when you implement a concurrent application.

Finally, we explained briefly the components of the Java concurrency API. It's a very rich API with low- and very high-level mechanisms that allow you to implement powerful concurrency applications easily. We also described the Java memory model, which determines how concurrent applications manage the memory and the execution order of the instructions internally.

In the next chapter, you will learn how to implement applications that use a lot of threads using the executor framework. This allows you to execute a big number of threads by controlling the resources you use and reducing the overhead introduced by thread creation (it reuses `Thread` objects to execute different tasks).

2
Managing Lots of Threads – Executors

When you implement a simple concurrent application, you create and execute a thread per concurrent task. This approach can have some important issues. Since **Java version 5**, the Java concurrency API includes the **executor framework** to improve the performance of concurrent applications with a lot of concurrent tasks. In this chapter, we will cover the following:

- An introduction to executors
- The first example – the k-nearest neighbors algorithm
- The second example – concurrency in a client/server environment

An introduction to executors

The basic mechanism to implement a concurrent application in Java is:

- **A class that implements the Runnable interface**: This is the code you want to implement in a concurrent way
- **An instance of the Thread class**: This is the thread that is going to execute the code in a concurrent way

With this approach, you're responsible for creating and manning the `Thread` objects and implementing the mechanisms of synchronization between the threads. However, it can have some problems, especially with those applications with a lot of concurrent tasks. If you create too many threads, you can degrade the performance of your application or even hang the entire system.

Java 5 included the executor framework, to solve these problems and provide an efficient solution, which would be easier for the programmers to use than the traditional concurrency mechanisms.

In this chapter, we will introduce the basic characteristics of the executor framework by implementing the following two examples using that framework:

- **The k-nearest neighbors algorithm**: This is a basic **machine-learning** algorithm used in classification. It determines the tag of a test example based on the tag of the *k* most similar examples in the train dataset.
- **Concurrency in a client/server environment**: Applications that serve information to thousands or millions of clients are critical nowadays. It is essential to implement the server side of the system in an optimal way.

In *Chapter 3, Getting the Maximum from Executors*, and *Chapter 4, Getting Data from the Tasks – The Callable and Future Interfaces*, we will introduce more advanced aspects of executors.

Basic characteristics of executors

The main characteristics of executors are:

- You don't need to create any `Thread` object. If you want to execute a concurrent task, you only create an instance of the task (for example, a class that implements the `Runnable` interface) and send it to the executor. It will manage the thread that will execute the task.
- Executors reduce the overhead introduced by thread creation reusing the threads. Internally, it manages a pool of threads named **worker-threads**. If you send a task to the executor and a worker-thread is idle, the executor uses that thread to execute the task.
- It's easy to control the resources used by the executor. You can limit the maximum number of worker-threads of your executor. If you send more tasks than worker-threads, the executor stores them in a queue. When a worker-thread finishes the execution of a task, it takes another from the queue.
- You have to finish the execution of an executor explicitly. You have to indicate to the executor that it has to finish its execution and kill the created threads. If you don't do this, it won't finish its execution and your application won't end.

Executors have more interesting characteristics that make them very powerful and flexible.

Basic components of the executor framework

The executor framework has various interfaces and classes that implement all the functionality provided by executors. The basic components of the framework are:

- **The Executor interface**: This is the basic interface of the executor framework. It only defines a method that allows the programmer to send a `Runnable` object to an executor.
- **The ExecutorService interface**: This interface extends the `Executor` interface and includes more methods to increase the functionality of the framework, such as the following:
    - Execute tasks that return a result: The `run()` method provided by the `Runnable` interface doesn't return a result, but with executors, you can have tasks that return a result
    - Execute a list of tasks with a single method call
    - Finish the execution of an executor and wait for its termination
- **The ThreadPoolExecutor class**: This class implements the `Executor` and `ExecutorService` interfaces. In addition, it includes some additional methods to get the status of the executor (number of worker-threads, number of executed tasks, and so on), methods to establish the parameters of the executor (minimum and maximum number or worker-threads, time that idle threads will wait for new tasks, and so on) and methods that allow programmers to extends and adapt its functionality.
- **The Executors class**: This class provides utility methods to create `Executor` objects and other related classes.

First example – the k-nearest neighbors algorithm

The k-nearest neighbors algorithm is a simple machine-learning algorithm used for supervised classification. The main components of this algorithm are:

- **A train dataset**: This dataset is formed by instances with one or more attributes that define every instance and a special attribute that determines the example or label of the instance
- **A distance metric**: This metric is used to determine the distance (or similarity) between the instances of the train dataset and the new instances you want to classify
- **A test dataset**: This dataset is used to measure the behavior of the algorithm

When it has to classify an instance, it calculates the distance against this instance and all the instances of the train dataset. Then, it takes the k-nearest instances and looks at the tag of those instances. The tag with the most instances is the tag assigned to the input instance.

In this chapter, we are going to work with the **Bank Marketing** dataset of the **UCI Machine Learning Repository**, which you can download from `http://archive.ics.uci.edu/ml/datasets/Bank+Marketing`. To measure the distance between instances, we are going to use the **Euclidean distance**. With this metric, all the attributes of our instances must have numerical values. Some of the attributes of the Bank Marketing dataset are categorical (that is to say, they can take one of some predefined values), so we can't use the Euclidean distance directly with this dataset. It's possible to assign ordinal numbers to each categorical value; for example, for marital status, 0 would be *single*, 1 would be *married*, and 2 would be *divorced*. However, this would imply that the *divorced* person is closer to *married* than to *single*, which is disputable. To make all the categorical values equally distant, we create separate attributes such as *married*, *single*, and *divorced*, which have only two values: 0 (*no*) and 1 (*yes*).

Our dataset has 66 attributes and two possible tags: *yes* and *no*. We also divided the data in two subsets:

- **The train dataset**: With 39,129 instances
- **The test dataset**: With 2,059 instances

As we explained in *Chapter 1, The First Step – Concurrency Design Principles*, we first implemented a serial version of the algorithm. Then, we looked for the parts of the algorithm that could be parallelized, and we used the executor framework to execute the concurrent tasks. In the following sections, we explain the serial implementation of the k-nearest neighbors algorithm and two different concurrent versions. The first one has a concurrency with very fine-grained granularity, whereas the second one has coarse-grained granularity.

K-nearest neighbors – serial version

We have implemented the serial version of the algorithm in the `KnnClassifier` class. Internally, this class stores the train dataset and the number k (the number of examples that we will use to determine the tag of an instance):

```
public class KnnClassifier {

    private List <? extends Sample> dataSet;
    private int k;
```

```
public KnnClassifier(List <? extends Sample> dataSet, int k) {
  this.dataSet=dataSet;
  this.k=k;
}
```

The `KnnClassifier` class only implements a method named `classify` that receives an `Sample` object with the instance we want to classify, and it returns a string with the tag assigned to that instance:

```
public String classify (Sample example) {
```

This method has three main parts—first, we calculate the distances between the input example and all the examples of the train dataset:

```
Distance[] distances=new Distance[dataSet.size()];

int index=0;

for (Sample localExample : dataSet) {
  distances[index]=new Distance();
  distances[index].setIndex(index);
  distances[index].setDistance
    (EuclideanDistanceCalculator.calculate(localExample,
      example));
  index++;
}
```

Then, we sort the examples from lower to higher distance, using the `Arrays.sort()` method:

```
Arrays.sort(distances);
```

Finally, we count the tag with most instances in the k-nearest examples:

```
Map<String, Integer> results = new HashMap<>();
for (int i = 0; i < k; i++) {
  Sample localExample = dataSet.get(distances[i].getIndex());
  String tag = localExample.getTag();
  results.merge(tag, 1, (a, b) -> a+b);
}
return Collections.max(results.entrySet(),
Map.Entry.comparingByValue()).getKey();
}
```

To calculate the distance between two examples, we can use the Euclidean distance implemented in an auxiliary class. This is the code of that class:

```
public class EuclideanDistanceCalculator {
  public static double calculate (Sample example1, Sample
     example2) {
    double ret=0.0d;

    double[] data1=example1.getExample();
    double[] data2=example2.getExample();

    if (data1.length!=data2.length) {
      throw new IllegalArgumentException ("Vector doesn't have the
         same length");
    }

    for (int i=0; i<data1.length; i++) {
      ret+=Math.pow(data1[i]-data2[i], 2);
    }
    return Math.sqrt(ret);
  }

}
```

We have also used the `Distance` class to store the distance between the `Sample` input and an instance of the train dataset. It only has two attributes: the index of the example of the train dataset and the distance to the input example. In addition, it implements the `Comparable` interface to use the `Arrays.sort()` method. Finally, the `Sample` class stores an instance. It only has an array of doubles and a string with the tag of that instance.

K-nearest neighbors – a fine-grained concurrent version

If you analyze the serial version of the k-nearest neighbors algorithm, you can find the following two points where you can parallelize the algorithm:

- **The computation of the distances**: Every loop iteration that calculates the distance between the input example and one of the examples of the train dataset is independent of the others
- **The sort of the distances**: Java 8 has included the `parallelSort()` method in the `Arrays` class to sort arrays in a concurrent way

In the first concurrent version of the algorithm, we are going to create a task per distance between examples that we're going to calculate. We are also going to make it possible to produce a concurrent sort of array of distances. We have implemented this version of the algorithm in a class named `KnnClassifierParallelIndividual`. It stores the train dataset, the k parameter, the `ThreadPoolExecutor` object to execute the parallel tasks, an attribute to store the number of worker-threads we want to have in the executor, and an attribute to store if we want to make a parallel sort.

We are going to create an executor with a fixed number of threads so that we can control the resources of the system that this executor is going to use. This number will be the number of processors available in the system we obtain with the `availableProcessors()` method of the `Runtime` class multiplied by the value of a parameter of the constructor named `factor`. Its value will be the number of threads you will have from the processor. We will always use the value 1, but you can test with other values and compare the results. This is the constructor of the classification:

```
public class KnnClassifierParallelIndividual {

    private List<? extends Sample> dataSet;
    private int k;
    private ThreadPoolExecutor executor;
    private int numThreads;
    private boolean parallelSort;

    public KnnClassifierParallelIndividual(List<? extends Sample>
       dataSet, int k, int factor, boolean parallelSort) {
       this.dataSet=dataSet;
       this.k=k;
       numThreads=factor*
          (Runtime.getRuntime().availableProcessors());
       executor=(ThreadPoolExecutor)
          Executors.newFixedThreadPool(numThreads);
       this.parallelSort=parallelSort;
    }
}
```

To create the executor, we have used the `Executors` utility class and its `newFixedThreadPool()` method. This method receives the number of worker-threads you want to have in the executor. The executor will never have more worker-threads than the number you specified in the constructor. This method returns an `ExecutorService` object, but we cast it to a `ThreadPoolExecutor` object to have access to methods provided but the class and not included in the interface.

This class also implements the `classify()` method that receives an example and returns a string.

First, we create a task for every distance we need to calculate and send them to the executor. Then, the main thread has to wait for the end of the execution of those tasks. To control that finalization, we have used a synchronization mechanism provided by the Java concurrency API: the `CountDownLatch` class. This class allows a thread to wait until other threads have arrived at a determined point of their code. It's initialized with the number of threads you want to wait for. It implements two methods:

- `getDown()`: This method decreases the number of threads you have to wait for
- `await()`: This method suspends the thread that calls it until the counter reaches zero

In this case, we initialize the `CountDownLatch` class with the number of tasks we are going to execute in the executor. The main thread calls the `await()` method and calls the `getDown()` method for every task, when it finishes its calculation:

```
public String classify (Sample example) throws Exception {

  Distance[] distances=new Distance[dataSet.size()];
  CountDownLatch endController=new
    CountDownLatch(dataSet.size());

  int index=0;
  for (Sample localExample : dataSet) {
    IndividualDistanceTask task=new
      IndividualDistanceTask(distances, index, localExample,
      example, endController);
    executor.execute(task);
    index++;
  }
  endController.await();
```

Then, depending on the value of the `parallelSort` attribute, we call the `Arrays.sort()` or `Arrays.parallelSort()` methods.

```
  if (parallelSort) {
    Arrays.parallelSort(distances);
  } else {
    Arrays.sort(distances);
  }
```

Finally, we calculate the tag assigned to the input examples. This code is the same as in the serial version.

The `KnnClassifierParallelIndividual` class also includes a method to shutdown the executor calling its `shutdown()` method. It you don't call this method, your application will never end because threads created by the executor are still alive and waiting for the new tasks to do. Previously submitted tasks are executed, and newly submitted tasks are rejected. The method doesn't wait for the finalization of the executor, it returns immediately:

```
public void destroy() {
   executor.shutdown();
}
```

A critical part of this example is the `IndividualDistanceTask` class. This is the class that calculates the distance between the input example and an example of the train dataset as a concurrent task. It stores the full array of distances (we are going to establish the value of one of its positions only), the index of the example of the train dataset, both examples, and the `CountDownLatch` object used to control the end of the tasks. It implements the `Runnable` interface, so it can be executed in the executor. This is the constructor of the class:

```
public class IndividualDistanceTask implements Runnable {

    private Distance[] distances;
    private int index;
    private Sample localExample;
    private Sample example;
    private CountDownLatch endController;

    public IndividualDistanceTask(Distance[] distances, int index,
      Sample localExample,
        Sample example, CountDownLatch endController) {
      this.distances=distances;
      this.index=index;
      this.localExample=localExample;
      this.example=example;
      this.endController=endController;
    }
```

The `run()` method calculates the distance between the two examples using the `EuclideanDistanceCalculator` class explained before and stores the result in the corresponding position of the distances:

```
public void run() {
  distances[index] = new Distance();
  distances[index].setIndex(index);
  distances[index].setDistance
    (EuclideanDistanceCalculator.calculate(localExample,
    example));
  endController.countDown();
}
```

 Note that although all the tasks share the array of distances, we don't need to use any synchronization mechanism because each task will modify a different position of the array.

K-nearest neighbors – a coarse-grained concurrent version

The concurrent solution presented in the previous section may have a problem. You are executing too many tasks. If you stop to think, in this case, we have more than 29,000 train examples, so you're going to launch 29,000 tasks per example you want to classify. On the other hand, we have created an executor with a maximum of `numThreads` worker-threads, so another option is to launch only `numThreads` tasks and split the train dataset in `numThreads` groups. We executed the examples with a quad-core processor, so each task will calculate the distances between the input example and approximately 7,000 train examples.

We have implemented this solution in the `KnnClassifierParallelGroup` class. It's very similar to the `KnnClassifierParallelIndividual` class with two main differences. First, the first part of the `classify()` method. Now, we will only have `numThreads` tasks, and we have to split the train dataset in `numThreads` subsets:

```
public String classify(Sample example) throws Exception {

    Distance distances[] = new Distance[dataSet.size()];
    CountDownLatch endController = new CountDownLatch(numThreads);

    int length = dataSet.size() / numThreads;
    int startIndex = 0, endIndex = length;
```

```
      for (int i = 0; i < numThreads; i++) {
        GroupDistanceTask task = new GroupDistanceTask(distances,
          startIndex, endIndex, dataSet, example, endController);
        startIndex = endIndex;
        if (i < numThreads - 2) {
         endIndex = endIndex + length;
        } else {
         endIndex = dataSet.size();
        }
        executor.execute(task);

      }
      endController.await();
```

We calculate the number of samples per task in the length variable. Then, we assign to each thread the start and end indexes of the samples they have to process. For all the threads except the last one, we add the length value to the start index to calculate the end index. For the last one, the last index is the size of the dataset.

Second, this class uses `GroupDistanceTask` instead of `IndividualDistanceTask`. The main difference between those classes is that the first one processes a subset of the train dataset, so it stores the full train dataset and the first and last positions of the dataset it has to process:

```
    public class GroupDistanceTask implements Runnable {
      private Distance[] distances;
      private int startIndex, endIndex;
      private Sample example;
      private List<? extends Sample> dataSet;
      private CountDownLatch endController;

      public GroupDistanceTask(Distance[] distances, int startIndex,
        int endIndex, List<? extends Sample> dataSet, Sample
        example, CountDownLatch endController) {
        this.distances = distances;
        this.startIndex = startIndex;
        this.endIndex = endIndex;
        this.example = example;
        this.dataSet = dataSet;
        this.endController = endController;
      }
```

The `run()` method processes a set of examples instead of only one example:

```
public void run() {
  for (int index = startIndex; index < endIndex; index++) {
    Sample localExample=dataSet.get(index);
    distances[index] = new Distance();
    distances[index].setIndex(index);
      distances[index].setDistance(EuclideanDistanceCalculator
        .calculate(localExample, example));
  }
  endController.countDown();
}
```

Comparing the solutions

Let's compare the different versions of the k-nearest neighbors algorithms we have implemented. We have the following five different versions:

- The serial version
- The fine-grained concurrent version with serial sorting
- The fine-grained concurrent version with concurrent sorting
- The coarse-grained concurrent version with serial sorting
- The coarse-grained concurrent version with concurrent sorting

To test the algorithm, we have used 2,059 test instances, which we take from the Bank Marketing dataset. We have classified all those examples using the five versions of the algorithm using the values of k as 10, 30, and 50, and measured their execution time. We have used the **JMH framework** (http://openjdk.java.net/projects/code-tools/jmh/) which allows you to implement microbenchmarks in Java. Using a framework for benchmarking is a better solution that simply measures time using the `currentTimeMillis()` or `nanoTime()` methods. These are the results:

Algorithm	K	Execution time (seconds)
Serial	10	100.296
	30	99.218
	50	99.458
Fine-grained serial sort	10	108.150
	30	105.196
	50	109.797

Algorithm	K	Execution time (seconds)
Fine-grained concurrent sort	10	84.663
	30	85,392
	50	83.373
Coarse-grained serial sort	10	78.328
	30	77.041
	50	76.549
Coarse-grained concurrent sort	10	54,017
	30	53.473
	50	53.255

We can draw the following conclusions:

- The selected values of the K parameter (10, 30, and 50) don't affect the execution time of the algorithm. The five versions present similar results for the three values.
- As it was expected, the use of the concurrent sort with the `Arrays.parallelSort()` method gives a great improvement in performance in the fine-grained and the coarse-grained concurrent versions of the algorithms.
- The fine-grained version of the algorithm gives the same or slightly worse results than the serial algorithm. The overhead introduced by the creation and management of concurrent tasks provokes these results. We execute too many tasks.
- The coarse-grained version, on the other hand, offers a great improvement of performance, with serial or parallel sorting.

So, the best version of the algorithm is the coarse-grained solution using parallel sorting. If we compare it with the serial version calculating the speedup:

$$S = \frac{T_{serial}}{T_{concurrent}} = \frac{99.218}{53.255} = 1.86$$

This example shows how a good election of a concurrent solution can give us a great improvement, and a bad election can give us a bad performance.

The second example – concurrency in a client/server environment

The **client/server model** is a software architecture in which applications are split into two parts: the server part that provides resources (data, operations, printer, storage, and so on) and the client part that uses the resources provided by the server. Traditionally, this architecture was used in the enterprise world, but with the boom of the Internet, it is still an actual topic. You can see a web application as a client/server application where the server part is the backend part of the application that is executed in a web server and the web navigator executes the client part of the application. **SOA** (short for **Service-Oriented Architecture**) is an other example of client/server architecture where the web services exposed are the server part and the different clients that consume them are the client part.

In a client/server environment, we usually have one server and a lot of clients that use the services provided by the server, so the performance of the server is a critical aspect when you have to design one of these systems.

In this section, we will implement a simple client/server application. It will make a search of data over the **World Development Indicators** of the **World Bank**, which you can download from here: `http://data.worldbank.org/data-catalog/world-development-indicators`. This data contains the values of different indicators over all the countries in the world from 1960 to 2014.

The main characteristics of our server will be:

- The client and the server will connect using sockets
- The client will send its queries in a string, and the server will respond to the results in another string
- The server can respond with three different queries:
    - **Query**: The format of this query is `q;codCountry;codIndicator;year` where `codCountry` is the code of the country, `codIndicator` is the code of the indicator, and `year` is an optional parameter with the year you want to query. The server will respond with the information in a single string.
    - **Report**: The format of this query is `r;codIndicator` where `codIndicator` is the code of the indicator you want to report. The server will respond with the mean value of that indicator for all countries over the years in a single string.
    - **Stop**: The format of this query is `z;`. The server stops its execution when it receives this command.
    - In other cases, the server returns an error message.

As in the previous example, we will show you how to implement a serial version of this client/server application. Then, we will show you how to implement a concurrent version using an executor. Finally, we will compare the two solutions to view the advantages of the use of concurrency in this case.

Client/server – serial version

The serial version of our server application has three main parts:

- The **DAO** (short for **Data Access Object**) part, responsible for access to the data and obtaining the results of the query
- The command part, formed by a command per kind of query
- The server part, which receives the queries, calls the corresponding command, and returns the results to the client

Let's see in detail each of these parts.

The DAO part

As we mentioned before, the server will make a search of data over the world development indicators of the World Bank. This data is in a CSV file. The DAO component in the application loads the entire file into a `List` object in memory. It implements a method per query it will attend that goes over the list looking for the data.

We don't include the code of this class here because it's simple to implement and it's not the main purpose of this book.

The command part

The command part is an intermediary between the DAO and the server parts. We have implemented a base abstract `Command` class to be the base class of all the commands:

```
public abstract class Command {

  protected String[] command;

  public Command (String [] command) {
    this.command=command;
  }

  public abstract String execute ();

}
```

Then, we have implemented a command for each query. The query is implemented in the `QueryCommand` class. The `execute()` method is as follows:

```java
public String execute() {
  WDIDAO dao=WDIDAO.getDAO();

  if (command.length==3) {
    return dao.query(command[1], command[2]);
  } else if (command.length==4) {
    try {
      return dao.query(command[1], command[2],
        Short.parseShort(command[3]));
    } catch (Exception e) {
      return "ERROR;Bad Command";
    }
  } else {
    return "ERROR;Bad Command";
  }
}
```

The report is implemented in `ReportCommand`. The `execute()` method is as follows:

```java
@Override
public String execute() {

  WDIDAO dao=WDIDAO.getDAO();
  return dao.report(command[1]);
}
```

The stop query is implemented in the `StopCommand` class. Its `execute()` method is as follows:

```java
@Override
public String execute() {
  return "Server stopped";
}
```

Finally, the error situations are processed by the `ErrorCommand` class. Its `execute()` method is as follows:

```java
@Override
public String execute() {
  return "Unknown command: "+command[0];
}
```

The server part

Finally, the server part is implemented in the `SerialServer` class. First of all, it initializes the DAO calling the `getDAO()` method. The main objective is that the DAO loads all the data:

```
public class SerialServer {

  public static void main(String[] args) throws IOException {
    WDIDAO dao = WDIDAO.getDAO();
    boolean stopServer = false;
    System.out.println("Initialization completed.");

    try (ServerSocket serverSocket = new
      ServerSocket(Constants.SERIAL_PORT)) {
```

After this, we have a loop that will be executed until the server receives a stop query. This loop does the following four steps:

- Receives a query for a client
- Parses and splits the elements of the query
- Calls the corresponding command
- Returns the results to the client

These four steps are shown in the following code snippet:

```
do {
  try (Socket clientSocket = serverSocket.accept();
    PrintWriter out = new PrintWriter
      (clientSocket.getOutputStream(), true);
    BufferedReader in = new BufferedReader(new
      InputStreamReader(clientSocket.getInputStream()));) {
  String line = in.readLine();
  Command command;

  String[] commandData = line.split(";");
  System.out.println("Command: " + commandData[0]);
  switch (commandData[0]) {
  case "q":
    System.out.println("Query");
    command = new QueryCommand(commandData);
    break;
  case "r":
    System.out.println("Report");
    command = new ReportCommand(commandData);
```

```
        break;
    case "z":
      System.out.println("Stop");
      command = new StopCommand(commandData);
      stopServer = true;
      break;
    default:
      System.out.println("Error");
      command = new ErrorCommand(commandData);
    }
    String response = command.execute();
    System.out.println(response);
    out.println(response);
  } catch (IOException e) {
    e.printStackTrace();
  }
} while (!stopServer);
```

Client/server – parallel version

The serial version of the server has a very important limitation. While it is processing one query, it can't attend to other queries. If the server needs an important amount of time to respond to every request, or to certain requests, the performance of the server will be very low.

We can obtain a better performance using concurrency. If the server creates a thread when it receives a request, it can delegate to the thread all the processes of the query and it can attend new request. This approach can also have some problems. If we receive a high number of queries, we can saturate the system creating too many threads. But if we use an executor with a fixed number of threads, we can control the resources used by our server and obtain a better performance than the serial version.

To convert our serial server to a concurrent one using an executor, we have to modify the server part. The DAO part is the same, and we have changed the names of the classes that implement the command part, but their implementation is almost the same. Only the stop query changes because now it has more responsibilities. Let's see the details of the implementation of the concurrent server part.

The server part

The concurrent server part is implemented in the `ConcurrentServer` part. We have added two elements not included in the serial server: a cache system, implemented in the `ParallelCache` class and a log system, implemented in the `Logger` class. First of all, it initializes the DAO part calling the `getDAO()` method. The main objective is that the DAO loads all the data and creates a `ThreadPoolExecutor` object using the `newFixedThreadPool()` method of the `Executors` class. This method receives the maximum number of worker-threads we want in our server. The executor will never have more than those worker-threads. To get the number of worker-threads, we get the number of cores of our system using the `availableProcessors()` method of the `Runtime` class:

```java
public class ConcurrentServer {

    private static ThreadPoolExecutor executor;

    private static ParallelCache cache;

    private static ServerSocket serverSocket;

    private static volatile boolean stopped = false;

    public static void main(String[] args) {

        serverSocket=null;
        WDIDAO dao=WDIDAO.getDAO();
        executor=(ThreadPoolExecutor) Executors.newFixedThreadPool
           (Runtime.getRuntime().availableProcessors());
        cache=new ParallelCache();
        Logger.initializeLog();

        System.out.println("Initialization completed.");
```

The `stopped` Boolean variable is declared as volatile because it will be changed from another thread. The `volatile` keyword ensures that when the `stopped` variable is set to `true` by another thread, this change will be visible in the main method. Without the `volatile` keyword, the change cannot be visible due to CPU caching or compiler optimizations. Then, we initialize `ServerSocket` to listen for the requests:

```java
serverSocket = new ServerSocket(Constants.CONCURRENT_PORT);
```

Managing Lots of Threads – Executors

We can't use a try-with-resources statement to manage the server socket. When we receive a `stop` command, we need to shut down the server, but the server is waiting in the `accept()` method of the `serverSocket` object. To force the server to leave that method, we need to explicitly close the server (we'll do that in the `shutdown()` method), so we can't leave the try-with-resources statement close the socket for us.

After this, we have a loop that will be executed until the server receives a stop query. This loop does three steps, as follows:

- Receives a query for a client
- Creates a task to process that query
- Sends the task to the executor

These three steps are shown in the following code snippet:

```
do {
  try {
    Socket clientSocket = serverSocket.accept();
    RequestTask task = new RequestTask(clientSocket);
    executor.execute(task);
  } catch (IOException e) {
    e.printStackTrace();
  }
} while (!stopped);
```

Finally, once the server has finished its execution (leaving the loop), we have to wait for the finalization of the executor using the `awaitTermination()` method. This method will block the main thread until the executor has finished its `execution()` method. Then, we shut down the cache system and wait for a message to indicate the end of the execution of the server, as follows:

```
executor.awaitTermination(1, TimeUnit.DAYS);
System.out.println("Shutting down cache");
cache.shutdown();
System.out.println("Cache ok");

System.out.println("Main server thread ended");
```

We have added two additional methods: the `getExecutor()` method, which returns the `ThreadPoolExecutor` object that is used to execute the concurrent tasks, and the `shutdown()` method, which is used to finish in an ordered way the executor of the server. It calls the `shutdown()` method of the executor and closes `ServerSocket`:

```
public static void shutdown() {
  stopped = true;
```

```
      System.out.println("Shutting down the server...");
      System.out.println("Shutting down executor");
      executor.shutdown();
      System.out.println("Executor ok");
      System.out.println("Closing socket");
      try {
        serverSocket.close();
        System.out.println("Socket ok");
      } catch (IOException e) {
        e.printStackTrace();
      }
      System.out.println("Shutting down logger");
      Logger.sendMessage("Shutting down the logger");
      Logger.shutdown();
      System.out.println("Logger ok");
    }
```

In the concurrent server, there is an essential part: the `RequestTask` class which processes every request of the clients. This class implements the `Runnable` interface, so it can be executed in an executor in a concurrent way. Its constructor receives the `Socket` parameter which will be used to communicate to the client:

```
public class RequestTask implements Runnable {

  private Socket clientSocket;

  public RequestTask(Socket clientSocket) {
    this.clientSocket = clientSocket;
  }
```

The `run()` method does the same things that are done by the serial server to respond to every requests:

- Receives a query for a client
- Parses and splits the elements of the query
- Calls the corresponding command
- Returns the results to the client

The following is its code snippet:

```
    public void run() {

      try (PrintWriter out = new
        PrintWriter(clientSocket.getOutputStream(),
        true);
```

```java
BufferedReader in = new BufferedReader(new
  InputStreamReader(
  clientSocket.getInputStream())););) {

String line = in.readLine();

Logger.sendMessage(line);
ParallelCache cache = ConcurrentServer.getCache();
String ret = cache.get(line);

if (ret == null) {
  Command command;

  String[] commandData = line.split(";");
  System.out.println("Command: " + commandData[0]);
  switch (commandData[0]) {
  case "q":
    System.err.println("Query");
    command = new ConcurrentQueryCommand(commandData);
    break;
  case "r":
    System.err.println("Report");
    command = new ConcurrentReportCommand(commandData);
    break;
  case "s":
    System.err.println("Status");
    command = new ConcurrentStatusCommand(commandData);
    break;
  case "z":
    System.err.println("Stop");
    command = new ConcurrentStopCommand(commandData);
    break;
  default:
    System.err.println("Error");
    command = new ConcurrentErrorCommand(commandData);
    break;
  }
  ret = command.execute();
  if (command.isCacheable()) {
    cache.put(line, ret);
  }
} else {
  Logger.sendMessage("Command "+line+" was found in the
  cache");
```

```
      }

      System.out.println(ret);
      out.println(ret);
    } catch (Exception e) {
      e.printStackTrace();
    } finally {
      try {
        clientSocket.close();
      } catch (IOException e) {
        e.printStackTrace();
      }
    }
  }
}
```

The command part

In the command part, we have renamed all the classes as you can see in the previous fragment of code. The implementation is the same except in the `ConcurrentStopCommand` class. Now, it calls the `shutdown()` method of the `ConcurrentServer` class to terminate the execution of the server in an ordered way. This is the `execute()` method:

```
@Override
public String execute() {
  ConcurrentServer.shutdown();
  return "Server stopped";
}
```

Also, now the `Command` class contains a new `isCacheable()` Boolean method that returns `true` if the command result is stored in the cache and `false` otherwise.

Extra components of the concurrent server

We have implemented some extra components in the concurrent server: a new command to return information about the status of the server, a cache system to store the results of the commands, time saving when a request is repeated, and a log system to write error and debug information. The following sections describe each of these components.

The status command

First of all, we have a new possible query. It has the format `s;` and is processed by the `ConcurrentStatusCommand` class. It gets `ThreadPoolExecutor` used by the server and obtains information about the status of the executor:

```java
public class ConcurrentStatusCommand extends Command {
  public ConcurrentStatusCommand (String[] command) {
    super(command);
    setCacheable(false);
  }
  @Override
  public String execute() {
    StringBuilder sb=new StringBuilder();
    ThreadPoolExecutor executor=ConcurrentServer.getExecutor();

    sb.append("Server Status;");
    sb.append("Actived Threads: ");
    sb.append(String.valueOf(executor.getActiveCount()));
    sb.append(";");
    sb.append("Maximum Pool Size: ");
    sb.append(String.valueOf(executor.getMaximumPoolSize()));
    sb.append(";");
    sb.append("Core Pool Size: ");
    sb.append(String.valueOf(executor.getCorePoolSize()));
    sb.append(";");
    sb.append("Pool Size: ");
    sb.append(String.valueOf(executor.getPoolSize()));
    sb.append(";");
    sb.append("Largest Pool Size: ");
    sb.append(String.valueOf(executor.getLargestPoolSize()));
    sb.append(";");
    sb.append("Completed Task Count: ");
    sb.append(String.valueOf(executor.getCompletedTaskCount()));
    sb.append(";");
    sb.append("Task Count: ");
    sb.append(String.valueOf(executor.getTaskCount()));
    sb.append(";");
    sb.append("Queue Size: ");
    sb.append(String.valueOf(executor.getQueue().size()));
    sb.append(";");
    sb.append("Cache Size: ");
    sb.append(String.valueOf
      (ConcurrentServer.getCache().getItemCount()));
    sb.append(";");
```

```
        Logger.sendMessage(sb.toString());
        return sb.toString();
    }
}
```

The information we obtain from the server is:

- `getActiveCount()`: This returns the approximate number of tasks that execute our concurrent tasks. There can be more threads in the pool, but they can be idle.
- `getMaximumPoolSize()`: This returns the maximum number of worker-threads the executor can have.
- `getCorePoolSize()`: This returns the core number of worker-threads the executor will have. This number determines the minimum number of threads the pool will have.
- `getPoolSize()`: This returns the current number of threads in the pool.
- `getLargestPoolSize()`: This returns the maximum number of threads of the pool during its execution.
- `getCompletedTaskCount()`: This returns the number of tasks the executor has executed.
- `getTaskCount()`: This returns the approximate number of tasks that have ever been scheduled for execution.
- `getQueue().size()`: This returns the number of tasks that are waiting in the queue of tasks.

As we have created our executor using the `newFixedThreadPool()` method of the `Executor` class, our executor will have the same maximum and core worker-threads.

The cache system

We have included a cache system in our parallel server to avoid the data search that has recently been made. Our cache system has three elements:

- **The CacheItem class**: This class represents every element stored in the cache. It has four attributes:
    - The command stored in the cache. We will store the `query` and `report` commands in the cache.
    - The response generated by that command.
    - The creation date of the item in the cache.
    - The last time this item was accessed in the cache.

- **The CleanCacheTask class**: If we store all the commands in the cache but never delete the elements stored in it, the cache will increase its size indefinitely. To avoid this situation, we can have a task that deletes elements in the cache. We are going to implement this task as a `Thread` object. There are two options:
    - You can have the maximum size in the cache. If the cache has more elements than the maximum size, you can delete the elements that have been accessed less recently.
    - You can delete from the cache the elements that haven't been accessed in a predefined period of time. We are going to use this approach.
- **The ParallelCache class**: This class implements the operations to store and retrieve elements in the cache. To store the data in the cache, we have used a `ConcurrentHashMap` data structure. As the cache will be shared between all the tasks of the server, we have to use a synchronization mechanism to protect the access to the cache avoiding data race conditions. We have three options:
    - We can use a non-synchronized data structure (for example, a `HashMap`) and add the necessary code to synchronize the types of access to this data structure, for example, with a lock. You can also convert a `HashMap` into a synchronized structure using the `synchronizedMap()` method of the `Collections` class.
    - Use a synchronized data structure, for example, `Hashtable`. In this case, we don't have data race conditions, but the performance can be better.
    - Use a concurrent data structure, for example, a `ConcurrentHashMap` class, which eliminates the possibility of data race conditions and it's optimized to work in a high concurrent environment. This is the option we're going to implement using an object of the `ConcurrentHashMap` class.

The code of the `CleanCacheTask` class is as follows:

```
public class CleanCacheTask implements Runnable {

  private ParallelCache cache;

  public CleanCacheTask(ParallelCache cache) {
    this.cache = cache;
  }
```

```
  @Override
  public void run() {
    try {
      while (!Thread.currentThread().interrupted()) {
        TimeUnit.SECONDS.sleep(10);
        cache.cleanCache();
      }
    } catch (InterruptedException e) {

    }
  }

}
```

The class has a `ParallelCache` object. Every 10 seconds, it executes the `cleanCache()` method of the `ParallelCache` instance.

The `ParallelCache` class has five different methods. First, the constructor of the class that initializes the elements of the cache. It creates the `ConcurrentHashMap` object and starts a thread that will execute the `CleanCacheTask` class:

```
public class ParallelCache {

  private ConcurrentHashMap<String, CacheItem> cache;
  private CleanCacheTask task;
  private Thread thread;
  public static int MAX_LIVING_TIME_MILLIS = 600_000;

  public ParallelCache() {
    cache=new ConcurrentHashMap<>();
    task=new CleanCacheTask(this);
    thread=new Thread(task);
    thread.start();
  }
```

Then, there are two methods to store and retrieve an element in the cache. We use the `put()` method to insert the element in the `HashMap` and the `get()` method to retrieve the element from the `HashMap`:

```
  public void put(String command, String response) {
    CacheItem item = new CacheItem(command, response);
    cache.put(command, item);

  }
```

```java
public String get (String command) {
  CacheItem item=cache.get(command);
  if (item==null) {
    return null;
  }
  item.setAccessDate(new Date());
  return item.getResponse();
}
```

Then, the method to clean the cache used by the `CleanCacheTask` class is:

```java
public void cleanCache() {
  Date revisionDate = new Date();
  Iterator<CacheItem> iterator = cache.values().iterator();

  while (iterator.hasNext()) {
    CacheItem item = iterator.next();
    if (revisionDate.getTime() - item.getAccessDate().getTime()
      > MAX_LIVING_TIME_MILLIS) {
      iterator.remove();
    }
  }
}
```

Finally, the method to shut down the cache that interrupts the thread executing the `CleanCacheTask` class and the method that returns the number of elements stored in the cache is:

```java
public void shutdown() {
  thread.interrupt();
}

public int getItemCount() {
  return cache.size();
}
```

The log system

In all the examples of this chapter, we write information in the console using the `System.out.println()` method. When you implement an enterprise application that is going to execute in a production environment, it's a better idea to use a log system to write debug and error information. In Java, `log4j` is the most popular log system. In this example, we are going to implement our own log system implementing the producer/consumer concurrency design pattern. The tasks that will use our log system will be the producer, and a special task (executed as a thread) that will write the log information into a file will be the consumer. The components of this log system are:

- **LogTask**: This class implements the log consumer that after every 10 seconds reads the log messages stored in the queue and writes them to a file. It will be executed by a `Thread` object.
- **Logger**: This is the main class of our log system. It has a queue where the producer will store the information and the consumer will read it. It also includes the method to add a message into the queue and a method to get all the messages stored in the queue and write them to disk.

To implement the queue, as happens with the cache system, we need a concurrent data structure to avoid any data inconsistency errors. We have two options:

- Use a **blocking data structure**, which blocks the thread when the queue is full (in our case, it will never be full) or empty
- Use a **non-blocking data structure**, which returns a special value if the queue is full or empty

We have chosen a non-blocking data structure, the `ConcurrentLinkedQueue` class, which implements the `Queue` interface. We use the `offer()` method to insert elements in the queue and the `poll()` method to get elements from it.

The `LogTask` class code is very simple:

```
public class LogTask implements Runnable {

  @Override
  public void run() {
    try {
```

```
      while (Thread.currentThread().interrupted()) {
        TimeUnit.SECONDS.sleep(10);
        Logger.writeLogs();
      }
    } catch (InterruptedException e) {
    }
    Logger.writeLogs();
  }
}
```

The class implements the `Runnable` interface and, in the `run()` method, calls the `writeLogs()` method of the `Logger` class every 10 seconds.

The `Logger` class has five different static methods. First of all, a static block of code that initializes and starts a thread that executes the `LogTask` and creates the `ConcurrentLinkedQueue` class used to store the log data:

```
public class Logger {

  private static ConcurrentLinkedQueue<String> logQueue = new
    ConcurrentLinkedQueue<String>();

  private static Thread thread;

  private static final String LOG_FILE = Paths.get("output",
    "server.log").toString();

  static {
    LogTask task = new LogTask();
    thread = new Thread(task);
  }
```

Then, there is a `sendMessage()` method that receives a string as a parameter and stores that message in the queue. To store the message, it uses the `offer()` method:

```
  public static void sendMessage(String message) {
    logQueue.offer(new Date()+": "+message);
  }
```

A critical method of this class is the `writeLogs()` class. It obtains and deletes all the log messages stored in the queue using the `poll()` method of the `ConcurrentLinkedQueue` class and writes them to a file:

```
  public static void writeLogs() {
    String message;
    Path path = Paths.get(LOG_FILE);
```

```java
      try (BufferedWriter fileWriter =
        Files.newBufferedWriter(path,StandardOpenOption.CREATE,
          StandardOpenOption.APPEND)) {
        while ((message = logQueue.poll()) != null) {
          fileWriter.write(new Date()+": "+message);
          fileWriter.newLine();
        }
      } catch (IOException e) {
        e.printStackTrace();
      }
    }
```

Finally, two methods: one to truncate the log file and another to finish the executor of the log system, which interrupts the thread that is executing `LogTask`:

```java
    public static void initializeLog() {
      Path path = Paths.get(LOG_FILE);
      if (Files.exists(path)) {
        try (OutputStream out = Files.newOutputStream(path,
            StandardOpenOption.TRUNCATE_EXISTING)) {

        } catch (IOException e) {
          e.printStackTrace();
        }
      }
      thread.start();
    }
    public static void shutdown() {
      thread.interrupt();
    }
```

Comparing the two solutions

Now it's time to test the serial and concurrent servers and see which has a better performance. We have automatized the tests implementing four classes that make queries to the servers. These classes are:

- `SerialClient`: This implements a possible client of the serial server. It makes nine requests using the query message and a query using the report message. It repeats the process 10 times, so it request 90 queries and 10 reports.
- `MultipleSerialClients`: This class simulates the existence of several clients at the same time. For this, we create a thread per `SerialClient` and execute them at the same time to see the performance of the server. We have tested from one to five concurrent clients.

- `ConcurrentClient`: It is analogue to the `SerialClient` class, but it calls the concurrent server instead of the serial one.
- `MultipleConcurrentClients`: It is analogue to the `MultipleSerialClients` class, but it calls the concurrent server instead of the serial one.

To test the serial server, you can follow these steps:

1. Launch the serial server and wait for its initialization.
2. Launch the `MultipleSerialClients` class, which launches one, then two, three, four, and finally, five `SerialClient` classes.

You can follow a similar process with the concurrent server:

1. Launch the concurrent server and wait for its initialization.
2. Launch the `MultipleConcurrentClients` class, which launches one, two, three, four, and finally, five `ConcurrentClient` classes.

To compare the execution times of both versions, we have implemented a microbenchmark using the JMH framework (http://openjdk.java.net/projects/code-tools/jmh/). We have implemented two executions based in the `SerialClient` and `ConcurrentClient` tasks. We have repeated this process 10 times calculating the mean time per number of concurrent clients. We launched the tests in a computer with a processor with four cores, so it can execute four parallel tasks at the same time.

These are the results of all these executions:

Concurrent clients	Serial server	Concurrent server	Speedup
1	7.404	5.144	1.43
2	9.344	4.491	2.08
3	19.641	9.308	2.11
4	29.180	12.842	2.27
5	30.542	16.322	1.87

The contents of the cells are the mean time of each client in seconds. We can draw the following conclusions:

- The performance of both kinds of servers is affected by the number of concurrent clients that send requests to our server
- In all cases, the execution times of the concurrent version are much lower than the execution times of the serial one

Other methods of interest

Throughout the pages of this chapter, we have used some classes of the Java concurrency API to implement basic functionalities of the executor framework. These classes also have other interesting methods. In this section, we collate some of them.

The `Executors` class provides other methods to create `ThreadPoolExecutor` objects. These methods are:

- `newCachedThreadPool()`: This method creates a `ThreadPoolExecutor` object that reuses a worker-thread if it's idle, but it creates a new one if it's necessary. There is no maximum number of worker-threads.
- `newSingleThreadExecutor()`: This method creates a `ThreadPoolExecutor` object that uses only a single worker-thread. The tasks you send to the executor are stored in a queue until the worker-thread can execute them.
- The `CountDownLatch` class provides the following additional methods:
    - `await(long timeout, TimeUnit unit)`: It waits till the internal counter arrives to zero of pass the time specified in the parameters. If the time passes, the method returns the `false` value.
    - `getCount()`: This method returns the actual value of the internal counter.

There are two types of concurrent data structures in Java:

- **Blocking data structures**: When you call a method and the library can't do that operation (for example, you try to obtain an element, and the data structure is empty), they block the thread until the operation can be done.
- **Non-blocking data structures**: When you call a method and the library can't do that operation (because the structure is empty or full), the method returns a special value or throws an exception.

There are data structures that implement both behaviors and data structures that implement only one. Usually, blocking data structures also implement the methods with non-blocking behavior, and non-blocking data structures don't implement the blocking methods.

The methods that implement the blocking operations are:

- `put()`, `putFirst()`, `putLast()`: These insert an element in the data structure. If it's full, it blocks the thread until there is space.
- `take()`, `takeFirst()`, `takeLast()`: These return and remove an element of the data structure. If it's empty, it blocks the thread until there is an element in it.

Managing Lots of Threads – Executors

The methods that implement the non-blocking operations are:

- `add()`, `addFirst()`, `addLast()`: These insert an element in the data structure. If it's full, the method throws an `IllegalStateException` exception.
- `remove()`, `removeFirst()`, `removeLast()`: These return and remove an element from the data structure. If it's empty, the method throws an `IllegalStateException` exception.
- `element()`, `getFirst()`, `getLast()`: These return but don't remove an element from the data structure. If it's empty, the method throws an `IllegalStateException` exception.
- `offer()`, `offerFirst()`, `offerLast()`: These insert an element value in the data structure. If it's full, they return the `false` Boolean value.
- `poll()`, `pollFirst()`, `pollLast()`: These return and remove an element from the data structure. If it's empty, they return the null value.
- `peek()`, `peekFirst()`, `peekLast()`: These return but don't remove an element from the data structure. If it's empty, they return the null value.

In *Chapter 9, Diving into Concurrent Data Structures and Synchronization Utilities*, we will describe concurrent data structures in more detail.

Summary

In simple concurrent applications, we execute concurrent tasks using the `Runnable` interface and the `Thread` class. We create and manage the threads and control their execution. We can't follow this approach in big concurrent applications because it can cause us many problems. For these cases, the Java concurrency API has introduced the executor framework. In this chapter, we presented the basic characteristics and components that form this framework. First of all, the `Executor` interface, which defines the basic method to send a `Runnable` task to an executor. This interface has a subinterface, the `ExecutorService` interface, which includes methods to send to the executor tasks that return a result (these tasks implement the `Callable` interface, as we will see in *Chapter 4, Getting Data from the Tasks – The Callable and Future Interfaces*) and a list of tasks.

The `ThreadPoolExecutor` class is the basic implementation of both interfaces: adding additional methods to get information about the status of the executor and the number of threads or tasks that are executing. The easiest way to create an object of this class is by using the `Executors` utility class, which includes methods to create different kinds of executors.

We showed you how to use executors and convert serial algorithms to concurrent ones using executors implementing two real-world examples. The first example is the k-nearest neighbors algorithm, applying it to the Bank Marketing dataset of the UCI machine learning repository. The second example is a client/server application to make queries over the World Development Indicators of the World Bank.

In both cases, the use of executors gave us a great improvement of performance.

In the next chapter, we will describe how to implement advanced techniques with executors. We are going to complete our client/server application adding the possibility of cancelling and executing tasks with higher priority before the tasks with a lower priority. We will also show you how to implement tasks that will execute periodically, implementing an RSS news reader.

3
Getting the Maximum from Executors

In *Chapter 2*, *Managing Lots of Threads – Executors*, we introduced the basic characteristics of executors as a way to improve the performance of concurrent applications that execute lots of concurrent tasks. In this chapter, we go a step further and explain advanced characteristics of executors that make them a powerful tool for your concurrent application. In this chapter, we will cover the following:

- Advanced characteristics of executors
- First example – an advanced server application
- Second example – executing periodic tasks
- Additional information about executors

Advanced characteristics of executors

An executor is a class that allows the programmers to execute concurrent tasks without being worried about the creation and management of threads. Programmers create `Runnable` objects and send them to the executor that creates and manages the necessary threads to execute those tasks. In *Chapter 2*, *Managing Lots of Threads – Executors*, we introduced the basic characteristics of the executor framework:

- How to create an executor and the different options we have when we create one
- How to send a concurrent task to an executor
- How to control the resources used by the executor
- How the executor, internally, uses a pool of threads to optimize the performance of the application

However, executors can give you many more options to make them a powerful mechanism in your concurrent application.

Cancellation of tasks

You can cancel the execution of a task after you send it to an executor. When you send a `Runnable` object to an executor using the `submit()` method, it returns an implementation of the `Future` interface. This class allows you to control the execution of the task. It has the `cancel()` method, which attempts to cancel the execution of the task. It receives a boolean value as a parameter. If it takes the `true` value and the executor is executing this task, the thread executing the task will be interrupted.

These are the situations when the task you want to cancel can't be canceled:

- The task has already been canceled
- The task has finished its execution
- The task is running and you supplied `false` as a parameter to the `cancel()` method
- Other reasons not specified in the API documentation

The `cancel()` method returns a boolean value to indicate whether the task has been canceled or not.

Scheduling the execution of tasks

The `ThreadPoolExecutor` class is the basic implementation of the `Executor` and `ExecutorService` interfaces. But the Java concurrency API provides an extension of this class to allow the execution of scheduled tasks. It's the `ScheduledThreadPoolExeuctor` class, and you can:

- Execute a task after a delay
- Execute a task periodically; this includes the execution of tasks at a fixed rate or with a fixed delay

Overriding the executor methods

The executor framework is a very flexible mechanism. You can implement your own executor extending one of the existing classes (`ThreadPoolExecutor` or `ScheduledThreadPoolExecutor`) to get the desired behavior. These classes include methods that make it easy to change how the executor works. If you override `ThreadPoolExecutor`, you can override the following methods:

- `beforeExecute()`: This method is invoked before the execution of a concurrent task in an executor. It receives the `Runnable` object that is going to be executed and the `Thread` object that will execute them. The `Runnable` object that this method receives is an instance of the `FutureTask` class and not the `Runnable` object you sent to the executor using the `submit()` method.

- `afterExecute()`: This method is invoked after the execution of a concurrent task in the executor. It receives the `Runnable` object that has been executed and a `Throwable` object that stores a possible exception thrown inside the task. As in the `beforeExecute()` method, the `Runnable` object is an instance of the `FutureTask` class.

- `newTaskFor()`: This method creates the task that is going to execute the `Runnable` object you sent using the `submit()` method. It must return an implementation of the `RunnableFuture` interface. By default, Open JDK 8 and Oracle JDK 8 returns an instance of the `FutureTask` class, but this circumstance can change in future implementations.

If you extend the `ScheduledThreadPoolExecutor` class, you can override the `decorateTask()` method. This method is like the `newTaskFor()` for the scheduled tasks. It allows you to override the tasks executed by the executor.

Changing some initialization parameters

You can also change the behavior of an executor by changing some parameters at its creation. The most useful ones are:

- `BlockingQueue<Runnable>`: Every executor uses an internal `BlockingQueue` to store the tasks that are waiting for its execution. You can pass any implementation of this interface as a parameter. For example, you can change the default order used by the executor to execute the tasks.

- `ThreadFactory`: You can specify an implementation of the `ThreadFactory` interface, and the executor will use that factory to create the threads that will execute the tasks. For example, you can use a `ThreadFactory` interface to create an extension of the `Thread` class that saves log information about the execution times of the tasks.

- **RejectedExecutionHandler**: After you call the `shutdown()` or the `shutdownNow()` method, all the tasks that are sent to the executor will be rejected. You can specify an implementation of the `RejectedExecutionHandler` interface to manage this situation.

The first example – an advanced server application

In *Chapter 2, Managing Lots of Threads – Executors*, we presented an example of a client/server application. We implemented a server to search data over the World Development Indicators of the World Bank and a client that makes multiple calls to that server to test the performance of the executor.

In this section, we will extend that example to add to it the following characteristics:

- You can cancel the execution of queries in the server, using a new cancellation query.
- You can control the order of execution of queries using a priority parameter. Tasks with higher priority will be executed first.
- The server will calculate the number of tasks and the total execution time used by the different users that use the server.

To implement these new characteristics, we have made the following changes to the server:

- We have added two parameters to every query. The first one is the name of the user that sends the query, and the other is the priority of the query. The new format of the queries are as follows:
    - **Query**: `q;username;priority;codCountry;codIndicator;year` where `username` is the name of the user, `priority` is the priority of the query, `codCountry` is the code of the country, `codIndicator` is the code of the indicator, and `year` is an optional parameter with the year you want to query.
    - **Report**: `r;username;priority;codIndicator` where `username` is the name of the user, `priority` is the priority of the query, and `codIndicator` is the code of the indicator you want to report.
    - **Status**: `s;username;priority` where `username` is the name of the user and `priority` is the priority of the query.
    - **Stop**: `z;username;priority` where `username` is the name of the user, and `priority` is the priority of the query.

- We have implemented a new query:
    - **Cancel**: `c;username;priority` where `username` is the name of the user, and `priority` is the priority of the query.
- We have implemented our own executor to:
    - Calculate the server use per user
    - Execute the tasks by priority
    - Control the rejection of tasks
    - We have adapted `ConcurrentServer` and `RequestTask` to take into account the new elements of the server

The rest of the elements of the server (the cache system, the log system, and the `DAO` class) are the same, so it won't be described again.

The ServerExecutor class

As we mentioned earlier, we have implemented our own executor to execute the tasks of the server. We also have implemented some additional but necessary classes to provide all the functionality. Let's describe these classes.

The statistics object

Our server will calculate the number of tasks that every user executes on it and the total execution time of these tasks. To store this data, we have implemented the `ExecutorStatistics` class. It has two attributes to store the information:

```
public class ExecutorStatistics {
    private AtomicLong executionTime = new AtomicLong(0L);
    private AtomicInteger numTasks = new AtomicInteger(0);
```

These attributes are `AtomicVariables` that support atomic operations on single variables. This allows you to use those variables in different threads without using any synchronization mechanisms. Then, it has two methods to increment the number of tasks and the execution time:

```
public void addExecutionTime(long time) {
    executionTime.addAndGet(time);
}
public void addTask() {
    numTasks.incrementAndGet();
}
```

Finally, we have added methods to get the value of both attributes, and we have overridden the `toString()` method to get the information in a readable way:

```
@Override
public String toString() {
    return "Executed Tasks: "+getNumTasks()+". Execution Time: 
      "+getExecutionTime();
}
```

The rejected task controller

When you create an executor, you can specify a class to manage its rejected tasks. A task is rejected by the executor when you submit it after the `shutdown()` or `shutdownNow()` methods has been invoked in the executor.

To control this circumstance, we have implemented the `RejectedTaskController` class. This class implements the `RejectedExecutionHandler` interface and implements the `rejectedExecution()` method:

```
public class RejectedTaskController implements 
  RejectedExecutionHandler {

    @Override
    public void rejectedExecution(Runnable task,
      ThreadPoolExecutor executor) {
        ConcurrentCommand command=(ConcurrentCommand)task;
        Socket clientSocket=command.getSocket();
        try {
            PrintWriter out = new 
               PrintWriter(clientSocket.getOutputStream(),true);

            String message="The server is shutting down."
                +" Your request can not be served."
                +" Shutting Down: "
                +String.valueOf(executor.isShutdown())
                +". Terminated: "
                +String.valueOf(executor.isTerminated())
                +". Terminating: "
                +String.valueOf(executor.isTerminating());
            out.println(message);
            out.close();
            clientSocket.close();
        } catch (IOException e) {
            e.printStackTrace();
        }
    }
}
```

The `rejectedExecution()` method is called once per task that is rejected and receives as parameters the task that has been rejected and the executor that has rejected the task.

The executor tasks

When you submit a `Runnable` object to an executor, it doesn't execute that `Runnable` object directly. It creates a new object, an instance of the `FutureTask` class, and it's this task that is executed by the worker thread of the executor.

In our case, to measure the execution time of the tasks, we have implemented our own `FutureTask` implementation in the `ServerTask` class. It extends the `FutureTask` class and implements the `Comparable` interface as follows:

```
public class ServerTask<V> extends FutureTask<V> implements
   Comparable<ServerTask<V>>{
```

Internally, it stores the query that is going to execute as a `ConcurrentCommand` object:

```
    private ConcurrentCommand command;
```

In the constructor, it uses the constructor of the `FutureTask` class and stores the `ConcurrentCommand` object:

```
        public ServerTask(ConcurrentCommand command) {
            super(command, null);
            this.command=command;
        }

        public ConcurrentCommand getCommand() {
            return command;
        }

        public void setCommand(ConcurrentCommand command) {
            this.command = command;
        }
```

Finally, it implements the `compareTo()` operation comparing the commands stored by the two `ServerTask` instances to compare. This can be seen in the following code:

```
        @Override
        public int compareTo(ServerTask<V> other) {
            return command.compareTo(other.getCommand());
        }
```

The executor

Now that we have the auxiliary classes of the executor, we have to implement the executor itself. We have implemented the `ServerExecutor` class with this purpose. It extends the `ThreadPoolExecutor` class and has some internal attributes, as follows:

- `startTimes`: This is a `ConcurrentHashMap` to store the start date of every task. The key of the class will be the `ServerTask` object (a `Runnable` object), and the value will be a `Date` object.
- `executionStatistics`: This is a `ConcurrentHashMap` to store the statistics of use per user. The key will be the username and the value will be a `ExecutorStatistics` object.
- `CORE_POOL_SIZE`, `MAXIMUM_POOL_SIZE`, and `KEEP_ALIVE_TIME`: These are constants to define the characteristics of the executor.
- `REJECTED_TASK_CONTROLLER`: This is a `RejectedTaskController` class attribute to control the tasks rejected by the executor.

This can be explained by the following code:

```
public class ServerExecutor extends ThreadPoolExecutor {
    private ConcurrentHashMap<Runnable, Date> startTimes;
    private ConcurrentHashMap<String, ExecutorStatistics>
      executionStatistics;
    private static int CORE_POOL_SIZE =
      Runtime.getRuntime().availableProcessors();
    private static int MAXIMUM_POOL_SIZE =
      Runtime.getRuntime().availableProcessors();
    private static long KEEP_ALIVE_TIME = 10;

    private static RejectedTaskController REJECTED_TASK_CONTROLLER
      = new RejectedTaskController();

    public ServerExecutor() {
        super(CORE_POOL_SIZE, MAXIMUM_POOL_SIZE, KEEP_ALIVE_TIME,
          TimeUnit.SECONDS, new PriorityBlockingQueue<>(),
          REJECTED_TASK_CONTROLLER);

        startTimes = new ConcurrentHashMap<>();
        executionStatistics = new ConcurrentHashMap<>();
    }
```

The constructor of the class calls to the parent constructor creating a `PriorityBlockingQueue` class to store the tasks that will be executed in the executor. This class orders the elements according to the result of the execution of the `compareTo()` method (so the elements stored in it have to implement the `Comparable` interface). The utilization of this class will allow us to execute our tasks by priority.

Then, we have overridden some methods of the `ThreadPoolExecutor` class. First is the `beforeExecute()` method. This method is executed before the execution of every task. It receives the `ServerTask` object as a parameter, and the thread that is going to execute the task. In our case, we store the actual date in the `ConcurrentHashMap` with the start dates of every task, as follows:

```
protected void beforeExecute(Thread t, Runnable r) {
    super.beforeExecute(t, r);
    startTimes.put(r, new Date());
}
```

The next method is the `afterExecute()` method. This method is executed after the execution of every task in the executor and receives the `ServerTask` object that has been executed as parameter and a `Throwable` object. This last parameter will have value only when an exception is thrown during the execution of the task. In our case, we will use this method to:

- Calculate the execution time of the task.
- Update the statistics of the user in the following manner:

```
@Override
protected void afterExecute(Runnable r, Throwable t) {
    super.afterExecute(r, t);
    ServerTask<?> task=(ServerTask<?>)r;
    ConcurrentCommand command=task.getCommand();

    if (t==null) {
        if (!task.isCancelled()) {
            Date startDate =
              startTimes.remove(r);
            Date endDate=new Date();
            long executionTime= endDate.getTime() -
              startDate.getTime();
                        ;
            ExecutorStatistics statistics =
              executionStatistics.computeIfAbsent
              (command.getUsername(), n -> new
              ExecutorStatistics());
```

```
                    statistics.addExecutionTime(executionTime);
                    statistics.addTask();
                    ConcurrentServer.finishTask
                        (command.getUsername(), command);
                }
                else {

                    String message="The task"
                        + command.hashCode() + "of user"
                        + command.getUsername() + "has been
                        cancelled.";
                    Logger.sendMessage(message);
                }

            } else {

                String message="The exception "
                        +t.getMessage()
                        +" has been thrown.";
                Logger.sendMessage(message);
            }
        }
```

Finally, we have overridden the `newTaskFor()` method. This method will be executed to convert the `Runnable` object that we send to the executor, using the `submit()` method in the instance of `FutureTask` that will be executed by the executor. In our case, we replace the default `FutureTask` class with our `ServerTask` object:

```
@Override
protected <T> RunnableFuture<T> newTaskFor(Runnable runnable,
   T value) {
    return new ServerTask<T>(runnable);
}
```

We have included an additional method in the executor to write all the statistics stored in the executor in the log system. This method will be called at the end of the execution of the server, as you will see later. We have the following code:

```
public void writeStatistics() {

    for(Entry<String, ExecutorStatistics> entry:
      executionStatistics.entrySet()) {
        String user = entry.getKey();
        ExecutorStatistics stats = entry.getValue();
        Logger.sendMessage(user+":"+stats);
    }
}
```

The command classes

The command classes execute the different queries you can send to the server. You can send five different queries to our server:

- **Query**: This is to get information about a country, an indicator, and optionally a year. It's implemented by the `ConcurrentQueryCommand` class.
- **Report**: This is to get information about an indicator. It's implemented by the `ConcurrentReportCommand` class.
- **Status**: This is to get information about the status of a server. It's implemented by the `ConcurrentStatusCommand` class.
- **Cancel**: This is to cancel the execution of the tasks of a user. It's implemented by the `ConcurrentCancelCommand` class.
- **Stop**: This is to stop the execution of the server. It's implemented by the `ConcurrentStopCommand` class.

We also have the `ConcurrentErrorCommand` class to manage the situation when an unknown command arrives at the server, and `ConcurrentCommand` that is the base class of all the commands.

The ConcurrentCommand class

This is the base class of every command. It includes the behavior common to all the commands that includes the following:

- Call the method that implements the specific logic of every command
- Write the results to the client
- Close all the resources used in the communication

The class extends the `Command` class and implements the `Comparable` and `Runnable` interfaces. In the example of *Chapter 2, Managing Lots of Threads – Executors*, the commands were simple classes, but in this example, the concurrent commands are `Runnable` objects that will be sent to the executor:

```
public abstract class ConcurrentCommand extends Command implements
   Comparable<ConcurrentCommand>, Runnable{
```

It has three attributes:

- `username`: This is to store the name of the user that sends the query.
- `priority`: This is to store the priority of the query. It will determine the order of execution of the query.
- `socket`: This is the socket used in the communication with the client.

The constructor of the class initializes these attributes:

```
private String username;
private byte priority;
private Socket socket;

public ConcurrentCommand(Socket socket, String[] command) {
    super(command);
    username=command[1];
    priority=Byte.parseByte(command[2]);
    this.socket=socket;

}
```

The main functionality of this class is in the abstract `execute()` method, which will be implemented by every concrete command to calculate and return the results of the query, and in the `run()` method. The `run()` method calls the `execute()` method, stores the result in the cache, writes the result in the socket, and closes all the resources used in the communication. We have the following:

```
@Override
public abstract String execute();

@Override
public void run() {

    String message="Running a Task: Username: "
            +username
            +"; Priority: "
            +priority;
    Logger.sendMessage(message);

    String ret=execute();

    ParallelCache cache = ConcurrentServer.getCache();

    if (isCacheable()) {
        cache.put(String.join(";",command), ret);
    }

    try {
        PrintWriter out = new
          PrintWriter(socket.getOutputStream(),true);
        out.println(ret);
```

```
            socket.close();
        } catch (IOException e) {
            e.printStackTrace();
        }
        System.out.println(ret);
    }
```

Finally, the `compareTo()` method uses the priority attribute to determine the order of the tasks. This will be used by the `PriorityBlockingQueue` class to order the tasks, so the tasks with a higher priority will be executed first. Take into account that a task has higher priority when the `getPriority()` method returns a lower value. If the `getPriority()` of a task returns 1, that task will have a higher priority than a task that `getPriority()` method returns 2:

```
    @Override
    public int compareTo(ConcurrentCommand o) {
        return Byte.compare(o.getPriority(), this.getPriority());
    }
```

Concrete commands

We have made minor changes in the classes that implement the different commands, and we added a new one implemented by the `ConcurrentCancelCommand` class. The main logic of these classes is included in the `execute()` method that calculates the response to the query and returns it as a string.

The `execute()` method of the new `ConcurrentCancelCommand` makes a call to the `cancelTasks()` method of the `ConcurrentServer` class. This method will stop the execution of all the pending tasks associated with the user passed as a parameter:

```
    @Override
    public String execute() {
        ConcurrentServer.cancelTasks(getUsername());

        String message = "Tasks of user "
                +getUsername()
                +" has been cancelled.";
        Logger.sendMessage(message);
        return message;
    }
```

The `execute()` method of `ConcurrentReportCommand` uses the `query()` method of the `WDIDAO` class to get the data requested by the user. In *Chapter 2, Managing Lots of Threads – Executors*, you can find the implementation of this method. The implementation is almost the same. The only difference is command array indices as follows:

```
@Override
public String execute() {

    WDIDAO dao=WDIDAO.getDAO();

    if (command.length==5) {
        return dao.query(command[3], command[4]);
    } else if (command.length==6) {
        try {
            return dao.query(command[3], command[4],
                Short.parseShort(command[5]));
        } catch (NumberFormatException e) {
            return "ERROR;Bad Command";
        }
    } else {
        return "ERROR;Bad Command";
    }
}
```

The `execute()` method of `ConcurrentQueryCommand` uses the `report()` method of the `WDIDAO` class to get the data. In *Chapter 2, Managing Lots of Threads – Executors*, you also can find the implementation of this method. The implementation here is almost the same. The only difference is the command array index:

```
@Override
public String execute() {

    WDIDAO dao=WDIDAO.getDAO();
    return dao.report(command[3]);
}
```

`ConcurrentStatusCommand` has an additional parameter in its constructor: the `Executor` object, which will execute the commands. This command uses this object to obtain information about the executor and send it as a response to the user. The implementation is almost the same as in *Chapter 2, Managing Lots of Threads – Executors*. We have used the same methods to get the status of the `Executor` object.

The `ConcurrentStopCommand` and `ConcurrentErrorCommand` are also the same as in *Chapter 2, Managing Lots of Threads – Executors*, so we haven't included their source code.

The server part

The server part receives the queries from the clients of the server and creates the command classes that executes the queries and sends them to the executor. It is implemented by two classes:

- The `ConcurrentServer` class: It includes the `main()` method of the server and additional methods to cancel tasks and finish the execution of the system
- The `RequestTask` class: This class creates the commands and sends them to the executor

The main difference with the example of *Chapter 2, Managing Lots of Threads – Executors* is the role of the `RequestTask` class. In the `SimpleServer` example, the `ConcurrentServer` class creates a `RequestTask` object per query and sends them to the executor. In this example, we will only have an instance of the `RequestTask` that will be executed as a thread. When the `ConcurrentServer` receives a connection, it stores the socket to communicate with the client in a concurrent list of pending connections. The `RequestTask` thread reads that socket, processes the data sent by the client, creates the corresponding command, and sends the command to the executor.

The main reason for this change is to leave in the tasks executed by the executor only the code of the queries and leave the preprocessed code outside the executor.

The ConcurrentServer class

The `ConcurrentServer` class needs some internal attributes to work properly:

- A `ParallelCache` instance to use the cache system.
- A `ServerSocket` instance to get the connections from the clients.
- A `boolean` value to know when it has to stop its execution.
- A `LinkedBlockingQueue` to store the sockets of the clients that sends a message to the server. These sockets will be processed by the `RequestTask` class.

- A `ConcurrentHashMap` to store the `Future` objects associated with every task executed in the executor. The key will be the username of the users that sends the queries, and the values will be another `Map` whose key will be the `ConcurrenCommand` objects, and the value will be the `Future` instance associated with that task. We use these `Future` instances to cancel the execution of tasks.
- A `RequestTask` instance to create the commands and sends them to the executor.
- A `Thread` object to execute the `RequestTask` object.

The code for this is as follows:

```
public class ConcurrentServer {
    private static ParallelCache cache;
    private static volatile boolean stopped=false;
    private static LinkedBlockingQueue<Socket> pendingConnections;
    private static ConcurrentMap<String,
        ConcurrentMap<ConcurrentCommand, ServerTask<?>>>
        taskController;
    private static Thread requestThread;
    private static RequestTask task;
```

The `main()` method of this class initializes these objects and opens the `ServerSocket` instance to listen to the connections from the clients. In addition, it creates the `RequestTask` object and executes it as a thread. It will be in a loop until the `shutdown()` method changes the value of the stopped attribute. After this, it waits for the finalization of the `Executor` object, using the `endTermination()` method of the `RequestTask` object, and shuts down the `Logger` system and the `RequestTask` object with the `finishServer()` method:

```
    public static void main(String[] args) {

        WDIDAO dao=WDIDAO.getDAO();
        cache=new ParallelCache();
        Logger.initializeLog();
        pendingConnections = new LinkedBlockingQueue<Socket>();
        taskController = new ConcurrentHashMap<String,
            ConcurrentHashMap<Integer, Future<?>>>();
        task=new RequestTask(pendingConnections, taskController);
        requestThread=new Thread(task);
        requestThread.start();

        System.out.println("Initialization completed.");
```

```
            serverSocket= new ServerSocket(Constants.CONCURRENT_PORT);
            do {
                try {
                    Socket clientSocket = serverSocket.accept();
                    pendingConnections.put(clientSocket);
                } catch (Exception e) {
                    e.printStackTrace();
                }
            } while (!stopped);
            finishServer();
            System.out.println("Shutting down cache");
            cache.shutdown();
            System.out.println("Cache ok" + new Date());

}
```

It includes two methods to shut down the executor of the server. The `shutdown()` method changes the value of the `stopped` variable and closes the `serverSocket` instance. The `finishServer()` method stops the executor, interrupts the thread that executes the `RequestTask` object, and shuts downs the `Logger` system. We divided this process into two parts to use the `Logger` system until the last instruction of the server:

```
    public static void shutdown() {
        stopped=true;
        try {
            serverSocket.close();
        } catch (IOException e) {
            e.printStackTrace();
        }
    }

    private static void finishServer() {
        System.out.println("Shutting down the server...");
        task.shutdown();
        System.out.println("Shutting down Request task");
        requestThread.interrupt();
        System.out.println("Request task ok");
        System.out.println("Closing socket");
        System.out.println("Shutting down logger");
        Logger.sendMessage("Shutting down the logger");
        Logger.shutdown();
        System.out.println("Logger ok");
        System.out.println("Main server thread ended");
    }
```

The server includes the method that cancels the tasks associated with a user. As we mentioned before, the `Server` class uses a nested `ConcurrentHashMap` to store all the tasks associated with a user. First, we obtain the `Map` with all the tasks of a user and then we process all the `Future` objects of those tasks calling to the `cancel()` method of the `Future` objects. We pass the value `true` as a parameter, so if the executor is running a task from that user, it will be interrupted. We have included the necessary code to avoid the cancellation of `ConcurrentCancelCommand`:

```java
public static void cancelTasks(String username) {

    ConcurrentMap<ConcurrentCommand, ServerTask<?>> userTasks
      = taskController.get(username);
    if (userTasks == null) {
       return;
    }
    int taskNumber = 0;

    Iterator<ServerTask<?>> it =
      userTasks.values().iterator();
    while(it.hasNext()) {
        ServerTask<?> task = it.next();
         ConcurrentCommand command = task.getCommand();
          if(!(command instanceof ConcurrentCancelCommand) &&
           task.cancel(true)) {
             taskNumber++;
             Logger.sendMessage("Task with code
              "+command.hashCode()+"cancelled:
              "+command.getClass().getSimpleName());
             it.remove();
         }
    }
    String message=taskNumber+" tasks has been cancelled.";
    Logger.sendMessage(message);
}
```

Finally, we have included a method to eliminate the `Future` object associated with tasks from our nested map of `ServerTask` objects when that task finishes its execution normally. It's the `finishTask()` method:

```java
public static void finishTask(String username,
   ConcurrentCommand command) {

    ConcurrentMap<ConcurrentCommand, ServerTask<?>> userTasks
      = taskController.get(username);
    userTasks.remove(command);
```

```
        String message = "Task with code "+command.hashCode()+"
            has finished";
        Logger.sendMessage(message);

    }
```

The RequestTask class

The `RequestTask` class is the intermediary between the `ConcurrentServer` class, which connects to the clients, and the `Executor` class, which executes the concurrent tasks. It opens the socket with the client, reads the query data, creates the adequate command, and sends it to the executor.

It uses some internal attributes:

- A `LinkedBlockingQueue` where the `ConcurrentServer` class stores the client sockets
- A `ServerExecutor` to execute the commands as concurrent tasks
- A `ConcurrentHashMap` to store the `Future` objects associated with the tasks

The constructor of the class initializes all these objects:

```
public class RequestTask implements Runnable {
    private LinkedBlockingQueue<Socket> pendingConnections;
    private ServerExecutor executor = new ServerExecutor();
    private ConcurrentMap<String, ConcurrentMap<ConcurrentCommand,
        ServerTask<?>>> taskController;
    public RequestTask(LinkedBlockingQueue<Socket>
        pendingConnections, ConcurrentHashMap<String,
        ConcurrentHashMap<Integer, Future<?>>> taskController) {
            this.pendingConnections = pendingConnections;
            this.taskController = taskController;
    }
```

The main method of this class is the `run()` method. It executes a loop until the thread is interrupted processing the sockets stored in the `pendingConnections` object. In this object, the `ConcurrentServer` class stores the sockets to communicate with the different clients that sends a query to the server. It opens the socket, reads the data, and creates the corresponding command. This also sends the command to the executor and stores the `Future` object in the double `ConcurrentHashMap` associated with the `hashCode` of the task and with the user that sent the query:

```
    public void run() {
        try {
            while (!Thread.currentThread().interrupted()) {
```

```java
try {
    Socket clientSocket =
      pendingConnections.take();
    BufferedReader in = new BufferedReader(new
      InputStreamReader
      (clientSocket.getInputStream()));
    String line = in.readLine();

    Logger.sendMessage(line);

    ConcurrentCommand command;

    ParallelCache cache =
      ConcurrentServer.getCache();
    String ret = cache.get(line);
    if (ret == null) {
        String[] commandData = line.split(";");
        System.out.println("Command: " +
          commandData[0]);
        switch (commandData[0]) {
        case "q":
            System.out.println("Query");
            command = new
              ConcurrentQueryCommand(clientSocket,
              commandData);
            break;
        case "r":
            System.out.println("Report");
            command = new
              ConcurrentReportCommand
              (clientSocket, commandData);
            break;
        case "s":
            System.out.println("Status");
            command = new
              ConcurrentStatusCommand(executor,
              clientSocket, commandData);
            break;
        case "z":
            System.out.println("Stop");
            command = new
              ConcurrentStopCommand(clientSocket,
              commandData);
            break;
```

```
                    case "c":
                        System.out.println("Cancel");
                        command = new
                          ConcurrentCancelCommand
                            (clientSocket, commandData);
                        break;
                    default:
                        System.out.println("Error");
                        command = new
                          ConcurrentErrorCommand(clientSocket,
                            commandData);
                        break;
                    }

                    ServerTask<?> controller =
                        (ServerTask<?>)executor.submit(command);
                    storeContoller(command.getUsername(),
                        controller, command);
                } else {
                    PrintWriter out = new
                        PrintWriter
                          (clientSocket.getOutputStream(),true);
                    out.println(ret);
                    clientSocket.close();
                }

            } catch (IOException e) {
                e.printStackTrace();
            }
        }
    } catch (InterruptedException e) {
        // No Action Required
    }
}
```

The storeController() method is the one that stores the Future object in the double ConcurrentHashMap:

```
private void storeContoller(String userName, ServerTask<?>
  controller, ConcurrentCommand command) {
    taskController.computeIfAbsent(userName, k -> new
      ConcurrentHashMap<>()).put(command, controller);
}
```

Finally, we have included two methods to manage the execution of the `Executor` class, one to call the `shutdown()` method for the executor and an other to wait for its finalization. Remember that you must explicitly call the `shutdown()` or `shutdownNow()` methods to end the execution of an executor. If not, the program won't terminate. Look at the following code:

```java
public void shutdown() {

    String message="Request Task: "
            +pendingConnections.size()
            +" pending connections.";
    Logger.sendMessage(message);
    executor.shutdown();
}

public void terminate() {
    try {
        executor.awaitTermination(1,TimeUnit.DAYS);
        executor.writeStatistics();
    } catch (InterruptedException e) {
        e.printStackTrace();
    }

}
```

The client part

Now it's time to test our server. In this case, we won't worry much about the execution time. The main objective of our test is to check whether the new features work well.

We have split the client part into the following two classes:

- **The ConcurrentClient class**: This implements an individual client of the server. Each instance of this class has a different username. It makes 100 queries, 90 of type query, and 10 of type report. The query queries have a priority of 5, and the report queries have lower priority (10).
- **The MultipleConcurrentClient class**: This measures the behavior of the multiple concurrent clients in parallel. We have tested the server with one to five concurrent clients. This class also tests the cancellation and the stop commands.

We have included an executor to execute the concurrent requests to the server to increase the level of concurrency of the client.

In the following image, you can see the results of the cancellation of tasks:

```
Fri Jul 03 18:50:39 CEST 2015: Running a Task: Username: USER_2; Priority: 10
Fri Jul 03 18:50:39 CEST 2015: Task with code 1133714432 has been cancelled. ConcurrentQueryCommand
Fri Jul 03 18:50:39 CEST 2015: Task with code 1330614123 has been cancelled. ConcurrentQueryCommand
Fri Jul 03 18:50:39 CEST 2015: Task with code 399789995 has been cancelled. ConcurrentQueryCommand
Fri Jul 03 18:50:39 CEST 2015: Task with code 693908051 has been cancelled. ConcurrentQueryCommand
Fri Jul 03 18:50:39 CEST 2015: 4 tasks has been cancelled.
Fri Jul 03 18:50:39 CEST 2015: Tasks of user USER_2 has been cancelled.
Fri Jul 03 18:50:39 CEST 2015: Task with code 1920227428 has finished
Fri Jul 03 18:50:39 CEST 2015: The task 1133714432 of user USER_2 has been cancelled.
Fri Jul 03 18:50:39 CEST 2015: The task 693908051 of user USER_2 has been cancelled.
Fri Jul 03 18:50:39 CEST 2015: q;USER_2;5;SXM;NY.ADJ.DNGY.GN.ZS
```

In this case, four tasks of the **USER_2** user have been canceled.

The following image shows the final statistics about the number of tasks and the execution time of every user:

```
Fri Jul 03 20:25:01 CEST 2015: Request Task: 0 pending connections.
Fri Jul 03 20:25:01 CEST 2015: Task with code 1733877831 has finished
Fri Jul 03 20:25:01 CEST 2015: USER_2:Executed Tasks: 400. Execution Time: 40440
Fri Jul 03 20:25:01 CEST 2015: USER_3:Executed Tasks: 300. Execution Time: 26684
Fri Jul 03 20:25:01 CEST 2015: USER_1:Executed Tasks: 501. Execution Time: 56295
Fri Jul 03 20:25:01 CEST 2015: admin:Executed Tasks: 1. Execution Time: 6
Fri Jul 03 20:25:01 CEST 2015: USER_4:Executed Tasks: 200. Execution Time: 16080
Fri Jul 03 20:25:01 CEST 2015: USER_5:Executed Tasks: 100. Execution Time: 7213
Fri Jul 03 20:25:01 CEST 2015: Shuttingdown the logger
```

The second example – executing periodic tasks

In the previous examples with executors, the tasks were executed once, and they were executed as soon as possible. The executor framework includes other executor implementation that gives us more flexibility about the execution time of the tasks. It's the `ScheduledThreadPoolExecutor` class that allows us to execute tasks *periodically* and to execute tasks *after a delay*.

In this section, you will learn how to execute periodic tasks implementing a **RSS feed** reader. This is a simple case where you need to make the same task (reading the news of a RSS feed) at regular intervals. Our example will have the following characteristics:

- Store the RSS sources in a file. We have chosen news about the world from some important newspapers, such as The New York Times, the Daily News, or The Guardian.

- We sent a `Runnable` object to the executor per RSS source. Every time the executor runs the object, it parses the RSS source and converts it to a list of `CommonInformationItem` objects with the content of the RSS.
- We use the **Producer/Consumer design pattern** to write the RSS news to disk. The producers will be the tasks of the executor that write every `CommonInformationItem` into a buffer. Only the new items will be stored in the buffer. The consumer will be an independent thread that reads the news from the buffer and writes them to a disk.
- The time between the finalization of the execution of a task and its next execution will be one minute.

We also have implemented the advanced version of the example where the time between two executions of a task can vary.

The common parts

As we mentioned earlier, we read an RSS feed and convert them to a list of objects. To parse the RSS file, we treat them as an XML file, and we have implemented a **SAX** (short for **Simple API for XML**) parser in the `RSSDataCapturer` class. It parses the file and creates a list of `CommonInformationItem`. This class stores the following information for every RSS item:

- **Title**: Title of the RSS item.
- **Date**: Date of the RSS item.
- **Link**: Link to the RSS item.
- **Description**: The text of the RSS item.
- **ID**: The ID of the RSS item. If the item doesn't include an ID, we calculate it.
- **Source**: The name of the RSS source.

We store the news into a disk using the Producer/Consumer design pattern, so we need a buffer to store the news and a `Consumer` class that, in this case, reads the news from the buffer and stores them into the disk.

We implemented the buffer in the `NewsBuffer` class. It has two internal attributes:

- **A LinkedBlockingQueue**: This is a concurrent data structure with blocking operations. If we want to obtain an item from the list and it's empty, the thread of the calling method will be blocked until there are elements in the list. We will use this structure to store `CommonInformationItems`.
- **A ConcurrentHashMap**: This is a concurrent implementation of a `HashMap`. We will use it to store the IDs of the news items stored in the buffer before.

We will only insert in the buffer the news that wasn't inserted earlier:

```java
public class NewsBuffer {
    private LinkedBlockingQueue<CommonInformationItem> buffer;
    private ConcurrentHashMap<String, String> storedItems;

    public NewsBuffer() {
        buffer=new LinkedBlockingQueue<>();
        storedItems=new ConcurrentHashMap<String, String>();
    }
```

We have two methods in the `NewsBuffer` class: one to store an item in the buffer that checks whether the item has been inserted before, and the other to obtain the next item from the buffer. We use the `compute()` method to insert elements in the `ConcurrentHashMap`. This method receives a lambda expression as a parameter with the key and the actual value associated with this key (null if the key has no associated value). In our case, we add the item to the buffer it has not been processed before. We use the `add()` and `take()` methods to to insert, obtain, and delete elements from the queue:

```java
    public void add (CommonInformationItem item) {
        storedItems.compute(item.getId(), (id, oldSource) -> {
            if(oldSource == null) {
              buffer.add(item);
              return item.getSource();
            } else {
              System.out.println("Item "+item.getId()+" has been
                processed before");
              return oldSource;
            }
        });
    }

    public CommonInformationItem get() throws
      InterruptedException {
        return buffer.take();
    }
}
```

The items of the buffer will be written to disk by the `NewsWriter` class that will be executed as an independent thread. It only has an internal attribute that points to the `NewsBuffer` class used in the application:

```java
public class NewsWriter implements Runnable {
    private NewsBuffer buffer;
    public NewsWriter(NewsBuffer buffer) {
        this.buffer=buffer;
    }
```

The `run()` method of this `Runnable` object takes `CommonInformationItem` instances from the buffer and saves them to a disk. As we use the blocking method `take`, if the buffer is empty, this thread will be blocked until there are elements in the buffer:

```
public void run() {
    try {
        while (!Thread.currentThread().interrupted()) {
            CommonInformationItem item=buffer.get();

            Path path=Paths.get
              ("output\\"+item.getFileName());

            try (BufferedWriter fileWriter =
              Files.newBufferedWriter(path,
              StandardOpenOption.CREATE)) {
                fileWriter.write(item.toString());
            } catch (IOException e) {
                e.printStackTrace();
            }

        }
    } catch (InterruptedException e) {
        //Normal execution
    }
}
```

The basic reader

The basic reader will use a standard `ScheduledThreadPoolExecutor` class to execute the tasks periodically. We will execute a task per RSS source, and there will be one minute between the termination of one execution of a task and the commencement of the next execution. These concurrent tasks are implemented in the `NewsTask` class. It has three internal attributes to store the name of the RSS feed, its URL, and the `NewsBuffer` class to store the news:

```
public class NewsTask implements Runnable {
    private String name;
    private String url;
    private NewsBuffer buffer;

    public NewsTask (String name, String url, NewsBuffer buffer) {
        this.name=name;
        this.url=url;
        this.buffer-buffer;
    }
```

The run() method of this Runnable object simply parses the RSS feed, gets a list of CommonItemInterface instances, and stores them in the buffer. This method will be executed in a periodic way. In every execution, the run() method will be executed from the beginning to the end:

```java
@Override
public void run() {
    System.out.println(name+": Running. " + new Date());
    RSSDataCapturer capturer=new RSSDataCapturer(name);
    List<CommonInformationItem> items=capturer.load(url);

    for (CommonInformationItem item: items) {
        buffer.add(item);
    }
}
```

In this example, we also have implemented another thread to implement the initialization of the executor and the tasks and the wait for the finalization of the execution. We have named this class NewsSystem. It has three internal attributes to store the path to the file with the RSS sources, the buffer to store the news, and a CountDownLatch object to control the end of its execution. The CountDownLatch class is a synchronization mechanism that allows you to make a thread wait for an event. We will detail the utilization of this class in *Chapter 9, Diving into Concurrent Data Structures and Synchronization Utilities*. We have the following code:

```java
public class NewsSystem implements Runnable {
    private String route;
    private ScheduledThreadPoolExecutor executor;
    private NewsBuffer buffer;
    private CountDownLatch latch=new CountDownLatch(1);

    public NewsSystem(String route) {
        this.route = route;
        executor = new
          ScheduledThreadPoolExecutor
            (Runtime.getRuntime().availableProcessors());
        buffer=new NewsBuffer();
    }
```

Getting the Maximum from Executors

In the `run()` method, we read all the RSS sources, create a `NewsTask` class for each one, and send them to our `ScheduledThreadPool` executor. We have created the executor using the `newScheduledThreadPool()` method of the `Executors` class, and we send the tasks to it using the `scheduleAtFixedDelay()` method. We also start the `NewsWriter` instance as a thread. The `run()` method waits for someone that tells it to finish its execution using the `await()` method of the `CountDownLatch` class and ends the execution of the `NewsWriter` task and of the `ScheduledExecutor`.

```java
@Override
public void run() {
    Path file = Paths.get(route);
    NewsWriter newsWriter=new NewsWriter(buffer);
    Thread t=new Thread(newsWriter);
    t.start();

    try (InputStream in = Files.newInputStream(file);
            BufferedReader reader = new BufferedReader(
                new InputStreamReader(in))) {
        String line = null;
        while ((line = reader.readLine()) != null) {
            String data[] = line.split(";");

            NewsTask task = new NewsTask(data[0], data[1],
                buffer);
            System.out.println("Task "+task.getName());
            executor.scheduleWithFixedDelay(task,0, 1,
                TimeUnit.MINUTES);
        }
    } catch (Exception e) {
        e.printStackTrace();
    }

    synchronized (this) {
        try {
            latch.await();
        } catch (InterruptedException e) {
            e.printStackTrace();
        }
    }

    System.out.println("Shutting down the executor.");
    executor.shutdown();
    t.interrupt();
    System.out.println("The system has finished.");

}
```

We also have implemented the `shutdown()` method. This method will notify the `NewsSystem` class to end its execution using the `countDown()` method of the `CountDownLatch` class. This method will wake up the `run()` method, so it will shut down the executor that is running the `NewsTask` objects:

```
public void shutdown() {
    latch.countDown();
}
```

The last class of this example is the `Main` class that implements the `main()` method of the example. It starts a `NewsSystem` instance as a thread, waits 10 minutes, and notifies the thread of its finalization, and consequently finishes the execution of the entire system, as follows:

```
public class Main {

    public static void main(String[] args) {

        // Creates the System an execute it as a Thread
        NewsSystem system=new NewsSystem("data\\sources.txt");

        Thread t=new Thread(system);

        t.start();

        // Waits 10 minutes
        try {
            TimeUnit.MINUTES.sleep(10);
        } catch (InterruptedException e) {
            e.printStackTrace();
        }

        // Notifies the finalization of the System
         (
        system.shutdown();
    }
```

When you execute this example, you see how the different tasks are executed in a periodic way and how the news items are written to a disk, as shown in the following screenshot:

```
Task Denver Post
Task New York Post
Task Newsday
Task The Guardian
Task Financial Times
The New York Times: Running. Fri Jul 03 21:58:36 CEST 2015
Daily News: Running. Fri Jul 03 21:58:36 CEST 2015
Washington Post: Running. Fri Jul 03 21:58:36 CEST 2015
Los Angeles Times: Running. Fri Jul 03 21:58:36 CEST 2015
Wall Street Journal: Running. Fri Jul 03 21:58:38 CEST 2015
Denver Post: Running. Fri Jul 03 21:58:38 CEST 2015
New York Post: Running. Fri Jul 03 21:58:38 CEST 2015
Newsday: Running. Fri Jul 03 21:58:38 CEST 2015
The Guardian: Running. Fri Jul 03 21:58:38 CEST 2015
Financial Times: Running. Fri Jul 03 21:58:38 CEST 2015
Daily News: Running. Fri Jul 03 21:59:38 CEST 2015
Los Angeles Times: Running. Fri Jul 03 21:59:38 CEST 2015
Washington Post: Running. Fri Jul 03 21:59:38 CEST 2015
The New York Times: Running. Fri Jul 03 21:59:38 CEST 2015
Wall Street Journal: Running. Fri Jul 03 21:59:39 CEST 2015
New York Post: Running. Fri Jul 03 21:59:39 CEST 2015
Newsday: Running. Fri Jul 03 21:59:39 CEST 2015
Denver Post: Running. Fri Jul 03 21:59:39 CEST 2015
```

The advanced reader

The basic news reader is an example of utilization of a `ScheduledThreadPoolExecutor` class, but we can go a step further. As occurs with `ThreadPoolExecutor`, we can implement our own `ScheduledThreadPoolExecutor` to obtain a particular behavior. In our case, we want that the delay time of our periodic task changes depending on the moment of the day. In this part, you will learn how to implement this behavior.

The first step is to implement a class that tells us the delay between two executions of a periodic task. We named this the `Timer` class. It only has a static method named `getPeriod()`, which returns the number of milliseconds between the end of one execution and the start of the next one. This is our implementation, but you can make your own:

```
public class Timer {
    public static long getPeriod() {
        Calendar calendar = Calendar.getInstance();
        int hour = calendar.get(Calendar.HOUR_OF_DAY);
```

```
            if ((hour >= 6) && (hour <= 8)) {
                return TimeUnit.MILLISECONDS.convert(1,
                    TimeUnit.MINUTES);
            }

            if ((hour >= 13) && (hour <= 14)) {
                return TimeUnit.MILLISECONDS.convert(1,
                    TimeUnit.MINUTES);
            }

            if ((hour >= 20) && (hour <= 22)) {
                return TimeUnit.MILLISECONDS.convert(1,
                    TimeUnit.MINUTES);
            }
            return TimeUnit.MILLISECONDS.convert(2, TimeUnit.MINUTES);
        }
    }
```

Next, we have to implement the internal tasks of our executor. When you send a `Runnable` object to an executor, externally, you see that object as the concurrent task but the executor converts this object into another task, an instance of the `FutureTask` class, that includes the `run()` method to execute the task and the methods of the `Future` interface to manage the execution of the task. To implement this example, we have to implement a class that extends the `FutureTask` class, and, as we will execute these tasks in a **scheduled executor**, it has to implement the `RunnableScheduledFuture` interface. This interface provides the `getDelay()` method that returns the time remaining to the next execution of a task. We have implemented these internal tasks in the `ExecutorTask` class. It has four internal attributes:

- The original `RunnableScheduledFuture` internal task created by the `ScheduledThreadPoolExecutor` class
- The scheduled executor that will execute the task
- The start date of the next execution of the task
- The name of the RSS feed

The code for this is as follows:

```
public class ExecutorTask<V> extends FutureTask<V> implements
    RunnableScheduledFuture<V> {
        private RunnableScheduledFuture<V> task;

        private NewsExecutor executor;
```

```java
        private long startDate;

        private String name;

        public ExecutorTask(Runnable runnable, V result,
          RunnableScheduledFuture<V> task,
          NewsExecutor executor) {
            super(runnable, result);
            this.task = task;
            this.executor = executor;
            this.name=((NewsTask)runnable).getName();
            this.startDate=new Date().getTime();
        }
```

We have overridden or implemented different methods in this class. The first one, the `getDelay()` method that, as we told you before, returns the time remaining to the next execution of a task in the given unit time:

```java
        @Override
        public long getDelay(TimeUnit unit) {
            long delay;
            if (!isPeriodic()) {
                delay = task.getDelay(unit);
            } else {
                if (startDate == 0) {
                    delay = task.getDelay(unit);
                } else {
                    Date now = new Date();
                    delay = startDate - now.getTime();
                    delay = unit.convert(delay,
                        TimeUnit.MILLISECONDS);
                }

            }

            return delay;
        }
```

The next one, the `compareTo()` method, compares two tasks, taking into account the start date of the next execution of the tasks:

```java
        @Override
        public int compareTo(Delayed object) {
            return Long.compare(this.getStartDate(),
                ((ExecutorTask<V>)object).getStartDate());
        }
```

Then, the `isPeriodic()` method returns `true` if the task is periodic or `false` if not:

```
@Override
public boolean isPeriodic() {
    return task.isPeriodic();
}
```

Finally, we have the `run()` method that implements the most important part of this example. First, we call the `runAndReset()` method of the `FutureTask` class. This method executes the task and resets its status, so it can be executed again. Then, we calculate the start date of the next execution using the `Timer` class, and finally, we have to insert the task again in the queue of the `ScheduledThreadPoolExecutor` class. If we don't do this final step, the task won't be executed again as follows:

```
@Override
public void run() {
    if (isPeriodic() && (!executor.isShutdown())) {
        super.runAndReset();
        Date now=new Date();
        startDate=now.getTime()+Timer.getPeriod();
        executor.getQueue().add(this);
        System.out.println("Start Date: "+new
           Date(startDate));
    }
}
```

Once we have the tasks for the executor, we have to implement the executor. We have implemented the `NewsExecutor` class that extends the `ScheduledThreadPoolExecutor` class. We have overridden the `decorateTask()` method. With this method, you can replace the internal task used by the scheduled executor. By default, it returns a default implementation of the `RunnableScheduledFuture` interface, but in our case, it will return an instance of the `ExecutorClass` instance:

```
public class NewsExecutor extends ScheduledThreadPoolExecutor {

    public NewsExecutor(int corePoolSize) {
        super(corePoolSize);
    }

    @Override
    protected <V> RunnableScheduledFuture<V> decorateTask(Runnable
      runnable,
          RunnableScheduledFuture<V> task) {
        ExecutorTask<V> myTask = new ExecutorTask<>(runnable,
          null, task, this);
        return myTask;
    }
}
```

We have to implement other versions of the `NewsSystem` and the `Main` classes to use the `NewsExecutor`. We have implemented `NewsAdvancedSystem` and `AdvancedMain` for this purpose.

Now you can run the advanced news system to see how the delay time between executions changes.

Additional information about executors

In this chapter, we have extended `ThreadPoolExecutor` and the `ScheduledThreadPoolExecutor` class and overridden some of their methods. But you can override more methods if you want a more particular behavior. These are some methods you can override:

- `shutdown()`: You must explicitly call this method to end the execution of the executor. You can override it to add some code to free additional resources used by your own executor.
- `shutdownNow()`: The difference between `shutdown()` and `shutdownNow()` is that the `shutdown()` method waits for the finalization of all the tasks that are waiting in the executor.
- `submit()`, `invokeall()`, or `invokeany()`: you call these methods to send concurrent tasks to the executor. You can override them if you need to do some actions before or after a task is inserted in the task queue of the executor. Note that adding a custom action before or after the task is enqueued is different than adding a custom action before or after it's executed, which we did while overriding `beforeExecute()` and `afterExecute()` methods.

In the news reader example, we use the `scheduleWithFixedDelay()` method to send tasks to the executor. But the `ScheduledThreadPoolExecutor` class has other methods to execute periodic tasks or tasks after a delay:

- `schedule()`: This method executes a task after the given delay. The task is executed only once.
- `scheduleAtFixedRate()`: This method executes a periodic task with the given period. The difference with the `scheduleWithFixedDelay()` method is that in the last one, the delay between two executions goes from the end of the first one to the start of the second one and in the first one the delay between two executions goes between the start of both.

Summary

In this chapter, we presented two examples that explored advanced characteristics of executors. In the first example, we continued with the client/server example of *Chapter 2, Managing Lots of Threads – Executors*. We implemented our own executor extending the `ThreadPoolExecutor` class to execute the tasks by priority and to measure the executing time of the tasks per user. We also included a new command to allow the cancellation of tasks.

In the second example, we explained how to use the `ScheduledThreadPoolExecutor` class to execute periodic tasks. We implemented two versions of a news reader. The first one showed how to use the basic functionality of the `ScheduledExecutorService`, and the second one showed how to override the behavior of the `ScheduledExecutorService` class to, for example, change the delay time between the two executions of a task.

In the next chapter, you will learn how to execute `Executor` tasks that return a result. If you extend the `Thread` class or implement the `Runnable` interface, the `run()` method doesn't return any result, but the executor framework includes the `Callable` interface that allows you to implement tasks that return a result.

4
Getting Data from the Tasks – The Callable and Future Interfaces

In *Chapter 2*, *Managing Lots of Threads – Executors,* and *Chapter 3*, *Getting the Maximum from Executors,* we introduced the executor framework to improve the performance of concurrent applications and showed you how to implement advanced characteristics to adapt this framework to your needs. In these chapters, all the tasks executed by the executor were based on the Runnable interface and its run() method that doesn't return a value. However, the executor framework allows us to execute other kind of tasks that return a result based on the Callable and Future interfaces. In this chapter, we will cover the following topics:

- An introduction to the Callable and Future interfaces
- First example – a best-matching algorithm for words
- Second example – building an inverted index of a collection of documents

Introducing the Callable and Future interfaces

The executor framework allows programmers to execute concurrent tasks without creating and managing threads. You create tasks and send them to the executor. It creates and manages the necessary threads.

In an executor, you can execute two kinds of tasks:

- **Tasks based on the Runnable interface**: These tasks implement the `run()` method that doesn't return any result.
- **Tasks based on the Callable interface**: These tasks implement the `call()` interface that returns an object as a result. The concrete type that will be returned by the `call()` method is specified by the generic type parameter of the `Callable` interface. To get the result returned by the task, the executor will return you an implementation of the `Future` interface for every task.

In previous chapters, you learned how to create executors, send tasks based on the `Runnable` interface to it, and personalize the executor to adapt it to your needs. In this chapter, you will learn how to work with tasks based on the `Callable` and `Future` interfaces.

The Callable interface

The `Callable` interface is very similar to the `Runnable` interface. The main characteristics of this interface are:

- It's a generic interface. It has a single type parameter that corresponds to the return type of the `call()` method.
- It declares the `call()` method. This method will be executed by the executor when it runs the task. It must return an object of the type specified in the declaration.
- The `call()` method can throw any checked exception. You can process the exceptions implementing your own executor and overriding the `afterExecute()` method.

The Future interface

When you send a `Callable` task to an executor, it will return you an implementation of the `Future` interface that allows you to control the execution and the status of the task and to get the result. The main characteristics of this interface are:

- You can cancel the execution of the task using the `cancel()` method. This method has a `boolean` parameter to specify whether you want to interrupt the task if it's running or not.
- You can check whether the task has been cancelled (with the `isCancelled()` method) or it has finished (with the `isDone()` method).

- You can get the value returned by the task using the `get()` method. There are two variants of this method. The first one doesn't have parameters and returns the value returned by the task if it has finished its execution. If the task hasn't finished its execution, it suspends the execution thread until the tasks finish. The second variant admits two parameters: a period of time and `TimeUnit` of that period. The main difference with the first one is that the thread waits for the period of time passed as a parameter. If the period ends and the task hasn't finished its execution, the method throws a `TimeoutException` exception.

First example – a best-matching algorithm for words

The main objective of a **best-matching algorithm** for words is to find the words most similar to a string passed as a parameter. To implement one of these algorithms you need the following:

- **A list of words**: In our case, we have used the **UK Advanced Cryptics Dictionary** (**UKACD**) that is a word list compiled for the crossword community. It has 250,353 words and idioms. It can be downloaded for free from `http://www.crosswordman.com/wordlist.html`.

- **A metric to measure the similarity between two words**: We have used the Levenshtein distance that is used to measure the difference between two sequences of **chars**. The **Levenshtein distance** is the minimal number of insertions, deletions, or substitutions, which is necessary to transform the first string into the second string. You can find a brief description of this metric in `https://en.wikipedia.org/wiki/Levenshtein_distance`.

In our example, you will implement two operations:

- The first operation returns a list of the most similar words to a **char sequence** using the Levenshtein distance.

- The second operation determines if a char sequence exists in our dictionary using the Levenshtein distance. It would be faster if we use the `equals()` method, but our version is a more interesting option for the objectives of the book.

You will implement serial and concurrent versions of these operations to verify that concurrency can help us in this case.

The common classes

In all the tasks implemented in this example, you will use the following three basic classes:

- The `WordsLoader` class that loads the list of words into a list of `String` objects.
- The `LevenshteinDistance` class that calculates the Levenshtein distance between two strings.
- The `BestMatchingData` class that stores the results of the best-matching algorithms. It stores a list of words and the distance of these words with the input string.

The UKACD is in a file with a word per line, so the `WordsLoader` class implements the `load()` static method that receives the path of the file that contains the list of words and returns a list of string objects with the 250,353 words.

The `LevenshteinDistance` class implements the `calculate()` method that receives two string objects as parameters and returns an `int` value with the distance between these two words. This is the code for this classification:

```java
public class LevenshteinDistance {

    public static int calculate (String string1, String string2) {
        int[][] distances=new
            int[string1.length()+1][string2.length()+1];

        for (int i=1; i<=string1.length();i++) {
            distances[i][0]=i;
        }

        for (int j=1; j<=string2.length(); j++) {
            distances[0][j]=j;
        }

        for(int i=1; i<=string1.length(); i++) {
            for (int j=1; j<=string2.length(); j++) {
                if (string1.charAt(i-1)==string2.charAt(j-1)) {
                    distances[i][j]=distances[i-1][j-1];
                } else {
                    distances[i][j]=minimum(distances[i-1][j],
                        distances[i][j-1],distances[i-1][j-1])+1;
                }
            }
        }
```

```
        return distances[string1.length()][string2.length()];
    }

    private static int minimum(int i, int j, int k) {
        return Math.min(i,Math.min(j, k));
    }
}
```

The `BestMatchingData` class has only two attributes: a list of string objects to store a list of words and an integer attribute named distance to store the distance of these words with the input string.

A best-matching algorithm – the serial version

First, we are going to implement the serial version of the best-matching algorithm. We are going to use this version as the starting point for the concurrent one and then we will compare the execution times of both versions to verify that concurrency help us to get better performance.

We have implemented the serial version of the best-matching algorithm in the following two classes:

- The `BestMatchingSerialCalculation` class that calculates the list of most similar words to the input string
- The `BestMatchingSerialMain` that includes the `main()` method that executes the algorithm, measures the execution time, and shows the results in the console

Let's analyze the source code of both classes.

The BestMatchingSerialCalculation class

This class has only one method named `getBestMatchingWords()` that receives two parameters: a string with the sequence we take as a reference and the list of string objects with all the words of the dictionary. It returns a `BestMatchingData` object with the results of the algorithm:

```
public class BestMatchingSerialCalculation {

    public static BestMatchingData getBestMatchingWords(String
      word, List<String> dictionary) {
        List<String> results=new ArrayList<String>();
        int minDistance=Integer.MAX_VALUE;
        int distance;
```

After the initialization of the internal variables, the algorithm processes all the words in the dictionary calculating the Levenshtein distance between these words and the string of reference. If the calculated distance for a word is less than the actual minimum distance, we clear the list of results and store the actual word into the list. If the calculated distance for a word is equal to the actual minimum distance, we add that word to the list of results:

```
for (String str: dictionary) {
    distance=LevenshteinDistance.calculate(word,str);
    if (distance<minDistance) {
        results.clear();
        minDistance=distance;
        results.add(str);
    } else if (distance==minDistance) {
        results.add(str);
    }
}
```

Finally, we create the `BestMatchingData` object to return the results of the algorithm:

```
    BestMatchingData result=new BestMatchingData();
    result.setWords(results);
    result.setDistance(minDistance);
    return result;
    }

}
```

The BestMachingSerialMain class

This is the main class of the example. It loads the UKACD file, calls `getBestMatchingWords()` with the string received as a parameter, and shows the results in the console including the execution time of the algorithm.

```
public class BestMatchingSerialMain {

    public static void main(String[] args) {

        Date startTime, endTime;
        List<String> dictionary=WordsLoader.load("data/UK Advanced
           Cryptics Dictionary.txt");

        System.out.println("Dictionary Size: "+dictionary.size());
```

```
            startTime=new Date();
            BestMatchingData result=
              BestMatchingSerialCalculation.getBestMatchingWords
              (args[0], dictionary);
            List<String> results=result.getWords();
            endTime=new Date();
            System.out.println("Word: "+args[0]);
            System.out.println("Minimum distance: "
              +result.getDistance());
            System.out.println("List of best matching words: "
              +results.size());
            results.forEach(System.out::println);
            System.out.println("Execution Time: "+(endTime.getTime()-
              startTime.getTime()));
        }

    }
```

Here, we used a new Java 8 language construct named **method reference** and a new `List.forEach()` method to output the result.

A best-matching algorithm – the first concurrent version

We have implemented two different concurrent versions of the best-matching algorithm. The first one is based on the `Callable` interface and the `submit()` method defined in the `AbstractExecutorService` interface.

We have implemented this version of the algorithm using the following three classes:

- The `BestMatchingBasicTask` class that implements the tasks that implement the `Callable` interface and will be executed in the executor
- The `BestMatchingBasicConcurrentCalculation` class that creates the executor and necessary tasks and sends them to the executor
- The `BestMatchingConcurrentMain` class that implements the `main()` method to execute the algorithm and shows the results in the console

Let's see the source code of these classes.

The BestMatchingBasicTask class

As we mentioned before, this class will implement the tasks that will obtain the list of best-matching words. This task will implement the `Callable` interface parameterized with the `BestMatchingData` class. This means that this class will implement the `call()` method, and this method will return a `BestMatchingData` object.

Each task will process a part of the dictionary and will return the results obtained for that part. We have used four internal attributes as follows:

- The first position (inclusive) of the dictionary it will analyze
- The last position (exclusive) of the dictionary it will analyze
- The dictionary as a list of string objects
- The reference input string

The code for this is the following:

```java
public class BestMatchingBasicTask implements Callable
  <BestMatchingData > {

    private int startIndex;

    private int endIndex;

    private List < String > dictionary;

    private String word;

    public BestMatchingBasicTask(int startIndex, int endIndex,
      List < String > dictionary, String word) {
        this.startIndex = startIndex;
        this.endIndex = endIndex;
        this.dictionary = dictionary;
        this.word = word;
    }
```

The `call()` method processes all the words between the `startIndex` and `endIndex` attributes and calculates the Levenshtein distance between those words and the input string. It will return only the nearest words to the input string. If during the process it finds a word nearer than the previous ones, it clears the result list and adds the new word to that list. If it finds a word that is at the same distance than the results found until now, it adds the word to the result list as follows:

```java
@Override
public BestMatchingData call() throws Exception {
    List<String> results=new ArrayList<String>();
```

```
            int minDistance=Integer.MAX_VALUE;
            int distance;
            for (int i=startIndex; i<endIndex; i++) {
                distance = LevenshteinDistance.calculate
                   (word,dictionary.get(i));
                if (distance<minDistance) {
                   results.clear();
                   minDistance=distance;
                   results.add(dictionary.get(i));
                } else if (distance==minDistance) {
                   results.add(dictionary.get(i));
                }
            }
```

At the end, we create a `BestMatchingData` object with the list of words we have found and their distance to the input string and return that object.

```
            BestMatchingData result=new BestMatchingData();
            result.setWords(results);
            result.setDistance(minDistance);
            return result;
        }
    }
```

The main difference with the tasks based on the `Runnable` interface is the return sentence included in the last line of the method. The `run()` method doesn't return a value, so those tasks cannot return a result. The `call()` method, on the other hand, returns an object (the class of that object is defined in the implements sentence), so this kind of tasks can return a result.

The BestMatchingBasicConcurrentCalculation class

This class is responsible for the creation of the necessary tasks to process the complete dictionary, the executor to execute those tasks, and to control the execution of the tasks in the executor.

It only has one method, `getBestMatchingWords()`, that receives two input parameters: the dictionary with the complete list of words and the reference string. It returns a `BestMatchingData` object with the results of the algorithm. First, we have created and initialized the executor. We have used the number of cores of the machine as the maximum number of threads we want to use on it.

```
    public class BestMatchingBasicConcurrentCalculation {
```

```
public static BestMatchingData getBestMatchingWords(String
  word, List<String> dictionary) throws InterruptedException,
  ExecutionException {

    int numCores = Runtime.getRuntime().availableProcessors();
    ThreadPoolExecutor executor = (ThreadPoolExecutor)
      Executors.newFixedThreadPool(numCores);
```

Then, we calculate the size of the parts of the dictionary each task will process and creates a list of `Future` objects to store the results of the tasks. When you send a task based on the `Callable` interface to an executor, you will get an implementation of the `Future` interface. You can use that object to:

- Know whether the task has been executed
- Get the result of the execution of the task (the object returned by the `call()` method)
- Cancel the execution of the tasks

The code for this is as follows:

```
int size = dictionary.size();
int step = size / numCores;
int startIndex, endIndex;
List<Future<BestMatchingData>> results = new
  ArrayList<>();
```

Then, we create the tasks, send them to the executor using the `submit()` method, and add the `Future` object that method returns to the list of `Future` objects. The `submit()` method returns immediately. It doesn't wait until the task is executed. We have the following code:

```
for (int i = 0; i < numCores; i++) {
    startIndex = i * step;
    if (i == numCores - 1) {
        endIndex = dictionary.size();
    } else {
        endIndex = (i + 1) * step;
    }
    BestMatchingBasicTask task = new
      BestMatchingBasicTask(startIndex, endIndex,
      dictionary, word);
    Future<BestMatchingData> future =
      executor.submit(task);
    results.add(future);
}
```

Chapter 4

Once we have sent the tasks to the executor, we call the shutdown() method of the executor to finish its execution and iterate over the list of Future objects to get the results of each task. We have used the get() method without any parameter. This method returns the object returned by the call() method if the task has finished its execution. If the task is not finished, the method puts the current thread to sleep the calling thread until the task has finished and the results are available.

We compose a result list with the results of the tasks, so we will only return the list with the words nearest to the reference string as follows:

```
executor.shutdown();
List<String> words=new ArrayList<String>();
int minDistance=Integer.MAX_VALUE;
for (Future<BestMatchingData> future: results) {
    BestMatchingData data=future.get();
    if (data.getDistance()<minDistance) {
        words.clear();
        minDistance=data.getDistance();
        words.addAll(data.getWords());
    } else if (data.getDistance()==minDistance) {
        words.addAll(data.getWords());
    }

}
```

Finally, we create and return a BestMatchingData object with the results of the algorithm:

```
BestMatchingData result=new BestMatchingData();
result.setDistance(minDistance);
result.setWords(words);
return result;
    }
}
```

The BestMatchingConcurrentMain class is very similar to BestMatchingSerialMain presented before. The only difference is the class used (BestMatchingBasicConcurrentCalculation instead of BestMatchingSerialCalculation), so we don't include the source code here. Note that we used neither thread-safe data structures nor synchronization as our concurrent tasks worked on independent pieces of data, and the final results were merged in a sequential manner after the concurrent tasks were terminated.

A best-matching algorithm – the second concurrent version

We have implemented the second version of the best-matching algorithm using the invokeAll() method of the AbstractExecutorService (implemented in the ThreadPoolExecutorClass). In the previous version, we have used the submit() method that receives a Callable object and returns a Future object. The invokeAll() method receives a List of Callable objects as a parameter and returns a List of Future ones. The first Future is associated with the first Callable and so on. There is another important difference between these two methods. Although the submit() method returns immediately, the invokeAll() method returns when all the Callable tasks have ended their execution. This means that all the Future objects returned will return true if you call their isDone() method.

To implement this version, we have used the BestMatchingBasicTask class implemented in the previous example and have implemented the BestMatchingAdvancedConcurrentCalculation class. The differences with the BestMatchingBasicConcurrentCalculation class are in the creation of the tasks and in the process of the results. In the creation of tasks, now we create a list and store it on the tasks we want to execute:

```
for (int i = 0; i < numCores; i++) {
    startIndex = i * step;
    if (i == numCores - 1) {
        endIndex = dictionary.size();
    } else {
        endIndex = (i + 1) * step;
    }
    BestMatchingBasicTask task = new
      BestMatchingBasicTask(startIndex, endIndex,
        dictionary, word);
    tasks.add(task);
}
```

To process the results, we call the invokeAll() method and then go over the list of Future objects returned:

```
results = executor.invokeAll(tasks);
executor.shutdown();
List<String> words = new ArrayList<String>();
int minDistance = Integer.MAX_VALUE;
for (Future<BestMatchingData> future : results) {
    BestMatchingData data = future.get();
```

```
            if (data.getDistance() < minDistance) {
                words.clear();
                minDistance = data.getDistance();
                words.addAll(data.getWords());
            } else if (data.getDistance()== minDistance) {
                words.addAll(data.getWords());
            }
        }
        BestMatchingData result = new BestMatchingData();
        result.setDistance(minDistance);
        result.setWords(words);
        return result;
    }
```

To execute this version, we have implemented `BestMatchingConcurrentAdvancedMain`. Its source code is very similar to the previous ones, so it's not included.

The word exists algorithm – a serial version

As part of this example, we have implemented another operation to check whether a string exists in our list of words. To check whether the word exists or not, we use the Levenshtein distance again. We consider that a word exists if it has a distance of 0 with a word of the list. It would be faster if we make the comparison using the `equals()` or `equalsIgnoreCase()` methods or reading the input words into a `HashSet` and using the `contains()` method (much more efficient than our version), but we consider that our version will be more useful for the purposes of the book.

As in previous examples, first, we have implemented the serial version of the operation to use it as a base to implement the concurrent one and compare the execution times of both versions.

To implement the serial version, we have used two classes:

- The `ExistSerialCalculation` class, which implements the `existWord()` method that compare the input string with all the words in the dictionary until it finds it
- The `ExistSerialMain` class, which launches the examples and measure the execution time

Let's analyze the source code of both the classes.

The ExistSerialCalculation class

This class has only one method, that is, the `existWord()` method. It receives two parameters: the word we are looking for and the complete list of words. It goes over the full list, which calculates the Levenshtein distance between the input word and the words in the list until it finds the word (the distance is 0), in which case it returns the `true` value, or it finishes the list of words without finding the word, in which case it returns the `false` value.

```
public class ExistSerialCalculation {

    public static boolean existWord(String word, List<String>
      dictionary) {
       for (String str: dictionary) {
           if (LevenshteinDistance.calculate(word, str) == 0) {
               return true;
           }
       }
       return false;
    }
}
```

The ExistSerialMain class

This class implements the `main()` method to call the `exist()` method. It gets the first parameter of the main method as the word we want to look for and calls that method. It measures its execution time and shows the results in the console.
We have the following code:

```
public class ExistSerialMain {

    public static void main(String[] args) {

        Date startTime, endTime;
        List<String> dictionary=WordsLoader.load("data/UK Advanced
          Cryptics Dictionary.txt");

        System.out.println("Dictionary Size: "+dictionary.size());

        startTime=new Date();
        boolean result=ExistSerialCalculation.existWord(args[0],
          dictionary);
        endTime=new Date();
```

```
            System.out.println("Word: "+args[0]);
            System.out.println("Exists: "+result);
            System.out.println("Execution Time: "+(endTime.getTime()-
               startTime.getTime()));
        }
    }
```

The word exists algorithm – the concurrent version

To implement the concurrent version of this operation, we have to take into account its most important characteristic. We don't need to process the whole list of words. When we find the word, we can finish the process of the list and return the result. This operation which does not process the whole input data and stops when some condition is fulfilled is called a **short-circuit operation**.

The `AbstractExecutorService` interface defines an operation (implemented in the `ThreadPoolExecutor` class) that fits perfectly with this idea. Its the `invokeAny()` method. This method sends to the executor the list of `Callable` tasks that receives as a parameter and returns the result of the first task that has finished its execution without throwing an exception. If all the tasks throw an exception, this method throws an `ExecutionException` exception.

As in previous examples, we have implemented different classes to implement this version of the algorithm:

- The `ExistBasicTask` class that implements the tasks we are going to execute in the executor
- The `ExistBasicConcurrentCalculation` class that creates the executor and the tasks, and send the tasks to the executor
- The `ExistBasicConcurrentMain` class that executes the examples measuring its running time

The ExistBasicTasks class

This class implements the tasks that are going to search for the word. It implements the `Callable` interface parameterized with the `Boolean` class. The `call()` method will return the `true` value if the task finds the word. It uses four internal attributes:

- The complete list of words
- The first word (included) in the list the task will process
- The last word (excluded) in the list the task will process
- The word the task will look for

Getting Data from the Tasks – The Callable and Future Interfaces

We have the following code:

```
public class ExistBasicTask implements Callable<Boolean> {

    private int startIndex;

    private int endIndex;

    private List<String> dictionary;

    private String word;

    public ExistBasicTask(int startIndex, int endIndex,
      List<String> dictionary, String word) {
        this.startIndex=startIndex;
        this.endIndex=endIndex;
        this.dictionary=dictionary;
        this.word=word;
    }
}
```

The `call` method will traverse the part of the list assigned to this task. It calculates the Levenshtein distance between the input word and the words of the list. If it finds the word, it will return the `true` value.

If the tasks process all its words and it doesn't find the word, it will throw an exception to adapt to the behavior of the `invokeAny()` method. If the task returns the `false` value in this case, the `invokeAny()` method will return the `false` value without waiting for the rest of the tasks. Maybe another task will find the word.

We have the following code:

```
        @Override
        public Boolean call() throws Exception {
            for (int i=startIndex; i<endIndex; i++) {
                if (LevenshteinDistance.calculate(word,
                  dictionary.get(i))==0) {
                    return true;
                }
            }
            if (Thread.interrupted()) {
                return false;
            }
            throw new NoSuchElementException("The word "+word+"
              doesn't exists.");
        }
```

The ExistBasicConcurrentCalculation class

This class will execute the search of the input word in the full list of words creating and executing the necessary tasks. It only implements one method named `existWord()`. It receives two parameters, the input string and the complete list of words, and returns a Boolean value indicating whether the word exists or not.

First, we create the executor to execute the tasks. We use the `Executor` class and create a `ThreadPoolExecutor` class with a maximum of threads determined by the number of available hardware threads of the machine as follows:

```
public class ExistBasicConcurrentCalculation {

    public static boolean existWord(String word, List<String>
      dictionary) throws InterruptedException, ExecutionException{
        int numCores = Runtime.getRuntime().availableProcessors();
        ThreadPoolExecutor executor = (ThreadPoolExecutor)
          Executors.newFixedThreadPool(numCores);
```

Then, we create the same number of tasks as the threads are running in the executor. Each task will process an equal part of the list of words. We create the tasks and store them in a list:

```
            int size = dictionary.size();
            int step = size / numCores;
            int startIndex, endIndex;
            List<ExistBasicTask> tasks = new ArrayList<>();

            for (int i = 0; i < numCores; i++) {
                startIndex = i * step;
                if (i == numCores - 1) {
                    endIndex = dictionary.size();
                } else {
                    endIndex = (i + 1) * step;
                }
                ExistBasicTask task = new ExistBasicTask(startIndex,
                  endIndex, dictionary,
                      word);
                tasks.add(task);
            }
```

Then, we use the `invokeAny()` method to execute the tasks in the executor. If the methods return a Boolean value, the word exists. We return that value. If the method throws an exception, the word doesn't exist. We print the exception in the console and return the `false` value. In both cases, we call the `shutdown()` method of the executor to terminate its execution as follows:

```
            try {
                Boolean result=executor.invokeAny(tasks);
                return result;
            } catch (ExecutionException e) {
                if (e.getCause() instanceof NoSuchElementException)
                    return false;
                throw e;
            } finally {
                executor.shutdown();
            }
        }
    }
```

The ExistBasicConcurrentMain class

This class implements the `main()` method of this example. It's equal to the `ExistSerialMain` class with one difference that uses the `ExistBasicConcurrentCalculation` class instead of the `ExistSerialCalculation`, so its source code is not included.

Comparing the solutions

Let's compare the different solutions (serial and concurrent) of the two operations we have implemented in this section. To test the algorithm, we have executed the examples using the JMH framework (http://openjdk.java.net/projects/code-tools/jmh/) that allows you to implement micro benchmarks in Java. Using a framework for benchmarking is a better solution that simply measures time using methods as `currentTimeMillis()` or `nanoTime()`. We have executed them 10 times in a computer with a four-core processor and calculated the medium execution time of those 10 times. Let's analyze the results of the executions.

Best-matching algorithms

In this case, we have implemented three versions of the algorithm:

- The serial version
- The concurrent version, sending a task once at a time
- The concurrent version, using the `invokeAll()` method

To test the algorithms, we have used three different strings that doesn't exist in the list of words:

- `Stitter`
- `Abicus`
- `Lonx`

These are the words returned by the best-matching algorithm for each word:

- `Stitter`: `sitter`, `skitter`, `slitter`, `spitter`, `stilter`, `stinter`, `stotter`, `stutter`, and `titter`
- `Abicus`: `abacus` and `amicus`
- `Lonx`: `lanx`, `lone`, `long`, `lox`, and `lynx`

The medium execution times and their standard deviation in milliseconds are discussed in the following table:

Algorithm	Stitter	Abicus	lonx
Serial	467.01 ± 23.40	408.03 ± 14.66	317.60 ± 28.78
Concurrent: `submit()` method	209.72 ± 74.79	184.10 ± 90.47	155.61 ± 65.43
Concurrent: `invokeAll()` method	217.66 ± 65.46	188.28 ± 81.28	160.43 ± 65.14

We can draw the following conclusions:

- The concurrent versions of the algorithm get a better performance than the serial one.
- The concurrent versions of the algorithm obtain similar results between them. All the concurrent versions have very high standard deviation values high. We can compare the concurrent version method with the serial version using the speed-up for the word `lonx` to see how concurrency improves the performance of our algorithm:

$$S = \frac{T_{serial}}{T_{concurrent}} = \frac{317.6}{155.61} = 2.04$$

Exist algorithms

In this case, we have implemented two versions of the algorithms:

- The serial version
- The concurrent version, using the `invokeAny()` method

To test the algorithm, we have used some strings:

- The string `xyzt` that doesn't exist in the list of words
- The string `stutter` that exists in the list of words near the end of the list
- The string `abacus` that exists in the list of words very close to the start of the list
- The string `lynx` that exists in the list of words just after the second half of the list

The medium execution times in milliseconds and their standard deviations are shown in the following table:

Algorithm	Word	Execution time (milliseconds)
Serial	abacus	50.70 ± 13.95
	lynx	194.41 ± 26.02
	stutter	398.11 ± 23.4
	xyzt	315.62 ± 28.7
Concurrent	abacus	50.72 ± 7.17
	lynx	69.15 ± 62.5
	stutter	126.74 ± 104.52
	xyzt	203.37 ± 76.67

We can draw the following conclusions:

- In general, the concurrent version of the algorithm provides better performance than the serial one.
- The position of a word in the list is a critical factor. With the `abacus` word, which appears at the beginning of the list, both algorithms give similar execution times, but with the `stutter` word, the difference is very big.
- The standard deviation in the concurrent case is very big.

If we compare the concurrent version with the serial one for the word `lynx` using the speed-up, the result is:

$$S = \frac{T_{serial}}{T_{concurrent}} = \frac{191.41}{69.15} = 2.76$$

The second example – creating an inverted index for a collection of documents

In the **information retrieval** world, an **inverted index** is a common data structure used to speed up the searches of text in a collection of documents. It stores all the words of the document collection and a list of the documents that contains that word.

To construct the index, we have to parse all the documents of the collection and construct the index in an incremental way. For every document, we extract the significant words of that document (deleting the most common words, also called stop words and maybe applying a stemming algorithm) and then add those words to the index. If a word exists in the index, we add the document to the list of documents associated with that word. If a word doesn't exist, add the word to the list of words of the index and associate the document to that word. You can add parameters to the association, as the **term frequency** of the word in the document that provides you more information.

When you make a search of a word or a list of words in the document collection, you use the inverted index to obtain the list of documents associated with each word and create a unique list with the results of the search.

In this section, you will learn how to use Java concurrency utilities to construct an inverted index file for a collection of documents. As the document collection, we have taken the Wikipedia pages with information about movies to construct a set of 100,673 documents. We have converted each Wikipedia page into a text file. You can download this document collection with all the information about the book.

To construct the inverted index, we don't delete any word and don't use any stemming algorithm too. We want to keep the algorithm as simple as possible to focus attention in the concurrency utilities.

The same principles explained here can be used to obtain other information about a document collection, for example, a vector representation of every document that can be used as an input for a **clustering algorithm**, as you will learn in *Chapter 6, Optimizing Divide and Conquer Solutions – The Fork/Join Framework*.

As with other examples, you will implement serial and concurrent versions of these operations to verify that concurrency can help us in this case.

Common classes

Both versions, serial and concurrent, have in common the classes to load the document collection into a Java object. We have used the following two classes:

- The Document class that stores the list of words contained in the document
- The DocumentParse class that converts a document stored in a file in a document object

Let's analyze the source code of both the classes.

The Document class

The Document class is very simple. It has only two attributes and the methods to get and set the values of those attributes. These attributes are:

- The name of the file, as a string.
- The vocabulary (that is, the list of words used in the document) as a HashMap. The **key** are the **words** and the values are the number of times the word appears in the document.

The DocumentParser class

As we mentioned earlier, this class converts a document stored in a file in a document in a Document object. It splits this word into three methods. The first one is the parse() method that receives the path to the file as a parameter and returns a HashMap with the vocabulary of that document. This method reads the file line by line and uses the parseLine() method to convert each line in a list of words and add them to the vocabulary as follows:

```
public class DocumentParser {

    public Map<String, Integer>  parse(String route) {
        Map<String, Integer> ret=new HashMap<String,Integer>();
        Path file=Paths.get(route);
```

```
          try ( BufferedReader reader =
            Files.newBufferedReader(file)) {
                String line = null;
                while ((line = reader.readLine()) != null) {
                    parseLine(line,ret);
                }
            } catch (IOException x) {
              x.printStackTrace();
            } catch (Exception e) {
              e.printStackTrace();
            }
        return ret;

    }
```

The `parseLine()` method processes the line extracting its words. We consider that a word is a sequence of alphabetical characters to continue with the simplicity of this example. We have used the `Pattern` class to extract the words and the `Normalizer` class to convert the words to lower case and delete the accents of the vowels as follows:

```
private static final Pattern PATTERN =
  Pattern.compile("\\P{IsAlphabetic}+");

private void parseLine(String line, Map<String, Integer> ret) {
  for(String word: PATTERN.split(line)) {
    if(!word.isEmpty())
      ret.merge(Normalizer.normalize(word,
        Normalizer.Form.NFKD).toLowerCase(), 1, (a, b) -> a+b);
  }
}
```

The serial version

The serial version of this example is implemented in the `SerialIndexing` class. This class has the `main()` method that reads all the documents, gets its vocabulary, and constructs the inverted index in an incremental way.

First, we initialize the necessary variables. The collection of documents is stored in the data directory, so we store all the documents in an array of `File` objects. We also initialize the `invertedIndex` object. We use a `HashMap` where the keys are the words and the values are a list of string objects with the name of the files that contain the word as follows:

```
public class SerialIndexing {

    public static void main(String[] args) {
```

Getting Data from the Tasks – The Callable and Future Interfaces

```
Date start, end;

File source = new File("data");
File[] files = source.listFiles();
Map<String, List<String>> invertedIndex=new
    HashMap<String,List<String>> ();
```

Then, we parse all the documents using the `DocumentParse` class and use the `updateInvertedIndex()` method to add the vocabulary obtained from each document into the inverted index. We measure the execution time of all the process. We have the following code:

```
start=new Date();
for (File file : files) {

    DocumentParser parser = new DocumentParser();

    if (file.getName().endsWith(".txt")) {
        Map<String, Integer> voc = parser.parse
            (file.getAbsolutePath());
        updateInvertedIndex(voc,invertedIndex,
            file.getName());
    }
}
end=new Date();
```

Finally, we show the results of the execution in the console:

```
System.out.println("Execution Time: "+(end.getTime()-
    start.getTime()));
System.out.println("invertedIndex:
    "+invertedIndex.size());
}
```

The `updateInvertedIndex()` method adds the vocabulary of a document into the inverted index structure. It processes all the words that form the vocabulary. If the word exists in the inverted index, we add the name of the document to the list of documents associated with that word. If the word doesn't exists, we add the word and associate the document with that word as follows:

```
private static void updateInvertedIndex(Map<String, Integer> voc,
    Map<String, List<String>> invertedIndex, String fileName) {
    for (String word : voc.keySet()) {
        if (word.length() >= 3) {
            invertedIndex.computeIfAbsent(word, k -> new
                ArrayList<>()).add(fileName);
        }
    }
}
```

The first concurrent version – a task per document

Now it's time to implement the concurrent version of the text indexing algorithm. Clearly, we can parallelize the process of every document. This includes reading the document from the file and processing every line to get the vocabulary of the document. The tasks can return that vocabulary as their result, so we can implement tasks based in the `Callable` interface.

In the previous example, we have used three methods to send `Callable` tasks to the executor:

- `submit()`
- `invokeAll()`
- `invokeAny()`

We have to process all the documents, so we have to discard the `invokeAny()` method. The other two methods are inconvenient. If we use the `submit()` method, we have to decide when we process the results of the task. If we send a task per document, we can process the results:

- After sending every task, this is nonviable
- After the finalization of all the tasks, we have to store a lot of `Future` objects
- After sending a group of tasks, we have to include code to synchronize both operations

All these approaches have a problem: we process the results of the tasks in a sequential way. If we use the `invokeAll()` method, we are in a situation similar to point 2. We have to wait for the finalization of all the tasks.

One possible option is to create other tasks to process the `Future` objects associated with every task, and the Java concurrency API provides us with an elegant solution to implement this solution with the `CompletionService` interface and its implementation, the `ExecutorCompletionService` class.

A `CompletionService` object is a mechanism that has an executor and allows you to decouple the production of tasks and the consumption of the results of those tasks. You can send tasks to the executor using the `submit()` method and get the results of the tasks when they finish using the `poll()` or `take()` methods. So, for our solution, we are going to implement the following elements:

- A `CompletionService` object to execute the tasks.

- A task per document to parse the document and generate its vocabulary. This task will be executed by the `CompletionService` object. These tasks are implemented in the `IndexingTask` class.
- Two threads to process the results of the tasks and construct the inverted index. These threads are implemented in the `InvertedIndexTask` class.
- A `main()` method to create and execute all the elements. This `main()` method is implemented in the `ConcurrentIndexingMain` class.

Let's analyze the source code of these classes.

The IndexingTask class

This class implements the tasks that will parse a document to obtain its vocabulary. It implements the `Callable` interface parameterized with the `Document` class. It has an internal attribute to store the `File` object that represents the document it has to parse. Take a look at the following code:

```java
public class IndexingTask implements Callable<Document> {
    private File file;
    public IndexingTask(File file) {
        this.file=file;
    }
}
```

In the `call()` method, it simply uses the `parse()` method of the `DocumentParser` class to parse the document and obtain the vocabulary and create and return the `Document` object with the data obtained:

```java
    @Override
    public Document call() throws Exception {
        DocumentParser parser = new DocumentParser();

        Map<String, Integer> voc =
          parser.parse(file.getAbsolutePath());

        Document document=new Document();
        document.setFileName(file.getName());
        document.setVoc(voc);
        return document;
    }
}
```

The InvertedIndexTask class

This class implements the tasks that get the `Document` objects generated by the `IndexingTask` objects and construct the inverted index. This tasks will be executed as `Thread` objects (we don't use an executor in this case), so they are based in the `Runnable` interface.

The `InvertedIndexTask` class uses three internal attributes:

- A `CompletionService` object parameterized with the `Document` class to get access to the objects returned by the `IndexingTask` objects.
- A `ConcurrentHashMap` to store the inverted index. The keys are the words and the values are `ConcurrentLinkedDeque` of string with the names of the files. In this case, we have to use concurrent data structures, and the ones used in the serial version are not synchronized.
- A Boolean value to indicate to the task that it can finish its work.

The code for this is as follows:

```
public class InvertedIndexTask implements Runnable {

    private CompletionService<Document> completionService;
    private ConcurrentHashMap<String,
      ConcurrentLinkedDeque<String>> invertedIndex;

    public InvertedIndexTask(CompletionService<Document>
      completionService,
          ConcurrentHashMap<String,
            ConcurrentLinkedDeque<String>> invertedIndex) {
        this.completionService = completionService;
        this.invertedIndex = invertedIndex;

    }
```

The `run()` method uses the method `take()` from `CompletionService` to obtain the `Future` object associated with a task. We implement a loop that will be running until the thread is interrupted. Once the thread has been interrupted, it processes all the pending `Future` objects using the `take()` method again. We update the inverted index using the `updateInvertedIndex()` method with the object returned by the `take()` method. We have the following method:

```
public void run() {
    try {
        while (!Thread.interrupted()) {
            try {
```

```
                Document document = 
                    completionService.take().get();
                updateInvertedIndex(document.getVoc(),
                    invertedIndex, document.getFileName());
            } catch (InterruptedException e) {
                break;
            }
        }
        while (true) {
            Future<Document> future = 
                completionService.poll();
            if (future == null)
                break;
            Document document = future.get();
            updateInvertedIndex(document.getVoc(),
                invertedIndex, document.getFileName());
        }
    } catch (InterruptedException | ExecutionException e) {
        e.printStackTrace();
    }
}
```

Finally, the `updateInvertedIndex` method receives the vocabulary obtained from a document, the inverted index, and the name of the file that has been processed as parameters. It processes all the words from the vocabulary. We use the `computeIfAbsent()` method to add the word to `invertedIndex` if it's not present:

```
        private void updateInvertedIndex(Map<String, Integer> voc,
            ConcurrentHashMap<String, ConcurrentLinkedDeque<String>>
            invertedIndex, String fileName) {
          for (String word : voc.keySet()) {
              if (word.length() >= 3) {
                  invertedIndex.computeIfAbsent(word, k -> new
                      ConcurrentLinkedDeque<>()).add(fileName);
              }
          }
        }
```

The ConcurrentIndexing class

This is the main class in the example. It creates and launches all the components, waits for its finalization, and prints the final execution time in the console.

First, it creates and initializes all the variables needed for its execution:

- An executor to run the `InvertedTask` tasks. As with the previous examples, we use the number of cores of the machine as the maximum number of work threads in the executor, but in this case, we leave one core to execute the independent threads.
- A `CompletionService` object to run the tasks. We use the executor created before to initialize this object.
- A `ConcurrentHashMap` to store the inverted index.
- An array of `File` objects with all the documents we have to process.

We have the following method:

```
public class ConcurrentIndexing {

    public static void main(String[] args) {

        int numCores=Runtime.getRuntime().availableProcessors();
        ThreadPoolExecutor executor=(ThreadPoolExecutor)
            Executors.newFixedThreadPool(Math.max(numCores-1, 1));
        ExecutorCompletionService<Document> completionService=new
            ExecutorCompletionService<>(executor);
        ConcurrentHashMap<String, ConcurrentLinkedDeque<String>>
            invertedIndex=new ConcurrentHashMap
            <String,ConcurrentLinkedDeque<String>> ();

        Date start, end;

        File source = new File("data");
        File[] files = source.listFiles();
```

Then, we process all the files of the array. For every file, we create a `InvertedTask` object and send it to the `CompletionService` class using the `submit()` method:

```
            start=new Date();
            for (File file : files) {
                IndexingTask task=new IndexingTask(file);
                completionService.submit(task);
            }
```

Then, we create two `InvertedIndexTask` objects to process the results returned by the `InvertedTask` tasks and execute them as normal `Thread` objects:

```
InvertedIndexTask invertedIndexTask=new
    InvertedIndexTask(completionService,invertedIndex);
Thread thread1=new Thread(invertedIndexTask);
thread1.start();
InvertedIndexTask invertedIndexTask2=new
    InvertedIndexTask(completionService,invertedIndex);
Thread thread2=new Thread(invertedIndexTask2);
thread2.start();
```

Once we have launched all the elements, we wait for the finalization of the executor using the `shutdown()` and the `awaitTermination()` methods. The `awaitTermination()` method will return when all the `InvertedTask` tasks have finished its execution, so we can finish the threads that execute the `InvertedIndexTask` tasks. To do this, we interrupt these threads (see my comment about `InvertedIndexTask`).

```
executor.shutdown();
try {
    executor.awaitTermination(1, TimeUnit.DAYS);
    thread1.interrupt();
    thread2.interrupt();
    thread1.join();
    thread2.join();
} catch (InterruptedException e) {
    e.printStackTrace();
}
```

Finally, we write the size of the inverted index and the execution time of all the process in the console:

```
end=new Date();
System.out.println("Execution Time: "+(end.getTime()-
    start.getTime()));
System.out.println("invertedIndex:
    "+invertedIndex.size());
    }

}
```

The second concurrent version – multiple documents per task

We have implemented a second concurrent version of this example. The basic principles are the same as the first version, but, in this case, each task will process more that one document instead of only one. The number of documents processed by each task will be an input parameter of the main method. We have tested the results with 100, 1,000, and 5,000 documents per task.

To implement this new approach, we are going to implement three new classes:

- The `MultipleIndexingTask` class, which is equivalent to the `IndexingTask` class, but it will process a list of documents instead of only one
- The `MultipleInvertedIndexTask` class, which is equivalent to the `InvertedIndexTask` class, but now the tasks will retrieve a list of `Document` objects instead of only one
- The `MultipleConcurrentIndexing` class, which is equivalent to the `ConcurrentIndexing` class but using the new classes

As much of the source code is similar to the previous version, we only show the differences.

The MultipleIndexingTask class

As we mentioned earlier, this class is similar to the `IndexingTask` class presented before. The main difference is that it uses a list of `File` objects instead of only one file:

```
public class MultipleIndexingTask implements
   Callable<List<Document>> {

    private List<File> files;

    public MultipleIndexingTask(List<File> files) {
        this.files = files;
    }
```

The `call()` method returns a list of `Document` objects instead of only one:

```
    @Override
    public List<Document> call() throws Exception {
        List<Document> documents = new ArrayList<Document>();
        for (File file : files) {
```

```
            DocumentParser parser = new DocumentParser();

            Hashtable<String, Integer> voc = parser.parse
              (file.getAbsolutePath());

            Document document = new Document();
            document.setFileName(file.getName());
            document.setVoc(voc);

            documents.add(document);
        }

        return documents;
    }
}
```

The MultipleInvertedIndexTask class

As we mentioned before, this class is similar to `InvertedIndexClass` presented earlier. The main difference is in the `run()` method. The `Future` object returned by the `poll()` method returns a list of `Document` objects, so we have to process the whole list.

```
        @Override
        public void run() {
            try {
                while (!Thread.interrupted()) {
                    try {
                        List<Document> documents =
                          completionService.take().get();
                        for (Document document : documents) {
                            updateInvertedIndex(document.getVoc(),
                              invertedIndex, document.getFileName());
                        }
                    } catch (InterruptedException e) {
                        break;
                    }
                }
                while (true) {
                    Future<List<Document>> future =
                      completionService.poll();
                    if (future == null)
                        break;
                    List<Document> documents = future.get();
                    for (Document document : documents) {
```

```
                updateInvertedIndex(document.getVoc(),
                    invertedIndex, document.getFileName());
            }
        }
    } catch (InterruptedException | ExecutionException e) {
        e.printStackTrace();
    }
}
```

The MultipleConcurrentIndexing class

As we mentioned earlier, this class is similar to the ConcurrentIndexing class. The only difference is the utilization of the new classes and the use of the first parameter to determine the number of documents processed per task. We have the following method:

```
start=new Date();
List<File> taskFiles=new ArrayList<>();
for (File file : files) {
    taskFiles.add(file);
    if (taskFiles.size()==NUMBER_OF_TASKS) {
        MultipleIndexingTask task=new
            MultipleIndexingTask(taskFiles);
        completionService.submit(task);
        taskFiles=new ArrayList<>();
    }
}
if (taskFiles.size()>0) {
    MultipleIndexingTask task=new
        MultipleIndexingTask(taskFiles);
    completionService.submit(task);
}

MultipleInvertedIndexTask invertedIndexTask=new
  MultipleInvertedIndexTask
    (completionService,invertedIndex);
Thread thread1=new Thread(invertedIndexTask);
thread1.start();
MultipleInvertedIndexTask invertedIndexTask2=new
  MultipleInvertedIndexTask
    (completionService,invertedIndex);
Thread thread2=new Thread(invertedIndexTask2);
thread2.start();
```

Comparing the solutions

Let's compare the solutions of the three versions of the example we have implemented. As we mentioned earlier, like document collection, we have taken the Wikipedia pages with information about movies to construct a set of 100,673 documents. We have converted each Wikipedia page in a text file. You can download this document collection with all the information about the book.

We have executed five different versions of the solutions:

- The serial version
- The concurrent version with one task per document
- The concurrent version with multiple tasks per document, with 100, 1,000, and 5,000 documents per task

The following table shows the execution time of the five versions:

Algorithm	Execution time (milliseconds)
Serial	69,480.50
Concurrent: one document per task	49,655.49
Concurrent: 100 documents per task	48,438.14
Concurrent: 1,000 documents per task	49,362.37
Concurrent: 5,000 documents per task	58,362.22

We can draw the following conclusions:

- Concurrent versions always obtain better performance than the serial one
- For the concurrent versions, if we increase the number of documents per task, we obtain worse results

If we compare the concurrent version with the serial one using the speed-up, the results are:

$$S = \frac{T_{serial}}{T_{concurrent}} = \frac{69480.50}{49655.49} = 1.4$$

Other methods of interest

In this chapter, we have used some methods of the `AbstractExecutorService` interface (implemented in the `ThreadPoolExecutor` class) and `CompletionService` interfaces (implemented in the `ExecutorCompletionService`) to manage the results of `Callable` tasks. However, there are other versions of the methods we have used and other methods we want to mention here.

About the `AbstractExecutorService` interface, let's discuss the following methods:

- `invokeAll (Collection<? extends Callable<T>> tasks, long timeout, TimeUnit unit)`: This method returns a list of `Future` objects associated with the list of `Callable` tasks passed as parameters when all the tasks have finished its execution or the timeout specified by the second and third parameters expires.

- `invokeAny (Collection<? Extends Callable<T>> tasks, long timeout, TimeUnit unit)`: This method returns the result of the first task of the list of `Callable` tasks passed as a parameter that finishes its execution without throwing an exception if it finishes before the timeout specified by the second and third parameters expires. If the timeout expires, the method throws a `TimeoutException` exception.

About the `CompletionService` interface, let's discuss the following methods:

- The `poll()` method: We have used a version of this method with two parameters, but there is also a version without parameters. From the internal data structures, this version retrieves and removes the `Future` object of the next task that has finished since the last call to the `poll()` or `take()` methods. If no tasks have finished, its execution returns a `null` value.

- The `take()` method: This method is similar to the previous one, but if no tasks have finished, it sleeps the thread until one task finishes its execution.

Summary

In this chapter, you learned the different mechanisms that you can use to work with tasks that return a result. These tasks are based on the Callable interface, which declares the call() method. This is a parameterized interface with the class returned by the call method.

When you execute a Callable task in an executor, you will always obtain an implementation of the Future interface. You can use this object to cancel the execution of the task, know if the task has finished its execution or get the result returned by the call() method.

You send Callable tasks to the executor using three different methods. With the submit() method, you send one task, and you will get immediately a Future object associated with this task. With the invokeAll() method, you send a list of tasks and will get a list of Future objects when all the tasks have finished its execution. With the invokeAny() method, you send a list of tasks, and you will receive the result (not a Future object) of the first task that finishes without throwing an exception. The rest of the tasks are canceled.

The Java concurrency API provides another mechanism to work with these kind of tasks. This mechanism is defined in the CompletionService interface and implemented in the ExecutorCompletionService class. This mechanism allows you to decouple the execution of tasks and the processing of their results. The CompletionService interface works internally with an executor and provides the submit() method to send tasks to the CompletionService interface and the poll() and take() methods to get the results of the tasks. These results are provided in the same order in which tasks finish their execution.

You also learned to implement these concepts with two real-world examples:

- A best-matching algorithm using the UKACD dataset
- An inverted index constructor, using a dataset with more than 1,00,000 documents with information of movies extracted from Wikipedia

In the next chapter, you will learn how to execute algorithms in a concurrent way that can be divided into phases, for example, a keyword extraction algorithm. You can implement that algorithm in the following three steps:

1. Step 1 – parse all the documents and extract all the words.
2. Step 2 – calculate the importance of each word on each document.
3. Step 3 – obtain the best keywords.

The main characteristic of these steps is that you must finish one completely before you can start the next one. Java concurrency API provides the Phaser class to facilitate the concurrent implementation of these algorithms. It allows you to synchronize all the tasks involved on it at the end of a phase, so none of them will start the next one until all have finished the current one.

5
Running Tasks Divided into Phases – The Phaser Class

The most important element in a concurrent API is the synchronization mechanisms it offers to the programmer. **Synchronization** is the coordination of two or more tasks to get the desired result. You can synchronize the execution of two or more tasks, when they have to be executed in a predefined order, or synchronize the access to a shared resource, when only one thread at a time can execute a fragment of code or modify a block of memory. Java 8 concurrency API provides a lot of synchronization mechanisms from the basic `synchronized` keyword or the `Lock` interface and their implementations to protect a critical section to the more advanced `CyclicBarrier` or `CountDownLatch` classes that allows you to synchronize the order of execution of different tasks. In Java 7, the concurrency API introduces the `Phaser` class. This class provides a powerful mechanism (**phaser**) to execute tasks divided into phases. The task can ask the Phaser class to wait until all other participants finish the phase. In this chapter, we will cover the following topics:

- An introduction to the `Phaser` class
- First example – a keyword extraction algorithm
- Second example – a genetic algorithm

An introduction to the Phaser class

The Phaser class is a synchronization mechanism designed to control the execution of algorithms that can be divided into phases in a concurrent way. If you have a process with clear defined steps so you have to finish the first one before you can start the second one and so on, you can use this class to make a concurrent version of your process. The main characteristics of the Phaser class are:

- The phaser must know the number of tasks it has to control. Java refers to this as the registration of the participants. A participant can register in a phaser any time.
- The tasks must inform the phaser when they finish a phase. The phaser will make that task sleep until all the participants have finished that phase.
- Internally, the phaser saves an integer number that stores the number of phase changes the phase has made.
- A participant can leave the control of the phaser any time. Java refers to this as the deregistration of the participants.
- You can execute custom code when the phaser makes a phase change.
- You can control the termination of the phaser. If a phaser is terminated, no new participants will be accepted and no synchronization between tasks will be made.
- You can use some methods to know the status and the number of participants of a phaser.

Registration and deregistration of participants

As we mentioned before, a phaser must know the number of tasks it has to control. It has to know how many different threads are executing the phase-divided algorithm to control the simultaneous phase change in a correct way.

Java refers to this process as the registration of participants. The normal situation is that participants are registered at the beginning of the execution, but a participant can be registered any time.

You can register a participant using different methods:

- When you create the Phaser object: The Phaser class provides four different constructors. Two of them are commonly used:
    - Phaser(): This constructor creates a phaser with zero participants
    - Phaser(int parties): This constructor creates a phaser with the given number of participants

- Explicitly, using one of these methods:
    - `bulkRegister(int parties)`: Register the given number of new participants at the same time
    - `register()`: Register one new participant

When one of the tasks controlled by the phaser finishes its execution, it must deregister from the phaser. If you don't do this, the phaser will wait endlessly for it in the next phase change. To deregister a participant, you can use this `arriveAndDeregister()` method. You use this method to indicate the phaser that this task has finished the current phase and it won't participate in the next phases.

Synchronizing phase changes

The main purpose of the phaser is to allow the implementation of algorithms that are clearly divided into phases in a concurrent way. None of the tasks can advance to the next phase until all the tasks have finished the previous phase. The `Phaser` class provides three methods to signal that the task finished the phase: `arrive()`, `arriveAndDeregister()`, and `arriveAndAwaitAdvance()`. If one of the tasks doesn't call one of these methods, the rest of the participant tasks will be blocked by the phaser indefinitely. To advance to the next phase, the following methods are used:

- `arriveAndAwaitAdvance()`: A task uses this method to indicate to the phaser that it has finished the current phase and wants to continue with the next one. The phaser will block the tasks until all the participant tasks have called one of the synchronization methods.

- `awaitAdvance(int phase)`: A task uses this method to indicate to the phaser that it wants to wait for the finalization of the current phase if the number we pass as a parameter and the actual phase of the phaser are equal. If they aren't equal, this method returns immediately.

Other functionalities

When all the participant tasks have finished the execution of a phase and before they continue with the next one, the `Phaser` class executes the `onAdvance()` method. This method receives the two following parameters:

- `phase`: This is the number of the phase that has finished. The first phase is the number zero
- `registeredParties`: This indicates the number of participant tasks

If you want to execute some code between two phases, for example, to sort or to transform some data, you can implement your own phaser extending the `Phaser` class and overriding this method.

A phaser can be in two states:

- **Active**: The phaser enters in this state when it's created and new participants are registered and continue on it until its termination. When it's in this state, it accepts new participants and works as it has been explained before.
- **Termination**: The phaser enters in this state when the `onAdvance()` method returns the `true` value. By default, it returns the `true` value when all the participants have been deregistered.

When a phaser is in the termination state, registration of new participants has no effect and synchronization methods return immediately.

Finally, the `Phaser` class provides some methods to get information about the status and participants in the phaser:

- `getRegisteredParties()`: This method returns the number of participants in the phaser
- `getPhase()`: This method returns the number of the current phase
- `getArrivedParties()`: This method returns the number of participants that have finished the current phase
- `getUnarrivedParties()`: This method returns the number of participants that haven't finished the current phase
- `isTerminated()`: This method returns `true` value if the phaser is in the termination state and `false` otherwise

First example – a keyword extraction algorithm

In this section, you are going to use a phaser to implement a **keyword extraction algorithm**. The main purpose of these kinds of algorithms is to extract the words from a text document or a collection of documents that define the document of the document inside the collection better. These terms can be used to summarize the documents, clustering them or to improve the information search process.

The most basic algorithm to extract the keywords of the documents in a collection (but it's still commonly used nowadays) is based on the **TF-IDF** measure where:

- **TF** (short for **term frequency**) is the number of times that a word appears in a document.
- **DF** (short for **document frequency**) is the number of documents that contains a word. The **IDF** (short for **inverse document frequency**) measures the information that word provides to distinguish a document from others. If a word is very common, it's IDF will be low, but if the word appears in only a few documents, it's IDF will be high.

The TF-IDF of the word *t* in the document *d* can be calculated using the following formula:

$$TF - IDF = TFxIDF = F_{t,d} x \log\left(\frac{N}{n_t}\right)$$

The attributes used in the preceding formula can be explained as follows:

- $F_{t,d}$ is the number of appearances of the word *t* in the document *d*   e.g. $F_{historical} = 3$, 40
- *N* is the number of documents in the collection   e.g. 1500
- n_t is the number of documents that contain the word *t*   e.g. 17

To obtain the keywords of a document, you can select the words with higher values of its TF-IDF.

The algorithm you are going to implement will calculate the best keywords in a document collection executing the following phases:

- **Phase 1**: Parse all the documents and extract the DF of all the words. Note that you will only have the exact values once you have parsed all the documents.
- **Phase 2**: Calculate the TF-IDF for all the words in all the documents. Select 10 keywords per document (the 10 words with a higher value of the TF-IDF measure).
- **Phase 3**: Obtain a list of the best keywords. We considered that those are the words that are a keyword of a higher number of documents.

To test the algorithm, we will use the Wikipedia pages with information about movies as the document collection. We have used the same collection in *Chapter 4, Getting Data from the Tasks – The Callable and Future Interfaces*. This collection is formed by 100,673 documents. We have converted each Wikipedia page in a text file. You can download this document collection with all the information about the book.

You are going to implement two different versions of the algorithm: a basic serial one and a concurrent one using the `Phaser` class. After this, we will compare the execution time of both versions to verify that concurrency provides us with better performance.

Common classes

Both versions of the algorithm share some common functionality to parse the documents and to store information about documents, keywords, and words. The common classes are:

- The `Document` class that stores the name of the file that contains the document and the words that form it
- The `Word` class that stores the string with the word and the measures of that word (TF, DF, and TF-IDF)
- The `Keyword` class that stores the string with the word and the number of documents in which the word is a keyword
- The `DocumentParser` class that extracts the words for a document

Let's see these classes in more detail.

The Word class

The `Word` class stores the information about a word. This information includes the whole word and the measures that affect it, that it's to say, it's TF in a document, it's global DF, and the resultant TF-IDF.

This class implements the `Comparable` interface because we're going to sort an array of words in order to obtain the ones with a higher TF-IDF. Refer to the following code:

```
public class Word implements Comparable<Word> {
```

Then, we declare the attributes of the class and implement the getters and setters (these ones are not included):

```
    private String word;
    private int tf;
    private int df;
    private double tfIdf;
```

We have implemented other methods of interest as follows:

- The constructor of the class, which initializes the word (with the word received as parameter) and the df attribute (with a value of 1).
- The addTf() method, which increments the tf attribute.
- The merge() method that receives a Word object and merges the same word from two different documents. It sums the tf and df attributes of both objects.

Then, we implement a special version of the setDf() method. It receives the value of the df attribute as a parameter and the total number of documents in the collection, and it calculates the tfIdf attribute:

```
public void setDf(int df, int N) {
    this.df = df;
    tfIdf = tf * Math.log(Double.valueOf(N) / df);
}
```

Finally, we implement the compareTo() method. We want the words ordered from a higher to lower tfIdf attribute:

```
@Override
public int compareTo(Word o) {
    return Double.compare(o.getTfIdf(), this.getTfIdf());
}
}
```

The Keyword class

The Keyword class stores information about a keyword. This information includes the whole word and the number of documents in which this word is a keyword.

As occurs with the Word class, it implements the Comparable interface because we're going to sort an array of keywords to obtain the best keywords:

```
public class Keyword implements Comparable<Keyword> {
```

Then, we declare the attributes of the class and implement the methods to establish and return its values (these ones are not included here):

```
private String word;
private int df;
```

Finally, we implement the `compareTo()` method. We want the keywords ordered from a higher to lower number of documents:

```
@Override
public int compareTo(Keyword o) {

    return Integer.compare(o.getDf(), this.getDf());
}
```

The Document class

The `Document` class stores the information about a document of the collection (remember that our collection has 100,673 documents) that includes the name of the file and the set of words that forms the document. That set of words, usually named the vocabulary of the document, is implemented as a `HashMap` using the whole word as a string as the key and a `Word` object as the value:

```
public class Document {
    private String fileName;
    private HashMap <String, Word> voc;
```

We have implemented a constructor that creates the `HashMap` and methods to get and set the name of the file and to return the vocabulary of the document (these methods are not included). We also have implemented a method to add a word in the vocabulary. If the word doesn't exist on it, we add to it. If the word exists in the vocabulary, we increment the `tf` attribute of the word. We have used the `computeIfAbsent()` method of the `voc` object. This method inserts the word in the `HashMap` if it doesn't exist and then increments the `tf` using the `addTf()` method:

```
public void addWord(String string) {
    voc.computeIfAbsent(string, k -> new Word(k)).addTf();
}
```

The `HashMap` class is not synchronized, but we can use it in our concurrent application because it will not be shared between different tasks. A `Document` object will be generated only by one task, so we won't have race conditions in our concurrent version derived by the utilization of the `HashMap` class.

The DocumentParser class

The `DocumentParser` class reads the content of a text file and converts it into a `Document` object. It splits the text into the words and stores them in the `Document` object to generate the vocabulary of the class. This class has two static methods. The first one is the `parse()` method that receives a string with the path of the file and returns a `Document` object. It opens the file and reads it line by line, using the `parseLine()` method to convert each line into a sequence of words, and stores them into the `Document` class:

```
public class DocumentParser {

    public static Document parse(String path) {
        Document ret = new Document();
        Path file = Paths.get(path);
        ret.setFileName(file.toString());

        try (BufferedReader reader =
          Files.newBufferedReader(file)) {
            for(String line : Files.readAllLines(file)) {
                parseLine(line, ret);
            }
        } catch (IOException x) {
            x.printStackTrace();
        }
        return ret;

    }
```

The `parseLine()` method receives the line to parse and the `Document` object to store the words as parameters.

First, it deletes the accents of the line using the `Normalizer` class and converts it into lowercase:

```
    private static void parseLine(String line, Document ret) {

        // Clean string
        line = Normalizer.normalize(line, Normalizer.Form.NFKD);
        line = line.replaceAll("[^\\p{ASCII}]", "");
        line = line.toLowerCase();
```

Then, we split the line in words using the `StringTokenizer` class and add those words to the `Document` object:

```
private static void parseLine(String line, Document ret) {

    // Clean string
    line = Normalizer.normalize(line, Normalizer.Form.NFKD);
    line = line.replaceAll("[^\\p{ASCII}]", "");
    line = line.toLowerCase();

    // Tokenizer

    for(String w: line.split("\\W+")) {
        ret.addWord(w);
    }
}

}
```

The serial version

We have implemented the serial version of our keyword algorithm in the `SerialKeywordExtraction` class. It defines the `main()` method you are going to execute to test the algorithm.

The first step is to declare the following necessary internal variables to execute the algorithm:

- Two `Date` objects to measure the execution time
- A string to store the name of the directory that contains the document collection
- An array of `File` objects to store the files with the document collection
- A `HashMap` to store the global vocabulary of the document collection
- A `HashMap` to store the keywords
- Two `int` values to measure statistic data about the execution

The following includes the declaration of these variables:

```
public class SerialKeywordExtraction {

    public static void main(String[] args) {

        Date start, end;
```

```
File source = new File("data");
File[] files = source.listFiles();
HashMap<String, Word> globalVoc = new HashMap<>();
HashMap<String, Integer> globalKeywords = new HashMap<>();
int totalCalls = 0;
int numDocuments = 0;

start = new Date();
```

Then, we have included the first phase of the algorithm. We parse all the documents using the `parse()` method of the `DocumentParser` class. This method returns a `Document` object that contains the vocabulary of that document. We add the document vocabulary to the global vocabulary using the `merge()` method of the `HashMap` class. If a word doesn't exist, it inserts it in the `HashMap`. If the word exists, two word objects are merged together summing the `Tf` and `Df` attributes:

```
if(files == null) {
    System.err.println("Unable to read the 'data'
      folder");
    return;
}
for (File file : files) {

    if (file.getName().endsWith(".txt")) {
        Document doc = DocumentParser.parse
          (file.getAbsolutePath());
        for (Word word : doc.getVoc().values()) {
            globalVoc.merge(word.getWord(), word,
              Word::merge);
        }
        numDocuments++;
    }
}
System.out.println("Corpus: " + numDocuments + "
  documents.");
```

After this phase, the `globalVocHashMap` class contains all the words of the document collection with their global TF (the total number of appearances of the word in the collection) and their DF.

Then, we have included the second phase of the algorithm. We are going to calculate the keywords of each document using the TF-IDF measure, as we explained before. We have to parse again each document to generate its vocabulary. We have to do this because we can't store in memory the vocabularies of 100,673 documents that form our document collection. If you work with a smaller document collection, you can try to parse the documents only once and store the vocabularies of all the documents in memory, but in our case, it's impossible. So, we parse all the documents again, and, to each word, we update the `Df` attribute using the values stored in the `globalVoc`. We also construct an array with all the words in the document:

```
for (File file : files) {
    if (file.getName().endsWith(".txt")) {
        Document doc =
            DocumentParser.parse(file.getAbsolutePath());
        List<Word> keywords = new ArrayList<>(
            doc.getVoc().values());

        int index = 0;
        for (Word word : keywords) {
            Word globalWord =
                globalVoc.get(word.getWord());
            word.setDf(globalWord.getDf(),
                numDocuments);
        }
```

Now, we have the list of keywords with all the words in the document with their TF-IDF calculated. We use the `sort()` method of the `Collections` class to sort the list getting the words with a higher value of TF-IDF in the first position. Then we get the first 10 words of that list to store them in the `globalKeywordsHashMap` using the `addKeyword()` method.

There is no special reason to choose the first 10 words. You can try other options, as a percentage of the words or a minimum value of the TF-IDF measure, and see their behavior:

```
            Collections.sort(keywords);

            int counter = 0;

            for (Word word : keywords) {
                addKeyword(globalKeywords, word.getWord());
                totalCalls++;
            }
        }
    }
```

Finally, we have included the third phase of our algorithm. We convert the `globalKeywordsHashMap` into a list of `Keyword` objects, use the `sort()` method of the `Collections` class to sort that array getting the keywords with a higher DF value in the first positions of the list, and write the first 100 words in the console.

Refer to the following code:

```
List<Keyword> orderedGlobalKeywords = new ArrayList<>();
for (Entry<String, Integer> entry :
  globalKeywords.entrySet()) {
  Keyword keyword = new Keyword();
  keyword.setWord(entry.getKey());
  keyword.setDf(entry.getValue());
  orderedGlobalKeywords.add(keyword);
}

Collections.sort(orderedGlobalKeywords);

if (orderedGlobalKeywords.size() > 100) {
    orderedGlobalKeywords = 
       orderedGlobalKeywords.subList(0, 100);
}
for (Keyword keyword : orderedGlobalKeywords) {
    System.out.println(keyword.getWord() + ": " +
       keyword.getDf());
}
```

As in the second phase, there is no special reason to choose the first 100 words. You can try other options if you want.

To finish the main method, we write the execution time and other statistic data in the console:

```
end = new Date();
System.out.println("Execution Time: " + (end.getTime() -
  start.getTime()));
System.out.println("Vocabulary Size: " +
  globalVoc.size());
System.out.println("Keyword Size: " +
  globalKeywords.size());
System.out.println("Number of Documents: " +
  numDocuments);
System.out.println("Total calls: " + totalCalls);

}
```

The `SerialKeywordExtraction` class also includes the `addKeyword()` method that updates the information of a keyword in the `globalKeywordsHashMap` class. If the word exists, the class updates its DF and if the word doesn't exists, inserts it. Refer to the following code:

```
      private static void addKeyword(Map<String, Integer>
        globalKeywords, String word) {
          globalKeywords.merge(word, 1, Integer::sum);
      }

}
```

The concurrent version

To implement the concurrent version of this example, we have used two different classes as follows:

- The `KeywordExtractionTasks` class that implements the tasks that are going to calculate the keywords in a concurrent way. We are going to execute the tasks as `Thread` objects, so this class implements the `Runnable` interface.
- The `ConcurrentKeywordExtraction` class that provides the `main()` method to execute the algorithm and creates, starts, and waits for the tasks to finish.

Let's see these classes in detail.

The KeywordExtractionTask class

As we mentioned before, this class implements the tasks that are going to calculate the final keyword list. It implements the `Runnable` interface, so we can execute them as a `Thread`, and internally uses some attributes, most of which are shared between all the tasks:

- **Two ConcurrentHashMap objects to store the global vocabulary and the global keywords**: We use the `ConcurrentHashMap` because these objects are going to be updated by all the tasks, so we have to use a concurrent data structure to avoid race conditions.

- **Two ConcurrentLinkedDeque of File objects to store the list of files that forms the document collection**: We use the `ConcurrentLinkedDeque` class because all the tasks are going to extract (`get` and `delete`) elements of the list simultaneously, so we have to use a concurrent data structure to avoid race conditions. If we use a normal `List`, the same `File` can be parsed twice by different tasks. We have two `ConcurrentLinkedDeque` because we have to parse the collection of documents twice. As we mentioned before, we parse the document collection extracting `File` objects from the data structures, so, when we have parsed the collection, the data structure will be empty.
- **A Phaser object to control the execution of the tasks**: As we explained before, our keyword extraction algorithm is executed in three phases. None of the tasks advanced to one phase until all the tasks have finished the previous one. We use the `Phaser` object to control this. If we don't control this, we will obtain inconsistent results.
- **The final step has to be executed by only one thread**: We are going to distinguish one main task from the others using a Boolean value. These main tasks will execute that final phase.
- **The total number of documents in the collection**: We need this value to calculate the TF-IDF measure.

We have included a constructor to initialize all these attributes:

```
public class KeywordExtractionTask implements Runnable {

    private ConcurrentHashMap<String, Word> globalVoc;
    private ConcurrentHashMap<String, Integer> globalKeywords;

    private ConcurrentLinkedDeque<File> concurrentFileListPhase1;
    private ConcurrentLinkedDeque<File> concurrentFileListPhase2;

    private Phaser phaser;

    private String name;
    private boolean main;

    private int parsedDocuments;
    private int numDocuments;

    public KeywordExtractionTask(
            ConcurrentLinkedDeque<File> concurrentFileListPhase1,
            ConcurrentLinkedDeque<File> concurrentFileListPhase2,
            Phaser phaser, ConcurrentHashMap<String, Word>
              globalVoc,
```

Running Tasks Divided into Phases – The Phaser Class

```
                ConcurrentHashMap<String, Integer> globalKeywords,
                int numDocuments, String name, boolean main) {
        this.concurrentFileListPhase1 = concurrentFileListPhase1;
        this.concurrentFileListPhase2 = concurrentFileListPhase2;
        this.globalVoc = globalVoc;
        this.globalKeywords = globalKeywords;
        this.phaser = phaser;
        this.main = main;
        this.name = name;
        this.numDocuments = numDocuments;
}
```

The `run()` method implements the algorithm with its three phases. First, we call the `arriveAndAwaitAdvance()` method of the phaser to wait for the creation of the other tasks. All the tasks will start their execution at the same moment. Then, as we explained in the serial version of the algorithm, we parse all the documents and build the `globalVocConcurrentHashMap` class with all the words and their global TF and DF values. To complete phase one, we call again the `arriveAndAwaitAdvance()` method to wait for the finalization of the other tasks before the execution of the second phase:

```
@Override
public void run() {
    File file;

    // Phase 1
    phaser.arriveAndAwaitAdvance();
    System.out.println(name + ": Phase 1");
    while ((file = concurrentFileListPhase1.poll()) != null) {
        Document doc =
          DocumentParser.parse(file.getAbsolutePath());
        for (Word word : doc.getVoc().values()) {
            globalVoc.merge(word.getWord(), word,
              Word::merge);
        }
        parsedDocuments++;
    }

    System.out.println(name + ": " + parsedDocuments + "
      parsed.");
    phaser.arriveAndAwaitAdvance();
```

As you can see, to get the `File` objects to process, we use the `poll()` method of the `ConcurrentLinkedDeque` class. This method *retrieves and removes* the first element of `Deque`, so the next task will obtain a different file to parse, and no file will be parsed twice.

The second phase calculates the `globalKeywords` structure, as we explained in the serial version of the algorithm. First, calculate the best 10 keywords of every document and then insert them in the `ConcurrentHashMap` class. The code is the same as in the serial version changing the serial data structures for the concurrent ones:

```
// Phase 2
System.out.println(name + ": Phase 2");
while ((file = concurrentFileListPhase2.poll()) != null) {

    Document doc =
      DocumentParser.parse(file.getAbsolutePath());
    List<Word> keywords = new
      ArrayList<>(doc.getVoc().values());

    for (Word word : keywords) {
      Word globalWord = globalVoc.get(word.getWord());
      word.setDf(globalWord.getDf(), numDocuments);
    }
    Collections.sort(keywords);

    if(keywords.size() > 10) keywords =
      keywords.subList(0, 10);
    for (Word word : keywords) {
      addKeyword(globalKeywords, word.getWord());
    }
}
System.out.println(name + ": " + parsedDocuments + "
  parsed.");
```

The final phase will be different for the main task and for the others. The main task uses the `arriveAndAwaitAdvance()` method of the `Phaser` class to wait for the finalization of the second phase of all the tasks before writing the best 100 keywords of the whole collection in the console. Finally, it uses the `arriveAndDeregister()` method to deregister from the phaser.

The rest of the tasks use the `arriveAndDeregister()` method to mark the finalization of the second phase, deregister from the phaser, and finish their execution.

Running Tasks Divided into Phases – The Phaser Class

When all the tasks have finished their work, all of them have deregistered themselves from the phaser. The phaser will have zero parties, and it will enter the termination state:

```java
if (main) {
    phaser.arriveAndAwaitAdvance();

    Iterator<Entry<String, Integer>> iterator =
        globalKeywords.entrySet().iterator();
    Keyword orderedGlobalKeywords[] = new
        Keyword[globalKeywords.size()];
    int index = 0;
    while (iterator.hasNext()) {
        Entry<String, AtomicInteger> entry =
            iterator.next();
        Keyword keyword = new Keyword();
        keyword.setWord(entry.getKey());
        keyword.setDf(entry.getValue().get());
        orderedGlobalKeywords[index] = keyword;
        index++;
    }

    System.out.println("Keyword Size: " +
        orderedGlobalKeywords.length);

    Arrays.parallelSort(orderedGlobalKeywords);
    int counter = 0;
    for (int i = 0; i < orderedGlobalKeywords.length;
      i++) {

        Keyword keyword = orderedGlobalKeywords[i];
        System.out.println(keyword.getWord() + ": " +
            keyword.getDf());
        counter++;
        if (counter == 100) {
            break;
        }
    }
}
phaser.arriveAndDeregister();

System.out.println("Thread " + name + " has finished.");
}
```

The ConcurrentKeywordExtraction class

The `ConcurrentKeywordExtraction` class initializes the shared objects, creates the tasks, executes them, and waits for its finalization. It implements the `main()` method that can receive an optional parameter. By default, we are doing the number of tasks determined by the `availableProcessors()` method of the `Runtime` class that returns the number of hardware threads available to the **Java Virtual Machine (JVM)**. If we receive a parameter, we convert it into an integer and use it as a multiplier of the number of available processors to determine the number of tasks we are going to create.

First, we initialize all the necessary data structures and parameters. To fill the two `ConcurrentLinkedDeque` structures, we use the `listFiles()` method of the `File` class to get an array of `File` objects with the files that end with the `txt` suffix.

We also create the `Phaser` object using the constructor without parameters, so all the tasks must register themselves in the phaser explicitly. Refer to the following code:

```
public class ConcurrentKeywordExtraction {

    public static void main(String[] args) {

        Date start, end;

        ConcurrentHashMap<String, Word> globalVoc = new
           ConcurrentHashMap<>();
        ConcurrentHashMap<String, Integer> globalKeywords = new
           ConcurrentHashMap<>();

        start = new Date();
        File source = new File("data");

        File[] files = source.listFiles(f ->
           f.getName().endsWith(".txt"));
        if (files == null) {
           System.err.println("The 'data' folder not found!");
           return;
        }
        ConcurrentLinkedDeque<File> concurrentFileListPhase1 = new
           ConcurrentLinkedDeque<>(Arrays.asList(files));
        ConcurrentLinkedDeque<File> concurrentFileListPhase2 = new
           ConcurrentLinkedDeque<>(Arrays.asList(files));

        int numDocuments = files.length();
        int factor = 1;
        if (args.length > 0) {
```

```
            factor = Integer.valueOf(args[0]);
        }

        int numTasks = factor *
            Runtime.getRuntime().availableProcessors();
        Phaser phaser = new Phaser();

        Thread[] threads = new Thread[numTasks];
        KeywordExtractionTask[] tasks = new
            KeywordExtractionTask[numTasks];
```

Then, we create the first task with the main parameter to `true` and the rest with the main parameter to `false`. After the creation of each task, we use the `register()` method of the `Phaser` class to register a new participant in the phaser as follows:

```
        for (int i = 0; i < numTasks; i++) {
            tasks[i] = new
                KeywordExtractionTask(concurrentFileListPhase1,
                    concurrentFileListPhase2, phaser, globalVoc,
                    globalKeywords, concurrentFileListPhase1.size(),
                    "Task" + i, i==0);
            phaser.register();
            System.out.println(phaser.getRegisteredParties() + "
                tasks arrived to the Phaser.");
        }
```

Then, we create and start the thread objects that run the tasks and wait for its finalization:

```
        for (int i = 0; i < numTasks; i++) {
            threads[i] = new Thread(tasks[i]);
            threads[i].start();
        }

        for (int i = 0; i < numTasks; i++) {
            try {
                threads[i].join();
            } catch (InterruptedException e) {
                e.printStackTrace();
            }
        }
```

Finally, we write some statistic information about the execution in the console, including the execution time:

```
System.out.println("Is Terminated: " +
    phaser.isTerminated());

end = new Date();
System.out.println("Execution Time: " + (end.getTime() -
    start.getTime()));
System.out.println("Vocabulary Size: " +
    globalVoc.size());
System.out.println("Number of Documents: " +
    numDocuments);

    }

}
```

Comparing the two solutions

Let's compare the serial and concurrent versions of our keyword extraction 100,673 documents. We have executed the examples using the JMH framework (http://openjdk.java.net/projects/code-tools/jmh/) that allows you to implement micro benchmarks in Java. Using a framework for benchmarking is a better solution that simply measures time using methods such as currentTimeMillis() or nanoTime(). We have executed them 10 times in a computer with a four-core processor and calculate the medium execution time of those 10 times.

Algorithm	Factor	Execution time (seconds)
Serial	N/A	194.45
Concurrent	1	64.52
	2	65.55
	3	68,23

We can draw the following conclusions:

- The concurrent version of the algorithm increases the performance of the serial version.
- If we use more tasks than the number of the available hardware threads, we don't get a better result. Just a little worse because of the extra synchronization work the phaser must do.

We compare the concurrent and serial versions of the algorithm calculating the speed-up using the following formula:

$$S = \frac{T_{serial}}{T_{concurrent}} = \frac{194.28}{64.52} = 3.01$$

The second example – a genetic algorithm

Genetic algorithms are adaptive heuristic search algorithms based on the natural selection principles use to generate good solutions to **optimization** and **search problems**. They work with possible solutions to a problem named **individuals** or **phenotypes**. Each individual has a representation formed by a set of properties named **chromosomes**. Normally, the individuals are represented by a sequence of bits, but you can choose the representation that better fits your problem.

You also need a function to determine whether a solution is good or bad named **fitness function**. The main objective of the genetic algorithm is to find a solution that maximizes or minimizes that function.

The genetic algorithm starts with a set of possible solutions to the problem. This set of possible solutions is named the population. You can generate this initial set randomly or use some kind of heuristic function to obtain better initial solutions.

Once you have the initial population, you begin an iterative process with three phases. Each step of that iterative process is called a generation. The phases of each generation are:

- **Selection**: You select the better individuals of your population. These are the individuals with a better value in the fitness function.
- **Crossover**: You cross the individuals selected in the previous step to generate the new individuals that form the new generation. This operation takes two individuals and generates two new individuals. The implementation of this operation depends on the problem you want to solve and the representation of the individuals you have chosen.
- **Mutation**: You can apply a mutation operator to alter the values of an individual. Normally, you will apply that operation to a very low number of individuals. While mutation is a very important operation to find a good solution, we don't apply it to simplify our example.

You repeat these three operations until you meet your finish criteria. These finish criteria can be:

- A fixed number of generations
- A predefined value of the fitness function
- A solution that meets the predefined criteria is found
- A time limit
- A manual stop

Normally, you will store the best individual you have found across the process outside of the population. This individual will be the solution proposed by the algorithm, and normally, it's going to be a better solution, as we generate new generations.

In this section, we are going to implement a genetic algorithm to solve the well-known **Travel Salesman Problem** (**TSP**). In this problem, you have a set of cities and the distances between them, and you want to find an optimal route to go through all the cities minimizing the total distance of the travel. As per other examples, we have implemented a serial version and a concurrent one using the `Phaser` class. The main characteristics of a genetic algorithm applied to the TSP problems are:

- **Individuals**: An individual represents the traversal order of the cities.
- **Crossover**: You have to create valid solutions after the crossover operation. You must visit each city only once.
- **Fitness function**: The main objective of the algorithm is to minimize the total distance to travel across the cities.
- **Finish criteria**: We are going to execute the algorithm a predefined number of generations.

For example, you can have a distance matrix with four cities as shown in the following table:

	City 1	City 2	City 3	City 4
City 1	0	11	6	9
City 2	7	0	8	2
City 3	7	3	0	3
City 4	10	9	4	0

This means that the distance between city 2 and city 1 is 7, but the distance between city 1 and city 2 is 11. An individual can be (2,4,3,1) and its fitness function is the sum of the distances between 2 and 4, 4 and 3, 3 and 1, and 1 and 2, that is, 2+4+7+11=24.

If you want to make the crossover between the individuals (1,2,3,4) and (1,3,2,4), you can't generate the individual (1,2,2,4) because you are visiting the city 2 twice. You can generate the individuals (1,2,4,3) and (1,3,4,2).

To test the algorithm, we have used two examples of the **City Distance Datasets** (http://people.sc.fsu.edu/~jburkardt/datasets/cities/cities.html) with 15 (lau15_dist) and 57 (kn57_dist) cities, respectively.

Common classes

Both versions use the following three common classes:

- The DataLoader class that loads the distance matrix from a file. We don't include the code of this class here. It has a static method that receives the name of the file and returns an int[][] matrix with the distances between the cities. The distances are stored in a csv file (we have made a little transformation in the original format), so it's easy to make the conversion.
- The Individual class stores the information of an individual of the population (a possible solution to the problem). To represent each individual, we have chosen an array of integer values that stores the order in which you visit the different cities.
- The GeneticOperators class implements the crossover, selection and evaluation of the population or an individual.

Let's see the details of the Individual and GeneticOperators classes.

The Individual class

This class stores each possible solution to our TSP problem. We call each possible solution, an individual, and its representation chromosomes. In our case, we represent each possible solution as an array of integers. That array contains the order in which our salesman will go through the cities. This class also has an integer value to store the result of the fitness function. We have the following code:

```
public class Individual implements Comparable<Individual> {
    private Integer[] chromosomes;
    private int value;
```

We have included two constructors. The first one receives the number of cities you must visit, and we create an empty array. The other receives an `Individual` object and copies its chromosomes as follows:

```java
public Individual(int size) {
    chromosomes=new Integer[size];
}

public Individual(Individual other) {
    chromosomes = other.getChromosomes().clone();

}
```

We have also implemented the `compareTo()` method to compare two individuals using the result of the fitness function:

```java
@Override
public int compareTo(Individual o) {
        return Integer.compare(this.getValue(), o.getValue());
}
```

Finally, we have included methods to get and set the values of the attributes.

The GeneticOperators class

This is a complex class because it implements the internal logic of the genetic algorithm. It provides methods to make the initialization, selection, crossover, and evaluation operations as were introduced at the beginning of this section. We are going to describe only the methods provided by this class, but not how they are implemented to avoid your unnecessary complexity. You can get the source code of the example to analyze the implementation of the methods.

The methods provided by this class are:

- `initialize(int numberOfIndividuals, int size)`: This creates a new population. The number of individuals of that population will be determined by the `numberOfIndividuals` parameter. The number of chromosomes (cities in our case) will be determined by the size parameter. It returns an array of `Individual` objects. It uses the method initialize(`Integer[]`) to initialize each Individual.

- `initialize(Integer[] chromosomes)`: It initializes the chromosomes of an individual in a random way. It generates valid individuals (you have to visit each city only once).

- `selection(Individual[] population)`: This method implements the selection operation to get the best individuals of a population. It returns that individuals in an array. The size of that array will be the half of the population size. You can test other criteria to determine the number of the selected individuals. We select the individuals with the best fit function.
- `crossover(Individual[] selected, int numberOfIndividuals, int size)`: This method receives the selected individuals of a generation as a parameter and generates the population of the next generation using the crossover operation. The number of individuals of the next generation will be determined by the parameter of the same name. The number of chromosomes of each individual will be determined by the size parameter. It uses the method crossover (`Individual, Individual, Individual, Individual`) to generate two new individuals from two selected ones.
- `crossover(Individual parent1, Individual parent2, Individual individual1, Individual individual2)`: This method performs the crossover operation taking the `parent1` and `parent2` individuals to generate the `individual1` and `individual2` individuals of the next generation.
- `evaluate(Individual[] population, int [][] distanceMatrix)`: This applies the fitness function to all the individuals of the population using the distance matrix it receives as a parameter. Finally, it sorts the population from the best to worst solution. It uses the method evaluate (`Individual, int [] []`) to evaluate each individual.
- `evaluate(Individual individual, int[][] distanceMatrix)`: This applies the fitness function to one individual.

With this class and its methods, you have all you need to implement a genetic algorithm to solve the TSP problem.

The serial version

We have implemented the serial version of the algorithm with the following two classes:

- The `SerialGeneticAlgorithm` class that implements the algorithm
- The `SerialMain` class that executes the algorithm with the input parameters and measures the execution time

Let's analyze both classes in detail.

The SerialGeneticAlgorithm class

This class implements the serial version of our genetic algorithm. Internally, it uses the following four attributes:

- The distance matrix with the distances between all the cities
- The number of generations
- The number of individuals in the population
- The number of chromosomes in each individual

The class also has a constructor to initialize all the attributes:

```
private int[][] distanceMatrix;

private int numberOfGenerations;
private int numberOfIndividuals;

private int size;

public SerialGeneticAlgorithm(int[][] distanceMatrix,
        int numberOfGenerations, int numberOfIndividuals) {
    this.distanceMatrix = distanceMatrix;
    this.numberOfGenerations = numberOfGenerations;
    this.numberOfIndividuals = numberOfIndividuals;
    size = distanceMatrix.length;
}
```

The main method of the class is the `calculate()` method. First, use the `initialize()` method to create the initial population. Then, evaluate the initial population and get its best individual as the first solution of the algorithm:

```
public Individual calculate() {
    Individual best;

    Individual[] population = GeneticOperators.initialize(
            numberOfIndividuals, size);
    GeneticOperators.evaluate(population, distanceMatrix);

    best = population[0];
```

Running Tasks Divided into Phases – The Phaser Class

Then, it executes a loop determined by the `numberOfGenerations` attribute. In each cycle, it uses the `selection()` method to obtain the selected individuals, use the `crossover()` method to calculate the next generation, evaluate this new generation, and if the best solution of the new generation is better than the best individual until now, we replace it. When the loop finishes, we return the best individual as the solution proposed by the algorithm:

```java
        for (int i = 1; i <= numberOfGenerations; i++) {
            Individual[] selected =
                GeneticOperators.selection(population);
            population = GeneticOperators.crossover(selected,
                numberOfIndividuals, size);
            GeneticOperators.evaluate(population, distanceMatrix);
            if (population[0].getValue() < best.getValue()) {
                best = population[0];
            }

        }

        return best;
    }
```

The SerialMain class

This class executes the genetic algorithm for the two datasets used in this section—the `lau15` with 15 cities and the `kn57` with 57 cities.

The `main()` method must receive two parameters. The first one is the number of generations we want to create, and the second parameter is the number of individuals we want to have in each generation:

```java
    public class SerialMain {

        public static void main(String[] args) {

            Date start, end;

            int generations = Integer.valueOf(args[0]);
            int individuals = Integer.valueOf(args[1]);
```

For each example, we load the distance matrix using the `load()` method of the `DataLoader` class, create the `SerialGeneticAlgorithm` object, execute the `calculate()` method measuring the execution time, and write the execution time and the result in the console:

```
for (String name : new String[] { "lau15_dist", "kn57_dist" })
{
  int[][] distanceMatrix = DataLoader.load(Paths.get("data",
    name + ".txt"));
  SerialGeneticAlgorithm serialGeneticAlgorithm = new
    SerialGeneticAlgorithm(distanceMatrix, generations,
    individuals);
    start = new Date();
    Individual result =
      serialGeneticAlgorithm.calculate();
    end = new Date();
  System.out.println
    ("=======================================");
  System.out.println("Example:"+name);
  System.out.println("Generations: " + generations);
  System.out.println("Population: " + individuals);
  System.out.println("Execution Time: " + (end.getTime() -
    start.getTime()));
  System.out.println("Best Individual: " + result);
  System.out.println("Total Distance: " +
    result.getValue());
  System.out.println
    ("=======================================");
}
```

The concurrent version

We have implemented the concurrent version of the genetic algorithm different classes:

- The `SharedData` class stores all the objects that will be shared between the tasks
- The `GeneticPhaser` class extends the `Phaser` class and overrides its `onAdvance()` method to execute code when all the tasks finish a phase
- The `ConcurrentGeneticTask` class implements the tasks that will implement the phases of the genetic algorithm
- The `ConcurrentGeneticAlgorithm` class will implement the concurrent version of the genetic algorithm using the previous classes
- The `ConcurrentMain` class will test the concurrent version of the genetic algorithm in our two datasets

Internally, the `ConcurrentGeneticTask` class will execute three phases. The first one is the selection phase and will only be executed by one task. The second one is the crossover phase where all the tasks will construct the new generation using the selected individuals, and the last phase is the evaluation phase where all the tasks will evaluate the individuals of the new generation.

Let's see in detail each of those classes.

The SharedData class

As we mentioned before, this class contains all the objects shared by the tasks. This include the following:

- The population array with all the individuals of a generation.
- The selected array with the selected individuals.
- An atomic integer called `index`. This is the only thread-safe object used to know the index of the individual a task has to generate or process.
- The best individual of all the generations that will be returned as the solution of the algorithm.
- The distance matrix with the distances between the cities.

All these objects will be shared by all the threads, but we only need to use one concurrent data structure. This is the only attribute that will be effectively shared by all the tasks. The rest of the objects will be only read (the distance matrix), or each task will access a different part of the object (the population and selected arrays), so we don't need to use concurrent data structures or synchronization mechanisms to avoid race conditions:

```
public class SharedData {

    private Individual[] population;
    private Individual selected[];
    private AtomicInteger index;
    private Individual best;
    private int[][] distanceMatrix;
}
```

This class also includes the getters and setters to get and establish the values of these attributes.

The GeneticPhaser class

We need to execute code on the phase changes of our tasks, so we have to implement our own phaser and override the `onAdvance()` method that is executed after all the parties have finished a phase and before they begin the execution of the next one. The `GeneticPhaser` class implements this phaser. It stores the `SharedData` object to work with it and receives it as a parameter to the constructor:

```
public class GeneticPhaser extends Phaser {

    private SharedData data;

    public GeneticPhaser(int parties, SharedData data) {
        super(parties);
        this.data=data;
    }
```

The `onAdvance()` method will receive the number of the phase to the phaser and the number of registered parties as parameters. The phaser internally stores the number of the phase as an integer that grows sequentially with every change of phase. On the contrary, our algorithm has only three phases that will be executed a lot of times. We have to convert the phaser phase number to the genetic algorithm phase number to know if the tasks are going to execute the selection, crossover, or evaluation phases. To do this, we calculate the remainder between the phase number of the phaser and three as follows:

```
    protected boolean onAdvance(int phase, int registeredParties) {
        int realPhase=phase%3;
        if (registeredParties>0) {
            switch (realPhase) {
            case 0:
            case 1:
                data.getIndex().set(0);
                break;
            case 2:
                Arrays.sort(data.getPopulation());
                if (data.getPopulation()[0].getValue() <
                  data.getBest().getValue()) {
                    data.setBest(data.getPopulation()[0]);
                }
                break;
            }
            return false;
        }
        return true;
    }
```

If the remainder is zero, the tasks have finished the selection phase and are going to execute the crossover phase. We initialize the index object with the value zero.

If the remainder is one, the tasks have finished the crossover phase and are going to execute the evaluation phase. We initialize the index object with the value zero.

Finally, if the remainder is two, the tasks have finished the evaluation phase and are going to start again with the selection phase. We sort the population based on the fitness function and update if necessary the best individual.

Take into account that this method will only be executed by one thread independently of the tasks. It will be executed in the thread of the task, which was the last to finish the previous phase (inside the `arriveAndAwaitAdvance()` call). The rest of the tasks will be sleeping and waiting for the phaser.

The ConcurrentGeneticTask class

This class implements the tasks that collaborate to execute the genetic algorithm. They execute the three phases (selection, crossover, and evaluation) of the algorithm. The selection phase will be executed by only one task (we called it the main task) while the rest of the phases will be executed by all the tasks.

Internally, it uses four attributes:

- A `GeneticPhaser` object to synchronize the tasks at the end of each phase
- A `SharedData` object to access the shared data
- The number of generations it has to calculate
- The Boolean flag that indicates whether it is the main task or not

All these attributes are initialized in the constructor of the class:

```
public class ConcurrentGeneticTask implements Runnable {
    private GeneticPhaser phaser;
    private SharedData data;
    private int numberOfGenerations;
    private boolean main;

    public ConcurrentGeneticTask(GeneticPhaser phaser, int
      numberOfGenerations, boolean main) {
        this.phaser = phaser;
        this.numberOfGenerations = numberOfGenerations;
        this.main = main;
        this.data = phaser.getData();
    }
```

The `run()` method implements the logic of the genetic algorithm. It has a loop to generate the specified generations. As we mentioned before, only the main task will execute the selection phase. The rests of the tasks will use the `arriveAndAwaitAdvance()` method to wait for the finalization of this phase. Refer to the following code:

```
@Override
public void run() {

    Random rm = new Random(System.nanoTime());
    for (int i = 0; i < numberOfGenerations; i++) {
        if (main) {
            data.setSelected(GeneticOperators.selection(data
                    .getPopulation()));
        }
        phaser.arriveAndAwaitAdvance();
```

The second phase is the crossover phase. We use the `AtomicInteger` variable index stored in the `SharedData` class to get the next position in the population array each task will calculate. As we mentioned before, the crossover operation generates two new individuals, so each task first reserves two positions in the population array. For this purpose, we use the `getAndAdd(2)` method that returns the actual value of the variable and increments its value by two units. It's an atomic variable, so we don't have to use any synchronization mechanism. It's inherent to the atomic variables. Refer to the following code:

```
// Crossover
int individualIndex;
do {
    individualIndex = data.getIndex().getAndAdd(2);
    if (individualIndex < data.getPopulation().length)
      {
        int secondIndividual = individualIndex++;

        int p1Index = rm.nextInt
          (data.getSelected().length);
        int p2Index;
        do {
            p2Index = rm.nextInt
                (data.getSelected().length);
        } while (p1Index == p2Index);

        Individual parent1 = data.getSelected()
          [p1Index];
```

Running Tasks Divided into Phases – The Phaser Class

```
            Individual parent2 = data.getSelected()
              [p2Index];
            Individual individual1 = data.getPopulation()
              [individualIndex];
            Individual individual2 = data.getPopulation()
              [secondIndividual];

            GeneticOperators.crossover(parent1, parent2,
              individual1, individual2);
          }
        } while (individualIndex <
          data.getPopulation().length);
        phaser.arriveAndAwaitAdvance();
```

When all the individuals of the new population have been generated, the tasks use the `arriveAndAwaitAdvance()` method to synchronize the end of the phase.

The last phase is the evaluation phase. We use the `AtomicInteger` index again. Each task gets the actual value of the variable, which represents the position of an individual in the population, and increments its value using the `getAndIncrement()` value. Once all the individuals have been evaluated, we use the `arriveAndAwaitAdvance()` method to synchronize the end of this phase. Remember that, when all the tasks have finished this phase, the `GeneticPhaser` class will execute the code that sorts the population array and updates, if necessary, the best individual variable as follows:

```
        // Evaluation
        do {
            individualIndex =
              data.getIndex().getAndIncrement();
            if (individualIndex < data.getPopulation().length)
              {
                GeneticOperators.evaluate(data.getPopulation()
                  [individualIndex], data.getDistanceMatrix());
            }
        } while (individualIndex <
          data.getPopulation().length);
        phaser.arriveAndAwaitAdvance();

    }

    phaser.arriveAndDeregister();
}
```

Finally, when all the generations have been calculated, the tasks use the `arriveAndDeregister()` method to indicate the end of its execution, so the phaser will enter in its finalization state.

The ConcurrentGeneticAlgorithm class

This class is the external interface of the genetic algorithm. Internally, it creates, starts, and waits for the finalization of the tasks that calculate the different generations. It uses four attributes: the number of generations, the number of individuals in each generation, the number of chromosomes of each individual, and the distance matrix as follows:

```java
public class ConcurrentGeneticAlgorithm {

    private int numberOfGenerations;
    private int numberOfIndividuals;
    private int[][] distanceMatrix;
    private int size;

    public ConcurrentGeneticAlgorithm(int[][] distanceMatrix, int
       numberOfGenerations, int numberOfIndividuals) {
       this.distanceMatrix=distanceMatrix;
       this.numberOfGenerations=numberOfGenerations;
       this.numberOfIndividuals=numberOfIndividuals;
       size=distanceMatrix.length;
    }
```

The `calculate()` method executes the genetic algorithm and returns the best individual. First, it creates the initial population using the `initialize()` method, evaluates that population, and creates and initialize a `SharedData` object with all the necessary data as follows:

```java
    public Individual calculate() {

        Individual[] population=
           GeneticOperators.initialize(numberOfIndividuals,size);
        GeneticOperators.evaluate(population,distanceMatrix);

        SharedData data=new SharedData();
        data.setPopulation(population);
        data.setDistanceMatrix(distanceMatrix);
        data.setBest(population[0]);
```

Then, it creates the tasks. We use the number of available hardware threads of the computer, returned by the method `availableProcessors()` of the `Runtime` class as the number of tasks we are going to create. We also create a `GeneticPhaser` object to synchronize the execution of those tasks as follows:

```
int numTasks=Runtime.getRuntime().availableProcessors();
GeneticPhaser phaser=new GeneticPhaser(numTasks,data);

ConcurrentGeneticTask[] tasks=new
  ConcurrentGeneticTask[numTasks];
Thread[] threads=new Thread[numTasks];

tasks[0]=new ConcurrentGeneticTask(phaser,
   numberOfGenerations, true);
for (int i=1; i< numTasks; i++) {
    tasks[i]=new ConcurrentGeneticTask(phaser,
       numberOfGenerations, false);
}
```

Then, we create the `Thread` objects to execute the tasks, start them, and wait for their finalization. Finally, we return the best individual stored in the `ShareData` object as follows:

```
for (int i=0; i<numTasks; i++) {
    threads[i]=new Thread(tasks[i]);
    threads[i].start();
}

for (int i=0; i<numTasks; i++) {
    try {
        threads[i].join();
    } catch (InterruptedException e) {
        e.printStackTrace();
    }
}

return data.getBest();
    }
}
```

The ConcurrentMain class

This class executes the genetic algorithm for the two datasets used in this section—the `lau15` with 15 cities and the `kn57` with 57 cities. Its code is analogous to the `SerialMain` class, but using the `ConcurrentGeneticAlgorithm` instead of `SerialGeneticAlgorithm`.

Comparing the two solutions

Now it's time to test both solutions and see which of them has the better performance. As we mentioned before, we have used two datasets from the City Distance Datasets (http://people.sc.fsu.edu/~jburkardt/datasets/cities/cities.html)—the lau15 with 15 cities and the kn57 with 57 cities. We also have tested different sizes for the population (100, 1,000, and 10,000 individuals) and the different number of generations (10, 100, and 1,000). To test the algorithm, we have executed the examples using the JMH framework (http://openjdk.java.net/projects/code-tools/jmh/) that allows you to implement micro benchmarks in Java. Using a framework for benchmarking is a better solution that simply measures time using such methods as currentTimeMillis() or nanoTime(). We have executed them 10 times on a computer with a four-core processor and calculated the medium execution time of those 10 times.

The Lau15 dataset

The execution times (in milliseconds) for the first dataset are:

	Population					
	100		1,000		10,000	
Generations	Serial	Concurrent	Serial	Concurrent	Serial	Concurrent
10	8.42	13.309	30.783	36.395	182.213	99.728
100	25.848	29.292	135.562	69.257	1488.457	688.840
1,000	117.929	71.771	1134.983	420.145	11810.518	4102.72

The Kn57 dataset

The execution times (in milliseconds) for the second dataset are:

	Population					
	100		1,000		10,000	
Generations	Serial	Concurrent	Serial	Concurrent	Serial	Concurrent
10	19.205	22.246	80.509	63.370	758.235	300.669
100	75.129	63.815	680.548	225.393	7406.392	2561.219
1,000	676.390	243.572	6796.780	2159.124	75315.885	26825.115

Conclusions

The behavior of the algorithms is similar to both datasets. You can see that as we have a low number of individuals and generations the serial versions of the algorithm have better execution times, but when the number of individuals or the number of generations grow, the concurrent version has a better throughput. For example, for the `kn57` dataset with 1,000 generations and 10,000 individuals the speed-up is:

$$S = \frac{T_{serial}}{T_{concurrent}} = \frac{75315.885}{26825.115} = 2.80$$

Summary

In this chapter, we explained one of the most powerful synchronization mechanisms provided by the Java concurrency API: the phaser. Its main objective is to provide synchronization between tasks that execute algorithms divided into phases. None of the tasks can begin the execution of a phase before the rest of the tasks have finished the previous one.

The phaser has to know how many tasks have to be synchronized. You have to register your tasks in the phaser using the constructor, the `bulkRegister()` method or the `register()` method.

Tasks can synchronize with the phaser in different ways. The most common are indicating to the phaser that it has finished the execution of one phase and wants to continue with the next one with the `arriveAndAwaitAdvance()` method. This method will sleep the thread until the rest of the tasks have finished the actual phase. But there are other methods you can use to synchronize your tasks. The method `arrive()` is used to notify to the phaser that you have finished the current phase, but you don't wait for the rest of the tasks (be very careful using this method). The `arriveAndDeregister()` method is used to notify the phaser that you have finished the current phase and you don't want to continue in the phaser (normally, because you have finished your job). Finally, the `awaitAdvance()` method can be used to wait for the finalization of the current phase.

You can control the phase change and execute code after all the tasks have finished the current phase and before they start the new one using the `onAdvance()` method. This method is called between the executions of two phases and receives as parameters the number of the phase and the number of participants in the phaser. You can extend the `Phaser` class and override this method to execute code between two phases.

A phaser can be in two states: active, when it is synchronizing tasks and in the termination state, when it has finished its job. A phaser will enter in the termination state when all the participants call the `arriveAndDeregister()` method or when the `onAdvance()` method returns the `true` value (by default, it always return `false`). When a `Phaser` class is in the termination state, it won't accept new participants and the synchronization methods will always return immediately.

We used the `Phaser` class to implement two algorithms: a keyword extraction algorithm and a genetic algorithm. In both cases, we got an important increase of throughput against the serial version of those algorithms.

In the next chapter, you will learn how to use another Java concurrency framework to solve special kind of problems. It's the Fork/Join framework, which has been developed to execute in a concurrent way those problems that can be solved using the divide and conquer algorithm. It's based in an executor with a special work-stealing algorithm that maximizes the performance of the executor.

6
Optimizing Divide and Conquer Solutions – The Fork/Join Framework

In *Chapter 2, Managing Lots of Threads – Executors*, *Chapter 3, Getting the Maximum from Executors*, and *Chapter 4, Getting Data from the Tasks – The Callable and Future Interfaces*, you learned how to work with executors as a mechanism to improve the performance of concurrent applications that executes lots of concurrent tasks. The Java 7 concurrency API introduces a special kind of executor through the Fork/Join framework. This framework is designed to implement optimal concurrent solutions to those problems that can be solved using the divide and conquer design paradigm. In this chapter, we will cover the following topics:

- An introduction to the Fork/Join framework
- The first example – the k-means clustering algorithm
- The second example – a data filtering algorithm
- The third example – the merge sort algorithm

An introduction to the Fork/Join framework

The executor framework, introduced in Java 5, provides a mechanism to execute concurrent tasks without creating, starting, and finishing threads. This framework uses a pool of threads that executes the tasks you send to the executor reusing them for multiple tasks. This mechanism provides some advantages to programmers and these are as follows:

- It's easier to program concurrent applications because you don't have to worry to create threads.
- It's easier to control the resources used by the executor and your application. You can create an executor that only uses a predefined number of threads. If you send more tasks, the executor stores them in a queue until a thread is available.
- Executors reduce the overhead introduced by thread creation reusing the threads. Internally, it manages a pool of threads that reuses threads to execute multiple tasks.

The divide and conquer algorithm is a very popular design technique. To solve a problem using this technique, you divide it into smaller problems. You repeat the process in a recursive way until the problems you have to solve are small enough to be solved directly. These kinds of problems can be solved using the executor, but to solve them in a more efficient way, the Java 7 concurrency API introduced the Fork/Join framework.

This framework is based on the `ForkJoinPool` class, which is a special kind of executor, two operations, the `fork()` and `join()` methods (and their different variants), and an internal algorithm named the **work-stealing algorithm**. In this chapter, you will learn the basic characteristics, limitations, and components of the Fork/Join framework implementing the following three examples:

- The k-means clustering algorithm applied to the clustering of a set of documents
- A data filter algorithm to get the data that meets certain criteria
- The merge sort algorithm to sort big groups of data in an efficient way

Basic characteristics of the Fork/Join framework

As we mentioned before, the Fork/Join framework must be used to implement solutions to problems based on the divide and conquer technique. You have to divide the original problem into smaller problems until they are small enough to be solved directly. With this framework, you will implement tasks whose main method will be something like this:

```
if ( problem.size() > DEFAULT_SIZE) {
    divideTasks();
    executeTask();
    taskResults=joinTasksResult();
    return taskResults;
} else {
    taskResults=solveBasicProblem();
    return taskResults;
}
```

The most important part is the one that allows you to divide and execute the child tasks in an efficient way and to get the results of those child tasks to calculate the results of the parent tasks. This functionality is supported by two methods provided by the `ForkJoinTask` class as follows:

- The `fork()` method: This method allows you to send a child task to the Fork/Join executor
- The `join()` method: This method allows you to wait for the finalization of a child task and returns its result

These methods have different variants, as you will see in the examples. The Fork/Join framework has another critical part: the work-stealing algorithm, which determines which tasks to be executed. When a task is waiting for the finalization of a child task using the `join()` method, the thread that is executing that task takes another task from the pool of tasks that are waiting and starts its execution. In this way, the threads of the Fork/Join executor are always executing a task by improving the performance of the application.

Java 8 includes a new feature in the Fork/Join framework. Now every Java application has a default `ForkJoinPool` named common pool. You can obtain it by calling the `ForkJoinPool.commonPool()` static method. You don't need to create one explicitly (although you can). This default Fork/Join executor will use by default the number of threads determined by the available processors of your computer. You can change this default behavior changing the value of the system property `java.util.concurrent.ForkJoinPool.common.parallelism`.

Some features of the Java API use the Fork/Join framework to implement concurrent operations. For example, the `parallelSort()` method of the `Arrays` class to sort an array in a parallel way and the parallel streams introduced in Java 8 (which will be described later in *Chapter 7, Processing Massive Datasets with Parallel Streams – The Map and Reduce Model* and *Chapter 8, Processing Massive Datasets with Parallel Streams – The Map and Collect Model*) use this framework.

Limitations of the Fork/Join framework

As the Fork/Join framework has been thought to solve a determined kind of problems, it has some limitations you have to take into account when you use it to implement your problem, which are as follows:

- The basic problems that you're not going to subdivide have to be not very large, but not very small. According to the Java API documentation, it should have between 100 and 10,000 basic computational steps.

- You should not use blocking I/O operations like reading user input or data from a network socket waiting until the data is available. Such operations will cause your CPU cores to become idle, reducing the parallelism level, so you will not achieve the full performance.

- You can't throw checked exceptions inside a task. You have to include the code to handle them (for example, wrapping into unchecked `RuntimeException`). Unchecked exceptions have a special treatment, as you will see in the examples.

Components of the Fork/Join framework

There are five basic classes in the Fork/Join framework:

- The `ForkJoinPool` class: This class implements the `Executor` and `ExecutorService` interfaces, and it is the `Executor` interface you're going to use to execute your Fork/Join tasks. Java provides you with a default `ForkJoinPool` object (named common pool), but you have some constructors to create one if you want. You can specify the parallelism level (the maximum number of running parallel threads). By default, it uses the number of available processors as the concurrency level.

- The `ForkJoinTask` class: This is the base abstract class of all of the Fork/Join tasks. It's an abstract class, and it provides the `fork()` and `join()` methods and some variants of them. It also implements the `Future` interface and provides methods to determine if the task finished in a normal way, if it was cancelled or if it throws an unchecked exception. The `RecursiveTask`, `RecursiveAction`, and `CountedCompleter` classes provide `compute()` abstract methods, which should be implemented in subclasses to perform actual computations.
- The `RecursiveTask` class: This class extends the `ForkJoinTask` class. It's also an abstract class, and it should be your start point to implement Fork/Join tasks that returns a result.
- The `RecursiveAction` class: This class extends the `ForkJoinTask` class. It's also an abstract class, and it should be your start point to implement Fork/Join tasks that don't return a result.
- The `CountedCompleter` class: This class extends the `ForkJoinTask` class. It's a new feature of the Java 8 API, and it should be your start point to implement tasks that trigger other tasks when they're completed.

The first example – the k-means clustering algorithm

The **k-means clustering** algorithm is a clustering algorithm to group a set of items not previously classified into a predefined number of k clusters. It's very popular within the data mining and machine learning world to organize and classify data in an unsupervised way.

Each item is normally defined by a vector of characteristics or attributes. All the items have the same number of attributes. Each cluster is also defined by a vector with the same number of attributes that represents all the items classified into that cluster. This vector is named the centroid. For example, if the items are defined by numeric vectors, the clusters are defined by the mean of the items classified into that cluster.

Basically, the algorithm has four steps:

1. **Initialization**: In the first step, you have to create the initial vectors that represent the K clusters. Normally, you will initialize those vectors randomly.
2. **Assignment**: Then, you classify each item into a cluster. To select the cluster, you calculate the distance between the item and every cluster. You will use a distance measure as the **Euclidean distance** to calculate the distance between the vector that represents the item and the vector to represents the cluster. You will assign the item to the cluster with the shortest distance.
3. **Update**: Once all the items have been classified, you have to recalculate the vectors that define each cluster. As we mentioned earlier, you normally calculate the mean of all the vectors of the items classified into the cluster.
4. **End**: Finally, you check whether some item has changed its assignment cluster. If there has been any change, you go to the assignment step again. Otherwise, the algorithm ends, and you have your items classified.

This algorithm has the following two main limitations:

- If you make a random initialization of the initial vectors of the clusters, as we suggested earlier, two executions to classify the same item set may give you different results.
- The numbers of cluster are previously predefined. A bad choice of this attribute will give you poor results from a classification point of view.

Despite of this, this algorithm is very popular to cluster different kinds of items. To test our algorithm, you are going to implement an application to cluster a set of documents. As a document collection, we have taken a reduced version of the Wikipedia pages with information about movies corpus we introduced in *Chapter 4, Getting Data from the Tasks – The Callable and Future Interfaces*. We only took 1,000 documents. To represent each document, we have to use the vector space model representation. With this representation, each document is represented as a numeric vector where each dimension of the vector represents a word or a term and its value is a metric that defines the importance of that word or term in the document.

When you represent a document collection using the vector space model, the vectors will have as many dimensions as the number of different words of the whole collection, so the vectors will have a lot of zero values because each document doesn't have all the words. You can use a more optimized representation in memory to avoid all those zero values and save memory increasing the performance of your application.

In our case, we have chosen **term frequency–inverse document frequency (tf-idf)** as the metric that defines the importance of each word and the 50 words with higher tf-idf as the terms that represents each document.

We use two files: the `movies.words` file stores a list of all the words used in the vectors, and the `movies.data` stores the representation of each document. The `movies.data` file has the following format:

```
10000202,rabona:23.039285705435507,1979:8.09314752937111,argentina:7
.953798614698405,la:5.440565539075689,argentine:4.058577338363469,ed
itor:3.0401515284855267,spanish:2.9692083275217134,image_size:1.3701
158713905104,narrator:1.1799670194306195,budget:0.286193223652206,s
tarring:0.25519156764102785,cast:0.2540127604060545,writer:0.239040-
44207902764,distributor:0.20430284744786784,cinematography:0.1825838
23735518,music:0.1675671228903468,caption:0.14545085918028047,runti
me:0.127767002869991,country:0.12493801913495534,producer:0.12321749
670640451,director:0.11592975672109682,links:0.07925582303812376,ima
ge:0.07786973207561361,external:0.07764427108746134,released:0.07447
174080087617,name:0.07214163435745059,infobox:0.06151153983466272,fi
lm:0.035415118094854446
```

Here, `10000202` is the identifier of the document, and the rest of the file follows the formant `word:tfxidf`.

As with other examples, we are going to implement the serial and concurrent versions and execute both versions to verify that the Fork/Join framework gives us an improvement of the performance of this algorithm.

The common classes

There are some parts that are shared between the serial and concurrent versions. These parts include:

- `VocabularyLoader`: This is a class to load the list of words that forms the vocabulary of our corpus.
- `Word`, `Document`, and `DocumentLoader`: These three classes to load the information about the documents. These classes have a little difference between the serial and concurrent versions of the algorithm.
- `DistanceMeasure`: This is a class to calculate the **Euclidean** distance between two vectors.
- `DocumentCluster`: This is a class to store the information about the clusters.

Let's see these classes in detail.

The VocabularyLoader class

As we mentioned before, our data is stored in two files. One of those files is the `movies.words` file. This file stores a list with all the words used in the documents. The `VocabularyLoader` class will transform that file into `HashMap`. The key of `HashMap` is the whole word, and the value is an integer value with the index of that word in the list. We use that index to determine the position of the word in the vector space model that represents each document.

The class has only one method, named `load()`, that receives the path of the file as a parameter and returns the `HashMap`:

```
public class VocabularyLoader {

    public static Map<String, Integer> load (Path path) throws
      IOException {
        int index=0;
        HashMap<String, Integer> vocIndex=new HashMap<String,
          Integer>();
        try(BufferedReader reader =
          Files.newBufferedReader(path)){
            String line = null;
            while ((line = reader.readLine()) != null) {
                vocIndex.put(line,index );
                index++;
            }
        }
        return vocIndex;

    }
}
```

The Word, Document, and DocumentLoader classes

These classes store all the information about the documents we will use in our algorithm. First, the `Word` class stores information about a word in a document. It includes the index of the word and the tf-idf of that word in the document. This class only includes those attributes (`int` and `double`, respectively), and implements the `Comparable` interface to sort two words using their tf-idf value, so we don't include the source code of this class.

The `Document` class stores all the relevant information about the document. First, an array of `Word` objects with the words in the document. This is our representation of the vector space model. We only store the words used in the document to save a lot of memory space. Then, a `String` with the name of the file that stores the document and finally a `DocumentCluster` object to know the cluster associated with the document. It also includes a constructor to initialize those attributes and methods to get and set their value. We only include the code of the `setCluster()` method. In this case, this method will return a Boolean value to indicate if the new value of this attribute is the same as the old value or a new one. We will use that value to determine if we stop the algorithm or not:

```
public boolean setCluster(DocumentCluster cluster) {
    if (this.cluster == cluster) {
        return false;
    } else {
        this.cluster = cluster;
        return true;
    }
}
```

Finally, the `DocumentLoader` class loads the information about the document. It includes a static method, `load()` that receives the path of the file, and the `HashMap` with the vocabulary and returns an `Array` of `Document` objects. It loads the file line by line and converts each line to a `Document` object. We have the following code:

```
public static Document[] load(Path path, Map<String, Integer> vocIndex) throws IOException{
    List<Document> list = new ArrayList<Document>();
    try(BufferedReader reader = Files.newBufferedReader(path)) {
        String line = null;
        while ((line = reader.readLine()) != null) {
            Document item = processItem(line, vocIndex);
            list.add(item);
        }
    }
    Document[] ret = new Document[list.size()];
    return list.toArray(ret);

}
```

To convert a line of the text file to a `Document` object, we use the `processItem()` method:

```
private static Document processItem(String line,Map<String,
  Integer> vocIndex) {

    String[] tokens = line.split(",");
    int size = tokens.length - 1;

    Document document = new Document(tokens[0], size);
    Word[] data = document.getData();

    for (int i = 1; i < tokens.length; i++) {
        String[] wordInfo = tokens[i].split(":");
        Word word = new Word();
        word.setIndex(vocIndex.get(wordInfo[0]));
        word.setTfidf(Double.parseDouble(wordInfo[1]));
        data[i - 1] = word;
    }
    Arrays.sort(data);
    return document;
}
```

As we mentioned earlier, the first item in the line is the identifier of the document. We obtain it from `tokens[0]`, and we pass it to the `Document` class constructor. Then, for the rest of the tokens, we split them again to obtain the information of every word that includes the whole word and the tf-idf value.

The DistanceMeasurer class

This class calculates the Euclidean distance between a document and a cluster (represented as a vector). The words in our word arrays after sorting are placed in the same order as in centroid array, but some words might be absent. For such words, we assume that tf-idf is zero, so the distance is just the square of the corresponding value from the centroid array:

```
public class DistanceMeasurer {

    public static double euclideanDistance(Word[] words, double[]
  centroid) {
        double distance = 0;

        int wordIndex = 0;
        for (int i = 0; i < centroid.length; i++) {
```

```
            if ((wordIndex < words.length)
               (words[wordIndex].getIndex() == i)) {
                distance += Math.pow(
                    (words[wordIndex].getTfidf() - centroid[i]), 2);
                wordIndex++;
            } else {
                distance += centroid[i] * centroid[i];
            }
        }
    }

    return Math.sqrt(distance);
    }
}
```

The DocumentCluster class

This class stores the information about each cluster generated by the algorithm. This information includes a list of all the documents associated with this cluster and the centroid of the vector that is the vector that represents the cluster. In this case, this vector has as many dimensions as words are in the vocabulary. The class has the two attributes, a constructor to initialize them, and methods to get and set their value. It also includes two very important methods. First, the `calculateCentroid()` method. It calculates the centroid of the cluster as the mean of the vectors that represents the documents associated with this cluster. We have the following code:

```
public void calculateCentroid() {

    Arrays.fill(centroid, 0);

    for (Document document : documents) {
        Word vector[] = document.getData();

        for (Word word : vector) {
            centroid[word.getIndex()] += word.getTfidf();
        }
    }

    for (int i = 0; i < centroid.length; i++) {
        centroid[i] /= documents.size();
    }
}
```

The second method is the `initialize()` method that receives a `Random` object and initializes the centroid vector of the cluster with random numbers as follows:

```
public void initialize(Random random) {
    for (int i = 0; i < centroid.length; i++) {
        centroid[i] = random.nextDouble();
    }
}
```

The serial version

Once we have described the common parts of the application, let's see how to implement the serial version of the k-means clustering algorithm. We are going to use two classes: `SerialKMeans`, which implements the algorithm, and `SerialMain`, which implements the `main()` method to execute the algorithm.

The SerialKMeans class

The `SerialKMeans` class implements the serial version of the k-means clustering algorithm. The main method of the class is the `calculate()` method. It receives the following as parameters:

- The array of `Document` objects with the information about the documents
- The number of clusters you want to generate
- The size of the vocabulary
- A seed for the random number generator

The method returns an `Array` of `DocumentCluster` object. Each cluster will have the list of documents associated with it. First, the document creates the `Array` of clusters determined by the `numberClusters` parameter and initializes them using the `initialize()` method and a `Random` object as follows:

```
public class SerialKMeans {

    public static DocumentCluster[] calculate(Document[]
      documents, int clusterCount, int vocSize, int seed) {
        DocumentCluster[] clusters = new
          DocumentCluster[clusterCount];

        Random random = new Random(seed);
        for (int i = 0; i < clusterCount; i++) {
            clusters[i] = new DocumentCluster(vocSize);
            clusters[i].initialize(random);
        }
```

Then, we repeat the assignment and update phases until all the documents stay in the same cluster. Finally, we return the array of clusters with the final organization of the documents as follows:

```
boolean change = true;

int numSteps = 0;
while (change) {
    change = assignment(clusters, documents);
    update(clusters);
    numSteps++;
}
System.out.println("Number of steps: "+numSteps);
return clusters;
}
```

The assignment phase is implemented in the `assignment()` method. This method receives the array of `Document` and `DocumentCluster` objects. For each document, it calculates the Euclidean distance between the document and all the clusters and assigns the document to the cluster with the lowest distance. It returns a Boolean value to indicate if one or more of the documents has changed their assigned cluster from one step to the next one. We have the following code:

```
private static boolean assignment(DocumentCluster[] clusters,
    Document[] documents) {

    boolean change = false;

    for (DocumentCluster cluster : clusters) {
        cluster.clearClusters();
    }

    int numChanges = 0;
    for (Document document : documents) {
        double distance = Double.MAX_VALUE;
        DocumentCluster selectedCluster = null;
        for (DocumentCluster cluster : clusters) {
            double curDistance =
            DistanceMeasurer.euclideanDistance(document.getData(),
            cluster.getCentroid());
            if (curDistance < distance) {
                distance = curDistance;
                selectedCluster = cluster;
            }
        }
```

```
            selectedCluster.addDocument(document);
            boolean result = document.setCluster(selectedCluster);
            if (result)
                numChanges++;
        }
        System.out.println("Number of Changes: " + numChanges);
        return numChanges > 0;
    }
```

The update step is implemented in the `update()` method. It receives the array of `DocumentCluster` with the information of the clusters, and it simply recalculates the centroid of each cluster:

```
        private static void update(DocumentCluster[] clusters) {
            for (DocumentCluster cluster : clusters) {
                cluster.calculateCentroid();
            }


        }
    }
```

The SerialMain class The `SerialMain` class includes the `main()` method to launch the tests of the k-means algorithm. First, it loads the data (words and documents) from the files:

```
    public class SerialMain {

        public static void main(String[] args) {
            Path pathVoc = Paths.get("data", "movies.words");

            Map<String, Integer>
              vocIndex=VocabularyLoader.load(pathVoc);
            System.out.println("Voc Size: "+vocIndex.size());

            Path pathDocs = Paths.get("data", "movies.data");
            Document[] documents = DocumentLoader.load(pathDocs,
              vocIndex);
            System.out.println("Document Size: "+documents.length);
```

Then, it initializes the number of clusters we want to generate and the seed for the random number generator. If they don't come as parameters of the `main()` method, we use a default value as follows:

```
if (args.length != 2) {
    System.err.println("Please specify K and SEED");
    return;
}
int K = Integer.valueOf(args[0]);
int SEED = Integer.valueOf(args[1]);
```

Finally, we launch the algorithm measuring its execution time and write the number of documents per cluster.

```
Date start, end;
start=new Date();
DocumentCluster[] clusters =
  SerialKMeans.calculate(documents, K ,vocIndex.size(),
  SEED);
end=new Date();
System.out.println("K: "+K+"; SEED: "+SEED);
System.out.println("Execution Time: "+(end.getTime()-
  start.getTime()));
System.out.println(
    Arrays.stream(clusters).map
       (DocumentCluster::getDocumentCount).sorted
       (Comparator.reverseOrder())
              .map(Object::toString).collect(
                Collectors.joining(", ", "Cluster sizes:
                ", "")));
    }
}
```

The concurrent version

To implement the concurrent version of the algorithm, we have used the Fork/Join framework. We have implemented two different tasks based on the `RecursiveAction` class. As we mentioned earlier, the `RecursiveAction` task is used when you want to use the Fork/Join framework with tasks that do not return a result. We have implemented the assignment and the update phases as tasks to be executed in a Fork/Join framework.

To implement the concurrent version of the k-means algorithm, we are going to modify some of the common classes to use concurrent data structures. Then, we are going to implement the two tasks, and finally, we are going to implement the `ConcurrentKMeans` that implements the concurrent version of the algorithm and the `ConcurrentMain` class to test it.

Two tasks for the Fork/Join framework – AssignmentTask and UpdateTask

As we mentioned earlier, we have implemented the assignment and update phases as tasks to be implemented in the Fork/Join framework.

The assignment phase assigns a document to the cluster that has the lowest Euclidean distance with the document. So, we have to process all the documents and calculate the Euclidean distances of all the documents and all the clusters. We are going to use the number of documents a task has to process as the measure to control whether we have to split the task or not. We start with the tasks that have to process all the documents and we are going to split them until we have tasks that have to process a number of documents lower than a predefined size.

The `AssignmentTask` class has the following attributes:

- The array of `ConcurrentDocumentCluster` objects with the data of the clusters
- The array of `ConcurrentDocument` objects with the data of the documents
- Two integer attributes, `start` and `end`, that determines the number of documents the task has to process
- An `AtomicInteger` attribute, `numChanges`, that stores the number of documents that have changed its assigned cluster from the last execution to the current one
- An integer attribute, `maxSize`, that stores the maximum number of documents a task can process

We have implemented a constructor to initialize all these attributes and methods to get and set its values.

The main method of these tasks is (as with every task) the `compute()` method. First, we check the number of documents the tasks have to process. If it's less or equal than the `maxSize` attribute, we process those documents. We calculate the Euclidean distance between each document and all the clusters and select the cluster with the lowest distance. If it's necessary, we increment the `numChanges` atomic variable using the `incrementAndGet()` method. The atomic variable can be updated by more than one thread at the same time without using synchronization mechanisms and without causing any memory inconsistencies. Refer to the following code:

```
protected void compute() {
    if (end - start <= maxSize) {
        for (int i = start; i < end; i++) {
            ConcurrentDocument document = documents[i];
            double distance = Double.MAX_VALUE;
            ConcurrentDocumentCluster selectedCluster = null;
            for (ConcurrentDocumentCluster cluster : clusters) {
                double curDistance =
                DistanceMeasurer.euclideanDistance
                (document.getData(), cluster.getCentroid());
                if (curDistance < distance) {
                    distance = curDistance;
                    selectedCluster = cluster;
                }
            }
            selectedCluster.addDocument(document);
            boolean result = document.setCluster(selectedCluster);
            if (result) {
                numChanges.incrementAndGet();
            }
        }
    }
```

If the number of documents the task has to process is too big, we split that set into two parts and create two new tasks to process each of those parts as follows:

```
    } else {
        int mid = (start + end) / 2;
        AssignmentTask task1 = new AssignmentTask(clusters,
            documents, start, mid, numChanges, maxSize);
        AssignmentTask task2 = new AssignmentTask(clusters,
            documents, mid, end, numChanges, maxSize);

        invokeAll(task1, task2);
    }
}
```

To execute those tasks in the Fork/Join pool, we have used the `invokeAll()` method. This method will return when the tasks have finished their execution.

The update phase recalculates the centroid of each cluster as the mean of all the documents. So, we have to process all the clusters. We are going to use the number of clusters a task has to process as the measure to control if we have to split the task or not. We start with a task that has to process all the clusters, and we are going to split it until we have tasks that have to process a number of clusters lower than a predefined size.

The `UpdateTask` class has the following attributes:

- The array of `ConcurrentDocumentCluster` objects with the data of the clusters
- Two integer attributes, `start` and `end`, that determine the number of clusters the task has to process
- An integer attribute, `maxSize`, that stores the maximum number of clusters a task can process

We have implemented a constructor to initialize all these attributes and methods to get and set its values.

The `compute()` method first checks the number of clusters the task has to process. If that number is less than or equal to the `maxSize` attribute, it processes those clusters and updates their centroid:

```
@Override
protected void compute() {
    if (end - start <= maxSize) {
        for (int i = start; i < end; i++) {
            ConcurrentDocumentCluster cluster = clusters[i];
            cluster.calculateCentroid();
        }
```

If the number of clusters the task has to process is too big, we are going to divide the set of clusters the task has to process in two and create two tasks to process each of that part as follows:

```
    } else {
        int mid = (start + end) / 2;
        UpdateTask task1 = new UpdateTask(clusters, start,
            mid, maxSize);
        UpdateTask task2 = new UpdateTask(clusters, mid, end,
            maxSize);
```

```
        invokeAll(task1, task2);
    }
}
```

The ConcurrentKMeans class

The `ConcurrentKMeans` class implements the concurrent version of the k-means clustering algorithm. As the serial version, the main method of the class is the `calculate()` method. It receives the following as parameters:

- The array of `ConcurrentDocument` objects with the information about the documents
- The number of clusters you want to generate
- The size of the vocabulary
- A seed for the random number generator
- The maximum number of items a Fork/Join tasks will process without splitting the task into other tasks

The `calculate()` method returns an array of the `ConcurrentDocumentCluster` objects with the information of the clusters. Each cluster has the list of documents associated with it. First, the document creates the array of clusters determined by the `numberClusters` parameter and initializes them using the `initialize()` method and a `Random` object:

```
public class ConcurrentKMeans {

    public static ConcurrentDocumentCluster[]
       calculate(ConcurrentDocument[] documents int numberCluster
       int vocSize, int seed, int maxSize) {
           ConcurrentDocumentCluster[] clusters = new
ConcurrentDocumentCluster[numberClusters];

           Random random = new Random(seed);
           for (int i = 0; i < numberClusters; i++) {
               clusters[i] = new ConcurrentDocumentCluster(vocSize);
               clusters[i].initialize(random);
           }
```

Then, we repeat the assignment and update phases until all the documents stay in the same cluster. Before the loop, we create `ForkJoinPool` that is going to execute that task and all of its subtasks. Once the loop has finished, as with other `Executor` objects, we have to use the `shutdown()` method with a Fork/Join pool to finish its executions. Finally, we return the array of clusters with the final organization of the documents:

```
boolean change = true;
ForkJoinPool pool = new ForkJoinPool();

int numSteps = 0;
while (change) {

    change = assignment(clusters, documents, maxSize,
       pool);
    update(clusters, maxSize, pool);
    numSteps++;
}
pool.shutdown();
System.out.println("Number of steps: "+numSteps);
   return clusters;
}
```

The assignment phase is implemented in the `assignment()` method. This method receives the array of clusters, the array of documents, and the `maxSize` attribute. First, we delete the list of associated documents to all the clusters:

```
private static boolean assignment(ConcurrentDocumentCluster[]
   clusters, ConcurrentDocument[] documents, int maxSize,
   ForkJoinPool pool) {

    boolean change = false;

    for (ConcurrentDocumentCluster cluster : clusters) {
        cluster.clearDocuments();
    }
```

Then, we initialize the necessary objects: an `AtomicInteger` to store the number of documents whose assigned cluster has changed and the `AssignmentTask` that will begin the process.

```
AtomicInteger numChanges = new AtomicInteger(0);
AssignmentTask task = new AssignmentTask(clusters,
   documents, 0, documents.length, numChanges, maxSize);
```

Then, we execute the tasks in the pool in an asynchronous way using the `execute()` method of `ForkJoinPool` and wait for its finalization with the `join()` method of the `AssignmentTask` object as follows:

```
pool.execute(task);
task.join();
```

Finally, we check the number of documents that has changed its assigned cluster. If there have been changes, we return the `true` value. Otherwise, we return the `false` value. We have the following code:

```
System.out.println("Number of Changes: " + numChanges);
return numChanges.get() > 0;
}
```

The update phase is implemented in the `update()` method. It receives the array of clusters and the `maxSize` parameters. First, we create an `UpdateTask` object to update all the clusters. Then, we execute that task in the `ForkJoinPool` object the method receives as parameter as follows:

```
private static void update(ConcurrentDocumentCluster[] 
   clusters, int maxSize, ForkJoinPool pool) {
      UpdateTask task = new UpdateTask(clusters, 0,
        clusters.length, maxSize, ForkJoinPool pool);
      pool.execute(task);
      task.join();
   }
}
```

The ConcurrentMain class

The `ConcurrentMain` class includes the `main()` method to launch the tests of the k-means algorithm. Its code is equal to the `SerialMain` class, but changing the serial classes for the concurrent ones.

Comparing the solutions

To compare the two solutions, we have executed different experiments changing the values of three different parameters:

- The k-parameter will establish the number of clusters we want to generate. We have tested the algorithms with the values 5, 10, 15, and 20.
- The seed for the `Random` number generator. This seed determines how the initial centroid positions. We have tested the algorithms with the values 1 and 13.

- For the concurrent algorithm, the `maxSize` parameter that determines the maximum number of items (documents or clusters), a task can process without being split into other tasks. We have tested the algorithms with the values 1, 20, and 400.

We have executed the experiments using the JMH framework (http://openjdk.java.net/projects/code-tools/jmh/) that allows you to implement micro benchmarks in Java. Using a framework for benchmarking is a better solution that simply measures time using methods such as `currentTimeMillis()` or `nanoTime()`. We have executed them 10 times in a computer with a four-core processor and calculated the medium execution time of those 10 times. These are the execution times we have obtained in milliseconds:

K	Seed	Serial	Concurrent		
			MaxSize=1	MaxSize=20	maxSize=400
5	1	6676.141	4696.414	3291.397	3179.673
10	1	6780.088	3365.731	2970.056	2825.488
15	1	12936.178	5308.734	4737.329	4490.443
20	1	19824.729	7937.820	7347.445	6848.873
5	13	3738.869	2714.325	1984.152	1916.053
10	13	9567.416	4693.164	3892.526	3739.129
15	13	12427.589	5598.996	4735.518	4468.721
20	13	18157.913	7285.565	6671.283	6325.664

We can draw the following conclusions:

- The seed has an important and unpredictable impact in the execution time. Sometimes, the execution times are lower with seed 13, but other times are lower with seed 1.
- When you increment the number of clusters, the execution time increments too.
- The `maxSize` parameter doesn't have much influence in the execution time. The parameter K or seed has a higher influence in the execution time. If you increase the value of the parameter, you will obtain better performance. The difference is bigger between 1 and 20 than between 20 and 400.
- In all the cases, the concurrent version of the algorithm has better performance than the serial one.

For example, if we compare the serial algorithm with parameters K=20 and seed=13 with the concurrent version with parameters K=20, seed=13, and maxSize=400 using the speed-up, we obtain the following result:

$$S = \frac{t_{serial}}{t_{concurrent}} = \frac{18157.913}{6325.664} = 2.87$$

The second example – a data filtering algorithm

Suppose that you have a lot of data that describes a list of items. For example, you have a lot of attributes (name, surname, address, phone number, and so on) of a lot of people. It's a common need to obtain the data that meets certain criteria, for example, you want to obtain people who live in a determined street or with a determined name.

In this section, you will implement one of those filtering programs. We have used the **Census-Income KDD** dataset from the UCI (you can download it from `https://archive.ics.uci.edu/ml/datasets/Census-Income+%28KDD%29`), that contains weighted census data extracted from the 1994 and 1995 current population surveys conducted by the U.S. Census Bureau.

In the concurrent version of this example, you will learn how to cancel tasks that are running in the Fork/Join pool and how to manage unchecked exceptions that can be thrown in a task.

Common parts

We have implemented some classes to read the data from a file and to filter the data. These classes are used by the serial and concurrent versions of the algorithm. These are the classes:

- The `CensusData` class: This class stores 39 attributes that define every person. It defines the attributes and methods to get and set their value. We are going to identify each attribute by a number. The `evaluateFilter()` method of this class contains the association between the number and the name of the attribute. You can check the file `https://archive.ics.uci.edu/ml/machine-learning-databases/census-income-mld/census-income.names` to get the details of every attribute.

- The `CensusDataLoader` class: This class loads the census data from a file. It has the `load()` method that receives the path to the file as an input parameter and returns an array of `CensusData` with the information of all the persons of the file.
- The `FilterData` class: This class defines a filter of data. A filter includes the number of an attribute and the value of that attribute.
- The `Filter` class: This class implements the methods to determine if a `CensusData` object meets the conditions of a list of filters.

We don't include the source code of these classes. They are very simple, and you can check the source code of the example.

The serial version

We have implemented the serial version of the filter algorithm in two classes. The `SerialSearch` class makes the filtering of data. It provides two methods:

- The `findAny()` method: It receives the array of `CensusData` object as a parameter with all the data from the file and a list of filters and returns a `CensusData` object with the first person it finds that meet all the criteria from the filters.
- The `findAll()` method: It receives the array of `CensusData` object as a parameter with all the data from the file and a list of filters and returns an array of `CensusData` objects with all the persons that meets all the criteria from the filter.

The `SerialMain` class implements the `main()` method of this version and tests it to measure the execution time of this algorithm in some circumstances.

The SerialSearch class

As we mentioned before, this class implements the filtering of data. It provides two methods. The first one, the `findAny()` method, looks for the first data object that meets the filters. When it finds the first data object, it finishes its execution. Refer to the following code:

```
public class SerialSearch {

    public static CensusData findAny (CensusData[] data,
       List<FilterData> filters) {
        int index=0;
        for (CensusData censusData : data) {
            if (Filter.filter(censusData, filters)) {
```

```
            System.out.println("Found: "+index);
            return censusData;
        }
        index++;
    }

    return null;
}
```

The second one, the `findAll()` method, returns an array of `CensusData` objects with all the objects that meet the filters as follows:

```
public static List<CensusData> findAll (CensusData[] data,
   List<FilterData> filters) {
    List<CensusData> results=new ArrayList<CensusData>();

    for (CensusData censusData : data) {
        if (Filter.filter(censusData, filters)) {
            results.add(censusData);
        }
    }
    return results;
  }
}
```

The SerialMain class

You're going to use this class to test the filtering algorithm in different circumstances. First, we load the data from the file as follows:

```
public class SerialMain {
    public static void main(String[] args) {
        Path path = Paths.get("data","census-income.data");

        CensusData data[]=CensusDataLoader.load(path);
        System.out.println("Number of items: "+data.length);

        Date start, end;
```

The first case we are going to test is to use the `findAny()` method to find an object that exists in the first places of the array. You construct a list of filters and then call the `findAny()` method with the data of the file and the list of filters:

```
List<FilterData> filters=new ArrayList<>();
FilterData filter=new FilterData();
filter.setIdField(32);
filter.setValue("Dominican-Republic");
filters.add(filter);
filter=new FilterData();
filter.setIdField(31);
filter.setValue("Dominican-Republic");
filters.add(filter);
filter=new FilterData();
filter.setIdField(1);
filter.setValue("Not in universe");
filters.add(filter);
filter=new FilterData();
filter.setIdField(14);
filter.setValue("Not in universe");
filters.add(filter);
start=new Date();
CensusData result=SerialSearch.findAny(data, filters);
System.out.println("Test 1 - Result:
  "+result.getReasonForUnemployment());
end=new Date();
System.out.println("Test 1- Execution Time:
  "+(end.getTime()-start.getTime()));
```

Our filters look for the following attributes:

- 32: This is the country of the birth father attribute
- 31: This is the country of the birth mother attribute
- 1: This is the class of the worker attributes; `Not in universe` is one of their possible values
- 14: This is the reason for unemployment attribute; `Not in universe` is one of their possible values

We are going to test other cases as follows:

- Use the `findAny()` method to find an object that exists in the last positions of the array
- Use the `findAny()` method to try to find an object that doesn't exist
- Use the `findAny()` method in an error situation

- Use the `findAll()` method to obtain all the objects that meet a list of filters
- Use the `findAll()` method in an error situation

The concurrent version

We are going to include more elements in our concurrent version:

- A task manager: When you use the Fork/Join framework, you start with one task and you split that task into two (or more) child tasks that you split again and again until your problem has the desired size. There can be situations when you want to finish the execution of all those tasks. For example, when you implement the `findAny()` method and you find an object that meets all the criteria, you don't need to continue with the execution of the rest of the tasks.
- A `RecursiveTask` class to implement the `findAny()` method: It's the `IndividualTask` class that extends `RecursiveTask`.
- A `RecursiveTask` class to implement the `findAll()` method: It's the `ListTask` class that extends `RecursiveTask`.

Let's see the details of all those classes.

The TaskManager class

We are going to use this class to control the cancellation of tasks. We are going to cancel the execution of tasks in the following two situations:

- You're executing the `findAny()` operation and you find an object that meets the requirements
- You're executing the `findAny()` or `findAll()` operations and there's an unchecked exception in one of the tasks

The class declares two attributes: `ConcurrentLinkedDeque` to store all the tasks we need to cancel and an `AtomicBoolean` variable to guarantee that only one task executes the `cancelTasks()` method:

```
public class TaskManager {

    private Set<RecursiveTask> tasks;
    private AtomicBoolean cancelled;

    public TaskManager() {
        tasks = ConcurrentHashMap.newKeySet();
        cancelled = new AtomicBoolean(false);
    }
```

Optimizing Divide and Conquer Solutions – The Fork/Join Framework

It defines methods to add a task to ConcurrentLinkedDeque, delete a task from the ConcurrentLinkedDeque, and cancel all the tasks stored in it. To cancel the tasks, we use the cancel() method defined in the ForkJoinTask class. The true parameter forces the interruption of the task if it is running as follows:

```
public void addTask(RecursiveTask task) {
    tasks.add(task);
}

public void cancelTasks(RecursiveTask sourceTask) {

    if (cancelled.compareAndSet(false, true)) {
        for (RecursiveTask task : tasks) {
            if (task != sourceTask) {
                if(cancelled.get()) {
                    task.cancel(true);
                }
                else {
                    tasks.add(task);
                }
            }
        }
    }
}

public void deleteTask(RecursiveTask task) {
    tasks.remove(task);
}
```

The cancelTasks() method receives a RecursiveTask object as a parameter. We're going to cancel all the tasks except the one that is calling this method. We don't want to cancel the tasks that have found the result. The compareAndSet(false, true) method sets the AtomicBoolean variable to true and returns true only if the current value is false. If the AtomicBoolean variable already has a true value, then false is returned. The whole operation is performed atomically, so it's guaranteed that the body of if statement will be executed at most once even if the cancelTasks() method is concurrently called several times from different threads.

The IndividualTask class

The `IndividualTask` class extends the `RecursiveTask` class parameterized with the `CensusData` task and implements the `findAny()` operation. It defines the following attributes:

- An array with all the `CensusData` objects
- The `start` and `end` attributes that determine the elements it has to process
- The `size` attribute that determines the maximum number of elements the task will process without splitting the task
- A `TaskManager` class to cancel the tasks if necessary
- The following code gives a list of filters to apply:

```
private CensusData[] data;
private int start, end, size;
private TaskManager manager;
private List<FilterData> filters;

public IndividualTask(CensusData[] data, int start, int
  end, TaskManager manager, int size, List<FilterData>
  filters) {
    this.data = data;
    this.start = start;
    this.end = end;
    this.manager = manager;
    this.size = size;
    this.filters = filters;
}
```

The main method of the class is the `compute()` method. It returns a `CensusData` object. If the number of elements the task has to process is less than the size attribute, it looks for the object directly. If the method finds the desired object, it returns the object and uses the method `cancelTasks()` to cancel the execution of the rest of the tasks. If the method doesn't find the desired object, it returns null. We have the following code:

```
if (end - start <= size) {
    for (int i = start; i < end && !
      Thread.currentThread().isInterrupted(); i++) {
        CensusData censusData = data[i];
        if (Filter.filter(censusData, filters)) {
            System.out.println("Found: " + i);
            manager.cancelTasks(this);
            return censusData;
```

```
            }
        }
        return null;
    }
```

If the number of items it has to process is more than the size attribute, we create two child tasks to process half of the elements:

```
} else {
    int mid = (start + end) / 2;
    IndividualTask task1 = new IndividualTask(data, start,
        mid, manager, size, filters);
    IndividualTask task2 = new IndividualTask(data, mid,
        end, manager, size, filters);
```

Then, we add the new created tasks to the task manager and deleted the actual tasks. If we want to cancel the tasks, we want to cancel only the tasks that are running:

```
manager.addTask(task1);
manager.addTask(task2);
manager.deleteTask(this);
```

Then, we send the tasks to `ForkJoinPool` with the `fork()` method that sends them in an asynchronous way and wait for its finalization with the `quietlyJoin()` method. The difference between the `join()` and `quietlyJoin()` methods is that the `join()` method launches and exception if the task is canceled or an unchecked exception is thrown inside the method while the `quietlyJoin()` method doesn't throw any exception.

```
task1.fork();
task2.fork();
task1.quietlyJoin();
task2.quietlyJoin();
```

Then, we delete the child tasks from the `TaskManager` class as follows:

```
manager.deleteTask(task1);
manager.deleteTask(task2);
```

Now, we obtain the results of the tasks using the `join()` method. If a task throws an unchecked exception, it will be propagated without special handling and cancellation will be just ignored as follows:

```
try {
    CensusData res = task1.join();
    if (res != null)
        return res;
```

```
                manager.deleteTask(task1);
        } catch (CancellationException ex) {
        }
        try {
            CensusData res = task2.join();
            if (res != null)
                return res;
            manager.deleteTask(task2);
        } catch (CancellationException ex) {
        }
        return null;
    }
}
```

The ListTask class

The `ListTask` class extends the `RecursiveTask` class parameterized with a `List` of `CensusData`. We are going to use this task to implement the `findAll()` operation. It's very similar to the `IndividualTask` task. Both use the same attributes, but they have differences in the `compute()` method.

First, we initialize a `List` object to return the results and check the number of elements the task has to process. If the number of elements the task has to process is less than the size attribute, add all the objects that meet the criteria specified in the filters to the list of results:

```
@Override
protected List<CensusData> compute() {
    List<CensusData> ret = new ArrayList<CensusData>();
    if (end - start <= size) {
        for (int i = start; i < end; i++) {
            CensusData censusData = data[i];
            if (Filter.filter(censusData, filters)) {
                ret.add(censusData);
            }
        }
    }
```

If the number of items it has to process is more than the size attribute, we will create two child tasks to process half of the elements:

```
            int mid = (start + end) / 2;
            ListTask task1 = new ListTask(data, start, mid, manager,
                size, filters);
            ListTask task2 = new ListTask(data, mid, end, manager,
                size, filters);
```

Then, we will add the new created tasks to the task manager and delete the actual tasks. The actual task won't be canceled; its child tasks will be canceled, as follows:

```
manager.addTask(task1);
manager.addTask(task2);
manager.deleteTask(this);
```

Then, we will send the tasks to `ForkJoinPool` with the `fork()` method that sends them in an asynchronous way and wait for its finalization with the `quietlyJoin()` method:

```
task1.fork();
task2.fork();
task2.quietlyJoin();
task1.quietlyJoin();
```

Then, we will delete the child tasks from `TaskManager`:

```
manager.deleteTask(task1);
manager.deleteTask(task2);
```

Now, we obtain the results of the tasks using the `join()` method. If a task throws an unchecked exception, it will be propagated without special handling and cancellation will be just ignored:

```
try {
 List<CensusData> tmp = task1.join();
 if (tmp != null)
   ret.addAll(tmp);
 manager.deleteTask(task1);
} catch (CancellationException ex) {
}
try {
 List<CensusData> tmp = task2.join();
 if (tmp != null)
   ret.addAll(tmp);
 manager.deleteTask(task2);
} catch (CancellationException ex) {
}
```

The ConcurrentSearch class

The ConcurrentSearch class implements the findAny() and findAll() methods. They have the same interface as the ones of the serial version. Internally, they initialize the TaskManager object and the first task and send to default ForkJoinPool using the execute method; they wait for the finalization of the task and write the results. This is the code of the findAny() method:

```java
public class ConcurrentSearch {

    public static CensusData findAny (CensusData[] data,
       List<FilterData> filters, int size) {
       TaskManager manager=new TaskManager();
       IndividualTask task=new IndividualTask(data, 0,
          data.length, manager, size, filters);
       ForkJoinPool.commonPool().execute(task);
       try {
          CensusData result=task.join();
          if (result!=null) {
             System.out.println("Find Any Result: 
                "+result.getCitizenship());
             return result;
          } catch (Exception e) {
             System.err.println("findAny has finished with an
                error: "+task.getException().getMessage());
          }


       return null;
    }
```

This is the code of the findAll() method:

```java
public static CensusData[] findAll (CensusData[] data,
   List<FilterData> filters, int size) {
   List<CensusData> results;
   TaskManager manager=new TaskManager();
   ListTask task=new ListTask(data,0,data.length,manager,
      size,filters);
   ForkJoinPool.commonPool().execute(task);
   try {
      results=task.join();
```

```
            return results;
        } catch (Exception e) {
            System.err.println("findAny has finished with an
                error: " + task.getException().getMessage());
        }
        return null;
    }
```

The ConcurrentMain class

The `ConcurrentMain` class is used to test the concurrent version of our object filter. It is identical to the `SerialMain` class, but uses the concurrent version of the operations.

Comparing the two versions

To compare the serial and concurrent versions of the filtering algorithm, we tested them in six different situations:

- **Test 1**: We test the `findAny()` method looking for an object that exists in the first positions of the `CensusData` array
- **Test 2**: We test the `findAny()` method looking for an object that exists in the last positions of the `CensusData` array
- **Test 3**: We test the `findAny()` method looking for an object that doesn't exist
- **Test 4**: We test the `findAny()` method in an error situation
- **Test 5**: We test the `findAll()` method in a normal situation
- **Test 6**: We test the `findAll()` method in an error situation

For the concurrent version of the algorithm, we have tested three different values of the size parameter that determines the maximum number of elements a task can process without forking in two child tasks. We have tested with 10, 200, and 2,000.

We have executed the tests using the JMH framework (http://openjdk.java.net/projects/code-tools/jmh/) that allows you to implement micro benchmarks in Java. Using a framework for benchmarking is a better solution that simply measures time using methods as `currentTimeMillis()` or `nanoTime()`. We have executed them 10 times in a computer with a four-core processor and calculated the medium execution time of those 10 times. As with other examples, we have measured the execution time in milliseconds:

Test case	Serial	Concurrent size = 10	Concurrent size = 200	Concurrent size = 2000	Best
Test 1	1.177	8.124	4.547	4.073	Serial
Test 2	95.237	157.412	34.581	35.691	Concurrent
Test 3	66.616	41.916	74.829	37.140	Concurrent
Test 4	0.540	25869.339	643.144	9.673	Serial
Test 5	61.752	37.349	40.344	22.911	Concurrent
Test 6	0.802	31663.607	231.440	7.706	Serial

We can draw the following conclusions:

- The serial version of the algorithm has better performance when we have to process a smaller number of elements.
- The concurrent version of the algorithm has better performance when we have to process all the elements or a bit amount of them.
- In error situations, the serial version of the algorithm has better performance than the concurrent version. The concurrent version has a very poor performance in this situation when the value of the `size` parameter is small.

In this case, concurrency does not always gives us an improvement of the performance.

The third example – the merge sort algorithm

The merge sort algorithm is a very popular sorting algorithm that is always implemented using the divide and conquer technique, so it's a very good candidate to test with the Fork/Join framework.

To implement the merge sort algorithm, we divide the unsorted lists into sublists of one element. Then, we merge those unsorted sublists to produce ordered sublists until we have processed all the sublists, and we have only the original list, but with all the elements sorted.

To make the concurrent version of our algorithm, we have used the new Fork/Join tasks, the `CountedCompleter` tasks, introduced in the Java 8 version. The most important characteristics of these tasks are that they include a method to be executed when all their child tasks have finished their execution.

To test out implementations, we have used the **Amazon product co-purchasing network metadata** (you can download it from https://snap.stanford.edu/data/amazon-meta.html). In particular, we have created a list with the salesrank of 542,184 products. We are going to test our versions of the algorithm, sorting this list of products, and compare the execution time with the `sort()` and `parallelSort()` methods of the `Arrays` class.

Shared classes

As we mentioned earlier, we have built a list of 542,184 products of Amazon with information about each product including an ID, its title, group, salesrank, number of reviews, number of similar products, and number of categories the product belongs to. We have implemented the `AmazonMetaData` class to store the information of a product. This class declares the necessary attributes and the methods to get and set their values. This class implements the `Comparable` interface to compare two instances of this class. We want to sort the elements by salesrank in ascending order. To implement the `compare()` method, we use the `compare()` method of the `Long` class to compare the salesrank of both objects as follows:

```
public int compareTo(AmazonMetaData other) {
    return Long.compare(this.getSalesrank(),
        other.getSalesrank());
}
```

We have also implemented `AmazonMetaDataLoader` that provides the `load()` method. This method receives a route to the file with the data as a parameter and returns an array of `AmazonMetaData` objects with the information of all the products.

> We don't include the source code of these classes to focus on the characteristics of the Fork/Join framework.

The serial version

We have implemented the serial version of the merge sort algorithm in the `SerialMergeSort` class, which implements the algorithm and the `SerialMetaData` class and provides the `main()` method to test the algorithm.

The SerialMergeSort class

The `SerialMergeSort` class implements the serial version of the merge sort algorithm. It provides the `mergeSort()` method that receives the following parameters:

- The array with all the data we want to sort
- The first element the method has to process (included)
- The last element the method has to process (not included)

If the method has to process only one element, it returns. Otherwise, it makes two recursive calls to the `mergeSort()` method. The first call will process the first half of the elements, and the second call will process the second half of the elements. Finally, we make a call to the `merge()` method to merge the two halves of the elements and get a sorted list of elements:

```java
public void mergeSort (Comparable data[], int start, int end) {
    if (end-start < 2) {
        return;
    }
    int middle = (end+start)>>>1;
    mergeSort(data,start,middle);
    mergeSort(data,middle,end);
    merge(data,start,middle,end);
}
```

We have used the `(end+start)>>>1` operator to obtain the mid-element to split the array. If you have, for example, 1.5 billions of elements (not that impossible with modern memory chips), it still fits the Java array. However, *(end+start)/2* will overflow resulting in a negative number array. You can find a detailed explanation of this problem at http://googleresearch.blogspot.ru/2006/06/extra-extra-read-all-about-it-nearly.html.

The `merge()` method merges two lists of elements to obtain a sorted list. It receives the following parameters:

- The array with all the data we want to sort
- The three elements (`start`, `mid`, and `end`) that determine the two parts of the array (start-mid, mid-end) we want to merge and sort

We create a temporary array to sort the elements, sort the elements in the array processing both parts of the list, and store the sorted list in the same positions of the original array. Check the following code:

```java
private void merge(Comparable[] data, int start, int middle,
    int end) {
    int length=end-start+1;
    Comparable[] tmp=new Comparable[length];
    int i, j, index;
    i=start;
    j=middle;
    index=0;
    while ((i<middle) && (j<end)) {
        if (data[i].compareTo(data[j])<=0) {
            tmp[index]=data[i];
            i++;
        } else {
            tmp[index]=data[j];
            j++;
        }
        index++;
    }

    while (i<middle) {
        tmp[index]=data[i];
        i++;
        index++;
    }

    while (j<end) {
        tmp[index]=data[j];
        j++;
        index++;
    }

    for (index=0; index < (end-start); index++) {
        data[index+start]=tmp[index];
    }
  }
}
```

The SerialMetaData class

The `SerialMetaData` class provides the `main()` method to test the algorithm. We're going to execute every sort algorithm 10 times to calculate the average execution time. First, we load the data from the file and create a copy of the array:

```
public class SerialMetaData {

    public static void main(String[] args) {
    for (int j=0; j<10; j++) {
        Path path = Paths.get("data","amazon-meta.csv");

        AmazonMetaData[] data = AmazonMetaDataLoader.load(path);
        AmazonMetaData data2[] = data.clone();
```

Then, we sort the first array using the `sort()` method of the `Arrays` class:

```
        Date start, end;

        start = new Date();
        Arrays.sort(data);
        end = new Date();
        System.out.println("Execution Time Java Arrays.sort(): "
           + (end.getTime() - start.getTime()));
```

Then, we sort the second array using our implementation of the merge sort algorithm:

```
        SerialMergeSort mySorter = new SerialMergeSort();
        start = new Date();
        mySorter.mergeSort(data2, 0, data2.length);
        end = new Date();
        System.out.println("Execution Time Java SerialMergeSort: "
           + (end.getTime() - start.getTime()));
```

Finally, we check that the sorted arrays are identical:

```
        for (int i = 0; i < data.length; i++) {
            if (data[i].compareTo(data2[i]) != 0) {
                System.err.println("There's a difference is
                   position " + i);
                System.exit(-1);
            }
        }
        System.out.println("Both arrays are equal");
    }
  }
}
```

The concurrent version

As we mentioned before, we are going to use the new Java 8 `CountedCompleter` class as the base class for our Fork/Join tasks. This class provides a mechanism to execute a method when all its child tasks have finished their execution. It's the `onCompletion()` method. So, we use the `compute()` method to divide the array and the `onCompletion()` method to merge the sublists into an ordered list.

The concurrent solution you are going to implement has three classes:

- The `MergeSortTask` class that extends the `CountedCompleter` class and implements the task that executes the merge sort algorithm
- The `ConcurrentMergeSort` task that launches the first task
- The `ConcurrentMetaData` class that provides the `main()` method to test the concurrent version of the merge sort algorithm

The MergeSortTask class

As we mentioned earlier, this class implements the tasks that are going to execute the merge sort algorithm. This class uses the following attributes:

- The array of data we want to sort
- The start and end positions of the array the task has to sort

The class also has a constructor to initialize its parameters:

```
public class MergeSortTask extends CountedCompleter<Void> {

    private Comparable[] data;
    private int start, end;
    private int middle;

    public MergeSortTask(Comparable[] data, int start, int end,
            MergeSortTask parent) {
        super(parent);

        this.data = data;
        this.start = start;
        this.end = end;
    }
```

The `compute()` method, if the difference between the start and end indexes are greater or equal that `1024`, we split the task into two child tasks to process two subsets of the original set. Both tasks use the `fork()` method to send a task to the `ForkJoinPool` in an asynchronous way. Otherwise, we execute `SerialMergeSorg.mergeSort()` to sort the part of the array (which have `1024` or less elements) and then we call the `tryComplete()` method. This method will internally call the `onCompletion()` method when the child task has finished its execution.
Take a look at the following code:

```java
@Override
public void compute() {
    if (end - start >= 1024) {
        middle = (end+start)>>>1;
        MergeSortTask task1 = new MergeSortTask(data, start,
            middle, this);
        MergeSortTask task2 = new MergeSortTask(data, middle,
            end, this);
        addToPendingCount(1);
        task1.fork();
        task2.fork();
    } else {
        new SerialMergeSort().mergeSort(data, start, end);
        tryComplete();
    }
}
```

In our case, we will use the `onCompletion()` method to make the merge and sort operations to obtain the sorted list. Once a task finishes the execution of the `onCompletion()` method, it calls `tryComplete()` over its parent to try to complete that task. The source code of the `onCompletion()` method is very similar to the `merge()` method of the serial version of the algorithm. Refer to the following code:

```java
@Override
public void onCompletion(CountedCompleter<?> caller) {
    if (middle==0) {
        return;
    }
    int length = end - start + 1;
    Comparable tmp[] = new Comparable[length];
    int i, j, index;
    i = start;
    j = middle;
    index = 0;
    while ((i < middle) && (j < end)) {
        if (data[i].compareTo(data[j]) <= 0) {
            tmp[index] = data[i];
```

```
                    i++;
                } else {
                    tmp[index] = data[j];
                    j++;
                }
                index++;
            }
            while (i < middle) {
                tmp[index] = data[i];
                i++;
                index++;
            }
            while (j < end) {
                tmp[index] = data[j];
                j++;
                index++;
            }
            for (index = 0; index < (end - start); index++) {
                data[index + start] = tmp[index];
            }
        }

    }
```

The ConcurrentMergeSort class

In the concurrent version, this class is very simple. It implements the `mergeSort()` method that receives the array of data to sort and the start index (which will always be 0) and the end index (which will always be the length of the array) to sort the array as parameters. We have chosen to maintain the same interface rather than the serial version.

The method creates a new `MergeSortTask`, sends it to the default `ForkJoinPool` using the `invoke()` method that returns when the task has finished its execution and the array is sorted.

```
    public class ConcurrentMergeSort {

        public void mergeSort (Comparable data[], int start, int end) {

            MergeSortTask task=new MergeSortTask(data, start,
                end,null);
            ForkJoinPool.commonPool().invoke(task);

        }
    }
```

The ConcurrentMetaData class

The `ConcurrentMetaData` class provides the `main()` method to test the concurrent version of the merge sort algorithm. In our case, the code is equal to the code of the `SerialMetaData` class, but using the concurrent versions of the classes and the `Arrays.parallelSort()` method instead of the `Arrays.sort()` method, so we don't include the source code of the class.

Comparing the two versions

We have executed our serial and concurrent versions of the merge sort algorithm and compared the execution times between them and against the methods `Arrays.sort()` and `Arrays.parallelSort()`. We have executed the four versions using the JMH framework (http://openjdk.java.net/projects/code-tools/jmh/) that allows you to implement micro benchmarks in Java. Using a framework for benchmarking is a better solution that simply measures time using methods as `currentTimeMillis()` or `nanoTime()`. We have executed them 10 times in a computer with a four-core processor and calculated the medium execution time of those 10 times. These are the execution times in millisecond we have obtained when we sort our dataset with 542,184 objects:

	Arrays.sort()	Serial merge sort	Arrays.parallelSort()	Concurrent merge sort
Execution time (ms)	561.324	711.004	261.418	353.846

We can draw the following conclusions:

- The method `Arrays.parallelSort()` obtains the best result. For serial algorithms, the `Arrays.sort()` method obtains better execution time than our implementation.
- For our implementations, the concurrent version of the algorithm has better performance than the serial one.

We can compare our serial and concurrent versions of the merge sort algorithm using the speed-up:

$$S = \frac{t_{serial}}{t_{concurrent}} = \frac{711.004}{353.846} = 2.01$$

Other methods of the Fork/Join framework

In the three examples of this chapter, we have used a lot of methods of the class that forms the Fork/Join framework, but there are other interesting methods you have to know.

We have used the methods `execute()` and `invoke()` from the `ForkJoinPool` class to send tasks to the pool. We can use another method named `submit()`. The main difference between them is that the `execute()` method sends the task to `ForkJoinPool` and returns immediately a void value, the `invoke()` method sends the task to the `ForkJoinPool` and returns when the task has finished its execution, and the `submit()` method sends the task to the `ForkJoinPool` and returns immediately a `Future` object to control the status of the task and obtain its result.

In all the examples of this chapter, we have used classes based on the `ForkJoinTask` class, but you can use the `ForkJoinPool` tasks based on the `Runnable` and `Callable` interfaces. To do this, you can use the method `submit()` that has versions that accept a `Runnable` object, a `Runnable` object with a result, and a `Callable` object.

The `ForkJoinTask` class provides the method `get(long timeout, TimeUnit unit)` to obtain the results returned by a task. This method waits for the period of time specified in the parameters for the result of the task. If the task finishes its execution before that period of time, the method returns the result. Otherwise, it throws a `TimeoutException` exception.

The `ForkJoinTask` provides an alternative to the `invoke()` method. It is the `quietlyInvoke()` method. The main difference between the two versions is that the `invoke()` method returns the result of the execution of the task or throws any exception if necessary. The `quietlyInvoke()` method don't return the result of the task and doesn't throw any exception. It's similar to the `quietlyJoin()` method used in the examples.

Summary

The divide and conquer design technique is a very popular approach to solve different kinds of problems. You divide the original problem into smaller problems and those problems into smaller ones until we have enough simple problems to solve it directly. In version 7, the Java concurrency API introduced a special kind of `Executor` optimized for these kinds of problems. It's the Fork/Join Framework. It's based on the following two operations:

- **fork**: This allows you to create a new child task

- **join**: This allows you to wait for the finalization of a child task and get its results

Using those operations, Fork/Join tasks have the following appearance:

```
if ( problem.size() > DEFAULT_SIZE) {
    childTask1=new Task();
    childTask2=new Task();
    childTask1.fork();
    childTask2.fork();
    childTaskResults1=childTask1.join();
    childTaskResults2=childTask2.join();
    taskResults=makeResults(childTaskResults1, childTaskResults2);
    return taskResults;
} else {
    taskResults=solveBasicProblem();
    return taskResults;
}
```

In this chapter, you have solved three different problems using the Fork/Join framework such as the k-means clustering algorithm, a data filtering algorithm, and the merge sort algorithm.

You have used default `ForkJoinPool`, provided by the API (this is a new feature of the Java 8 version), and created a new `ForkJoinPool` object. You have also used the three types of `ForkJoinTasks`:

- The `RecursiveAction` class, used as the base class for those `ForkJoinTasks` that don't return a result.
- The `RecursiveTask` class, used as the base class for those `ForkJoinTasks` that return a result.
- The `CountedCompleter` class, introduced in Java 8 and used as the base class for those `ForkJoinTasks` that need to execute a method or launch another task when all its child subtasks finish their execution.

In the next chapter, you will learn how to use the MapReduce programming technique using the new Java 8 **parallel streams** to get the best performance processing very big datasets.

7
Processing Massive Datasets with Parallel Streams – The Map and Reduce Model

Undoubtedly, the most important innovations introduced in Java 8 are **lambda** expressions and **stream** API. A stream is a sequence of elements that can be processed in a sequential or parallel way. We can transform the stream applying the intermediate operations and then perform a final computation to get the desired result (a list, an array, a number, and so on). In this chapter, we will cover the following topics:

- An introduction to streams
- The first example – a numerical summarization application
- The second example – an information retrieval search tool

An introduction to streams

A stream is a sequence of data (it is not a data structure) that allows you to apply a sequence of operations in a sequential or concurrent way to filter, convert, sort, reduce, or organize those elements to obtain a final object. For example, if you have a stream with the data of your employees, you can use a stream to:

- Count the total number of employees
- Calculate the average salary of all employees who live in a particular place
- Obtain a list of the employees who haven't met their objectives
- Any operation that implies work with all or part of the employees

Streams are greatly influenced by functional programming (the **Scala** programming language provides a very similar mechanism), and they were thought to work with lambda expressions. A stream API resembles **LINQ** (short for **Language-Integrated Query**) queries available in C# language and, to some extent, could be compared with SQL queries.

In the following sections, we will explain the basic characteristics of streams and the parts you will find in a stream.

Basic characteristics of streams

The main characteristics of a stream are:

- A stream does not store its elements. The stream takes the elements from its source and sends them across all the operations that form the pipeline.

- You can work with streams in parallel without any extra work. When you create a stream, you can use the `stream()` method to create a sequential stream or `parallelStream()` to create a concurrent one. The `BaseStream` interface defines the `sequential()` methods to obtain a sequential version of the stream and `parallel()` to obtain a concurrent version of the stream. You can convert a sequential stream to parallel and a parallel to sequential as many times as you want. Take into account that when the terminal stream operation is performed, all the stream operations will be processed according to the last setting. You cannot instruct a stream to perform some operations sequentially and other operations concurrently. Internally, parallel streams in Oracle JDK 8 and Open JDK 8 use an implementation of the Fork/Join framework to execute the concurrent operations.

- Streams are greatly influenced by the functional programming and the Scala programming language. You can use the new lambda expressions as a way to define the algorithm to be executed in an operation over a stream.

- Streams can't be reusable. When you obtain a stream, for example, from a list of values, you can use that stream only once. If you want to perform another operation on the same data, you have to create one more stream.

- Streams make a lazy processing of data. They don't obtain the data until it's necessary. As you will learn later, a stream has an origin, some intermediate operations, and a terminal operation. The data isn't processed until the terminal operation needs it, so the stream processing doesn't begin until the terminal operation is executed.

- You can't access the elements of the stream in a different way. When you have a data structure, you can access one determined element stored in it, for example, indicating its position or its key. Stream operations usually process the elements uniformly, so the only thing you have is the element itself. You don't know the position of the element in the stream and the neighbor elements. In the case of parallel streams, the elements can be processed in any order.
- Stream operations don't allow you to modify the stream source. For example, if you use a list as the stream source, you can store the processing result into the new list, but you cannot add, remove, or replace the elements of the original list. Although this sounds restrictive, it's a very useful feature as you can return the stream created from your internal collection without a fear that the list will be modified by the caller.

Sections of a stream

A stream has three different sections:

- A **source** that generates the data consumed by the stream.
- Zero or more **intermediate operations**, which generate another stream as an output.
- One **terminal operation** that generates an object, which can be a simple object or a collection as an array, a list, or a hash table. There can be also terminal operations that don't produce any explicit result.

Sources of a stream

The source of the stream generates the data that will be processed by the Stream object. You can create a stream from different sources. For example, the Collection interface has included the stream() methods in Java 8 to generate a sequential stream and parallelStream() to generate a parallel one. This allows you to generate a stream to process all the data from almost all the data structures implemented in Java as lists (ArrayList, LinkedList, and so on), sets (HashSet, EnumSet), or concurrent data structures (LinkedBlockingDeque, PriorityBlockingQueue, and so on). Another data structure that can generate streams is an array. The Array class includes four versions of the stream() method to generate a stream from the array. If you pass an array of int numbers to the method, it will generate IntStream. This is a special kind of stream implemented to work with integer numbers (you can still use Stream<Integer> instead of IntStream, but performance might be significantly worse). Similarly, you can create LongStream or DoubleStream from the long[] or double[] array.

Of course, if you pass an array of object to the `stream()` method, you will obtain a generic stream of the same type. In this case, there is no `parallelStream()` method, but once you have obtained the stream, you can call the `parallel()` method defined in the `BaseStream` interface to convert the sequential stream into a concurrent one.

Other interesting functionality provided by the `Stream` API is that you can generate and stream to process the content of a directory or a file. The `Files` class provides different methods to work with files using streams. For example, the `find()` method returns a stream with the `Path` objects of the files in a file tree that meet certain conditions. The `list()` method returns a stream of the `Path` objects with the contents of a directory. The `walk()` method returns a stream of the `Path` objects processing all the objects in a directory tree using a depth-first algorithm. But the most interesting method is the `lines()` method that creates a stream of `String` objects with the lines of a file, so you can process its content using a stream. Unfortunately, all of the methods mentioned here parallelize badly unless you have many thousands of elements (files or lines).

Also, you can create a stream using two methods provided by the `Stream` interface: the `generate()` and `iterate()` methods. The `generate()` method receives a `Supplier` parameterized with an object type as a parameter and generates an infinite sequential stream of objects of that type. The `Supplier` interface has the `get()` method. Every time the stream needs a new object it will call this method to obtain the next value of the stream. As we mentioned earlier, streams process the data in a lazy way, so there is no problem with the infinite nature of the stream. You will use other methods that will convert that stream in finite way. The `iterate()` method is similar, but in this case, the method receives a seed and a `UnaryOperator`. The first value is the result of apply the `UnaryOperator` to the seed; the second value is the result of apply the `UnaryOperator` to the first result, and so on. This method should be avoided as much as possible in concurrent applications because of their performance.

There's also more stream sources as follows:

- `String.chars()`: This returns a `IntStream` with the `char` values of the `String`.
- `Random.ints()`, `Random.doubles()`, or `Random.longs()`: This returns `IntStream`, `DoubleStream`, and `LongStream`, respectively with pseudorandom values. You can specify the range of numbers between the random numbers or the number or random values that you want to obtain. For example, you can generate pseudorandom numbers between 10 and 20 using `new Random.ints(10,20)`.

- The `SplittableRandom` class: This class provides the same methods as the `Random` class to generate pseudorandom `int`, `double`, and `long` values, but is more suitable for parallel processing. You can check the Java API documentation to get the details of this class.
- The `Stream.concat()` method: This receives two streams as parameters and creates a new stream with the elements of the first stream followed by the elements of the second stream.

You can generate streams from other sources, but we think they are not significant.

Intermediate operations

The most important characteristic of an intermediate operation is that they return another stream as their result. The objects of the input and output stream can be of a different type, but an intermediate operation always will generate a new stream. You can have zero or more intermediate operations in a stream. The most important intermediate operations provided by the `Stream` interface are:

- `distinct()`: This method returns a stream with unique values. All the repeated elements will be eliminated
- `filter()`: This method returns a stream with the elements that meet certain criteria
- `flatMap()`: This method is used to convert a stream of streams (for example, a stream of list, sets, and so on) in a single stream
- `limit()`: This method returns a stream that contains at the most the specified number of the original elements in the encounter order starting from the first element
- `map()`: This method is used to transform the elements of a stream for one type to another
- `peek()`: This method returns the same stream, but it executes some code; normally, it is used to write log messages
- `skip()`: This method ignores the first elements (the concrete number is passed as parameter) of the stream
- `sorted()`: This method sorts the elements of the stream

Terminal operations

A terminal operation returns an object as a result. It never returns a stream. In general, all streams will end with a terminal operation that returns the final result of all the sequence of operations. The most important terminal operations are:

- `collect()`: This method provides a way to reduce the number of elements of the source stream organizing the elements of the stream in a data structure. For example, you want to group the elements of your stream by any criterion.
- `count()`: This returns the number of elements of the stream.
- `max()`: This returns the maximum element of the stream.
- `min()`: This returns the minimum element of the stream.
- `reduce()`: This method transforms the elements of the stream in a unique object that represents the stream.
- `forEach()`/`forEachOrdered()`: This methods apply an action to every element in the stream. The second method uses the order of the elements of the stream if the stream has a defined order.
- `findFirst()`/`findAny()`: This returns 1 or the first element of the stream, respectively, if they exist.
- `anyMatch()`/`allMatch()`/`noneMatch()`: They receive a predicate as a parameter and return a Boolean value to indicate if any, all, or none elements of the stream match the predicate.
- `toArray()`: This method returns an array with the elements of the stream.

MapReduce versus MapCollect

MapReduce is a programming model to process very large datasets in distributed environments with a lot of machines working in a cluster. It has two steps generally implemented by two methods:

- **Map**: This filters and transforms the data
- **Reduce**: This applies a summary operation in the data

To make this operation in a distributed environment, we have to split the data and then distribute over the machines of the cluster. This programming model has been used for a long time in the functional programming world. Google recently developed a framework based on this principle, and in the **Apache Foundation**, the **Hadoop** project is very popular as an open source implementation of this model.

Java 8 with streams allows programmers to implement something very similar to this. The `Stream` interface defines intermediate operations (`map()`, `filter()`, `sorted()`, `skip()`, and so on) that can be considered as map functions, and it provides the `reduce()` method as a terminal operation whose main objective is to make a reduction of the elements of the stream as the reduction of the MapReduce model.

The main idea of the `reduce` operation is to create a new intermediate result based on a previous intermediate result and a stream element. The alternative way of reduction (also named mutable reduction) is to incorporate the new resulting item into the mutable container (for example, adding it into `ArrayList`). This kind of reduction is performed by the `collect()` operation, and we will name it as a **MapCollect** model.

We will see how to work with the MapReduce model in this chapter and how to work with the MapCollect model in *Chapter 8, Processing Massive Datasets with Parallel Streams – The Map and Collect Model*.

The first example – a numerical summarization application

One of the most common needs when you have a big set of data is to process its elements to measure certain characteristics. For example, if you have a set with the products purchased in a shop, you can count the number of products you have sold, the number of units per product you have sold, or the average amount that each customer spent on it. We have named that process **numerical summarization**.

In this chapter, we are going to use streams to obtain some measures of the **Bank Marketing** dataset of the **UCI Machine Learning Repository** that you can download from http://archive.ics.uci.edu/ml/datasets/Bank+Marketing. Specifically, we have used the `bank-additional-full.csv` file. This dataset stores information about marketing campaigns of a Portuguese banking institution.

Unlike other chapters, in this case, we explain the concurrent version using streams and then how to implement a serial equivalent version to verify that concurrency improves performance with streams too. Take into account that concurrency is transparent for the programmer, as we mentioned in the introduction of the chapter.

The concurrent version

Our numerical summarization application is very simple. It has the following components:

- `Record`: This class defines the internal structure of every record of the file. It defines the 21 attributes of every record and the corresponding `get()` and `set()` method to establish their values. Its code is very simple, so it won't be included in the book.
- `ConcurrentDataLoader`: This class will load the `bank-additional-full.csv` file with the data and convert it to a list of `Record` objects. We will use streams to load the data and make the conversion.
- `ConcurrentStatistics`: This class implements the operations that we will use to make the calculations over the data.
- `ConcurrentMain`: This class implements the `main()` method to call the operations of the `ConcurrentStatistics` class and measure its execution time.

Let's describe the last three classes in detail.

The ConcurrentDataLoader class

The `ConcurrentDataLoader` class implements the `load()` method that loads the file with the Bank Marketing dataset and converts it to a list of `Record` objects. First, we use the method `readAllLines()` of the `Files` method to load the file and convert its contents in a list of `String` objects. Every line of the file will be converted in an element of the list:

```
public class ConcurrentDataLoader {

    public static List<Record> load(Path path) throws IOException {
        System.out.println("Loading data");

        List<String> lines = Files.readAllLines(path);
```

Then, we apply the necessary operations to the stream to get the list of `Record` objects:

```
        List<Record> records = lines
                .parallelStream()
                .skip(1)
                .map(l -> l.split(";"))
                .map(t -> new Record(t))
                .collect(Collectors.toList());
```

The operations we use are:

- `parallelStream()`: We create a parallel stream to process all the lines of the file.
- `skip(1)`: We ignore the first item of the stream; in this case, the first line of the file, which contains the headers of the file.
- `map (l -> l.split(";"))`: We convert each string in a `String[]` array dividing the line by the `;` character. We use a lambda expression where `l` represents the input parameter and `l.split()` will generate the array of strings. We call this method in a stream of strings, and it will generate a stream of `String[]`.
- `map(t -> new Record(t))`: We convert each array of string in a `Record` object using the constructor of the `Record` class. We use a lambda expression where `t` represents the array of strings. We call this method in a stream of `String[]`, and we generate a stream of `Record` objects.
- `collect(Collectors.toList())`: This method converts the stream into a list. We will work with the `collect` method in more detail in *Chapter 8, Processing Massive Datasets with Parallel Streams – The Map and Collect Model*.

As you can see, we have made the transformation in a compact, elegant, and concurrent way without the utilization of any thread, task, or framework. Finally, we return the list of `Record` objects, as follows:

```
        return records;
    }
}
```

The ConcurrentStatistics class

The `ConcurrentStatistics` class implements the methods that make the calculus over the data. We have seven different operations to obtain information about the dataset. Let's describe each of them.

Job information from subscribers

The main objective of this method is to obtain the number of people per job type (field job) for those people who have subscribed a bank deposit (field subscribe equals to `yes`).

This is the source code of this method:

```java
public class ConcurrentStatistics {

    public static void jobDataFromSubscribers(List<Record>
      records) {
        System.out.println
            ("*******************************************");
        System.out.println("Job info for Deposit subscribers");

        ConcurrentMap<String, List<Record>> map =
          records.parallelStream()
                .filter(r -> r.getSubscribe().equals("yes"))
                .collect(Collectors.groupingByConcurrent
                    (Record::getJob));

        map.forEach((k, l) -> System.out.println(k + ": " +
          l.size()));

        System.out.println
            ("*******************************************");
    }
}
```

The method receives the list of `Record` objects as input parameters. First, we use a stream to obtain a `ConcurrentMap<String, List<Record>>` object where there are different job types and the list includes the records of each job type. This stream starts with the `parallelStream()` method to create a parallel stream. Then, we use the `filter()` method to select those `Record` objects with the subscribe attribute to `yes`. Finally, we use the `collect()` method passing the `Collectors.groupingByConcurrent()` method to group the actual elements of the stream by the values of the job attribute. Take into account that the `groupingByConcurrent()` method is an unordered collector. The records collected into the list can be in arbitrary order, not in the original order (unlike the simple `groupingBy()` collector).

Once we have the `ConcurrentMap` object, we use the `forEach()` method to write the information on the screen.

Age data from subscribers

The main objective of this method is to obtain statistical information (maximum, minimum, and average values) from the age of the subscribers of a bank deposit (field subscribe equals to `yes`).

This is the source code of the method:

```java
public static void ageDataFromSubscribers(List<Record>
  records) {

    System.out.println
      ("*****************************************");
    System.out.println("Age info for Deposit subscribers");



    DoubleSummaryStatistics statistics =
      records.parallelStream()
         .filter(r -> r.getSubscribe().equals("yes"))
         .collect(Collectors.summarizingDouble
           (Record::getAge));

    System.out.println("Min: " + statistics.getMin());
    System.out.println("Max: " + statistics.getMax());
    System.out.println("Average: " + statistics.getAverage());
    System.out.println
      ("*****************************************");
}
```

This method receives the list of `Record` objects as input parameters and uses a stream to get a `DoubleSummaryStatistics` object with the statistical information. First, we use the `parallelStream()` method to get a parallel stream. Then, we use the `filter()` method to obtain the subscribers of a bank deposit. Finally, we use the `collect()` method with the `Collectors.summarizingDouble()` parameter to obtain the `DoubleSummaryStatistics` object. This class implements the `DoubleConsumer` interface and collects statistical data of the values it receives in the `accept()` method. This `accept()` method is called internally by the `collect()` method of the stream. Java provides the `IntSummaryStatistics` and `LongSummaryStatistics` classes also to obtain statistical data from the `int` and `long` values. In this case, we use the `max()`, `min()`, and `average()` methods to obtain the maximum, minimum, and average values, respectively.

Marital data from subscribers

The main objective of this method is to obtain the different marital status (field marital) of the subscribers of a bank deposit (field subscribe equals to `yes`).

This is the source code of the method:

```java
public static void maritalDataFromSubscribers(List<Record>
  records) {

    System.out.println
      ("*****************************************");
    System.out.println("Marital info for Deposit subscribers");

    records.parallelStream()
        .filter(r -> r.getSubscribe().equals("yes"))
        .map(r -> r.getMarital())
        .distinct()
        .sorted()
        .forEachOrdered(System.out::println);
    System.out.println
      ("*****************************************");
}
```

The method receives the list of `Record` objects as input parameters and uses the `parallelStream()` method to get a parallel stream. Then, we use the `filter()` method to only get the subscribers of a bank deposit. Then, we use the `map()` method to obtain a stream of `String` objects with the marital status of all the subscribers. With the `distinct()` method, we take only the unique values, and with the `sorted()` method, we sort those values alphabetically. Finally, we are using `forEachOrdered()` to print the result. Be careful not to use `forEach()` here as it will print the results in no particular order, which would make the `sorted()` step useless. The `forEach()` operation is useful when the elements order is not important and may work much faster for parallel streams than `forEachOrdered()`.

Campaign data from nonsubscribers

One of the most common mistakes we have when we use streams is to try to reuse a stream. We will show you the consequences of this mistake with this method, the main objective of which is to obtain the maximum number of contacts (attribute campaign).

The first version of the method is to try to reuse a stream. This is its source code:

```java
public static void campaignDataFromNonSubscribersBad
  (List<Record> records) {

    System.out.println
      ("*****************************************");
    System.out.println("Number of contacts for Non
      Subscriber");
```

```
            IntStream stream = records.parallelStream()
                    .filter(Record::isNotSubscriber)
                    .mapToInt(r -> r.getCampaign());

            System.out
                    .println("Max number of contacts: " +
                      stream.max().getAsInt());
            System.out
                    .println("Min number of contacts: " +
                      stream.min().getAsInt());
            System.out.println
                ("*******************************************");
    }
```

The method receives the list of `Record` objects as input parameters. First, we create an `IntStream` object using that list. With the `parallelStream()` method, we create a parallel stream. Then, we use the `filter()` method to get the nonsubscribers and the `mapToInt()` method to convert a stream of `Record` objects in an `IntStream` object replacing each object by the value of the `getCampaign()` method.

We try to use that stream to get the maximum value, with the `max()` method, and the minimum value, with the `min()` method. If we execute this method, we will obtain `IllegalStateException` in the second call with the message **the stream has already been operated upon or closed**.

We can solve this problem creating two different streams, one to obtain the maximum and the other to obtain the minimum. This is the source code of this option:

```
        public static void campaignDataFromNonSubscribersOk
           (List<Record> records) {

            System.out.println
               ("*******************************************");
            System.out.println("Number of contacts for Non
               Subscriber");
            int value = records.parallelStream()
                    .filter(Record::isNotSubscriber)
                    .map(r -> r.getCampaign())
                    .mapToInt(Integer::intValue)
                    .max()
                    .getAsInt();

            System.out.println("Max number of contacts: " + value);
```

```java
            value = records.parallelStream()
                    .filter(Record::isNotSubscriber)
                    .map(r -> r.getCampaign())
                    .mapToInt(Integer::intValue)
                    .min()
                    .getAsInt();

        System.out.println("Min number of contacts: " + value);
        System.out.println
            ("*******************************************");
    }
```

Another option is to use the `summaryStatistics()` method to obtain an `IntSummaryStatistics` object, as we showed in a previous method.

Multiple data filter

The main objective of this method is to obtain the number of records that meet at most one of the following conditions:

- The `defaultCredit` attribute takes the value `true`
- The `housing` attribute takes the value `false`
- The `loan` attribute takes the value `false`

One solution to implement this method is to implement a filter that checks whether the elements meet one of these conditions. You can implement other solutions with the `concat()` method provided by the `Stream` interface. This is the source code:

```java
        public static void multipleFilterData(List<Record> records) {

            System.out.println
                ("*******************************************");
            System.out.println("Multiple filter");

            Stream<Record> stream1 = records.parallelStream()
                    .filter(Record::isDefaultCredit);
            Stream<Record> stream2 = records.parallelStream()
                    .filter(r -> !(r.isHousing()));
            Stream<Record> stream3 = records.parallelStream()
                    .filter(r -> !(r.isLoan()));

            Stream<Record> complete = Stream.concat(stream1, stream2);
            complete = Stream.concat(complete, stream3);
```

```
            long value =
              complete.parallel().unordered().distinct().count();

            System.out.println("Number of people: " + value);
            System.out.println
              ("*****************************************");
    }
```

This method receives the list of Record objects as input parameters. First, we create three streams with the elements that meet each of the conditions and then we use the concat() method to generate a single stream. The concat() method only creates a stream with the elements of the first stream followed by the elements of the second stream. For this reason, with the final stream, we use the parallel() method to convert the final stream in a parallel once, the unordered() method to get an unordered stream that will give us better performance in the distinct() method with parallel streams and the distinct() method to get only unique values, and the count() method to obtain the number of elements in the stream.

This is not the most optimal solution. We have used it to show you how the concat() and distinct() methods work. You can implement the same in a more optimal way using the following code

```
            public static void multipleFilterDataPredicate (List<Record>
              records) {

            System.out.println
              ("*****************************************");
            System.out.println("Multiple filter with Predicate");

            Predicate<Record> p1 = r -> r.isDefaultCredit();
            Predicate<Record> p2 = r -> !r.isHousing();
            Predicate<Record> p3 = r -> !r.isLoan();

            Predicate<Record> pred = Stream.of(p1, p2, p3)
                        .reduce(Predicate::or).get();

            long value =
              records.parallelStream().filter(pred).count();

            System.out.println("Number of people: " + value);
            System.out.println
              ("*****************************************");
    }
```

We create a stream of three predicates and reduce them via the `Predicate::or` operation to create the compound predicate, which is `true` when either of the input predicates is `true`. You can also use the `Predicate::and` reduction operation to create a predicate, which is `true` when all the input predicates are `true`.

Duration data from nonsubscribers

The main objective of this method is to obtain the 10 longest phone calls (duration attribute) to people that finally didn't subscribe a bank deposit (field subscribe equals to `no`).

This is the source code of this method:

```java
public static void durationDataForNonSubscribers(List<Record>
   records) {

   System.out.println
      ("******************************************");
   System.out.println("Duration data for non subscribers");
   records.parallelStream().filter(r -> r.isNotSubscriber())
      .sorted(Comparator.comparingInt (Record::getDuration)
      .reversed()).limit(10)
      .forEachOrdered(
         r -> System.out.println("Education: "
            + r.getEducation() + "; Duration: " +
            r.getDuration()));
   System.out.println
      ("******************************************");
}
```

The method receives the list of `Record` objects as input parameters and uses the `parallelStream()` method to get a parallel stream. We use the `filter()` method to get the nonsubscribers. Then, we use the `sorted()` method and we pass a comparator. The comparator is created using the `Comparator.comparingInt()` static method. As we need to sort in reverse order (biggest duration first), we simply add the `reversed()` method to the created comparator. The `sorted()` method uses that comparator to compare and sort the elements of the stream, so we can obtain the elements sorted as we want.

Once the elements have been sorted, we get the first 10 results using the `limit()` method and print the result using the `forEachOrdered()` method.

People aged between 25 and 50

The main objective of this method is to obtain the number of people in the file with an age between 25 and 50.

This is the source code of this:

```
public static void peopleBetween25and50(List<Record> records) {

    System.out.println
        ("*****************************************");
    System.out.println("People between 25 and 50");
    int count=records.parallelStream()
      .map(r -> r.getAge())
      .filter(a -> (a >=25 ) && (a <=50))
      .mapToInt(a -> 1)
      .reduce(0, Integer::sum);
    System.out.println("People between 25 and 50: "+count);
    System.out.println
        ("*****************************************");
}
```

The method receives the list of `Record` objects as input parameters and uses the `parallelStream()` method to get a parallel stream. Then, we use the `map()` method to transform the stream of `Record` objects into a stream of `int` values replacing each object by the value of its age attribute. Then, we use the `filter()` method to select only the people with an age of 25 and 50 and the `map()` method again to convert each value into `1`. Finally, we use the `reduce()` method to sum all those 1s and obtain the total number of people between 25 and 50. The first parameter of the `reduce()` method is the identity value, and the second parameter is the operation that is used to obtain a single value from all the elements of the stream. In this case, we use the `Integer::sum` operation. The first sum is between the initial and the first value of the stream, the second sum between the result of the first sum and the second value of the stream, and so on.

The ConcurrentMain class

The `ConcurrentMain` class implements the `main()` method to test the `ConcurrentStatistic` class. First, we implement the `measure()` method that measures the execution time of a task:

```
public class ConcurrentMain {
    static Map<String, List<Double>> totalTimes = new
       LinkedHashMap<>();
    static List<Record> records;

    private static void measure(String name, Runnable r) {
        long start = System.nanoTime();
        r.run();
```

```
            long end = System.nanoTime();
            totalTimes.computeIfAbsent(name, k -> new
                ArrayList<>()).add((end - start) / 1_000_000.0);
    }
```

We use a map to store all the execution times of every method. We are going to execute each method 10 times to see how the execution time decreases after the first execution. Then, we include the `main()` method code. It uses the `measure()` method to measure the execution time of every method and repeats this process 10 times:

```
        public static void main(String[] args) throws IOException {
            Path path = Paths.get("data\\bank-additional-full.csv");

            for (int i = 0; i < 10; i++) {
                records = ConcurrentDataLoader.load(path);
                measure("Job Info", () ->
                    ConcurrentStatistics.jobDataFromSubscribers
                        (records));
                measure("Age Info", () ->
                    ConcurrentStatistics.ageDataFromSubscribers
                        (records));
                measure("Marital Info", () ->
                    ConcurrentStatistics.maritalDataFromSubscribers
                        (records));
                measure("Multiple Filter", () ->
                    ConcurrentStatistics.multipleFilterData(records));
                measure("Multiple Filter Predicate", () ->
                    ConcurrentStatistics.multipleFilterDataPredicate
                        (records));
                measure("Duration Data", () ->
                    ConcurrentStatistics.durationDataForNonSubscribers
                        (records));
                measure("Number of Contacts Bad: ", () ->
                    ConcurrentStatistics
                        .campaignDataFromNonSubscribersBad(records));
                measure("Number of Contacts", () ->
                    ConcurrentStatistics
                        .campaignDataFromNonSubscribersOk(records));
                measure("People Between 25 and 50", () ->
                    ConcurrentStatistics.peopleBetween25and50(records));
            }
```

Finally, we write in the console all the execution times and the average execution time, as follows:

```
times.stream().map(t -> String.format("%6.2f",
    t)).collect(Collectors.joining(" ")), times
    .stream().mapToDouble
    (Double::doubleValue).average().getAsDouble()));
    }
}
```

The serial version

In this case, the serial version is almost equal to the concurrent one. We only replace all the calls to the `parallelStream()` method by calls to the `stream()` method to obtain a sequential stream instead of a parallel stream. We also have to delete the call to the `parallel()` method we use in one of the samples and change the call to the `groupingByConcurrent()` method to `groupingBy()`.

Comparing the two versions

We have executed both versions of the operations to test if the use of parallel streams provides us with a better performance. We have executed them using the JMH framework (http://openjdk.java.net/projects/code-tools/jmh/) that allows you to implement micro benchmarks in Java. Using a framework for benchmarking is a better solution that simply measures time using methods such as `currentTimeMillis()` or `nanoTime()`. We have executed them 10 times in a computer with a four-core processor and calculated the medium execution time of those 10 times. Take into account that we have implemented a special class to execute the JMH tests. You can find these classes in the `com.javferna.packtpub.mastering.numericalSummarization.benchmark` package of the source code. These are the results in milliseconds:

Operation	Sequential streams	Parallel streams
Job info	13.704	9.550
Age info	7.218	5.512
Marital info	8.551	6.783
Multiple filter	27.002	23.668
Multiple filter with predicate	9.413	6.963
Duration data	41.762	23.641
Number of contacts	22.148	13.059
People between 25 and 50	9.102	6.014

We can see how parallel streams always get a better performance than the serial streams. This is the speed-up for all the examples:

Operation	Speed-up
Job info	1.30
Age info	1.25
Marital info	1.16
Multiple filter	1.08
Duration data	1.51
Number of contacts	1.64
People between 25 and 50	1.37

The second example – an information retrieval search tool

According to Wikipedia (https://en.wikipedia.org/wiki/Information_retrieval), **information retrieval** is:

> *"The activity obtaining information resources relevant to an information need from a collection of information resources."*

Usually, the information resources are a collection of documents and the information need is a set of words, which summarizes our need. To make a fast search over the document collection, we use a data structure named **inverted index**. It stores all the words of the document collection, and for each word, a list of the documents that contains that word. In *Chapter 4, Getting Data from the Tasks – The Callable and Future Interfaces*, you constructed an inverted index of a document collection constructed with the Wikipedia pages with information about movies to construct a set of 100,673 documents. We have converted each Wikipedia page in a text file. This inverted index is stored in a text file where each line contains the word, its document frequency, and all the documents in which the word appears with the `tfxidf` attribute of the word in the document. The documents are sorted by the value of the `tfxidf` attribute. For example, a line of the file looks like this:

```
velankanni:4,18005302.txt:10.13,20681361.txt:10.13,45672176.txt:10
    .13,6592085.txt:10.13
```

This line contains the `velankanni` word with a DF of 4. It appears in the `18005302.txt` document with a `tfxidf` value of `10.13`, in the `20681361.txt` document with a `tfxidf` value of `10.13`, in the document `45672176.txt` with a `tfxidf` value of `10.13`, and in the `6592085.txt` document with a `tfxidf` value of `10.13`.

In this chapter, we will use the stream API to implement different versions of our search tool and obtain information about the inverted index.

An introduction to the reduction operation

As we mentioned earlier in this chapter, the `reduce` operation applies a summary operation to the elements of a stream to generate a single summary result. This single result can be of the same type as the elements of the stream of an other type. A simple example of the `reduce` operation is calculating the sum of a stream of numbers.

The stream API provides the `reduce()` method to implement reduction operations. This method has the following three different versions:

- `reduce(accumulator)`: This version applies the `accumulator` function to all the elements of the stream. There is no initial value in this case. It returns an `Optional` object with the final result of the `accumulator` function or an empty `Optional` object if the stream is empty. This `accumulator` function must be an `associative` function. It implements the `BinaryOperator` interface. Both parameters could be either the stream elements or the partial results returned by previous accumulator calls.

- `reduce(identity, accumulator)`: This version must be used when the final result and the elements of the stream has the same type. The identity value must be an identity value for the `accumulator` function. That is to say, if you apply the `accumulator` function to the identity value and any value V, it must return the same value V: `accumulator(identity,V)=V`. That identity value is used as the first result for the accumulator function and is the returned value if the stream has no elements. As in the other version, the accumulator must be an `associative` function that implements the `BinaryOperator` interface.

- `reduce(identity, accumulator, combiner)`: This version must be used when the final result has a different type than the elements of the stream. The identity value must be an identity for the `combiner` function, that is to say, `combiner(identity,v)=v`. A `combiner` function must be compatible with the `accumulator` function, that is to say, `combiner(u,accumulator(identity,v))=accumulator(u,v)`. The `accumulator` function takes a partial result and the next element of the stream to generate a partial result, and the combiner takes two partial results to generate another partial result. Both functions must be associative, but in this case, the `accumulator` function is an implementation of the `BiFunction` interface and the `combiner` function is an implementation of the `BinaryOperator` interface.

The `reduce()` method has a limitation. As we mentioned before, it must return a single value. You shouldn't use the `reduce()` method to generate a collection or a complex object. The first problem is performance. As the documentation of the stream API specifies, the `accumulator` function returns a new value every time it processes an element. If your `accumulator` function works with collections, every time it processes an element it creates a new collection, which is very inefficient. Another problem is that, if you work with parallel streams, all the threads will share the identity value. If this value is a mutable object, for example, a collection, all the threads will be working over the same collection. This does not comply with the philosophy of the `reduce()` operation. In addition, the `combiner()` method will always receive two identical collections (all the threads are working over only one collection), that also doesn't comply the philosophy of the `reduce()` operation.

If you want to make a reduction that generates a collection or a complex object, you have the following two options:

- Apply a mutable reduction with the `collect()` method. *Chapter 8, Processing Massive Datasets with Parallel Streams – The Map and Collect Model*, explains in detail how to use this method in different situations.
- Create the collection and use the `forEach()` method to fill the collection with the required values.

In this example, we will use the `reduce()` method to obtain information about the inverted index and the `forEach()` method to reduce the index to the list of relevant documents for a query.

The first approach – full document query

In our first approach, we will use all the documents associated with a word. The steps of this implementation of our search process are:

1. We select in the inverted index the lines corresponding with the words of the query.
2. We group all the document lists in a single list. If a document appears associated with two or more different words, we sum the `tfxidf` value of those words in the document to obtain the final `tfxidf` value of the document. If a document is only associated with one word, the `tfxidf` value of that word will be the final `tfxidf` value for that document.
3. We sort the documents using its `tfxidf` value, from high to low.
4. We show to the user the 100 documents with a higher value of `tfxidf`.

We have implemented this version in the `basicSearch()` method of the `ConcurrentSearch` class. This is the source code of the method:

```java
public static void basicSearch(String query[]) throws
   IOException {

Path path = Paths.get("index", "invertedIndex.txt");
HashSet<String> set = new HashSet<>(Arrays.asList(query));
QueryResult results = new QueryResult(new
   ConcurrentHashMap<>());

try (Stream<String> invertedIndex = Files.lines(path)) {

    invertedIndex.parallel()
      .filter(line -> set.contains(Utils.getWord(line)))
      .flatMap(ConcurrentSearch::basicMapper)
      .forEach(results::append);

    results
      .getAsList()
      .stream()
      .sorted()
      .limit(100)
      .forEach(System.out::println);

    System.out.println("Basic Search Ok");
  }

}
```

We receive an array of string objects with the words of the query. First, we transform that array in a set. Then, we use a *try-with-resources* stream with the lines of the `invertedIndex.txt` file, which is the file that contains the inverted index. We use a *try-with-resources* so we don't have to worry about opening or closing the file. The aggregate operations of the stream will generate a `QueryResult` object with the relevant documents. We use the following methods to obtain that list:

- `parallel()`: First, we obtain a parallel stream to improve the performance of the search process.
- `filter()`: We select the lines that associated the word in the set with the words in the query. The `Utils.getWord()` method obtains the word of the line.
- `flatMap()`: We convert the stream of strings where each string is a line of the inverted index in a stream of `Token` objects. Each token contains the `tfxidf` value of a word in a file. Of every line, we will generate as many tokens as files containing that word.
- `forEach()`: We generate the `QueryResult` object adding every token with the `add()` method of that class.

Once we have created the `QueryResult` object, we create other streams to obtain the final list of results using the following methods:

- `getAsList()`: The `QueryResult` object returns a list with the relevant documents
- `stream()`: To create a stream to process the list
- `sorted()`: To sort the list of documents by its `tfxidf` value
- `limit()`: To get the first 100 results
- `forEach()`: To process the 100 results and write the information in the screen

Let's describe the auxiliary classes and methods used in the example.

The basicMapper() method

This method converts a stream of strings into a stream of `Token` objects. As we will describe later in detail, a token stores the `tfxidf` value of a word in a document. This method receives a string with a line of the inverted index. It splits the line into the tokens and generates as many `Token` objects as documents containing the word. This method is implemented in the `ConcurrentSearch` class. This is the source code:

```
public static Stream<Token> basicMapper(String input) {
    ConcurrentLinkedDeque<Token> list = new
      ConcurrentLinkedDeque();
    String word = Utils.getWord(input);
```

```
        Arrays
            .stream(input.split(","))
            .skip(1)
            .parallel()
            .forEach(token -> list.add(new Token(word, token)));

        return list.stream();
    }
```

First, we create a `ConcurrentLinkedDeque` object to store the `Token` objects. Then, we split the string using the `split()` method and use the `stream()` method of the `Arrays` class to generate a stream. Skip the first element (which contains the information of the word) and process the rest of the tokens in parallel. For each element, we create a new `Token` object (we pass to the constructor the word and the token that has the `file:tfxidf` format) and add it to the stream. Finally, we return a stream using the `stream()` method of the `ConcurrenLinkedDeque` object.

The Token class

As we mentioned earlier, this class stores the `tfxidf` value of a word in a document. So, it has three attributes to store this information, as follows:

```
    public class Token {

        private final String word;
        private final double tfxidf;
        private final String file;
```

The constructor receives two strings. The first one contains the word, and the second one contains the file and the `tfxidf` attribute in the `file:tfxidf` format, so we have to process it as follows:

```
    public Token(String word, String token) {
        this.word=word;
        String[] parts=token.split(":");
        this.file=parts[0];
        this.tfxidf=Double.parseDouble(parts[1]);
    }
```

Finally, we have added methods to obtain (not to set) the values of the three attributes and to convert an object to a string, as follows:

```
    @Override
    public String toString() {
        return word+":"+file+":"+tfxidf;
    }
```

The QueryResult class

This class stores the list of documents relevant to a query. Internally, it uses a map to store the information of the relevant documents. The key is the name of the file that stores the document, and the value is a `Document` object that also contains the name of the file and the total `tfxidf` value of that document to the query, as follows:

```
public class QueryResult {

    private Map<String, Document> results;
```

We use the constructor of the class to indicate the concrete implementation of the `Map` interface we will use. We use a `ConcurrentHashMap` to the concurrent version and a `HashMap` in the serial version:

```
public QueryResult(Map<String, Document> results) {
    this.results=results;
}
```

The class includes the `append` method that inserts a token in the map, as follows:

```
public void append(Token token) {
    results.computeIfAbsent(token.getFile(), s -> new
        Document(s)).addTfxidf(token.getTfxidf());
}
```

We use the `computeIfAbsent()` method to create a new `Document` object if there is no `Document` object associated with the file or to obtain the corresponding one if already exists and add the `tfxidf` value of the token to the total `tfxidf` value of the document using the `addTfxidf()` method.

Finally, we have included a method to obtain the map as a list, as follows:

```
public List<Document> getAsList() {
    return new ArrayList<>(results.values());
}
```

The `Document` class stores the name of the file as a string and the total `tfxidf` value as `DoubleAdder`. This class is a new feature of Java 8 and allows us to sum values to the variable from different threads without worrying about synchronization. It implements the `Comparable` interface to sort the documents by its `tfxidf` value, so the documents with biggest `tfxidf` will be first. Its source code is very simple, so it is not included.

The second approach – reduced document query

The first approach creates a new `Token` object per word and file. We have noted that common words, for example, `the`, take a lot of documents associated and a lot of them have low values of `tfxidf`. We have changed our mapper method to take into account only 100 files per word, so the number of `Token` objects generated will be smaller.

We have implemented this version in the `reducedSearch()` method of the `ConcurrentSearch` class. This method is very similar to the `basicSearch()` method. It only changes the stream operations that generate the `QueryResult` object, as follows:

```
invertedIndex.parallel()
  .filter(line -> set.contains(Utils.getWord(line)))
  .flatMap(ConcurrentSearch::limitedMapper)
  .forEach(results::append);
```

Now, we use the `limitedMapper()` method as function in the `flatMap()` method.

The limitedMapper() method

This method is similar to the `basicMapper()` method, but, as we mentioned earlier, we only take into account the first 100 documents associated with every word. As the documents are sorted by its `tfxidf` value, we are using the 100 documents in which the word is more important, as follows:

```
public static Stream<Token> limitedMapper(String input) {
    ConcurrentLinkedDeque<Token> list = new
      ConcurrentLinkedDeque();
    String word = Utils.getWord(input);

    Arrays.stream(input.split(","))
      .skip(1)
      .limit(100)
      .parallel()
      .forEach(token -> {
        list.add(new Token(word, token));
      });

    return list.stream();
}
```

The only difference with the `basicMapper()` method is the `limit(100)` call that takes the first 100 elements of the stream.

The third approach – generating an HTML file with the results

While working with a search tool using a web search engine (for example, Google), when you make a search, it returns you the results of your search (the 10 most important) and for every result the title of the document and a fragment of the document where the words you have searched for appears.

Our third approach to the search tool is based on the second approach but by adding a third stream to generate an HTML file with the results of the search. For every result, we will show the title of the document and three lines where one of the words introduced in the query appears. To implement this, you need access to the files that appears in the inverted index. We have stored them in a folder named docs.

This third approach is implemented in the htmlSearch() method of the ConcurrentSearch class. The first part of the method to construct the QueryResult object with the 100 results is equal to the reducedSearch() method, as follows:

```
public static void htmlSearch(String query[], String fileName)
   throws IOException {
   Path path = Paths.get("index", "invertedIndex.txt");
   HashSet<String> set = new HashSet<>(Arrays.asList(query));
   QueryResult results = new QueryResult(new
      ConcurrentHashMap<>());

   try (Stream<String> invertedIndex = Files.lines(path)) {

      invertedIndex.parallel()
         .filter(line -> set.contains(Utils.getWord(line)))
         .flatMap(ConcurrentSearch::limitedMapper)
         .forEach(results::append);
```

Then, we create the file to write the output and the HTML headers in it:

```
         path = Paths.get("output", fileName +
            "_results.html");
         try (BufferedWriter fileWriter =
            Files.newBufferedWriter(path,
            StandardOpenOption.CREATE)) {

            fileWriter.write("<HTML>");
            fileWriter.write("<HEAD>");
            fileWriter.write("<TITLE>");
            fileWriter.write("Search Results with Streams");
            fileWriter.write("</TITLE>");
```

```
                    fileWriter.write("</HEAD>");
                    fileWriter.write("<BODY>");
                    fileWriter.newLine();
```

Then, we include the stream that generates the results in the HTML file:

```
                    results.getAsList()
                .stream()
                .sorted()
                .limit(100)
                .map(new ContentMapper(query)).forEach(l -> {
                    try {
                        fileWriter.write(l);
                        fileWriter.newLine();
                    } catch (IOException e) {
                        e.printStackTrace();
                    }
                });

                fileWriter.write("</BODY>");
                fileWriter.write("</HTML>");

        }
```

We have used the following methods:

- `getAsList()` to get the list of relevant documents for the query.
- `stream()` to generate a sequential stream. We can't parallelize this stream. If we try to do it, the results in the final file won't be sorted by the `tfxidf` value of the documents.
- `sorted()` to sort the results by its `tfxidf` attribute.
- `map()` to convert a `Result` object into a string with the HTML code for each result using the `ContentMapper` class. We will explain the details of this class later.
- `forEach()` to write the `String` objects returned by the `map()` method in the file. The methods of the `Stream` object can't throw a checked exception, so we have to include the try-catch block that will throw.

Let's see the details of the `ContentMapper` class.

The ContentMapper class

The `ContentMapper` class is an implementation of the `Function` interface that converts a `Result` object in an HTML block with the title of the document and three lines that include one or more words of the query.

The class uses an internal attribute to store the query and implements a constructor to initialize that attribute, as follows:

```
public class ContentMapper implements Function<Document, String> {
    private String query[];

    public ContentMapper(String query[]) {
        this.query = query;
    }
```

The title of the document is stored in the first line of the file. We use a try-with-resources instruction and the `lines()` method of the `Files` class to create and stream `String` objects with the lines of the file and take the first one with the `findFirst()` to obtain the line as a string:

```
public String apply(Document d) {
    String result = "";

    try (Stream<String> content =
      Files.lines(Paths.get("docs",d.getDocumentName()))) {
        result = "<h2>" + d.getDocumentName() + ": "
                + content.findFirst().get()
                + ": " + d.getTfxidf() + "</h2>";
    } catch (IOException e) {
        e.printStackTrace();
        throw new UncheckedIOException(e);
    }
```

Then, we use a similar structure, but in this case, we use the `filter()` method to get only the lines that contain one or more words of the query, the `limit()` method to take three of those lines. Then, we use the `map()` method to add the HTML tags for a paragraph (`<p>`) and the `reduce()` method to complete the HTML code with the selected lines:

```
    try (Stream<String> content =
        Files.lines(Paths.get
        ("docs",d.getDocumentName()))) {
    result += content
            .filter(l -> Arrays.stream(query).anyMatch
                (l.toLowerCase()::contains))
            .limit(3)
```

```
                .map(l -> "<p>"+l+"</p>")
                .reduce("",String::concat);
            return result;
        } catch (IOException e) {
            e.printStackTrace();
            throw new UncheckedIOException(e);
        }
    }
}
```

The fourth approach – preloading the inverted index

The three previous solutions have a problem when they are executed in parallel. As we mentioned earlier, parallel streams are executed using the common Fork/Join pool provided by the Java concurrency API. In *Chapter 6, Optimizing Divide and Conquer Solutions – The Fork/Join Framework*, you learned that you shouldn't use I/O operations as read or write data in a file inside the tasks. This is because when a thread has blocked reading or writing data from or to a file, the framework doesn't use the work-stealing algorithm. As we use a file as the source of our streams, we are penalizing our concurrent solution.

One solution to this problem is to read the data to a data structure and then create our streams from that data structure. Obviously, the execution time of this approach will be smaller when we compare it with the other approaches, but we want to compare the serial and concurrent versions to see (as we expect) that the concurrent version gives us better performance than the serial version. The bad part of this approach is that you need to have your data structure in memory, so you will need a big amount of memory.

This fourth approach is implemented in the `preloadSearch()` method of the `ConcurrentSearch` class. This method receives the query as an `Array` of `String` and an object of the `ConcurrentInvertedIndex` class (we will see the details of this class later) with the data of the inverted index as parameters. This is the source code of this version:

```
        public static void preloadSearch(String[] query,
          ConcurrentInvertedIndex invertedIndex) {

          HashSet<String> set = new HashSet<>(Arrays.asList(query));
          QueryResult results = new QueryResult(new
            ConcurrentHashMap<>());
```

```
            invertedIndex.getIndex()
                .parallelStream()
                .filter(token -> set.contains(token.getWord()))
                .forEach(results::append);

            results
                .getAsList()
                .stream()
                .sorted()
                .limit(100)
                .forEach(document -> System.out.println(document));

            System.out.println("Preload Search Ok.");
    }
```

The `ConcurrentInvertedIndex` class has `List<Token>` to store all the `Token` objects read from the file. It has two methods, `get()` and `set()` for this list of elements.

As in other approaches, we use two streams: the first one to get a `ConcurrentLinkedDeque` of `Result` objects with the whole list of results and the second one to write the results in the console. The second one doesn't change over other versions, but the first one changes. We use the following methods in this stream:

- `getIndex()`: First, we obtain the list of `Token` objects
- `parallelStream()`: Then, we create a parallel stream to process all the elements of the list
- `filter()`: We select the token associated with the words in the query
- `forEach()`: We process the list of tokens adding them to the `QueryResult` object using the `append()` method

The ConcurrentFileLoader class

The `ConcurrentFileLoader` class loads into memory the contents of the `invertedIndex.txt` file with the information of the inverted index. It provides a static method named `load()` that receives a path with the route of the file where the inverted index is stored and returns an `ConcurrentInvertedIndex` object. We have the following code:

```
    public class ConcurrentFileLoader {

        public ConcurrentInvertedIndex load(Path path) throws
            IOException {
```

```
        ConcurrentInvertedIndex invertedIndex = new
           ConcurrentInvertedIndex();
        ConcurrentLinkedDeque<Token> results=new
           ConcurrentLinkedDeque<>();
```

We open the file using a *try-with-resources* structure and create a stream to process all the lines:

```
        try (Stream<String> fileStream = Files.lines(path)) {
            fileStream
            .parallel()
            .flatMap(ConcurrentSearch::limitedMapper)
            .forEach(results::add);
        }

        invertedIndex.setIndex(new ArrayList<>(results));
        return invertedIndex;
    }
}
```

We use the following methods in the stream:

- `parallel()`: We convert the stream into a parallel one
- `flatMap()`: We convert the line into a stream of `Token` objects using the `limitedMapper()` method of the `ConcurrentSearch` class
- `forEach()`: We process the list of `Token` objects adding them to a `ConcurrentLinkedDeque` object using the `add()` method

Finally, we convert the `ConcurrentLinkedDeque` object into `ArrayList` and set it in the `InvertedIndex` object using the `setIndex()` method.

The fifth approach – using our own executor

To go further with this example, we're going to test another concurrent version. As we mentioned in the introduction of this chapter, parallel streams use the common Fork/Join pool introduced in Java 8. However, we can use a trick to use our own pool. If we execute our method as a task of the Fork/Join pool, all the operations of the stream will be executed in the same Fork/Join pool. To test this functionality, we have added the `executorSearch()` method to the `ConcurrentSearch` class. This method receives the query as an array of `String` objects as a parameter, the `InvertedIndex` object, and a `ForkJoinPool` object. This is the source code of this method:

```
        public static void executorSearch(String[] query,
           ConcurrentInvertedIndex invertedIndex, ForkJoinPool pool) {
```

```
            HashSet<String> set = new HashSet<>(Arrays.asList(query));
            QueryResult results = new QueryResult(new
              ConcurrentHashMap<>());

            pool.submit(() -> {
                invertedIndex.getIndex()
                    .parallelStream()
                    .filter(token -> set.contains(token.getWord()))
                    .forEach(results::append);

                results
                    .getAsList()
                    .stream()
                    .sorted()
                    .limit(100)
                    .forEach(document ->
                        System.out.println(document));
            }).join();

            System.out.println("Executor Search Ok.");

        }
```

We execute the content of the method, with its two streams, as a task in the Fork/Join pool using the `submit()` method, and wait for its finalization using the `join()` method.

Getting data from the inverted index – the ConcurrentData class

We have implemented some methods to get information about the inverted index using the `reduce()` method in the `ConcurrentData` class.

Getting the number of words in a file

The first method calculates the number of words in a file. As we mentioned earlier in this chapter, the inverted index stores the files in which a word appears. If we want to know the words that appear in a file, we have to process all the inverted index. We have implemented two versions of this method. The first one is implemented in `getWordsInFile1()`. It receives the name of the file and the `InvertedIndex` object as parameters, as follows:

```
        public static void getWordsInFile1(String fileName,
            ConcurrentInvertedIndex index) {
            long value = index
                    .getIndex()
```

```
                .parallelStream()
                .filter(token -> fileName.equals(token.getFile()))
                .count();
        System.out.println("Words in File "+fileName+": "+value);
    }
```

In this case, we get the list of Token objects using the getIndex() method and create a parallel stream using the parallelStream() method. Then, we filter the tokens associated with the file using the filter() method, and finally, we count the number of words associated with that file using the count() method.

We have implemented another version of this method using the reduce() method instead of the count() method. It's the getWordsInFile2() method:

```
    public static void getWordsInFile2(String fileName,
        ConcurrentInvertedIndex index) {

        long value = index
                .getIndex()
                .parallelStream()
                .filter(token -> fileName.equals(token.getFile()))
                .mapToLong(token -> 1)
                .reduce(0, Long::sum);
        System.out.println("Words in File "+fileName+": "+value);
    }
```

The start of the sequence of operations is the same as the previous one. When we have obtained the stream of Token objects with the words of the file, we use the mapToInt() method to convert that stream into a stream of 1 and then the reduce() method to sum all the 1 numbers.

Getting the average tfxidf value in a file

We have implemented the getAverageTfxidf() method that calculates the average tfxidf value of the words of a file in the collection. We have used here the reduce() method to show how it works. You can use other methods here with better performance:

```
    public static void getAverageTfxidf(String fileName,
        ConcurrentInvertedIndex index) {

        long wordCounter = index
                .getIndex()
                .parallelStream()
                .filter(token -> fileName.equals(token.getFile()))
```

```
            .mapToLong(token -> 1)
            .reduce(0, Long::sum);

    double tfxidf = index
            .getIndex()
            .parallelStream()
            .filter(token -> fileName.equals(token.getFile()))
            .reduce(0d, (n,t) -> n+t.getTfxidf(), (n1,n2) ->
                n1+n2);

    System.out.println("Words in File "+fileName+":
        "+(tfxidf/wordCounter));
}
```

We use two streams. The first one calculates the number of words in a file and has the same source code as the `getWordsInFile2()` method. The second one calculates the total `tfxidf` value of all the words in the file. We use the same methods to get the stream of `Token` objects with the words in the file and then we use the `reduce` method to sum the `tfxidf` value of all the words. We pass the following three parameters to the `reduce()` method:

- `0`: This is passed as the identity value.
- `(n,t) -> n+t.getTfxidf()`: This is passed as the `accumulator` function. It receives a `double` number and a `Token` object and calculates the sum of the number and the `tfxidf` attribute of the token.
- `(n1,n2) -> n1+n2`: This is passed as the `combiner` function. It receives two numbers and calculates their sum.

Getting the maximum and minimum tfxidf values in the index

We have also used the `reduce()` method to calculate the maximum and minimum `tfxidf` values of the inverted index in the `maxTfxidf()` and `minTfxidf()` methods:

```
    public static void maxTfxidf(ConcurrentInvertedIndex index) {
        Token token = index
                .getIndex()
                .parallelStream()
                .reduce(new Token("", "xxx:0"), (t1, t2) -> {
                    if (t1.getTfxidf()>t2.getTfxidf()) {
                        return t1;
                    } else {
                        return t2;
```

```
            }
        });
        System.out.println(token.toString());
}
```

The method receives the ConcurrentInvertedIndex as a parameter. We use the getIndex() to obtain the list of Token objects. Then, we use the parallelStream() method to create a parallel stream over the list and the reduce() method to obtain the Token with the biggest tfxidf. In this case, we use the reduce() method with two parameters: an identity value and an accumulator function. The identity value is a Token object. We don't care about the word and the file name, but we initialize its tfxidf attribute with the value 0. Then, the accumulator function receives two Token objects as parameters. We compare the tfxidf attribute of both objects and return the one with greater value.

The minTfxidf() method is very similar, as follows:

```
public static void minTfxidf(ConcurrentInvertedIndex index) {
    Token token = index
            .getIndex()
            .parallelStream()
            .reduce(new Token("", "xxx:1000000"), (t1, t2) ->
            {
                if (t1.getTfxidf()<t2.getTfxidf()) {
                    return t1;
                } else {
                    return t2;
                }
            });
    System.out.println(token.toString());
}
```

The main difference is that in this case, the identity value is initialized with a very high value for the tfxidf attribute.

The ConcurrentMain class

To test all the methods explained in the previous sections, we have implemented the ConcurrentMain class that implements the main() method to launch our tests. In these tests, we have used the following three queries:

- query1, with the words james and bond
- query2, with the words gone, with, the, and wind
- query3, with the words rocky

We have tested the three queries with the three versions of our search process measuring the execution time of each test. All the tests have a code similar to this:

```java
public class ConcurrentMain {

    public static void main(String[] args) {

        String query1[]={"james","bond"};
        String query2[]={"gone","with","the","wind"};
        String query3[]={"rocky"};

         Date start, end;

        bufferResults.append("Version 1, query 1, concurrent\n");
        start = new Date();
        ConcurrentSearch.basicSearch(query1);
        end = new Date();
        bufferResults.append("Execution Time: "
                + (end.getTime() - start.getTime()) + "\n");
```

To load the inverted index from a file to an `InvertedIndex` object, you can use the following code:

```java
ConcurrentInvertedIndex invertedIndex = new
    ConcurrentInvertedIndex();
ConcurrentFileLoader loader = new ConcurrentFileLoader();
invertedIndex =
    loader.load(Paths.get("index","invertedIndex.txt"));
```

To create the `Executor` to use in the `executorSearch()` method, you can use the following code:

```java
ForkJoinPool pool = new ForkJoinPool();
```

The serial version

We have implemented a serial version of this example with the `SerialSearch`, `SerialData`, `SerialInvertendIndex`, `SerialFileLoader`, and `SerialMain` classes. To implement that version, we have made the following changes:

- Use sequential streams instead of parallel ones. You have to delete the use of the `parallel()` method to convert the streams in parallel or replace the method `parallelStream()` to create a parallel stream for the `stream()` method to create a sequential one.
- In the `SerialFileLoader` class, use `ArrayList` instead of `ConcurrentLinkedDeque`.

Comparing the solutions

Let's compare the solutions of the serial and concurrent versions of all the methods we have implemented. We have executed them using the JMH framework (http://openjdk.java.net/projects/code-tools/jmh/), which allows you to implement micro benchmarks in Java. Using a framework for benchmarking is a better solution that simply measures time using methods such as currentTimeMillis() or nanoTime(). We have executed them 10 times in a computer with a four-core processor so a concurrent algorithm can become theoretically four times faster than a serial one. Take into account that we have implemented a special class to execute the JMH tests. You can find these classes in the com.javferna.packtpub.mastering.irsystem.benchmark package of the source code.

For the first query, with the words james and bond, these are the execution times obtained in milliseconds:

	Serial	Concurrent
Basic search	3516.674	3301.334
Reduced search	3458.351	3230.017
HTML search	3298.996	3298.632
Preload search	153.414	105.195
Executor search	154.679	102.135

For the second query, with the words gone, with, the, and wind, these are the execution times obtained in milliseconds:

	Serial	Concurrent
Basic search	3446.022	3441.002
Reduced search	3249.930	3260.026
HTML search	3299.625	3379.277
Preload search	154.631	113.757
Executor search	156.091	106.418

For the third query, with the words `rocky`, these are the execution times obtained in milliseconds:

	Serial	Concurrent
Basic search	3271.308	3219.990
Reduced search	3318.343	3279.247
HTML search	3323.345	3333.624
Preload search	151.416	97.092
Executor search	155.033	103.907

Finally, these are the average execution times in milliseconds for the methods that return information about the inverted index:

	Serial	Concurrent
`getWordsInFile1`	131.066	81.357
`getWordsInFile2`	132.737	84.112
`getAverageTfxidf`	253.067	166.009
`maxTfxidf`	90.714	66.976
`minTfxidf`	84.652	68.158

We can draw the following conclusions:

- When we read the inverted index to obtain the list of relevant documents, we obtain worse execution times. In this case, the execution times between the concurrent and serial versions are very similar.
- When we work with a preload version of the inverted index, concurrent versions of the algorithms give us better performance in all cases.
- For the methods that give us information about the inverted index, concurrent versions of the algorithms always give us better performance.

We can compare the parallel and sequential streams for the three queries in this end using the speed-up:

$$S_{query1} = \frac{T_{serial\ pre-load}}{T_{concurrent\ pre-load}} = \frac{150.827}{106.353} = 1.42$$

$$S_{query2} = \frac{T_{serial\ pre-load}}{T_{concurrent\ pre-load}} = \frac{155.915}{105.708} = 1,47$$

$$S_{query3} = \frac{T_{serial\ pre-load}}{T_{concurrent\ pre-load}} = \frac{149.404}{96.605} = 1,55$$

Finally, in our third approach, we generate an HTML web page with the results of the queries. These are the first results with the query `james bond`:

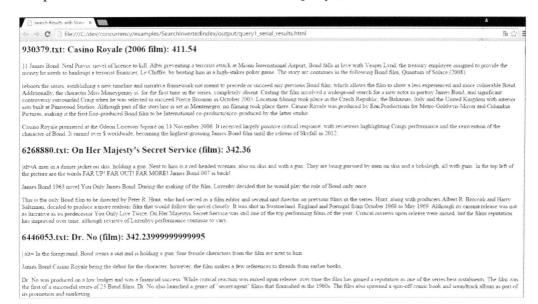

Processing Massive Datasets with Parallel Streams – The Map and Reduce Model

For the query `gone with the wind`, these are the first results:

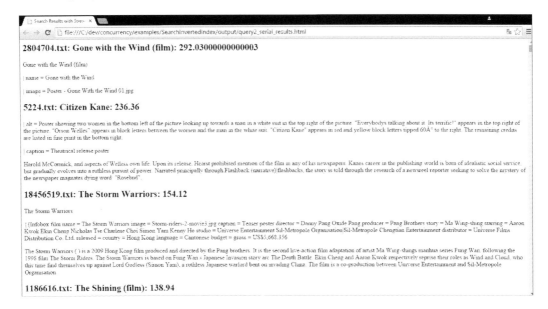

Finally, these are the first results for the query `rocky`:

Summary

In this chapter, we were introduced to streams, a new feature introduced in Java 8 inspired by functional programming and got ready to work with the new lambda expressions. A stream is a sequence of data (it is not a data structure) that allows you to apply a sequence of operations in a sequential or concurrent way to filter, convert, sort, reduce, or organize those elements to obtain a final object.

You also learned the main characteristics of the streams that we have to take into account when we use streams in our sequential or concurrent applications.

Finally, we used streams in two samples. In the first sample, we used almost all the methods provided by the `Stream` interface to calculate statistical data of a big dataset. We used the Bank Marketing dataset of the UCI Machine Learning Repository with its 45,211 records. In the second sample, we implemented different approaches to a search application in an inverted index to obtain the most relevant documents to a query. This is one of the most common tasks in the information retrieval field. For this purpose, we used the `reduce()` method as the terminal operation of our streams.

In the next chapter, we will continue working with streams, but with more focus on the `collect()` terminal operation.

8
Processing Massive Datasets with Parallel Streams – The Map and Collect Model

In *Chapter 7, Processing Massive Datasets with Parallel Streams – The Map and Reduce Model*, we introduced the concept of stream, the new Java 8 feature. A stream is a sequence of elements that can be processed in a parallel or sequential way. In this chapter, you will learn how to work with streams with the following topics:

- The `collect()` method
- The first example – searching data without indexing
- The second example – a recommendation system
- The third example – common contacts in a social network

Using streams to collect data

In *Chapter 7, Processing Massive Datasets with Parallel Streams – The Map and Reduce Model*, we made an introduction to streams. Let's remember their most important characteristics:

- Streams' elements are not stored in the memory
- Streams can't be reusable
- Streams make a lazy processing of data
- The stream operation cannot modify the stream source
- Streams allow you to chain operations so the output of one operation is the input of the next one

A stream is formed by the following three main elements:

- A source that generates stream elements
- Zero or more intermediate operations that generate output as another stream
- One terminal operation that generates a result that could be either a simple object, array, collection, map, or anything else

The `Stream` API provides different terminal operations, but there are two more significant operations for their flexibility and power. In *Chapter 7, Processing Massive Datasets with Parallel Streams – The Map and Reduce Model*, you learned how to use the `reduce()` method, and in this chapter, you will learn how to use the `collect()` method. Let's make an introduction to this method.

The collect() method

The `collect()` method allows you to transform and group the elements of the stream generating a new data structure with the final results of the stream. You can use up to three different data types: an input data type, the data type of the input elements that come from the stream, an intermediate data type used to store the elements while the `collect()` method is running, and an output data type returned by the `collect()` method.

There are two different versions of the `collect()` method. The first version accepts the following three functional parameters:

- **Supplier**: This is a function that creates an object of the intermediate data type. If you use a sequential stream, this method will be called once. If you use a parallel stream, this method may be called many times and must produce a fresh object every time.
- **Accumulator**: This function is called to process an input element and store it in the intermediate data structure.
- **Combiner**: This function is called to merge two intermediate data structures into one. This function will be only called with parallel streams.

This version of the `collect()` method works with two different data types: the input data type of the elements that comes from the stream and the intermediate data type that will be used to store the intermediate elements and to return the final result.

The second version of the `collect()` method accepts an object that implements the `Collector` interface. You can implement this interface by yourself, but it's easier to use the `Collector.of()` static method. The arguments of this method are as follows:

- **Supplier**: This function creates an object of the intermediate data type, and it works as seen earlier
- **Accumulator**: This function is called to process an input element, transform it if necessary, and store it in the intermediate data structure
- **Combiner**: This function is called to merge two intermediate data structures into one, and it works as seen earlier
- **Finisher**: This function is called to transform the intermediate data structure into a final data structure if you need to make a final transformation or computation
- **Characteristics**: You can use this final variable argument to indicate some characteristics of the collector you are creating

Actually, there's slight difference between the two versions. The three-param collect accepts a combiner, that is `BiConsumer`, and it must merge the second intermediate result into the first one. Unlike it, this combiner is `BinaryOperator` and should return the combiner. Therefore, it has the freedom to merge either the second inside the first or the first inside the second, or create a new intermediate result. There is another version of the `of()` method, which accepts the same arguments except the finisher; in this case, the finishing transformation is not performed.

Java provides you with some predefined collectors in the `Collectors` factory class. You can get those collectors using one of its static methods. Some of those methods are:

- `averagingDouble()`, `averagingInt()`, and `averagingLong()`: This returns a collector that allows you to calculate the arithmetic mean of a `double`, `int`, or `long` function.
- `groupingBy()`: This returns a collector that allows you to group the elements of a stream by an attribute of its objects generating a map where the keys are the values of the selected attribute and the values are a list of the objects that have a determined value.
- `groupingByConcurrent()`: This is similar to the previous one except for two important differences. The first one is that it may work faster in the parallel but slower in the sequential mode than the `groupingBy()` method. The second and most important difference is that `groupingByConcurrent()` function is an unordered collector. The items in the lists are not guaranteed to be in the same order as in the stream. The `groupingBy()` collector on the other hand guarantees the ordering.

- `joining()`: This returns a `Collector` factory class that concatenates the input elements into a string.
- `partitioningBy()`: This returns a `Collector` factory class that makes a partition of the input elements based on the results of a predicate.
- `summarizingDouble()`, `summarizingInt()`, and `summarizingLong()`: These return a `Collector` factory class that calculates summary statistics of the input elements.
- `toMap()`: This returns a `Collector` factory class that allows you to transform input elements into a map based on two mapping functions.
- `toConcurrentMap()`: This is similar to the previous one, but in a concurrent way. Without custom merger, `toConcurrentMap()` is just faster for parallel streams. As occurs with `groupingByConcurrent()`, this is an unordered collector too, whereas `toMap()` uses the encounter order to make the conversion.
- `toList()`: This returns a `Collector` factory class that stores the input elements into a list.
- `toCollection()`: This method allows you to accumulate the input elements into a new `Collection` factory class (`TreeSet`, `LinkedHashSet`, and so on) in the encounter order. The method receives an implementation of the `Supplier` interface that creates the collection as a parameter.
- `maxBy()` and `minBy()`: This returns a `Collector` factory class that produces the maximal and minimal element according to the comparator passed as a parameter.
- `toSet()`: This returns a `Collector` that stores the input elements into a set.

The first example – searching data without an index

In *Chapter 7, Processing Massive Datasets with Parallel Streams – The Map and Reduce Model*, you learned how to implement a search tool to look for the documents similar to an input query using an inverted index. This data structure makes the search operation easier and faster, but there will be situations where you will have to make a search operation over a big set of data and you won't have an inverted index to help you. In these cases, you have to process all the elements of the dataset to get the correct results. In this example, you will see one of these situations and how the `reduce()` method of the `Stream` API can help you.

To implement this example, you will use a subset of the **Amazon product co-purchasing network metadata** that includes information about 548,552 products sold by Amazon, which includes title, salesrank, and the lists of similar products, categories, and reviews. You can download this dataset from `https://snap.stanford.edu/data/amazon-meta.html`. We have taken the first 20,000 products and stored each product record in a separate file. We have changed the format of some of the fields to ease the data processing. All the fields have the `property:value` format.

Basic classes

We have some classes that are shared between the concurrent and serial versions. Let's see the details of each one.

The Product class

The `Product` class stores the information about a product. The following are the `Product` classes:

- `id`: This is a unique identifier of the product.
- `asin`: This is the Amazon standard identification number.
- `title`: This is the title of the product.
- `group`: This is the group of the product. This attribute can take the values `Baby Product`, `Book`, `CD`, `DVD`, `Music`, `Software`, `Sports`, `Toy`, `Video`, or `Video Games`.
- `salesrank`: This indicates the Amazon salesrank.
- `similar`: This is the number of similar items included in the file.
- `categories`: This is a list of `String` objects with the categories assigned to the product.
- `reviews`: This is a list of `Review` objects with the reviews (user and value) assigned to the product.

This class includes only the definition of the attributes and the corresponding `getXXX()` and `setXXX()` methods, so its source code is not included.

The Review class

As we mentioned earlier, the `Product` class includes a list of `Review` objects with the information of the reviews made by the users to a product. This class stores the information of each review in the following two attributes:

- `user`: The internal code of the user that made the review
- `value`: The score given by the user to the product

This class includes only the definition of the attributes and the corresponding `getXXX()` and `setXXX()` methods, so its source code is not included.

The ProductLoader class

The `ProductLoader` class allows you to load the information of a product from a file to a `Product` object. It implements the `load()` method that receives a `Path` object with the path to the file with the information of the product and returns a `Product` object. This is its source code:

```
public class ProductLoader {
    public static Product load(Path path) {
        try (BufferedReader reader =
          Files.newBufferedReader(path)) {
            Product product=new Product();
            String line=reader.readLine();
            product.setId(line.split(":")[1]);
            line=reader.readLine();
            product.setAsin(line.split(":")[1]);
            line=reader.readLine();
            product.setTitle(line.substring
                (line.indexOf(':')+1));
            line=reader.readLine();
            product.setGroup(line.split(":")[1]);
            line=reader.readLine();
            product.setSalesrank(Long.parseLong
                (line.split(":")[1]));
            line=reader.readLine();
            product.setSimilar(line.split(":")[1]);
            line=reader.readLine();

            int numItems=Integer.parseInt(line.split(":")[1]);

            for (int i=0; i<numItems; i++) {
                line=reader.readLine();
                product.addCategory(line.split(":")[1]);
```

```
            }

            line=reader.readLine();
            numItems=Integer.parseInt(line.split(":")[1]);
            for (int i=0; i<numItems; i++) {
                line=reader.readLine();
                String tokens[]=line.split(":");
                Review review=new Review();
                review.setUser(tokens[1]);
                review.setValue(Short.parseShort(tokens[2]));
                product.addReview(review);
            }
            return product;
        } catch (IOException x) {
            throw newe UncheckedIOException(x);
        }

    }
}
```

The first approach – basic search

The first approach receives a word as the input query and searches all the files that store the information of the products whether that word is included in one of the fields that define the product, no matter which. It will only show the name of the file that includes the word.

To implement this basic approach, we have implemented the `ConcurrentMainBasicSearch` class that implements the `main()` method. First, we initialize the query and the base path that stores all the files:

```
public class ConcurrentMainBasicSearch {

    public static void main(String args[]) {
        String query = args[0];
        Path file = Paths.get("data");
```

We need only one stream to generate a list of strings with the results as follows:

```
        try {
            Date start, end;
            start = new Date();
            ConcurrentLinkedDeque<String> results = Files
                    .walk(file, FileVisitOption.FOLLOW_LINKS)
                    .parallel()
```

```
            .filter(f -> f.toString().endsWith(".txt"))
            .collect(ArrayList<String>::new,
                    new ConcurrentStringAccumulator
                        (query),
                    List::addAll);
    end = new Date();
```

Our stream contains the following elements:

- We start the stream with the `walk()` method of the `Files` class passing the base `Path` object of our collection of files as a parameter. This method will return all the files as a stream and directories stored under that route.
- Then, we convert the stream into a concurrent one using the `parallel()` method.
- We are only interested in the files that ends with the `.txt` extension, so we filter them using the `filter()` method.
- Finally, we use the `collect()` method to convert the stream of `Path` objects into `ConcurrentLinkedDeque` of `String` objects with the names of the files.

We use the three parameters version of the `collect()` method using the following functional parameters:

- **Supplier**: We use the `new` method reference of the `ArrayList` class to create a new data structure per thread to store the corresponding results.
- **Accumulator**: We have implemented our own accumulator in the `ConcurrentStringAccumulator` class. We will describe the details of this class later.
- **Combiner**: We use the `addAll()` method of the `ConcurrentLinkedDeque` class to join two data structures. In this case, all the elements from the second collection will be added to the first one. The first collection will be used for further combining or as a final result.

Finally, we write the results obtained with the stream in the console:

```
            System.out.println("Results for Query: "+query);
            System.out.println("*************");
            results.forEach(System.out::println);
            System.out.println("Execution Time: "+(end.getTime()-
                start.getTime()));
        } catch (IOException e) {
            e.printStackTrace();
        }
    }
}
```

The accumulator functional parameter will be executed each time we want to process a path of the stream to evaluate whether we have to include its name into the result list. To implement this functionality, we have implemented the `ConcurrentStringAccumulator` class. Let's see the details of this class.

The ConcurrentStringAccumulator class

The `ConcurrentStringAccumulator` class loads a file with the information of a product to determine whether it contains the term of the query. It implements the `BiConsumer` interface because we want to use it as a parameter of the `collect()` method. We have parameterized that interface with the `List<String>` and `Path` classes:

```
public class ConcurrentStringAccumulator implements
   BiConsumer<List<String>, Path> {
```

It defines the query as an internal attribute that is initialized in the constructor as follows:

```
private String word;

public ConcurrentStringAccumulator (String word) {
    this.word=word.toLowerCase();
}
```

Then, we implement the `accept()` method defined in the `BiConsumer` interface. This method receives two parameters: one of the `ConcurrentLinkedDeque<String>` classes and one of the `Path` classes.

To load the file and determine whether it contains the query, we use the following stream:

```
@Override
public void accept(List<String> list, Path path) {
    boolean result;

try (Stream<String> lines = Files.lines(path)) {
        result = lines
                .parallel()
                .map(l -> l.split(":")[1].toLowerCase())
                .anyMatch(l -> l.contains(word))
```

Our stream contains the following elements:

- We create the stream of `String` objects using the `lines()` method of the `Files` class in a try-with-resources sentence. This method receives a `Path` object that points to a file as a parameter and returns a stream with all the lines of the file.
- Then, we use the `parallel()` method to convert the stream into a concurrent one.
- Then, we use the `map()` method to get the values of every property. As we mentioned in the introduction of this section, every line has the `property:value` format.
- Finally, we use the `anyMatch()` method to know whether there is any property whose value contains the query term.

If the counter variable has a value bigger than 0, the file contains the query term, and we include the name of the file in the `ConcurrentLinkedDeque` class with the results:

```
            if (counter>0) {
                list.add(path.toString());
            }
        } catch (Exception e) {
            System.out.println(path);
            e.printStackTrace();
        }
    }

}
```

The second approach – advanced search

Our basic search has some drawbacks:

- We look for the query term in all the properties, but maybe we only want to look for it in some of them, for example, in the title
- We only show the name of the file, but it would be more informative if we show additional information as the title of the product

To solve these problems, we are going to implement the `ConcurrentMainSearch` class that implements the `main()` method. First, we initialize the query and the base `Path` object that stores all the files:

```
public class ConcurrentMainSearch {
    public static void main(String args[]) {
        String query = args[0];
        Path file = Paths.get("data");
```

Then, we generate a `ConcurrentLinkedDeque` class of `Product` objects using the following stream:

```
try {
    Date start, end;
    start=new Date();
    ConcurrentLinkedDeque<Product> results = Files
            .walk(file, FileVisitOption.FOLLOW_LINKS)
            .parallel()
            .filter(f -> f.toString().endsWith(".txt"))
            .collect(ArrayList<Product>::new,
                    new ConcurrentObjectAccumulator
                        (query),
                    List::addAll);
    end=new Date();
```

This stream has the same elements as the one we implemented in the basic approach with the following two changes:

- In the `collect()` method, we use the `ConcurrentObjectAccumulator` class in the accumulator parameter
- We parameterize the `ConcurrentLinkedDeque` class with the `Product` one

Finally, we write the results in the console, but in this case, we write the title of each product:

```
    System.out.println("Results");
    System.out.println("*************");
    results.forEach(p ->
        System.out.println(p.getTitle()));
    System.out.println("Execution Time: "+(end.getTime()-
        start.getTime()));

    } catch (IOException e) {
        e.printStackTrace();
    }
  }
}
```

You can change this code to write whatever information about the product, as the salesrank or the categories.

The most important change between this implementation and the previous one is the `ConcurrentObjectAccumulator` class. Let's see the details of this class.

The ConcurrentObjectAccumulator class

The `ConcurrentObjectAccumulator` class implements the `BiConsumer` interface parameterized with the `ConcurrentLinkedDeque<Product>` and `Path` classes because we want to use it in the `collect()` method. It defines an internal attribute named `word` to store the query term. This attribute is initialized in the constructor of the class:

```
public class ConcurrentObjectAccumulator implements
        BiConsumer<List<Product>, Path> {

    private String word;

    public ConcurrentObjectAccumulator(String word) {
        this.word = word;
    }
```

The implementation of the `accept()` method (defined in the `BiConsumer` interface) is very simple:

```
@Override
public void accept(List<Product> list, Path path) {

    Product product=ProductLoader.load(path);

    if (product.getTitle().toLowerCase().contains
      (word.toLowerCase())) {
        list.add(product);
    }

}

}
```

The method receives the `Path` object that points to the file we are going to process as a parameter and the `ConcurrentLinkedDeque` class to store the results. We load the file in a `Product` object using the `ProductLoader` class and then check whether the title of the product contains the query term. If it contains the query, we add the `Product` object to the `ConcurrentLinkedDeque` class.

A serial implementation of the example

As with the rest of the examples in this book, we have implemented a serial version of both versions of the search operations to verify that the concurrent stream allows us to get an improvement of the performance.

You can implement the serial equivalent of the four classes described earlier by deleting the `parallel()` calls in the `Stream` objects to make the streams concurrent.

With the source code of the book, we have included the `SerialMainBasicSearch`, `SerialMainSearch`, `SerialStringAccumulator`, and `SerialObjectAccumulator` classes that are the serial equivalent ones with the changes commented earlier.

Comparing the implementations

We have tested our implementations (the two approaches: serial and concurrent versions) to compare their execution times. To test them, we have used three different queries:

- Patterns
- Java
- Tree

For every query, we have executed the two search operations (basic and object) for the serial and parallel stream. We have executed them using the JMH framework (http://openjdk.java.net/projects/code-tools/jmh/) that allows you to implement micro benchmarks in Java. Using a framework for benchmarking is a better solution that simply measures time using the methods such as `currentTimeMillis()` or `nanoTime()`. We have executed them 10 times in a computer with a four-core processor and calculated the medium execution time of those 10 times. These are the results in milliseconds:

	String search			Object search		
	Java	Patterns	Tree	Java	Patterns	Tree
Serial	4318.551	4372.565	4364.674	4573.985	4588.957	4591.100
Concurrent	32402.969	2428.729	2412.747	2190.053	2173.511	2173.936

We can draw the following conclusions:

- The results obtained with different queries are very similar
- With serial streams, the execution time of the string search is better than the execution time of the object search
- With concurrent streams, the execution time of the object search is better than the execution time of the string search
- Concurrent streams get better performance than serial ones in all cases

If we compare the concurrent and serial versions, for example, for the object search with the query patterns using the speed-up, we obtain the following result:

$$S = \frac{T_{serial}}{T_{concurrent}} = \frac{4588.957}{2173.511} = 2.11$$

The second example – a recommendation system

A **recommendation system** recommends a product or a service to a customer based on the products/services he has bought/used and on the products/services bought/used by the users that have bought/used the same services as him.

We have used the example explained in the previous section to implement a recommendation system. Each description of a product includes the reviews of a number of customers to a product. This review includes the score the customer gives to the product.

In this example, you will use these reviews to get a list of the products that may be interesting to a customer. We will obtain the list of the products purchased by a customer. In order to get that list, a list of the users who have purchased those products and the list of products purchased by those users are sorted using the average score given in the reviews. That will be the suggested products for the user.

Common classes

We have added two new classes to the ones used in the previous section. These classes are:

- `ProductReview`: This class extends the product class with two new attributes
- `ProductRecommendation`: This class stores the information of the recommendation of a product

Let's see the details of both classes.

The ProductReview class

The `ProductReview` class extends the `Product` class adding two new attributes:

- `buyer`: This attribute stores the name of a customer of the product
- `value`: This attribute stores the value given by this customer to the product in his review

The class includes the definition of the attributes: the corresponding `getXXX()` and `setXXX()` methods, a constructor to create a `ProductReview` object from a `Product` object, and the values for the new attributes. It's very simple, so its source code is not included.

The ProductRecommendation class

The `ProductRecommendation` class stores the necessary information for a product recommendation that includes the following:

- `title`: The title of the product we are recommending
- `value`: The score of that recommendation, which is calculated as the average score of all the reviews for that product

This class includes the definition of the attributes, the corresponding `getXXX()` and `setXXX()` methods, and the implementation of the `compareTo()` methods (the class implements the `Comparable` interface) that will allow us to sort the recommendations in descending order by its value. It's very simple, so its source code is not included.

The recommendation system – the main class

We have implemented our algorithm in the `ConcurrentMainRecommendation` class to obtain the list of recommended products to a customer. This class implements the `main()` method that receives as a parameter the ID of the customer whose recommended products we want to obtain. We have the following code:

```
public static void main(String[] args) {
    String user = args[0];
    Path file = Paths.get("data");
    try {
        Date start, end;
        start=new Date();
```

Processing Massive Datasets with Parallel Streams – The Map and Collect Model

We have used different stream to transform the data in the final solution. The first one loads the whole list of the `Product` objects from its files:

```
List<Product> productList = Files
    .walk(file, FileVisitOption.FOLLOW_LINKS)
    .parallel()
    .filter(f -> f.toString().endsWith(".txt"))
    .collect(ConcurrentLinkedDeque<Product>::new
      ,new ConcurrentLoaderAccumulator(),
        ConcurrentLinkedDeque::addAll);
```

This stream has the following elements:

- We start the stream with the `walk()` method of the `Files` class. This method will create a stream to process all the files and directories under the data directory.
- Then, we use the `parallel()` method to convert the stream into a concurrent one.
- Then, we get the files with the extension `.txt` only.
- Finally, we use the `collect()` method to obtain a `ConcurrentLinkedDeque` class of the `Product` objects. It's very similar to the one used in the previous section with the difference that we use another accumulator object. In this case, we use the `ConcurrentLoaderAccumulator` class that we will describe later.

Once we have the list of products, we are going to organize those products in a map using the identifier of the customer as the key for that map. We use the `ProductReview` class to store the information of the customers of the products. We will create as many `ProductReview` objects as reviews have a `Product`. We use the following stream to make the transformation:

```
Map<String, List<ProductReview>>
   productsByBuyer=productList
      .parallelStream()
      .<ProductReview>flatMap(p ->
         p.getReviews().stream().map(r -> new
         ProductReview(p, r.getUser(), r.getValue())))
      .collect(Collectors.groupingByConcurrent( p ->
         p.getBuyer()));
```

This stream has the following elements:

- We start stream with the `parallelStream()` method of the `productList` object, so we create a concurrent stream.
- Then, we use the `flatMap()` method to convert the stream of `Product` objects we have into a unique stream of `ProductReview` objects.
- Finally, we use the `collect()` method to generate the final map. In this case, we have used the predefined collector generated by the `groupingByConcurrent()` method of the `Collectors` class. The returned collector will generate a map where the keys will be the different values of the buyer attributes and the values of a list of `ProductReview` objects with the information of the products purchased by that user. This transformation will be done, as the method name indicates, in a concurrent way.

The next stream is the most important stream of this example. We take the products purchased by a customer and generate the recommendations to that customer. It's a two-phase process made by one stream. In the first phase, we obtain the users that purchased the products purchased by the original customer. In the second phase, we generate a map with the products purchased by those customers with all the reviews of the products made by those customers. This is the code for that stream:

```
Map<String,List<ProductReview>>
    recommendedProducts=productsByBuyer.get(user)
        .parallelStream()
        .map(p -> p.getReviews())
        .flatMap(Collection::stream)
        .map(r -> r.getUser())
        .distinct()
        .map(productsByBuyer::get)
        .flatMap(Collection::stream)
        .collect(Collectors.groupingByConcurrent(p ->
           p.getTitle()));
```

We have the following elements in that stream:

- First, we get the list of products purchased by the user and generate a concurrent stream using the `parallelStream()` method.
- Then, we get all the reviews for that products using the `map()` method.
- At this moment, we have a stream of `List<Review>`. We convert that stream into a stream of `Review` objects. Now we have a stream with all the reviews of the products purchased by the user.

- Then, we transform that stream into a stream of `String` objects with the names of the users who made the reviews.
- Then, we get the unique names of the users with the `distinct()` method. Now we have a stream of `String` objects with the names of the users who purchased the same products as the original user.
- Then, we use the `map()` method to transform each customer into its list of purchased products.
- At this moment, we have a stream of `List<ProductReview>` objects. We convert that stream into a stream of `ProductReview` objects using the `flatMap()` method.
- Finally, we generate a map of products using the `collect()` method and the `groupingByConcurrent()` collector. The keys of the map will be the title of the product and the values of the list of `ProductReview` objects with the reviews made by the customers obtained earlier.

To finish our recommendation algorithm, we need one last step. For every product, we want to calculate its average score in the reviews and sort the list in descending order to show in the first place the top-rated products. To make that transformation, we use an additional stream:

```
            List<ProductRecommendation> recommendations =
            recommendedProducts
                    .entrySet()
                    .parallelStream()
                    .map(entry -> new
                    ProductRecommendation(
                        entry.getKey(),
                        entry.getValue().stream().mapToInt(p ->
                            p.getValue()).average().getAsDouble()))
                    .sorted()
                    .collect(Collectors.toList());
        end=new Date();
        recommendations. forEach(pr -> System.out.println
           (pr.getTitle()+": "+pr.getValue()));

            System.out.println("Execution Time: "+(end.getTime()-
               start.getTime()));

        } catch (IOException e) {
            e.printStackTrace();
        }
    }
}
```

We process the map obtained in the previous step. For each product, we process its list of reviews generating a `ProductRecommendation` object. The value of this object is calculated as the average value of each review using a stream using the `mapToInt()` method to transform the stream of `ProductReview` objects into a stream of integers and the `average()` method to get the average value of all the numbers in the string.

Finally, in the recommendations `ConcurrentLinkedDeque` class, we have a list of `ProductRecommendation` objects. We sort that list using an other stream with the `sorted()` method. We use that stream to write the final list in the console.

The ConcurrentLoaderAccumulator class

To implement this example, we have used the `ConcurrentLoaderAccumulator` class used as the accumulator function in the `collect()` method that transforms the stream of `Path` objects with the routes of all the files to process into the `ConcurrentLinkedDeque` class of `Product` objects. This is the source code of this class:

```
public class ConcurrentLoaderAccumulator implements
        BiConsumer<ConcurrentLinkedDeque<Product>, Path> {

    @Override
    public void accept(ConcurrentLinkedDeque<Product> list, Path
      path) {

        Product product=ProductLoader.load(path);
        list.add(product);

    }
}
```

It implements the `BiConsumer` interface. The `accept()` method uses the `ProducLoader` class (explained earlier in this chapter) to load the product information from the file and add the resultant `Product` object in the `ConcurrentLinkedDeque` class received as parameters.

The serial version

As with other examples in the book, we have implemented a serial version of this example to check that parallel streams improve the performance of the application. To implement this serial version, we have to follow these steps:

- Replace the `ConcurrentLinkedDeque` data structure by the `List` or `ArrayList` data structures
- Change the `parallelStrem()` method by the `stream()` method
- Change the `gropingByConcurrent()` method by the `groupingBy()` method

You can see the serial version of this example in the source code of the book.

Comparing the two versions

To compare the serial and concurrent versions of our recommendation system, we have obtained the recommended products for three users:

- A2JOYUS36FLG4Z
- A2JW67OY8U6HHK
- A2VE83MZF98ITY

For these three users, we have executed both versions using the JMH framework (http://openjdk.java.net/projects/code-tools/jmh/) that allows you to implement micro benchmarks in Java. Using a framework for benchmarking is a better solution that simply measures time using the methods such as `currentTimeMillis()` or `nanoTime()`. We have executed them 10 times in a computer with a four-core processor and calculated the medium execution time of those 10 times. These are the results in milliseconds:

	A2JOYUS36FLG4Z	A2JW67OY8U6HHK	A2VE83MZF98ITY
Serial	4848.672	4830.051	4817.216
Concurrent	2454.003	2458.003	2527.194

We can draw the following conclusions:

- The results obtained are very similar for the three users
- The execution time of concurrent streams is always better than the execution time of the sequential ones

If we compare the concurrent and serial versions, for example, the second user using the speed-up, we obtain the following result:

$$S = \frac{T_{serial}}{T_{concurrent}} = \frac{4830.051}{2458.03} = 1.97$$

The third example – common contacts in a social network

Social networks are transforming our society and the way people relate to each other. Fackebook, Linkedin, Twitter, or Instagram have millions of users who use these networks to share life moments with their friends, make new professional contacts, promote their professional brand, meet new people, or simply know the latest trends in the world.

We can see a social network as a graph where users are the nodes of the graph and relations between users are the arcs of the graph. As occurs with graphs, there are social networks such as Facebook, where relations between users are undirected or bidirectional. If user *A* is connected with user *B*, user *B* is connected with *A* too. On the contrary, there are social networks such as Twitter where relations between users are directed. We say in this case that user *A* follows user *B*, but the contrary is not necessarily true.

In this section, we are going to implement an algorithm to calculate the common contacts for every pair of users in a social network with bidirectional relations between users. We are going to implement the algorithm described in http://stevekrenzel.com/finding-friends-with-mapreduce. The main steps of that algorithm are as follows.

Our data source will be a file where we store every user with their contacts:

```
A-B,C,D,
B-A,C,D,E,
C-A,B,D,E,
D-A,B,C,E,
E-B,C,D,
```

This means that user A has users B, C, and D as contacts. Take into account that the relations are bidirectional, so if B is a contact for A, A will be a contact for B too and both relations have to be represented in the file. So, we have elements with the following two parts:

- A user identifier
- The list of contacts for that user

In the next step, we generate a set of elements with three parts per every element. The three parts are:

- A user identifier
- The user identifier of a friend
- The list of contacts for that user

Thus, for user A, we will generate the following elements:

```
A-B-B,C,D
A-C-B,C,D
A-D-B,C,D
```

We follow the same process for all the elements. We are going to store the two user identifiers alphabetically sorted. Thus, for user B, we generate the following elements:

```
A-B-A,C,D,E
B-C-A,C,D,E
B-D-A,C,D,E
B-E-A,C,D,E
```

Once we have generated all the new elements, we group them for the two user identifiers. For example, for the tuple A-B we will generate the following group:

```
A-B-(B,C,D),(A,C,D,E)
```

Finally, we calculate the intersection between the two lists. The resultant lists are the common contacts between the two users. For example, users A and B have in common the contacts C and D.

To test our algorithm, we have used two datasets:

- The test sample presented earlier.
- The social circles: the Facebook dataset that you can download from https://snap.stanford.edu/data/egonets-Facebook.html contains the contact information of 4,039 users from Facebook. We have transformed the original data into the data format used by our example.

Base classes

As with other examples in the book, we have implemented the serial and concurrent versions of this example to verify that parallel streams improve the performance of our application. Both versions share some classes.

The Person class

The `Person` class stores the information about every person in the social network that includes the following:

- It's user ID, stored in the ID attribute
- The list of contacts of that user, stored as a list of `String` objects in the contacts attribute

The class declares both attributes and the corresponding `getXXX()` and `setXXX()` methods. We also need a constructor to create the list and a method named `addContact()` to add a single contact to the list of contacts. The source code of this class is very simple, so it won't be included here.

The PersonPair class

The `PersonPair` class extends the `Person` class adding the attribute to store the second user identifier. We called this attribute `otherId`. This class declares the attribute and implements the corresponding `getXXX()` and `setXXX()` methods. We need an additional method named `getFullId()` that returns a string with the two user identifiers separated by a `,` character. The source code of this class is very simple, so it won't be included here.

The DataLoader class

The `DataLoader` class loads the file with the information of the users and their contacts and converts it into a list of `Person` objects. It implements only a static method named `load()` that receives the path of the file as a `String` object as a parameter and returns the list of `Person` objects.

As we mentioned earlier, the file has the following format:

```
User-C1,C2,C3...CN
```

Here, `User` is the identifier of the user, and `C1`, `C2`, `C3`…. `CN` are the identifiers of the contacts of that user.

The source code of this class is very simple, so it won't be included here.

The concurrent version

First, let's analyze the concurrent version of this algorithm.

The CommonPersonMapper class

The `CommonPersonMapper` class is an auxiliary class that will be used later. It will generate all the `PersonPair` objects you can generate from a `Person` object. This class implements the `Function` interface parameterized with the `Person` and `List<PersonPair>` classes.

It implements the `apply()` method defined in the `Function` interface. First, we initialize the `List<PersonPair>` object that we're going to return and obtain and sort the list of contacts for the person:

```
public class CommonPersonMapper implements Function<Person,
    List<PersonPair>> {

    @Override
    public List<PersonPair> apply(Person person) {

        List<PersonPair> ret=new ArrayList<>();

        List<String> contacts=person.getContacts();
        Collections.sort(contacts);
```

Then, we process the whole list of contacts creating the `PersonPair` object per contact. As we mentioned earlier, we store the two contacts sorted in alphabetical order. The lesser one in the ID field and the other in the `otherId` field:

```
        for (String contact : contacts) {
            PersonPair personExt=new PersonPair();
            if (person.getId().compareTo(contact) < 0) {
                personExt.setId(person.getId());
                personExt.setOtherId(contact);
            } else {
                personExt.setId(contact);
                personExt.setOtherId(person.getId());
            }
```

Finally, we add the list of contacts to the new object and the object to the list of results. Once we have processed all the contacts, we return the list of results:

```
            personExt.setContacts(contacts);
            ret.add(personExt);
        }
        return ret;
    }
}
```

The ConcurrentSocialNetwork class

The `ConcurrentSocialNetwork` is the main class of this example. It implements only a static method named `bidirectionalCommonContacts()`. This method receives the list of persons of the social network with their contacts and returns a list of `PersonPair` objects with the common contacts between every pair of users who are contacts.

Internally, we use two different streams to implement our algorithm. We use the first one to transform the input list of `Person` objects into a map. The keys of this map will be the two identifiers of every pair of users, and the value will be a list of `PersonPair` objects with the contacts of both users. So, these lists will always have two elements. We have the following code:

```
public class ConcurrentSocialNetwork {

    public static List<PersonPair> bidirectionalCommonContacts(
            List<Person> people) {

        Map<String, List<PersonPair>> group =
          people.parallelStream()
                .map(new CommonPersonMapper())
                .flatMap(Collection::stream)
                .collect(Collectors.groupingByConcurrent
                    (PersonPair::getFullId));
```

This stream has the following components:

- We create the stream using the `parallelStream()` method of the input list.
- Then, we use the `map()` method and the `CommonPersonMapper` class explained earlier to transform every `Person` object in a list of `PersonPair` objects with all the possibilities for that object.
- At this moment, we have a stream of `List<PersonPair>` objects. We use the `flatMap()` method to convert that stream into a stream of `PersonPair` objects.
- Finally, we use the `collect()` method to generate the map using the collector returned by the `groupingByConcurrent()` method using the value returned by the `getFullId()` method as the keys for the map.

Then, we create a new collector using the `of()` method of the `Collectors` class. This collector will receive a `Collection` of string as input, use an `AtomicReference<Collection<String>>` as intermediate data structure, and return a `Collection` of string as the return type.

```
Collector<Collection<String>,
  AtomicReference<Collection<String>>, Collection<String>>
  intersecting = Collector.of(
        () -> new AtomicReference<>(null), (acc, list) ->
        {
          acc.updateAndGet(set -> set == null ? new
            ConcurrentLinkedQueue<>(list) :
            set).retainAll(list);
        }, (acc1, acc2) -> {
          if (acc1.get() == null)
            return acc2;
          if (acc2.get() == null)
            return acc1;
          acc1.get().retainAll(acc2.get());
          return acc1;
        }, (acc) -> acc.get() == null ?
          Collections.emptySet() : acc.get(),
          Collector.Characteristics.CONCURRENT,
          Collector.Characteristics.UNORDERED);
```

The first parameter of the `of()` method is the supplier function. This supplier is called always when we need to create an intermediate structure of data. In serial streams, this method is called only once, but in concurrent streams, this method will be called once per thread.

```
() -> new AtomicReference<>(null),
```

In our case, we simply create a new `AtomicReference` to store the `Collection<String>` object.

The second parameter of the `of()` method is the accumulator function. This function receives an intermediate data structure and an input value as parameters:

```
(acc, list) -> {
    acc.updateAndGet(set -> set == null ? new
        ConcurrentLinkedQueue<>(list) : set).retainAll(list);
},
```

In our case, the `acc` parameter is an `AtomicReference` and the `list` parameter is a `ConcurrentLinkedDeque`. We use the `updateAndGet()` method of the `AtomicReference`. This method updates the current value and returns the new value. If the `AtomicReference` is `null`, we create a new `ConcurrentLinkedDeque` with the elements of the list. If the `AtomicReference` is not null, it will store a `ConcurrentLinkedDeque`. We use the `retainAll()` method to add all the elements of the list.

The third parameter of the `of()` method is the combiner function. This function is only called in parallel streams, and it receives two intermediate data structures as a parameter to generate only one.

```
(acc1, acc2) -> {
    if (acc1.get() == null)
        return acc2;
    if (acc2.get() == null)
        return acc1;
    acc1.get().retainAll(acc2.get());
    return acc1;
},
```

In our case, if one of the parameters is null, we return the other. Otherwise, we use the `retainAll()` method in the `acc1` parameter and returns the result.

The fourth parameter of the `of()` method is the finisher function. This function converts the final intermediate data structure in the data structure we want to return. In our case, the intermediate and final data structures are the same, so no conversion is needed.

```
(acc) -> acc.get() == null ? Collections.emptySet() : acc.get(),
```

Finally, we use the last parameter to indicate to the collector that the collector is concurrent, that is to say, the accumulator function can be called concurrently with the same result container from multiple threads, and unordered, that is to say, this operation will not preserve the original order of the elements.

As we have defined the collector now, we have to convert the map generated with the first stream into a list of `PersonPair` objects with the common contacts of each pair of users. We use the following code:

```
        List<PersonPair> peopleCommonContacts = group.entrySet()
            .parallelStream()
          .map((entry) -> {
            Collection<String> commonContacts =
              entry.getValue()
                .parallelStream()
                .map(p -> p.getContacts())
                .collect(intersecting);
            PersonPair person = new PersonPair();
            person.setId(entry.getKey().split(",")[0]);
            person.setOtherId(entry.getKey().split
              (",")[1]);
            person.setContacts(new ArrayList<String>
              (commonContacts));
            return person;
          }).collect(Collectors.toList());

      return peopleCommonContacts;
    }
  }
```

We use the `entySet()` method to process all the elements of the map. We create a `parallelStream()` method to process all the `Entry` objects and then use the `map()` method to convert every list of `PersonPair` objects into a unique `PersonPair` object with the common contacts.

For each entry, the key is the identifier of a pair of users concatenated with, as separator and the value is a list of two `PersonPair` objects. The first one contains the contacts of one user, and the other contains the contacts of the other user.

We create a stream for that list to generate the common contacts of both users with the following elements:

- We create the stream using the `parallelStream()` method of the list
- We use the `map()` method to replace each `PersonPair()` object for the list of contacts stored in it
- Finally, we use our collector to generate `ConcurrentLinkedDeque` with the common contacts

Finally, we create a new `PersonPair` object with the identifier of both users and the list of common contacts. We add that object to the list of results. When all the elements of the map have been processed, we can return the list of results.

The ConcurrentMain class

The `ConcurrentMain` class implements the `main()` method to test our algorithm. As we mentioned earlier, we have tested it with the following two datasets:

- A very simple dataset to test the correctness of the algorithm
- A dataset based on real data from Facebook

This is the source code of this class:

```
public class ConcurrentMain {

    public static void main(String[] args) {

        Date start, end;
        System.out.println("Concurrent Main Bidirectional - 
          Test");
        List<Person> people=DataLoader.load("data","test.txt");
        start=new Date();
        List<PersonPair> peopleCommonContacts=
          ConcurrentSocialNetwork.bidirectionalCommonContacts
          (people);
        end=new Date();
        peopleCommonContacts.forEach(p -> System.out.println
          (p.getFullId()+": "+getContacts(p.getContacts())));
        System.out.println("Execution Time: "+(end.getTime()-
          start.getTime())); 

        System.out.println("Concurrent Main Bidirectional - 
          Facebook");
        people=DataLoader.load("data","facebook_contacts.txt");
        start=new Date();
```

```
            peopleCommonContacts=
              ConcurrentSocialNetwork.bidirectionalCommonContacts
              (people);
            end=new Date();
            peopleCommonContacts.forEach(p -> System.out.println
              (p.getFullId()+": "+getContacts(p.getContacts())));
            System.out.println("Execution Time: "+(end.getTime()-
              start.getTime()));

        }

        private static String formatContacts(List<String> contacts) {
            StringBuffer buffer=new StringBuffer();
            for (String contact: contacts) {
                buffer.append(contact+",");
            }
            return buffer.toString();
        }
}
```

The serial version

As with other examples in this book, we have implemented a serial version of this example. This version is equal to the concurrent one making the following changes:

- Replace the `parallelStream()` method by the `stream()` method
- Replace the `ConcurrentLinkedDeque` data structure by the `ArrayList` data structure
- Replace the `groupingByConcurrent()` method by the `groupingBy()` method
- Don't use the final parameter in the `of()` method

Comparing the two versions

We have executed both versions with both datasets using the JMH framework (http://openjdk.java.net/projects/code-tools/jmh/) that allows you to implement micro benchmarks in Java. Using a framework for benchmarking is a better solution that simply measures time using methods such as `currentTimeMillis()` or `nanoTime()`. We have executed them 10 times in a computer with a four-core processor and calculated the medium execution time of those 10 times. These are the results in milliseconds:

	Example	Facebook
Serial	0.861	7002.485
Concurrent	1.352	5303.990

We can draw the following conclusions:

- For the example dataset, the serial version obtains a better execution time. The reason for this result is that the example dataset has few elements.
- For the Facebook dataset, the concurrent version obtains a better execution time.

If we compare the concurrent and serial versions for the Facebook dataset, we obtain the following results:

$$S = \frac{T_{serial}}{T_{concurrent}} = \frac{7002.485}{5303.990} = 1.32$$

Summary

In this chapter, we used the different versions of the `collect()` method provided by the `Stream` framework to transform and group the elements of a `Stream`. This and *Chapter 7, Processing Massive Datasets with Parallel Streams – The Map and Reduce Model*, teach you how to work with the whole stream API.

Basically, the `collect()` method needs a collector that processes the data of the stream and generates a data structure returned by the set of aggregate operations that forms the stream. A collector works with three different data structures — the class of the input elements, an intermediate data structure used while processing the input elements, and a final data structure that is returned.

We used the different versions of the `collect()` method to implement a search tool that must look for a query in a set of files without an inverted index, a recommendation system, and a tool to calculate the common contacts between two users in a social network.

In the next chapter, we will take a deep look at the concurrent data structures and synchronization mechanisms provided by the Java concurrent API.

9
Diving into Concurrent Data Structures and Synchronization Utilities

Among of the most important elements in every computer program are **data structures**. Data structures allow us to store the data that our applications read, transform, and write in different ways according to our needs. The selection of an adequate data structure is a critical point to get good performance. A bad choice can degrade the performance of an algorithm considerably. Java concurrency API includes some data structures designed to be used in concurrent applications without provoking data inconsistencies or loss of information.

Another critical point in concurrent applications are **synchronization mechanisms**. You use them to implement mutual exclusion by creating a critical section, that is to say, a piece of code that can only be executed by one thread at a time. But you can also use synchronization mechanisms to implement dependencies between threads when, for example, a concurrent task must wait for the finalization of another task. Java concurrency API includes basic synchronization mechanisms, like the synchronized keyword and very high-level utilities, such as the CyclicBarrier class or the Phaser class you used in *Chapter 5, Running Tasks Divided into Phases – The Phaser Class*.

In this chapter, we will cover the following topics:

- Concurrent data structures
- Synchronization mechanisms

Concurrent data structures

Every computer program works with data. They get the data from a database, a file, or another source, transform that data, and then write the transformed data into a database, a file, or another destination. The programs work with data stored in memory and use data structures to store the data in memory.

When you implement a concurrent application, you must be very careful with the utilization of data structures. If different threads can modify the data stored in a unique data structure, you have to use a synchronization mechanism to protect the modifications over that data structure. If you don't do this, you can have a data race condition. Your application may sometimes work correctly, but next time may crash with a random exception, stuck in an infinite loop, or silently produce an incorrect result. The outcome will depend on the order of execution.

To avoid data race conditions you can:

- Use a non-synchronized data structure and add the synchronization mechanisms by yourself
- Use a data structure provided by the Java concurrency API that implements the synchronization mechanism internally and is optimized to be used in concurrent applications

The second option is the most recommended. Through the pages of this section, you will review the most important concurrent data structures giving special importance to Java 8's new features.

Blocking and non-blocking data structures

Java concurrency API provides two kinds of concurrent data structures:

- **Blocking data structures**: This kind of data structure provides methods to insert and delete data on it where, when the operation cannot be done immediately (for example, if you want to take an element and the data structure is empty), the thread that made the call will be blocked until the operation can be done
- **Non-blocking data structures**: This kind of data structure provides methods to insert and delete data on it that, when the operation cannot be done immediately, return a special value or throw an exception

Sometimes, we have a non-blocking equivalent for the blocking data structure. For example, the ConcurrentLinkedDeque class is a non-blocking data structure and the LinkedBlockingDeque is the blocking equivalent. Blocking data structures have methods that behave like non-blocking data structures. For example, the Deque interface defines the pollFirst() method that does not block returns null if the deque is empty. Every blocking queue implementation implements this method as well.

The **Java collections framework (JCF)** provides a set of different data structures that can be used in sequential programming. The Java concurrent API extends those structures, providing others that can be used in concurrent applications. This includes:

- **Interfaces**: This extends the interfaces provided by the JCF, adding some methods that can be used in concurrent applications
- **Classes**: This implements the previous interfaces to provide implementations that can be used in the applications

In the following sections, we make an introduction to the interfaces and classes you can use in concurrent applications.

Interfaces

First, let's describe the most important interfaces implemented by the concurrent data structures.

BlockingQueue

A **queue** is a linear data structure that allows you to insert elements at the end of the queue and get elements from the start. It's a **First-In-First-Out (FIFO)** data structure where the first elements introduced in the queue are the first ones that are processed.

The JCF defines the Queue interface that defines the basic operations to be implemented in a queue. This interface provides methods to:

- Insert an element at the end of the queue
- Retrieve and remove an element from the head of the queue
- Retrieve without removing an element from the head of the queue

The interface defines two versions of these methods that have different behaviors when the method can be done (for example, if you want to retrieve an element of an empty queue):

- Methods that throw an exception
- Methods that return a special value, for example `false` or `null`

The next table includes the names of the methods for every operation:

Operation	Exception	Special value
Insert	`add()`	`offer()`
Retrieve and remove	`remove()`	`poll()`
Retrieve but don't remove	`element()`	`peek()`

The `BlockingDeque` interface extends the `Queue` interface, adding methods that block the calling thread if the operation can be done. These methods are:

Operation	Blocks
Insert	`put()`
Retrieve and remove	`take()`
Retrieve without removing	N/A

BlockingDeque

A **deque** is a linear data structure, like the queue, but allows you to insert and delete elements from both sides of the data structure. The JCF defines the `Deque` interface that extends the `Queue` interface. In addition to the methods provided by the `Queue` interface, it provides methods to insert, retrieve and remove, and retrieve without removing at both ends:

Operation	Exception	Special value
Insert	`addFirst()`, `addLast()`	`offerFirst()`, `offerLast()`
Retrieve and remove	`removeFirst()`, `removeLast()`	`pollFirst()`, `pollLast()`
Retrieve without removing	`getFirst()`, `getLast()`	`peekFirst()`, `peekLast()`

The `BlockingDeque` interface extends the `Deque` interface, adding the methods that block the calling threads when the operation can't be done:

Operation	Blocks
Insert	`putFirst()`, `putLast()`
Retrieve and remove	`takeFirst()`, `takeLast()`
Retrieve without removing	N/A

ConcurrentMap

A **map** (sometimes also called an **associative array**) is a data structure that allows you to store (key, value) pairs. The JCF provides the `Map` interface that defines the basic operations to work with the map. This includes methods to:

- `put()`: Insert a (key, value) pair into the map
- `get()`: Return the value associated with a key
- `remove()`: Remove the (key, value) pair associated with the specified key
- `containsKey()` and `containsValue()`: Return true if the map contains the specified key of the value

This interface has been modified in Java 8 to include the following new methods. You will learn how to work with these methods later in this chapter:

- `forEach()`: This method executes the given function over all the elements of the map.
- `compute()`, `computeIfAbsent()`, and `computeIfPresent()`: These methods allows you to specify a function that calculates the new value associated with a key.
- `merge()`: This method allows you to specify merging a (key, value) pair into an existing map. If the key isn't in the map, it's inserted directly. If not, the function specified is executed.

`ConcurrentMap` extends the `Map` interface to provide the same methods to concurrent applications. Notice that in Java 8 (unlike Java 7), the `ConcurrentMap` interface doesn't add new methods to the `Map` interface.

TransferQueue

This interface extends the `BlockingQueue` interface and adds methods to transfer elements from producers to consumers, where producers can wait until a consumer takes off its element. The new methods added by this interface are:

- `transfer()`: Transfer an element to a consumer and wait (blocking the calling thread) until the element is consumed.
- `tryTransfer()`: Transfer an element if there is a consumer waiting. If not, this method returns the `false` value and doesn't insert the element in the queue.

Classes

The Java concurrency API provides different implementations of the interfaces described before. Some of them don't add any new characteristics but others add new interesting functionality.

LinkedBlockingQueue

This class implements the `BlockingQueue` interface to provide a queue with blocking methods that optionally can have a limited number of elements. It also implements the `Queue`, `Collection`, and `Iterable` interfaces.

ConcurrentLinkedQueue

This class implements the `Queue` interface to provide a thread-save unlimited queue. Internally, it uses a non-blocking algorithm to guarantee that there won't be a data race in your application.

LinkedBlockingDeque

This class implements the `BlockingDeque` interface to provide a deque with blocking methods that optionally can have a limited number of elements. It has more functionality than `LinkedBlockingQueue` but may have more overhead, thus `LinkedBlockingQueue` should be used when deque features are unnecessary.

ConcurrentLinkedDeque

This class implements the `Deque` interface to provide a thread-save unlimited deque that allows you to add and delete elements at both ends of the deque. It has more functionality than `ConcurrentLinkedQueue`, but may have more overhead as occurs with `LinkedBlockingDeque`.

ArrayBlockingQueue

This class implements the `BlockingQueue` interface to provide an implementation of a blocking queue with a limited number of elements based on an array. It also implements the `Queue`, `Collection`, and `Iterable` interfaces. Unlike non-concurrent array-based data structures (`ArrayList` and `ArrayDeque`), `ArrayBlockingQueue` allocates an array of a fixed size specified in the constructor and never resizes it.

DelayQueue

This class implements the `BlockingDeque` interface to provide an implementation of a queue with blocking methods and an unlimited number of elements. The elements of this queue must implement the `Delayed` interface, so they have to implement the `getDelay()` method. If that method returns a negative or zero value, the delay has expired and the element can be taken of the queue. The head of the queue is the element with the most negative value of delay.

LinkedTransferQueue

This class provide an implementation of the `TransferQueue` interface. It provides a blocking queue with an unlimited number of elements, and with the possibility of using them as a communication channel between producers and consumer where producers can wait for consumers to process their elements.

PriorityBlockingQueue

This class provide an implementation of the `BlockingQueue` interface where the elements can be polled according to their natural order or by a comparator specified in the constructor of the class. The head of this queue is determined by the sorting order of the elements.

ConcurrentHashMap

This class provides an implementation of the `ConcurrentMap` interface. It provides a thread-safe hash table. In addition to the methods added in the `Map` interface in the Java 8 version, this class has added other ones:

- `search()`, `searchEntries()`, `searchKeys()`, and `searchValues()`: These methods allows you to apply a search function over the (key, value) pairs, over the keys, or over the values. The search function can be a lambda expression, and the method ends when the search function returns a not-null value. That is the result of the execution of the method.

- `reduce()`, `reduceEntries()`, `reduceKeys()`, and `reduceValues()`: These methods allows you to apply a `reduce()` operation to transform the (key, value) pairs, the keys, or the entries as occurs with streams (Refer to *Chapter 8, Processing Massive Datasets with Parallel Streams – The Map and Collect Model* to get more details about the `reduce()` method).

More methods have been added (`forEachValue`, `forEachKey`, and so on), but they are not covered here.

Using the new features

In this section, you will learn how to use the new features introduced in Java 8 to the concurrent data structures.

First example with ConcurrentHashMap

In *Chapter 8, Processing Massive Datasets with Parallel Streams – The Map and Collect Model*, you implemented an application to make a search in a dataset from 20,000 Amazon products. We have taken that information from the Amazon product co-purchasing network metadata, which includes information about 548,552 products including title, salesrank, and similar products. You can download this dataset from https://snap.stanford.edu/data/amazon-meta.html. In that example, you used a `ConcurrentHashMap<String, List<ExtendedProduct>>` named `productsByBuyer` to store information about the products purchased by a user. The keys of this map are the identifier of the user, and the values a list of the products purchased by the user. You're going to use that map to learn how to work with the new methods of the `ConcurrentHashMap` class.

The forEach() method

This method allows you to specify a function that will be executed on every (key, value) pair of `ConcurrentHashMap`. There are many versions of this method, but the most basic version has only a `BiConsumer` function that can be expressed as a lambda expression. For example, you can use this method to print how many products every user has purchased, using the following code:

```
productsByBuyer.forEach( (id, list) ->
   System.out.println(id+": "+list.size()));
```

This basic version is a part of the usual `Map` interface and is always executed sequentially. In this code, we have used a lambda expression where `id` is the key of the element and `list` is the value of the element.

In this other example, we have used the `forEach()` method to calculate the average rating given per every user.

```
productsByBuyer.forEach( (id, list) -> {
    double average=list.stream().mapToDouble(item ->
       item.getValue()).average().getAsDouble();
    System.out.println(id+": "+average);
});
```

In this code, we have also used a lambda expression where `id` is the key of the element and `list` is its value. We have used a stream applied to the list of products to calculate the average rating.

Other versions of this method are as follows:

- `forEach(parallelismThreshold, action)`: This is the version of the method you have to use in concurrent applications. If the map has more elements than the number specified in the first parameter, this method will be executed in parallel.
- `forEachEntry(parallelismThreshold, action)`: The same as the previous, but in this case the action is an implementation of the `Consumer` interface that receives a `Map.Entry` object with the key and the value of the element. You can also use a lambda expression in this case.
- `forEachKey(parallelismThreshold, action)`: The same as the previous, but in this case the action will be applied only over the keys of `ConcurrentHashMap`.
- `forEachValue(parallelismThreshold, action)`: The same as the previous, but in this case the action will be applied only over the values of `ConcurrentHashMap`.

Current implementation uses the common `ForkJoinPool` instance to execute the parallel tasks.

The search() method

This method applies a search function to all the elements of `ConcurrentHashMap`. This search function can return a null value or a value different from null. The `search()` method will return the first non-null value returned by the search function. This method receives two parameters:

- `parallelismThreshold`: If the map has more elements than the number specified by this parameter, this method will be executed in parallel.

- **searchFunction**: This is an implementation of the `BiFunction` interface that can be expressed as a lambda expression. This function receives as parameters the key and the value of each element and, as we mentioned before, has to return a non-null value if you find what you are searching for and a null value if you don't.

For example, you can use this function to find the first book that contains a word:

```
ExtendedProduct firstProduct=productsByBuyer.search(100,
    (id, products) -> {
        for (ExtendedProduct product: products) {
            if (product.getTitle()
                .toLowerCase().contains("java")) {
                return product;
            }
        }
    return null;
});
if (firstProduct!=null) {
    System.out.println(firstProduct.getBuyer()+":"+
        firstProduct.getTitle());
}
```

In this case, we use 100 as `parallelismThreshold` and a lambda expression to implement the search function. In this function, for every element, we process all the products of the list. If we find a product that contains the word `java`, we return that product. This is the value returned by the `search()` method. Finally, we write the buyer and the title of the product in the console.

There are other versions of this method:

- `searchEntries(parallelismThreshold, searchFunction)`: In this case, the search function is an implementation of the `Function` interface that receives as a parameter a `Map.Entry` object
- `searchKeys(parallelismThreshold, searchFunction)`: In this case, the search function is applied only over the keys of `ConcurrentHashMap`
- `searchValues(parallelismThreshold, searchFunction)`: In this case, the search function is applied only over the values of `ConcurrentHashMap`

The reduce() method

This method is similar to the `reduce()` method provided by the `Stream` framework, but in this case you work directly with the elements of `ConcurrentHashMap`. This method receive three parameters:

- `parallelismThreshold`: If `ConcurrentHashMap` has more elements than the number specified in this parameter, this method will be executed in parallel.
- `transformer`: This parameter is an implementation of the `BiFunction` interface that can be expressed as a lambda function. It receives as a parameter a key and a value and returns a transformation of these elements.
- `reducer`: This parameter is an implementation of the `BiFunction` interface that can be expressed as a lambda function too. It receives as parameters two objects returned by the transformer function. The objective of this function is to group those two objects into a single one.

As an example of this method, we will obtain a list of products that have a review with a value of 1 (the worst value). We have used two auxiliary variables. The first one is `transformer`. It is a `BiFunction` interface that we will use as the `transformer` element of the `reduce()` method:

```
BiFunction<String, List<ExtendedProduct>, List<ExtendedProduct>>
    transformer = (key, value) -> value.stream().filter(product ->
    product.getValue() == 1).collect(Collectors.toList());
```

This function will receive the key, which is the `id` of a user, and a list of `ExtendedProduct` objects with the products purchased by that user. We process all the products of the list and return the products that have a rating of one.

The second variable is the reducer `BinaryOperator`. We use it as the reducer function of the `reduce()` method:

```
BinaryOperator<List<ExtendedProduct>> reducer = (list1, list2) ->{
        list1.addAll(list2);
        return list1;
};
```

The reduce receives two lists of `ExtendedProduct` and concatenates them into a single one using the `addAll()` method.

Now, we only have to implement the call to the `reduce()` method:

```
List<ExtendedProduct> badReviews=productsByBuyer.reduce(10,
    transformer, reducer);
badReviews.forEach(product -> {
    System.out.println(product.getTitle()+":"+
      product.getBuyer()+":"+product.getValue());
});
```

There are other versions of the `reduce()` method:

- `reduceEntries()`, `reduceEntriesToDouble()`, `reduceEntriesToInt()`, and `reduceEntriesToLong()`: In this case, the transformer and reducer functions work over `Map.Entry` objects. The last three versions return respectively a `double`, an `int`, and a `long` value.
- `reduceKeys()`, `reduceKeysToDouble()`, and `reduceKeysToInt()`, `reduceKeysToLong()`: In this case, the transformer and reducer functions work over the keys of the map. The last three versions return respectively a `double`, an `int`. and a `long` value.
- `reduceToInt()`, `reduceToDouble()`, and `reduceToLong()`: In this case, the transformer function works over the keys and values and the reducer method works over `int`, `double`, or `long` number respectively. These methods return an `int`, `double`, and `long` values.
- `reduceValues()`, `reduceValuesToDouble()`, `reduceValuesToInt()`, and `reduceValuesToLong()`: In this case, the transformer and reducer functions work over the values of the map. The last three versions return a `double`, an `int`, and a `long` value respectively.

The compute() method

This method (which is defined in the `Map` interface) receives as parameters the key of an element and an implementation of the `BiFunction` interface that can be expressed as a lambda expression. This function will receive the key and value of the element if the key exists in `ConcurrentHashMap` or null if the key doesn't exist in `ConcurrentHashMap`. The method will replace the value associated with the key with the value returned by the function, insert them in `ConcurrentHashMap` if it doesn't exist, or remove the item if `null` is returned for a previously existing item. Note that during the `BiFunction` execution, one or several map entries can be locked. Thus, your `BiFunction` should not work for very long and should not try to update any other entries in the same map. Otherwise a deadlock might occur.

For example, we can use this method with the new atomic variable introduced in Java 8 named `LongAdder` to calculate the number of bad reviews associated with every product. We create a new `ConcurrentHashMap` named counter. The keys will be the title of the products and the value an object of the `LongAdder` class to count how many bad reviews every product has.

```
ConcurrentHashMap<String, LongAdder> counter=new
   ConcurrentHashMap<>();
```

We process all the elements of `badReviews` `ConcurrentLinkedDeque` calculated in the previous section and use the `compute()` method to create and update the `LongAdder` associated with every product.

```
badReviews.forEach(product -> {
    counter.computeIfAbsent(product.getTitle(), title -> new
       LongAdder()).increment();
});
counter.forEach((title, count) -> {
    System.out.println(title+":"+count);
});
```

Finally, we write the results in the console.

Another example with ConcurrentHashMap

There is another method added in the `ConcurrentHashMap` class and defined in the Map interface. It's the `merge()` method that allows you to merge a (key, value) pair into the map. If the key doesn't exist in `ConcurrentHashMap`, it is inserted directly. If the key exists, you have to define which will be the new value associated with that key from the old one and the new one. This method receives three parameters:

- The key we want to merge.
- The value we want to merge.
- An implementation of `BiFunction` that can be expressed as a lambda expression. This function receives as parameters the old value and the new value associated with the key. The method will associate with the key the value returned by this function. `BiFunction` is executed under a partial lock of the map, so it's guaranteed that it's not concurrently executed for the same key.

For example, we have split the 20,000 products of Amazon used in the previous section in files by the year of the review. For every year, we load `ConcurrentHashMap` where the products are the keys and a list of reviews are the values. So, we can load the reviews of 1995 and 1996 with the following code:

```
Path path=Paths.get("data\\amazon\\1995.txt");
ConcurrentHashMap<BasicProduct,
    ConcurrentLinkedDeque<BasicReview>>
    products1995=BasicProductLoader.load(path);
showData(products1995);

path=Paths.get("data\\amazon\\1996.txt");
ConcurrentHashMap<BasicProduct,
    ConcurrentLinkedDeque<BasicReview>>
    products1996=BasicProductLoader.load(path);
System.out.println(products1996.size());
showData(products1996);
```

If we want to merge both versions of `ConcurrentHashMap` into one, we can use the following code:

```
products1996.forEach(10,(product, reviews) -> {
    products1995.merge(product, reviews, (reviews1,
        reviews2) -> {
        System.out.println("Merge for:
            "+product.getAsin());
        reviews1.addAll(reviews2);
        return reviews1;
    });
});
```

We process all the elements of the 1996 `ConcurrentHashMap` and for every (key, value) pair, we call the `merge()` method over the 1995 `ConcurrentHashMap`. The `merge` function will receive two lists of reviews, so we only have to concatenate them into one.

An example with the ConcurrentLinkedDeque class

The `Collection` interface has also included new methods in Java 8. Most of the concurrent data structures implement this interface, so we can use these new features with them. Two of them are the `stream()` and `parallelStream()` methods used in *Chapter 7, Processing Massive Datasets with Parallel Streams – The Map and Reduce Model* and *Chapter 8, Processing Massive Datasets with Parallel Streams – The Map and Collect Model*. Let's see how to use the other two using `ConcurrentLinkedDeque` with the 20,000 products we have used in the previous sections.

The removeIf() method

This method has a default implementation in the `Collection` interface that is not concurrent and is not overridden by the `ConcurrentLinkedDeque` class. This method receives an implementation of the `Predicate` interface as a parameter that will receive an element of the `Collection` as a parameter and should return a `true` or a `false` value. The method will process all the elements of the `Collection` and will delete those that obtain a `true` value with the predicate.

For example, if you want to delete all the products with a salesrank higher than 1,000, you can use the following code:

```
System.out.println("Products: "+productList.size());
productList.removeIf(product -> product.getSalesrank() >
   1000);
System.out.println("Products; "+productList.size());
productList.forEach(product -> {
    System.out.println(product.getTitle()+":
       "+product.getSalesrank());
});
```

The spliterator() method

This method returns an implementation of the `Spliterator` interface. A **spliterator** defines the data source that can be used by the `Stream` API. You rarely need to use spliterator directly, but sometimes you may want to create your own spliterator to produce a custom source for the stream (for example, if you implement your own data structure). If you have your own spliterator implementation, you can create a stream on top of it using `StreamSupport.stream(mySpliterator, isParallel)`. Here, `isParallel` is a Boolean value that determines whether the created stream will be parallel or not. A spliterator is like an iterator in the sense that you can use it to traverse all the elements in the collection, but you can split them to make that traversal in a concurrent way.

A spliterator has eight different characteristics that define its behavior:

- CONCURRENT: The spliterator source may be safely concurrently modified
- DISTINCT: All the elements returned by the spliterator are distinct
- IMMUTABLE: The spliterator source cannot be modified
- NONNULL: The spliterator never returns a `null` value
- ORDERED: The elements returned by the spliterator are ordered (which means their order matters)

- `SIZED`: The spliterator is capable of returning an exact number of elements with the `estimateSize()` method
- `SORTED`: The spliterator source is sorted
- `SUBSIZED`: If you use the `trySplit()` method to divide this spliterator, the resulting spliterators will be `SIZED` and `SUBSIZED`

The most useful methods of this interface are:

- `estimatedSize()`: This method will give you an estimation of the number of elements in the spliterator.
- `forEachRemaining()`: This method allows you to apply an implementation of the `Consumer` interface, which can be represented with a lambda function, to the elements of the spliterator that haven't yet been processed.
- `tryAdvance()`: This method allows you to apply an implementation of the `Consumer` interface, which can be represented with a lambda function, to the next element to process by the spliterator if there is one.
- `trySplit()`: This method tries to split the spliterator in two parts. The caller spliterator will process some elements and the returned spliterator will process the others. If the spliterator is `ORDERED`, the returned spliterator must process a strict prefix of the elements and the call must process the strict suffix.
- `hasCharacteristics()`: This method allows you to check the properties of the spliterator.

Let's see an example of this method with the `ArrayList` data structure, with 20,000 products.

First, we need an auxiliary task that will process a set of products to convert their title to lowercase. This task will have a `Spliterator` as an attribute:

```
public class SpliteratorTask implements Runnable {

    private Spliterator<Product> spliterator;

    public SpliteratorTask (Spliterator<Product> spliterator) {
        this.spliterator=spliterator;
    }
```

```java
    @Override
    public void run() {
        int counter=0;
        while (spliterator.tryAdvance(product -> {
            product.setTitle(product.getTitle().toLowerCase());
        })) {
            counter++;
        };
        System.out.println(Thread.currentThread().getName()
          +":"+counter);
    }

}
```

As you can see, this task writes the number of products processed when it finishes its execution.

In the main method, once we have loaded `ConcurrentLinkedQueue` with the 20,000 products, we can obtain the spliterator, check some of its properties, and look at its estimated size.

```java
Spliterator<Product> split1=productList.spliterator();
System.out.println(split1.hasCharacteristics
  (Spliterator.CONCURRENT));
System.out.println(split1.hasCharacteristics
  (Spliterator.SUBSIZED));
System.out.println(split1.estimateSize());
```

Then, we can divide the spliterator using the `trySplit()` method and look at the size of the two spliterators:

```java
Spliterator<Product> split2=split1.trySplit();
System.out.println(split1.estimateSize());
System.out.println(split2.estimateSize());
```

Finally, we can execute two tasks in an executor, one for the spliterator, to see that every spliterator has really processed the expected number of elements.

```java
ThreadPoolExecutor executor=(ThreadPoolExecutor)
   Executors.newCachedThreadPool();
executor.execute(new SpliteratorTask(split1));
executor.execute(new SpliteratorTask(split2));
```

In the following screenshot, you can see the results of the execution of this example:

```
<terminated> ConcurrentSpliteratorMain [Java Application] C:\Program File
false
true
20000
10000
10000
pool-1-thread-1:10000
pool-1-thread-2:10000
```

You can see how before splitting the spliterator, the `estimatedSize()` method returns 20,000 elements. After the execution of the `trySplit()` method, both spliterators have 10,000 elements. These are the elements processed by each of the tasks.

Atomic variables

Atomic variables were introduced in Java 1.5 to provide atomic operations over `integer`, `long`, `boolean`, `reference`, and `Array` objects. They provide some methods to increment, decrement, establish the value, return the value, or establish the value if its current value is equal to a predefined one.

In Java 8, four new classes has been added. These are `DoubleAccumulator`, `DoubleAdder`, `LongAccumulator`, and `LongAdder`. In a previous section, we used the `LongAdder` class to count the number of bad reviews of the products. This class provides similar functionality to `AtomicLong`, but it has better performance when you frequently update the cumulative sum from different threads and request the result only at the end of the operation. The `DoubleAdder` function is equal to it but with double values. The main objective of both classes is to have a counter that can be updated by different threads in a consistent way. The most important methods of these classes are:

- `add()`: Increment the value of the counter with the value specified as a parameter
- `increment()`: Equivalent to `add(1)`
- `decrement()`: Equivalent to `add(-1)`
- `sum()`: This method returns the current value of the counter

Take into account that the `DoubleAdder` class doesn't have the `increment()` and `decrement()` methods.

The `LongAccumulator` and `DoubleAccumulator` classes are similar but they have a very important difference. They have a constructor where you specify two parameters:

- The identity value of the internal counter
- A function to accumulate the new value into the accumulator

Note that the function must not depend on the order of accumulation. In this case, the most important methods are:

- `accumulate()`: This method receives a `long` value as a parameter. It applies the function to increment or decrement the counter to the current value and the parameter.
- `get()`: Returns the current value of the counter.

For example, the following code will write 362,880 in the console in all the executions:

```
LongAccumulator accumulator=new LongAccumulator((x,y)
    -> x*y, 1);

IntStream.range(1, 10).parallel().forEach(x ->
    accumulator.accumulate(x));

System.out.println(accumulator.get());
```

We use a commutative operation inside the accumulator so the result is the same for any input order.

Synchronization mechanisms

Synchronization of tasks is the coordination between those tasks to get the desired results. In concurrent applications, we can have two kinds of synchronizations:

- **Process synchronization**: We use this kind of synchronization when we want to control the order of execution of the tasks. For example, a task must wait for the finalization of other tasks before it starts its execution.
- **Data synchronization**: We use this kind of synchronization when two or more tasks access the same memory object. In this case, you have to protect the access in the write operations to that object. If you don't do this, you can have a data race condition where the final results of a program vary from one execution to another.

The Java concurrency API provides mechanisms that allow you to implement both types of synchronization. The most basic synchronization mechanism provided by the Java language is the `synchronized` keyword. This keyword can be applied to a method or to a block of code. In the first case, only one thread can execute the method at a time. In the second case, you have to specify a reference to an object. In this case, only one block of code protected by an object can be executed at the same time.

Java also provide other synchronization mechanisms:

- The `Lock` interface and its implementation classes: This mechanism allows you to implement a critical section to guarantee that only one thread will execute that block of code.
- The `Semaphore` class that implements the well-known **semaphore** synchronization mechanism introduced by *Edsger Dijkstra*.
- `CountDownLatch` allows you to implement a situation where one or more threads wait for the finalization of other threads.
- `CyclicBarrier` allows you to synchronize different tasks in a common point.
- `Phaser` allows you to implement concurrent tasks divided into phases. We made a detailed description of this mechanism in *Chapter 5, Running Tasks Divided into Phases – The Phaser Class*.
- `Exchanger` allows you to implement a point of data interchange between two tasks.
- `CompletableFuture`, a new feature of Java 8, extends the `Future` mechanism of the executor tasks to generate the result of a task in an asynchronous way. You can specify tasks to be executed after the result is generated, so you can control the order of the execution of the tasks.

In the following section, we will show you how to use these mechanisms, giving special attention to the `CompletableFuture` mechanism introduced in the Java 8 version.

The CommonTask class

We have implemented a class named the `CommonTask` class. This class will sleep the calling thread during a random period of time between `0` and `10` seconds. This is its source code:

```
public class CommonTask {

    public static void doTask() {
```

```
            long duration = ThreadLocalRandom.current().nextLong(10);
            System.out.printf("%s-%s: Working %d seconds\n",new
               Date(),Thread.currentThread().getName(),duration);
            try {
                TimeUnit.SECONDS.sleep(duration);
            } catch (InterruptedException e) {
                e.printStackTrace();
            }
        }
    }
}
```

All the tasks we're going to implement in the following sections will use this class to simulate its execution time.

The Lock interface

One of the most basic synchronization mechanisms is the Lock interface and its implementation classes. The basic implementation class is the ReentrantLock class. You can use this class to implement a critical section in an easy way. For example, the following task gets a lock in the first line of its code using the lock() method and releases it in the last line using the unlock() method. Only one task can execute the code between these two sentences at the same time.

```
    public class LockTask implements Runnable {

        private static ReentrantLock lock = new ReentrantLock();
        private String name;

        public LockTask(String name) {
            this.name=name;
        }

        @Override
        public void run() {
            try {
                lock.lock();
                System.out.println("Task: " + name + "; Date: " + new
                   Date() + ": Running the task");
                CommonTask.doTask();
                System.out.println("Task: " + name + "; Date: " + new
                   Date() + ": The execution has finished");
            } finally {
```

```
            lock.unlock();
        }

    }
}
```

You can check this if, for example, you execute ten tasks in an executor using the following code:

```
public class LockMain {

    public static void main(String[] args) {
        ThreadPoolExecutor executor=(ThreadPoolExecutor)
          Executors.newCachedThreadPool();
        for (int i=0; i<10; i++) {
            executor.execute(new LockTask("Task "+i));
        }
        executor.shutdown();
        try {
            executor.awaitTermination(1, TimeUnit.DAYS);
        } catch (InterruptedException e) {
            e.printStackTrace();
        }
    }
}
```

In the following image, you can see the result of an execution of this example. You can see how only one task is executed at a time.

```
Problems  @ Javadoc  Declaration  Search  Console  Progress
<terminated> LockMain [Java Application] C:\Program Files\Java\jre1.8.0_65\bin\javaw.exe (8/11/2015 23:49:13)
Task: Task 0; Date: Sun Nov 08 23:49:13 CET 2015: Running the task
Sun Nov 08 23:49:13 CET 2015-pool-1-thread-1: Working 0 seconds
Task: Task 0; Date: Sun Nov 08 23:49:14 CET 2015: The execution has finished
Task: Task 1; Date: Sun Nov 08 23:49:14 CET 2015: Running the task
Sun Nov 08 23:49:14 CET 2015-pool-1-thread-2: Working 1 seconds
Task: Task 1; Date: Sun Nov 08 23:49:15 CET 2015: The execution has finished
Task: Task 2; Date: Sun Nov 08 23:49:15 CET 2015: Running the task
Sun Nov 08 23:49:15 CET 2015-pool-1-thread-3: Working 0 seconds
Task: Task 2; Date: Sun Nov 08 23:49:15 CET 2015: The execution has finished
Task: Task 3; Date: Sun Nov 08 23:49:15 CET 2015: Running the task
Sun Nov 08 23:49:15 CET 2015-pool-1-thread-4: Working 2 seconds
Task: Task 3; Date: Sun Nov 08 23:49:17 CET 2015: The execution has finished
Task: Task 4; Date: Sun Nov 08 23:49:17 CET 2015: Running the task
Sun Nov 08 23:49:17 CET 2015-pool-1-thread-5: Working 2 seconds
```

The Semaphore class

The semaphore mechanism was introduced by Edsger Dijkstra in 1962 and is used to control the access to one or more shared resources. This mechanism is based on an internal counter and two methods named `wait()` and `signal()`. When a thread calls the `wait()` method, if the internal counter has a value bigger than 0, then the semaphore decrements the internal counter and the thread gets access to the shared resource. If the internal counter has a value of 0, the thread is blocked until some thread calls the `signal()` method. When a thread calls the `signal()` method, the semaphore looks to see whether there are some threads waiting in the `waiting` state (they have called the `wait()` method). If there are no threads waiting, it increments the internal counter. If there are threads waiting for the semaphore, it gets one of those threads, which will return for the `wait()` method and access the shared resource. The other threads that were waiting continue waiting for their turn.

In Java, semaphores are implemented in the `Semaphore` class. The `wait()` method is called `acquire()` and the `signal()` method is called `release()`. For example, in this example, we have used this task where a `Semaphore` class is protecting its code:

```java
public class SemaphoreTask implements Runnable{
    private Semaphore semaphore;
    public SemaphoreTask(Semaphore semaphore) {
        this.semaphore=semaphore;
    }
    @Override
    public void run() {
        try {
            semaphore.acquire();
            CommonTask.doTask();
        } catch (InterruptedException e) {
            e.printStackTrace();
        } finally {
            semaphore.release();
        }
    }
}
```

In the main program, we execute ten tasks that share a `Semaphore` class initialized with two shared resources, so we will have two tasks running at the same time.

```
public static void main(String[] args) {

    Semaphore semaphore=new Semaphore(2);
    ThreadPoolExecutor executor=(ThreadPoolExecutor)
      Executors.newCachedThreadPool();

    for (int i=0; i<10; i++) {
        executor.execute(new SemaphoreTask(semaphore));
    }

    executor.shutdown();
    try {
        executor.awaitTermination(1, TimeUnit.DAYS);
    } catch (InterruptedException e) {
        e.printStackTrace();
    }
}
```

The following screenshot shows the results of an execution of this example. You can see how two tasks are running at the same time:

```
<terminated> SemaphoreMain [Java Application] C:\Program Files\Java\jre1.8.0_65\bin\javaw.exe (9/1
Mon Nov 09 00:55:20 CET 2015-pool-1-thread-2: Working 4 seconds
Mon Nov 09 00:55:20 CET 2015-pool-1-thread-1: Working 1 seconds
Mon Nov 09 00:55:21 CET 2015-pool-1-thread-3: Working 2 seconds
Mon Nov 09 00:55:23 CET 2015-pool-1-thread-4: Working 7 seconds
Mon Nov 09 00:55:24 CET 2015-pool-1-thread-5: Working 9 seconds
Mon Nov 09 00:55:30 CET 2015-pool-1-thread-6: Working 5 seconds
Mon Nov 09 00:55:33 CET 2015-pool-1-thread-7: Working 9 seconds
Mon Nov 09 00:55:35 CET 2015-pool-1-thread-8: Working 2 seconds
```

The CountDownLatch class

This class provides a mechanism to wait for the finalization of one or more concurrent tasks. It has an internal counter that must be initialized with the number of tasks we are going to wait for. Then, the `await()` method sleeps the calling thread until the internal counter arrives at zero and the `countDown()` method decrements that internal counter.

For example, in this task we use the `countDown()` method to decrement the internal counter of the `CountDownLatch` object it receives as a parameter in its constructor.

```java
public class CountDownTask implements Runnable {

    private CountDownLatch countDownLatch;

    public CountDownTask(CountDownLatch countDownLatch) {
        this.countDownLatch=countDownLatch;
    }

    @Override
    public void run() {
        CommonTask.doTask();
        countDownLatch.countDown();

    }
}
```

Then, in the `main()` method, we execute the tasks in an executor and wait for their finalization using the `await()` method of `CountDownLatch`. The object is initialized with the number of tasks we want to wait for.

```java
public static void main(String[] args) {

    CountDownLatch countDownLatch=new CountDownLatch(10);

    ThreadPoolExecutor executor=(ThreadPoolExecutor)
      Executors.newCachedThreadPool();

    System.out.println("Main: Launching tasks");
    for (int i=0; i<10; i++) {
        executor.execute(new CountDownTask(countDownLatch));
    }

    try {
        countDownLatch.await();
    } catch (InterruptedException e) {
        e.printStackTrace();
    }
    System.out.

    executor.shutdown();
}
```

The following screenshot shows the results of an execution of this example:

```
Problems  @ Javadoc  Declaration  Search  Console  Progress
<terminated> CountDownMain [Java Application] C:\Program Files\Java\jre1.8.0_65\bin\javaw.exe (9/11/2015
Main: Launching tasks
Mon Nov 09 01:02:41 CET 2015-pool-1-thread-3: Working 6 seconds
Mon Nov 09 01:02:41 CET 2015-pool-1-thread-5: Working 3 seconds
Mon Nov 09 01:02:41 CET 2015-pool-1-thread-2: Working 5 seconds
Mon Nov 09 01:02:41 CET 2015-pool-1-thread-10: Working 2 seconds
Mon Nov 09 01:02:41 CET 2015-pool-1-thread-1: Working 8 seconds
Mon Nov 09 01:02:41 CET 2015-pool-1-thread-9: Working 3 seconds
Mon Nov 09 01:02:41 CET 2015-pool-1-thread-6: Working 3 seconds
Mon Nov 09 01:02:41 CET 2015-pool-1-thread-8: Working 0 seconds
Mon Nov 09 01:02:41 CET 2015-pool-1-thread-4: Working 9 seconds
Mon Nov 09 01:02:41 CET 2015-pool-1-thread-7: Working 1 seconds
Main: Tasks finished at Mon Nov 09 01:02:50 CET 2015
```

The CyclicBarrier class

This class allows you to synchronize some tasks in a common point. All tasks will wait in that point until all have arrived. Internally, it also manages an internal counter with the tasks that haven't arrived at that point yet. When a task arrives at the determined point, it has to execute the `await()` method to wait for the rest of the tasks. When all the tasks have arrived, the `CyclicBarrier` object wakes them up so they continue with their execution.

This class allows you to execute another task when all the parties have arrived. To configure this, you have to specify a runnable object in the constructor of the object.

For example, we have implemented the following Runnable that uses a `CyclicBarrier` object to wait for other tasks:

```java
public class BarrierTask implements Runnable {

    private CyclicBarrier barrier;

    public BarrierTask(CyclicBarrier barrier) {
        this.barrier=barrier;
    }

    @Override
    public void run() {
        System.out.println(Thread.currentThread().getName()+":
            Phase 1");
```

```
            CommonTask.doTask();
            try {
                barrier.await();
            } catch (InterruptedException e) {
                e.printStackTrace();
            } catch (BrokenBarrierException e) {
                e.printStackTrace();
            }
            System.out.println(Thread.currentThread().getName()+":
              Phase 2");

        }
    }
```

We have also implemented another `Runnable` object that will be executed by `CyclicBarrier` when all the tasks have executed the `await()` method.

```
    public class FinishBarrierTask implements Runnable {

        @Override
        public void run() {
            System.out.println("FinishBarrierTask: All the tasks have
              finished");
        }
    }
```

Finally, in the `main()` method, we execute ten tasks in an executor. You can see how `CyclicBarrier` is initialized with the number of tasks we want to synchronize and with an object of the `FinishBarrierTask` object:

```
        public static void main(String[] args) {
            CyclicBarrier barrier=new CyclicBarrier(10,new
              FinishBarrierTask());

            ThreadPoolExecutor executor=(ThreadPoolExecutor)
              Executors.newCachedThreadPool();

            for (int i=0; i<10; i++) {
                executor.execute(new BarrierTask(barrier));
            }

            executor.shutdown();

            try {
```

```
            executor.awaitTermination(1, TimeUnit.DAYS);
        } catch (InterruptedException e) {
            e.printStackTrace();
        }
    }
}
```

The following screenshot shows the results of an execution of this example:

```
Mon Nov 09 01:22:35 CET 2015-pool-1-thread-7: Working 3 seconds
Mon Nov 09 01:22:35 CET 2015-pool-1-thread-1: Working 5 seconds
FinishBarrierTask: All the tasks have finished
pool-1-thread-5: Phase 2
pool-1-thread-2: Phase 2
pool-1-thread-4: Phase 2
pool-1-thread-8: Phase 2
pool-1-thread-9: Phase 2
pool-1-thread-7: Phase 2
pool-1-thread-10: Phase 2
pool-1-thread-1: Phase 2
pool-1-thread-3: Phase 2
pool-1-thread-6: Phase 2
```

You can see how when all the tasks arrive at the point where the await() method is called, FinishBarrierTask is executed and then all the tasks continue with their execution.

The CompletableFuture class

This is a new synchronization mechanism introduced in the Java 8 concurrency API. It extends the Future mechanism, giving it more power and flexibility. It allows you to implement an event-driving model linking tasks that will only be executed when others have finished. As with the Future interface, CompletableFuture must be parameterized with the type of the result that will be returned by the operation. As with a Future object, the CompletableFuture class represents a result of an asynchronous computation, but the result of CompletableFuture can be established by any thread. It has the complete() method to establish the result when the computation ends normally, and the method completeExceptionally() when the computation ends with an exception. If two or more threads call the complete() or completeExceptionally() methods over the same CompletableFuture, only the first call will take effect.

First, you can create `CompletableFuture` using its constructor. In this case, you have to establish the result of the task using the `complete()` method as we explained before. But you can also create one using the `runAsync()` or `supplyAsync()` methods. The `runAsync()` method executes a `Runnable` object and returns `CompletableFuture<Void>` so that computation can't return any result. The `supplyAsync()` method executes an implementation of the `Supplier` interface parametrized with the type that will be returned by this computation. The `Supplier` interface provides the `get()` method. In that method, we have to include the code of the task and return the result generated by it. In this case, the result of `CompletableFuture` will be the result of the `Supplier` interface.

This class provides a lot of methods that allow you to organize the order of execution of tasks implementing an event-driving model where one task doesn't start its execution until a previous one has finished. These are some of those methods:

- `thenApplyAsync()`: This method receives as a parameter an implementation of the `Function` interface that can be represented as a lambda expression. This function will be executed when the calling `CompletableFuture` has been completed. This method will return `CompletableFuture` to get the result of the `Function`.

- `thenComposeAsync()`: This method is analogous to `thenApplyAsync`, but is useful when the supplied function returns `CompletableFuture` too.

- `thenAcceptAsync()`: This method is similar to the previous one but the parameter is an implementation of the `Consumer` interface that can be also specified as a lambda expression; in this case, the computation won't return a result.

- `thenRunAsync()`: This method is equivalent to the previous one but in this case receives a `Runnable` object as a parameter.

- `thenCombineAsync()`: This method receives two parameters. The first one is another `CompletableFuture` instance. The other is an implementation of the `BiFunction` interfaces that can be specified as a lambda function. This `BiFunction` will be executed when both `CompletableFuture` (the calling one and the parameter) have been completed. This method will return `CompletableFuture` to get the result of the `BiFunction`.

- `runAfterBothAsync()`: This method receives two parameters. The first one is another `CompletableFuture`. The other is an implementation of the `Runnable` interface that will be executed when both `CompletableFuture` (the calling one and the parameter) have been completed.

- `runAfterEitherAsync()`: This method is equivalent to the previous one, but the Runnable task is executed when one of the CompletableFuture objects is completed.
- `allOf()`: This method receives as a parameter a variable list of CompletableFuture objects. It will return a CompletableFuture<Void> object that will return its result when all the CompletableFuture objects have been completed.
- `anyOf()`: This method is equivalent to the previous one, but the returned CompletableFuture returns its result when one of the CompletableFuture is completed.

Finally, if you want to obtain the result returned by CompletableFuture, you can use the `get()` or `join()` methods. Both methods block the calling thread until CompletableFuture has been completed and then returns its result. The main difference between both methods is that `get()` throws ExecutionException, which is a checked exception, but `join()` throws RuntimeException (which is an unchecked exception). Thus, it's easier to use `join()` inside non-throwing lambdas (like Supplier, Consumer, or Runnable).

Most of the methods explained before have the Async suffix. This means that these methods will be executed in a concurrent way using the ForkJoinPool.commonPool instance. Those methods that have versions without the Async suffix will be executed in a serial way (that is to say, in the same thread where CompletableFuture is executed) and with the Async suffix and an executor instance as an additional parameter. In this case, CompletableFuture will be executed asynchronously in the executor passed as a parameter.

Using the CompletableFuture class

In this example, you will learn how to use the CompletableFuture class to implement the execution of some asynchronous tasks in a concurrent way. We will use our collection of 20,000 products of Amazon to implement the following tree of tasks:

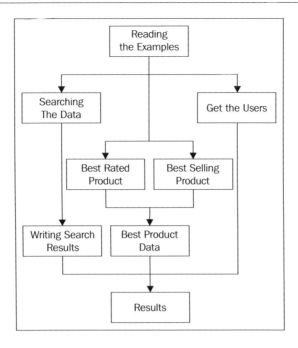

First, we're going to use the examples. Then, we will execute four concurrent tasks. The first one will make a search of products. When the search finishes, we will write the results to a file. The second one will obtain the best-rated product. The third one will obtain the best-selling product. When these both finish, we will concatenate their information using another task. Finally, the fourth task will get a list with the users who have purchased a product. The `main()` program will wait for the finalization of all the tasks and then will write the results.

Let's see the details of the implementation.

Auxiliary tasks

In this example, we will use some auxiliary tasks. The first one is `LoadTask`, which will load the product information from the disk and will return a list of `Product` objects.

```
public class LoadTask implements Supplier<List<Product>> {

    private Path path;

    public LoadTask (Path path) {
        this.path=path;
    }
```

```java
        @Override
        public List<Product> get() {
            List<Product> productList=null;
            try {
                productList = Files.walk(path,
                    FileVisitOption.FOLLOW_LINKS).parallel()
                        .filter(f -> f.toString().endsWith(".txt"))
                            .map(ProductLoader::load).collect
                                (Collectors.toList());
            } catch (IOException e) {
                e.printStackTrace();
            }

            return productList;
        }
    }
```

It implements the `Supplier` interface to be executed as `CompletableFuture`. Inside, it uses a stream to process and parse all the files obtaining a list of products.

The second task is `SearchTask`, which will implement the search in the list of `Product` objects, looking for the ones that contain a word in the title. This task is an implementation of the `Function` interface.

```java
    public class SearchTask implements Function<List<Product>,
        List<Product>> {

        private String query;

        public SearchTask(String query) {
            this.query=query;
        }

        @Override
        public List<Product> apply(List<Product> products) {
            System.out.println(new Date()+": CompletableTask: start");
            List<Product> ret = products.stream()
                    .filter(product -> product.getTitle()
                        .toLowerCase().contains(query))
                    .collect(Collectors.toList());
            System.out.println(new Date()+": CompletableTask: end: 
              "+ret.size());
            return ret;
        }

    }
```

It receives List<Product> with the information of all the products a return List<Product> with the products that meet the criteria. Internally, it creates the stream on the input list, filters it, and collects the result to another list.

Finally, the WriteTask is going to write the products obtained in the search task in a File. In our case, we generate an HTML file, but feel free to write this information in the format you want. This task implements the Consumer interface, so its code must be something like the follow:

```java
public class WriteTask implements Consumer<List<Product>> {

    @Override
    public void accept(List<Product> products) {
        // implementation is omitted
    }
}
```

The main() method

We have organized the execution of the tasks in the main() method. First, we execute the LoadTask using the supplyAsync() method of the CompletableFuture class.

```java
public class CompletableMain {

    public static void main(String[] args) {
        Path file = Paths.get("data","category");

        System.out.println(new Date() + ": Main: Loading
          products");
        LoadTask loadTask = new LoadTask(file);
        CompletableFuture<List<Product>> loadFuture =
          CompletableFuture
                .supplyAsync(loadTask);
```

Then, with the resultant CompletableFuture, we use thenApplyAsync() to execute the search task when the load task has been completed.

```java
        System.out.println(new Date() + ": Main: Then apply for
          search");

        CompletableFuture<List<Product>> completableSearch =
          loadFuture
                .thenApplyAsync(new SearchTask("love"));
```

Once the search task has been completed, we want to write the results of the execution in a file. As this task won't return a result, we use the `thenAcceptAsync()` method:

```
CompletableFuture<Void> completableWrite =
    completableSearch
        .thenAcceptAsync(new WriteTask());

completableWrite.exceptionally(ex -> {
    System.out.println(new Date() + ": Main: Exception "
            + ex.getMessage());
    return null;
});
```

We have used the exceptionally() method to specify what we want to do if the write task throws an exception.

Then, we use the `thenApplyAsync()` method over the `completableFuture` object to execute the task to get the list of users who purchased a product. We specify this task as a lambda expression. Take into account that this task will be executed in parallel with the search task.

```
System.out.println(new Date() + ": Main: Then apply for
    users");

CompletableFuture<List<String>> completableUsers =
    loadFuture
        .thenApplyAsync(resultList -> {

            System.out.println(new Date()
                    + ": Main: Completable users: start");
                            List<String> users =
                                resultList.stream()
        .flatMap(p -> p.getReviews().stream())
        .map(review -> review.getUser())
        .distinct()
        .collect(Collectors.toList());
            System.out.println(new Date()
                    + ": Main: Completable users: end");

            return users;
});
```

In parallel with these tasks, we also executed the tasks using the `thenApplyAsync()` method to find the best-rated product and the best-selling product. We have defined these tasks using a lambda expression too.

```java
System.out.println(new Date()
        + ": Main: Then apply for best rated
          product....");

CompletableFuture<Product> completableProduct = loadFuture
        .thenApplyAsync(resultList -> {
            Product maxProduct = null;
            double maxScore = 0.0;

            System.out.println(new Date()
                    + ": Main: Completable product:
                      start");
            for (Product product : resultList) {
                if (!product.getReviews().isEmpty()) {
                    double score =
                        product.getReviews().stream()
                            .mapToDouble(review ->
                                review.getValue())
                            .average().getAsDouble();
                    if (score > maxScore) {
                        maxProduct = product;
                        maxScore = score;
                    }
                }
            }
            System.out.println(new Date()
                    + ": Main: Completable product: end");
            return maxProduct;
        });

System.out.println(new Date()
        + ": Main: Then apply for best selling
          product....");
CompletableFuture<Product> completableBestSellingProduct =
    loadFuture
        .thenApplyAsync(resultList -> {
            System.out.println(new Date() + ": Main:
                Completable best selling: start");
            Product bestProduct = resultList
                .stream()
```

```
            .min(Comparator.comparingLong
               (Product::getSalesrank))
            .orElse(null);
                System.out.println(new Date()
                        + ": Main: Completable best selling:
                   end");
                return bestProduct;

    });
```

As we mentioned before, we want to concatenate the results of the last two tasks. We can do this using the `thenCombineAsync()` method to specify a task that will be executed after both tasks have been completed.

```
            CompletableFuture<String> completableProductResult =
               completableBestSellingProduct
            .thenCombineAsync(
                completableProduct,
                   (bestSellingProduct, bestRatedProduct) -> {
            System.out.println(new Date() + ": Main: Completable
                product result: start");
            String ret = "The best selling product is "
                + bestSellingProduct.getTitle() + "\n";
            ret += "The best rated product is "
                + bestRatedProduct.getTitle();
            System.out.println(new Date()
                + ": Main: Completable product result: end");
            return ret;
    });
```

Finally, we wait for the end of the final tasks using the `allOf()` and `join()` methods and write the results using the `get()` method to obtain them.

```
            System.out.println(new Date() + ": Main: Waiting for
               results");
            CompletableFuture<Void> finalCompletableFuture =
               CompletableFuture
                    .allOf(completableProductResult, completableUsers,
                        completableWrite);
            finalCompletableFuture.join();

            try {
                System.out.println("Number of loaded products: "
                        + loadFuture.get().size());
                System.out.println("Number of found products: "
                        + completableSearch.get().size());
```

```
            System.out.println("Number of users: "
                    + completableUsers.get().size());
            System.out.println("Best rated product: "
                    + completableProduct.get().getTitle());
            System.out.println("Best selling product: "
                    + completableBestSellingProduct.get()
                    .getTitle());
            System.out.println("Product result:
               "+completableProductResult.get());
        } catch (InterruptedException | ExecutionException e) {
            e.printStackTrace();
        }
    }
```

In the following screenshot, you can see the results of an execution of this example:

```
Tue Nov 10 01:23:17 CET 2015: Main: Loading products....
Tue Nov 10 01:23:17 CET 2015: Main: Then apply for search....
Tue Nov 10 01:23:17 CET 2015: Main: Then apply for users....
Tue Nov 10 01:23:17 CET 2015: Main: Then apply for best rated product....
Tue Nov 10 01:23:17 CET 2015: Main: Then apply for best selling product....
Tue Nov 10 01:23:17 CET 2015: Main: Waiting for results
Tue Nov 10 01:23:40 CET 2015: Main: Completable product: start
Tue Nov 10 01:23:40 CET 2015: Main: Completable best selling: start
Tue Nov 10 01:23:40 CET 2015: Main: Completable users: start
Tue Nov 10 01:23:40 CET 2015: Main: Completable best selling: end
Tue Nov 10 01:23:40 CET 2015: CompletableTask: start
Tue Nov 10 01:23:41 CET 2015: CompletableTask: end: 208
Tue Nov 10 01:23:41 CET 2015: WriteTask: start
Tue Nov 10 01:23:41 CET 2015: WriteTask: end
Tue Nov 10 01:23:41 CET 2015: Main: Completable product: end
Tue Nov 10 01:23:41 CET 2015: Main: Completable product result: start
Tue Nov 10 01:23:41 CET 2015: Main: Completable product result: end
Tue Nov 10 01:23:41 CET 2015: Main: Completable users: end
Number of loaded products: 20000
Number of found products: 208
Number of users: 158288
Best rated product: Patterns of Preaching
Best selling product: The Da Vinci Code
Product result: The best selling product is The Da Vinci Code
The best rated product is Patterns of Preaching
Tue Nov 10 01:23:41 CET 2015: Main: end
```

First, the `main()` method executes all the configuration and waits for the finalization of the tasks. The execution of the tasks follows the order we have configured.

Summary

In this chapter, we have reviewed two components of all concurrent applications. The first one is data structures. Every program uses them to store in memory the information it has to process. We have quickly been introduced to the concurrent data structures to make a detailed description of the new features introduced in the Java 8 Concurrency API that affect the `ConcurrentHashMap` class and the classes that implement the `Collection` interface.

The second one is the synchronization mechanisms that allow you to protect your data when more than one concurrent task wants to modify them, and to control the order of execution of the tasks if necessary. In this case, we have also quickly been introduced to the synchronization mechanisms, giving a detailed description of `CompletableFuture`, a new feature of the Java 8 concurrency API.

In the next chapter, we will show you how you can implement complete concurrent systems integrating the different parts that can also be concurrent and using different classes to implement its concurrency.

10
Integration of Fragments and Implementation of Alternatives

From *Chapter 2*, *Managing Lots of Threads – Executors*, to *Chapter 8*, *Processing Massive Datasets with Parallel Streams – The Map and Collect Model*, you implemented different examples using the most important parts of the Java concurrency API. Usually, these examples are real, but most of the times, these examples can be parts of a bigger system. For example, in *Chapter 4*, *Getting Data from the Tasks – The Callable and Future Interfaces*, you implemented an application to construct an inverted index to be used in an information retrieval system. In *Chapter 6*, *Optimizing Divide and Conquer Solutions – The Fork/Join Framework*, you implemented the k-means clustering algorithm to cluster a set of documents. However, you can implement a full information retrieval application that reads a set of documents, represents them using the vector space model, and clusters them using the K-NN algorithm. In these cases, you have different parts that may use different concurrency technologies (executors, streams, and so on), but they have to synchronize and communicate between them to get the desired results.

Moreover, all the examples presented in this book can be implemented using other components of the Java concurrency API. We will discuss some of those alternatives too.

In this chapter, we will cover the following topics:

- Big-block synchronization mechanisms
- An example of a document clustering application
- Implementation alternatives

Big-block synchronization mechanisms

Big computer applications are formed by different components that work together to get the desired functionality. Those components have to synchronize and communicate between them. In *Chapter 9, Diving into Concurrent Data Structures and Synchronization Utilities*, you learned that you can use different Java classes to synchronize tasks and communicate between them. But this task organization is more complicated when the components you want to synchronize are concurrent systems too that can use different mechanisms to implement their concurrency. For example, you have a component in an application that uses the Fork/Join framework to generate their results that are used by other tasks synchronized using the `Phaser` class.

In these cases, you can use the following two mechanisms to synchronize and communicate those components:

- **Shared memory**: The systems share a data structure to pass information between them.
- **Message passing**: One of the systems sends a message to one or more systems. There are different ways to implement this. In object-oriented programming languages such as Java, the most basic message passing mechanism is when an object calls a method of an other object. You can also use **Java Message Service (JMS)**, buffers, or other data structures. You can have the following two kinds of message passing techniques:
    - **Synchronous**: In this case, the class that sends the message waits until the receiver has processed its message
    - **Asynchronous**: In this case, the class that sends the message doesn't wait for a receiver that processes its message

In this section, you're going to implement an application to cluster documents formed by four subsystems that communicate and synchronize between them to cluster the documents.

An example of a document clustering application

This application will read a set of documents and will organize them using the k-means clustering algorithms. To achieve this, we will use four components:

- **The Reader system**: This system will read all the documents and convert every document into a list of `String` objects.

- **The Indexer system**: This system will process the documents and convert them into a list of words. At the same time, it will generate the global vocabulary of the set of documents with all the words that appear on them.
- **The Mapper system**: This system will convert each list of words into a mathematical representation using the vector space model. The value of each item will be the **Tf-Idf** (short for **term frequency–inverse document frequency**) metric.
- **The Clustering system**: This system will use the k-means clustering algorithm to cluster the documents.

All these systems are concurrent and use their own tasks to implement their functionality. Let's see how you can implement this example.

The four systems of k-means clustering

Let's see how to implement the Reader, Indexer, Mapper, and Clustering systems.

The Reader system

We have implemented this system in the `DocumentReader` class. This class implements the `Runnable` interface and internally uses three attributes:

- A `ConcurrentLinkedDeque` class of `String` objects with all the names of the files you have to process
- A `ConcurrentLinkedQueue` class of `TextFile` objects to store the documents
- A `CountDownLatch` object to control the end of the execution of the tasks

The constructor of the class initializes these attributes (the three are received as parameters by the constructor) and the `run()` method given here implements all the functionality:

```
String route;
System.out.println(Thread.currentThread().getName()+":
  Reader start");

while ((route = files.pollFirst()) != null) {
    Path file = Paths.get(route);

    TextFile textFile;
    try {
        textFile = new TextFile(file);
        buffer.offer(textFile);
```

```
            } catch (IOException e) {
                e.printStackTrace();
            }
        }
        System.out.println(Thread.currentThread().getName()+":
          Reader end: "+buffer.size());
        readersCounter.countDown();
    }
}
```

First, we read the content of all the files. For every file, we create an object of the `TextFile` class. This class contains the name and the content of the text file. It has a constructor that receives a `Path` object with the route of the file. Finally, we write a message in the console and use the `countDown()` method of the `CountDownLatch` object to indicate the finalization of this task.

This is the code of the `TextFile` class. Internally, it has two attributes to store the file name and its contents. It uses the `readAllLines()` method of the `Files` class to convert the content of the file into a `List<String>` data structure:

```
public class TextFile {

    private String fileName;
    private List<String> content;

    public TextFile(String fileName, List<String> content) {
        this.fileName = fileName;
        this.content = content;
    }

    public TextFile(Path path) throws IOException {
        this(path.getFileName().toString(),
            Files.readAllLines(path));
    }

    public String getFileName() {
        return fileName;
    }

    public List<String> getContent() {
        return content;
    }
}
```

The Indexer system

This system is implemented in the `Indexer` class that also implements the `Runnable` interface. In this case, we use five internal attributes as follows:

- A `ConcurrentLinkedQueue` of `TextFile` with the content of all the documents
- A `ConcurrentLinkedDeque` of `Document` objects to store the list of words that forms each document
- A `CountDownLatch` object to control the finalization of the `Reader` system
- A `CountDownLatch` object to indicate the finalization of the tasks of this system
- A `Vocabulary` object to store all the words that form the document collection

The constructor of the class initializes this attributes (receives all of them as parameters):

```
public class Indexer implements Runnable {

    private ConcurrentLinkedQueue<TextFile> buffer;
    private ConcurrentLinkedDeque<Document> documents;
    private CountDownLatch readersCounter;
    private CountDownLatch indexersCounter;
    private Vocabulary voc;
```

The `run()` method implements all the functionality, as shown here:

```
@Override
public void run() {
    System.out.println(Thread.currentThread().getName()+":
      Indexer start");
    do {
        TextFile textFile= buffer.poll();
        if (textFile!=null) {
            Document document= parseDoc(textFile);
```

First, it gets `TextFile` from the queue and if it's not `null`, uses the `parseDoc()` method to convert it into a `Document` object. Then, it processes all the words of the document to store them in the global vocabulary object and stores the document in the list of documents, as you can see in the following code:

```
            document.getVoc().values()
                .forEach(voc::addWord);
```

```
                documents.offer(document);
            }
        } while ((readersCounter.getCount()>0) ||
            (!buffer.isEmpty()));
```

This process is repeated while the `Reader` systems are running or there are still documents in the buffer. Finally, the `run()` method shown in the snippet mentioned later writes a message in the console and uses the `countDown()` method of the `CountDownLatch` object to indicate that this task has finished its execution:

```
        indexersCounter.countDown();
        System.out.println(Thread.currentThread().getName()+":
            Indexer end");
    }
```

The `parseDoc()` method receives `List<String>` with the contents of the document and return a `Document` object. It creates a `Document` object to process all the lines using the `forEach()` method as follows:

```
    private Document parseDoc(TextFile textFile) {
        Document doc=new Document();

        doc.setName(textFile.getFileName());
        textFile.getContent().forEach(line ->
            parseLine(line,doc));

        return doc;
    }
```

The `parseLine()` method will split the line into its words and store them into the `doc` object as follows:

```
    private static void parseLine(String inputLine, Document doc) {

        // Clean string
        String line=new String(inputLine);
        line = Normalizer.normalize(line, Normalizer.Form.NFKD);
        line = line.replaceAll("[^\\p{ASCII}]", "");
        line = line.toLowerCase();

        // Tokenizer
        StringTokenizer tokenizer = new StringTokenizer(line,
                " ,.;:-{}[]¿?¡!|\\=*+/()\"@\t~#<>", false);
        while (tokenizer.hasMoreTokens()) {
            doc.addWord(tokenizer.nextToken());
        }
    }
```

You can include an optimization in the code presented before precompiling the regular expression used in the `replaceAll()` method:

```
static final Pattern NON_ASCII = Pattern.compile("[^\\p{ASCII}]");
    line = NON_ASCII.matcher(line).replaceAll("");
}
```

The Mapper system

This system is implemented in the `Mapper` class that also implements the `Runnable` interfaces. Internally, it use the following two attributes:

- A `ConcurrentLinkedDeque` of `Document` objects with the information of all the documents
- A `Vocabulary` object with all the words in the entire collection

The code for this is as follows:

```
public class Mapper implements Runnable {

    private ConcurrentLinkedDeque<Document> documents;
    private Vocabulary voc;
```

The constructor of the class initializes those attributes, and the `run()` method implements the functionality of this system:

```
public void run() {
    Document doc;
    int counter=0;
    System.out.println(Thread.currentThread().getName()+":
      Mapper start");
    while ((doc=documents.pollFirst())!=null) {
        counter++;
```

First, it gets a document from the `Deque` object of documents using the `pollFirst()` method. Then, it processes all the words in the document calculating the `tfxidf` measure and creating a new `Attribute` object to store those values. Those attributes are stored in a list.

```
            List<Attribute> attributes=new ArrayList<>();
            doc.getVoc().forEach((key, item) -> {
                Word word=voc.getWord(key);
                item.setTfxidf(item.getTfxidf()/word.getDf());
                Attribute attribute=new Attribute();
                attribute.setIndex(word.getIndex());
                attribute.setValue(item.getTfxidf());
                attributes.add(attribute);
            });
```

Finally, we convert the list into an array of `Attribute` objects and store that array in the `Document` object:

```
            Collections.sort(attributes);
            doc.setExample(attributes);
        }
        System.out.println(Thread.currentThread().getName()+":
          Mapper end: "+counter);


    }
```

The Clustering system

This system implements the k-means clustering algorithm. You can use the elements presented in *Chapter 5, Running Tasks Divided into Phases – The Phaser Class*, to implement this system. That implementation has the following elements:

- **The DistanceMeasurer class**: This class calculates the Euclidean distance between an array of `Attribute` objects with the information of a document and the centroid of a cluster
- **The DocumentCluster class**: This stores the information about a cluster: the centroid and the documents of that cluster
- **The AssigmentTask class**: This extends the `RecursiveAction` class (of the Fork/Join framework) and executes the assignment task of the algorithm where we calculate the distance between each document and all the clusters to decide the cluster of every document
- **The UpdateTask class**: This extends the `RecursiveAction` class (of the Fork/Join framework) and executes the updated task of the algorithm that recalculates the centroid of every cluster as the average of the documents stored on it
- **The ConcurrentKMeans class**: This class has the static method `calculate()` that executes the clustering algorithm and returna an array of `DocumentCluster` objects with all the clusters generated

We have only added a new class, the `ClusterTask` class that implements the `Runnable` interface and will call the `calculate()` method of the `ConcurrentKMeans` class. Internally, it uses two attributes as follows:

- An array of `Document` objects with the information of all the documents
- The `Vocabulary` object with all the words of the collection

The constructor initializes those attributes, and the `run()` method implements the logic of the task. We call the `calculate()` method of the `ConcurrentKMeans` class passing to the five parameters as follows:

- The array of `Document` objects with the information of all the documents.
- The `Vocabulary` object with all the words of the collection.
- The number of clusters we want to generate. In this case, we use `10` as the number of clusters.
- The seed used to initialize the centroids of the clusters. In this case, we use `991` as a seed.
- The reference size to split the tasks in subtasks used in the Fork/Join framework. In this case, we use `10` as that minimum size.

This is the code of that class:

```
@Override
public void run() {
    System.out.println("Documents to cluster:
      "+documents.length);
    ConcurrentKMeans.calculate(documents, 10,
      voc.getVocabulary().size(), 991, 10);
}
```

The main class of the document clustering application

Once we have implemented all the elements we use in our application, we have to implement the `main()` method of our system. In this case, this method is critical because it's responsible for the launching of the systems and the creation of the elements needed to synchronize them. The `Reader` and `Indexer` systems will be executing at the same time. They will be using a buffer to share information between them. When the reader reads a document, it will write the list of `String` objects in the buffer and then proceed to process the next document. It doesn't wait for a task that processes that `List`. This is an example of **asynchronous message passing**. The `Indexer` system will take the documents from the buffer, process them, and generate the `Vocabulary` object with all the words of the documents. All the tasks executed by the `Indexer` system share the same instance of the `Vocabulary` class. This is an example of **shared memory**.

Integration of Fragments and Implementation of Alternatives

The main class will wait for the finalization of the `Reader` and `Indexer` systems in a synchronous way using the `await()` method of a `CountDownLatch` object. This method blocks the execution of the calling thread until its internal counter arrives at 0.

Once both systems have finished their execution, the `Mapper` system will use the `Vocabulary` object and the `Document` information to obtain the vector space model representation of each document. When the `Mapper` has finished its execution, the `Clustering` system clusters all the documents. We have used the `CompletableFuture` class to synchronize the end of the `Mapper` system with the start of the `Clustering` system. This is another example of asynchronous communication between two systems.

We have implemented the main class in the `ClusteringDocs` class.

First, we create a `ThreadPoolExecutor` object and obtain `ConcurrentLinkedDeque` with the files that contain the documents using the `readFileNames()` method:

```
public class ClusteringDocs {

    private static int NUM_READERS = 2;
    private static int NUM_WRITERS = 4;

    public static void main(String[] args) throws
       InterruptedException {

        ThreadPoolExecutor executor=(ThreadPoolExecutor)
           Executors.newCachedThreadPool();
        ConcurrentLinkedDeque<String> files=readFiles("data");
        System.out.println(new Date()+":"+files.size()+" files
           read.");
```

Then, we create the buffer of documents, `ConcurrentLinkedDeque`, to store the `Document` objects, the `Vocabulary` object, and two `CountDownLatch` objects—one to control the end of the tasks of the `Reader` system and other to control the end of the tasks of the `Indexer` system. We have the following code:

```
            ConcurrentLinkedQueue<List<String>> buffer=new
               ConcurrentLinkedQueue<>();
            CountDownLatch readersCounter=new CountDownLatch(2);
            ConcurrentLinkedDeque<Document> documents=new
               ConcurrentLinkedDeque<>();
            CountDownLatch indexersCounter=new CountDownLatch(4);
            Vocabulary voc=new Vocabulary();
```

Then, we launch the two tasks to execute the Reader system of the DocumentReader class and another four tasks to execute the Indexer system of the Indexer class. All these tasks are executed in the Executor object we have created earlier:

```
System.out.println(new Date()+":"+"Launching the tasks");
for (int i=0; i<NUM_READERS; i++) {
    DocumentReader reader=new
        DocumentReader(files,buffer,readersCounter);
    executor.execute(reader);

}

for (int i=0; i<NUM_WRITERS; i++) {
    Indexer indexer=new Indexer(documents, buffer,
        readersCounter, indexersCounter, voc);
    executor.execute(indexer);
}
```

Then, the main() method waits for the finalization of this tasks; first, for the DocumentReader tasks and then for the Indexer tasks as follows:

```
System.out.println(new Date()+":"+"Waiting for the
    readers");
readersCounter.await();

System.out.println(new Date()+":"+"Waiting for the
    indexers");
indexersCounter.await();
```

Then, we convert the ConcurrentLinkedDeque class of Document objects in an array:

```
Document[] documentsArray=new Document[documents.size()];
documentsArray=documents.toArray(documentsArray);
```

We launch the Indexer system executing four tasks of the Mapper class using the runAsync() method of the CompletableFuture class as follows:

```
System.out.println(new Date()+":"+"Launching the
    mappers");
CompletableFuture<Void>[] completables =
    Stream.generate(() -> new Mapper(documents, voc))
        .limit(4)
        .map(CompletableFuture::runAsync)
        .toArray(CompletableFuture[]::new);
```

Then, we launch the `Clustering` system to launch one tasks of the `ClusterTask` class (remember that these tasks will launch other tasks to execute the algorithm). The `main()` method uses the `allOf()` method of the `CompletableFuture` class to wait for the finalization of the `Mapper` tasks and then uses the `thenRunAsync()` method to launch the clustering algorithm when the `Mapper` system has finished:

```
System.out.println(new Date()+":"+"Launching the cluster
    calculation");

CompletableFuture<Void> completableMappers=
    CompletableFuture.allOf(completables);
ClusterTask clusterTask=new ClusterTask(documentsArray,
    voc);
CompletableFuture<Void> completableClustering=
    completableMappers.thenRunAsync(clusterTask);
```

Finally, we wait for the finalization of the `Clustering` system using the `get()` method and finish the execution of the program as follows:

```
System.out.println(new Date()+":"+"Wating for the cluster
    calculation");
try {
    completableClustering.get();
} catch (InterruptedException | ExecutionException e) {
    e.printStackTrace();
}

System.out.println(new Date()+":"+"Execution finished");
executor.shutdown();
}
```

The `readFileNames()` method receives a string as a parameter that must be the path to the directory where the collection of documents is stored and generates a `ConcurrentLinkedDeque` class of `String` objects with the name of the files contained in that directory.

Testing our document clustering application

To test this application, we have used a subset of 10,052 documents of the 100,673 documents with information about movies taken from Wikipedia as the collection of documents. In the following image, you can see the results of the first part of the execution—from the start of the execution until the indexer execution ends:

```
 Problems  @ Javadoc   Declaration   Search   Console ⊠   Progress
<terminated> ClusteringDocs [Java Application] C:\Program Files\Java\jre1.8.0_65\bin\javaw.exe (22/11/2015 1:30:57)
Sun Nov 22 01:30:57 CET 2015:10052 files readed.
Sun Nov 22 01:30:57 CET 2015:Launching the tasks
pool-1-thread-2: Reader start
pool-1-thread-1: Reader start
pool-1-thread-3: Indexer start
Sun Nov 22 01:30:57 CET 2015:Waiting for the readers
pool-1-thread-5: Indexer start
pool-1-thread-4: Indexer start
pool-1-thread-6: Indexer start
pool-1-thread-2: Reader end: 6
pool-1-thread-1: Reader end: 6
Sun Nov 22 01:31:45 CET 2015:Waiting for the indexers
pool-1-thread-6: Indexer end
pool-1-thread-4: Indexer end
pool-1-thread-5: Indexer end
pool-1-thread-3: Indexer end
```

The following image shows the rest of the execution of the examples:

```
pool-1-thread-3: Indexer end
Sun Nov 22 01:31:45 CET 2015:Launching the mappers
Sun Nov 22 01:31:45 CET 2015:Launching the cluster calculation
Sun Nov 22 01:31:45 CET 2015:Wating for the cluster calculation
ForkJoinPool.commonPool-worker-0: Mapper start
ForkJoinPool.commonPool-worker-1: Mapper start
ForkJoinPool.commonPool-worker-2: Mapper start
ForkJoinPool.commonPool-worker-1: Mapper end: 3408
ForkJoinPool.commonPool-worker-1: Mapper start
ForkJoinPool.commonPool-worker-0: Mapper end: 3229
ForkJoinPool.commonPool-worker-2: Mapper end: 3415
ForkJoinPool.commonPool-worker-1: Mapper end: 0
Documents to cluser: 10052
Step
Number of Changes: 10052
Step
Number of Changes: 7
Step
Number of Changes: 6
Step
Number of Changes: 2
Step
Number of Changes: 0
Sun Nov 22 01:35:22 CET 2015:Execution finished
```

You can see how the tasks are synchronized as seen earlier in this chapter. First, the `Reader` and `Indexer` tasks are executed in a concurrent way. When they finish, the mapper makes the transformation of the data, and finally, the clustering algorithm organizes the examples.

Implementation of alternatives with concurrent programming

Most of the examples we have implemented through the chapters of this book can be implemented using other components of the Java concurrency API. In this section, we will describe how to implement some of these alternatives.

The k-nearest neighbors' algorithm

You have implemented the k-nearest neighbors' algorithm in *Chapter 2*, *Managing Lots of Threads – Executors*, using an executor. This is a simple machine-learning algorithm used for supervised classification. You have a training set of previous classified examples. To obtain the class of a new example, you calculate the distance from this example to the training set of examples. The majority of classes in the nearest examples are the classes selected for the example. You can also implement this algorithm with one of the following components of the concurrency API:

- **Threads**: You can implement this example using `Thread` objects. You have to execute the tasks executed in the executor using normal threads. Each thread will calculate the distance between the example and a subset of the training set, and it will save that distance in a data structure shared between all the threads. When all the threads have finished, you can sort the data structure using the distance and calculate the class of the example.

- **Fork/Join framework**: As in the previous solution, each task will calculate the distance between the example and the subset of the training set. In this case, you define the maximum number of examples in those subsets. If a task has to process more examples, you divide that task into two child tasks. After you have joined the two tasks, you have to generate a unique data structure with the results of the two subtasks. At the end, you will have a data structure with all the distances that you can sort to obtain the class of the example.

- **Streams**: You create a stream from the training data and map each training example in a structure that contains the distance between the example you want to classify and that example. Then, you sort that structure, get the closest ones using `limit()` and calculate the final resultant class.

Building an inverted index of a collection of documents

We have implemented this example in *Chapter 4, Getting Data from the Tasks – The Callable and Future Interfaces*, using an executor. An inverted index is a data structure used in the information retrieval field to speed up the searches of information. It stores the words presented in a document collection and for each word, the documents where they appear. When you make a search of information, you don't need to process the documents. You look at the inverted index to extract the documents where the words you have inserted appear and construct the result list. You can also implement this algorithm with one of the following components of the concurrency API:

- **Threads**: Each thread will process a subset of documents. This process includes obtaining the vocabulary of the document and updating a common data structure with the global index. When all the threads have finished their execution, you can create the file in a sequential way.
- **Fork/Join framework**: You define the maximum number of documents a task can process. If a task has to process more documents, you split that task into two subtasks. The result of each task will be a data structure with the inverted index of the documents processed by those tasks or its subtasks. After joining the two subtasks, you construct a unique inverted index from the inverted indexes of its subtasks.
- **Streams**: You create a stream to process all the files. You map each file in the object with its vocabulary and then you reduce that vocabulary stream to get the inverted index.

A best-matching algorithm for words

You have implemented this example in *Chapter 4, Getting Data from the Tasks – The Callable and Future Interfaces*. The main objective of this algorithm is to find the words most similar to a string passed as a parameter. You can also implement this algorithm using one of the following components of the concurrency API:

- **Threads**: Each thread will calculate the distance between the searched word and a sublist of the whole list of words. Each thread will generate a partial result that will be merged into the final result for a shared class between all the threads.

- **Fork/Join framework**: Each task will calculate the distance between the searched word and a sublist of the whole list of words. If the list is too big, you have to split the task into two subtasks. Each task will return a partial result. After joining the two subtasks, the task will integrate the two sublists into one. The original task will return the final result.
- **Streams**: You create a stream for the whole list of word, map each word with a data structure that includes the distance between the searched word and that word, sort that list, and get the results.

A genetic algorithm

You have implemented this example in *Chapter 5, Running Tasks Divided into Phases – The Phaser Class*. A **genetic algorithm** is an adaptive heuristic search algorithm based on the natural selection principles used to generate good solutions to **optimization** and **search problems**. There are different approaches to use the multiple threads for a genetic algorithm. The most classical one is to create *islands*. Each thread represents an island where a part of the population evolves. Sometimes, migrations between islands occur while transferring some individuals from one island to another. After the algorithm finishes, the best specie across all the islands is selected. Such an approach reduces the contention considerably as threads rarely talk to each other.

There are also other approaches well-described in many publications and websites. For example, this handouts set summarizes the approaches pretty well at https://cw.fel.cvut.cz/wiki/_media/courses/a0m33eoa/prednasky/08pgas-handouts.pdf.

You can also implement this algorithm using one of the following components of the concurrency API:

- **Threads**: The population with all the individuals must be a shared data structure. You can implement the three phases in the following way: the selection phase in a sequential way; the crossover phase with threads, where each thread will generate a predefined number of individuals; and the evaluation phase, with threads too. Each thread will evaluate a predefined number of individuals.
- **Executor**: You can implement something similar to the previous one executing the tasks in an executor instead of independent threads.
- **Fork/Join framework**: The main idea is the same, but in this case, your tasks will be divided until they process a predefined number of individuals. The join part in this case doesn't do anything because the results of the tasks will be stored in the common data structure.

A keyword extraction algorithm

You have implemented this example in *Chapter 5, Running Tasks Divided into Phases – The Phaser Class*. We use this kind of algorithm to extract a small set of words that describes a document. We try to find the most informative words using measures such as the Tf-Idf. You can also implement this example using the following components of the concurrency API:

- **Threads**: You need two kinds of threads. The threads of the first group will process the document set to obtain the document frequency of every word. You need a shared data structure that stores the vocabulary of the collection. The threads of the second group will process the documents again to obtain the keywords of each document and update a structure that maintains the whole list of keywords.

- **Fork/Join framework**: The main idea is similar to the previous version. You need two kinds of tasks. The first one to obtain the global vocabulary of the collection of documents. Each task will calculate the vocabulary of a subset of documents. If that subset is too big, the task will execute two subtasks. After joining the subtasks, it will group the two vocabularies obtained into one. The second group of tasks will calculate the list of keywords. Each task will calculate the list of keywords of a subset of documents. If that subset is too big, it will execute two subtasks. When those tasks finish, the parent task will generate a list of keywords with the lists returned by the child tasks.

- **Streams**: You create a stream to process all the documents. You map each document with an object that contains the vocabulary of the document and reduce it to get the global vocabulary. You generate another stream to process all the documents again, map each document with an object that contains its keywords, and reduce it to generate the final list of keywords.

A k-means clustering algorithm

You have implemented this algorithm in *Chapter 6, Optimizing Divide and Conquer Solutions – The Fork/Join Framework*. This algorithm classifies a set of elements into a previous defined number of clusters. You don't have any information about the class of the elements, so this is an unsupervised learning algorithm that tries to find similar items. You can also implement this example using the following components of the concurrency API:

- **Threads**: You will have two kinds of threads. The first one will assign a cluster to the examples. Each thread will process a subset of the examples set. The second kind of thread will update the centroid of the clusters. The clusters and the examples must be data structures shared by all the threads.

- **Executor**: You can implement the idea presented before but executing the tasks in an executor instead of using independent threads.

A filtering data algorithm

You have implemented this algorithm in *Chapter 6, Optimizing Divide and Conquer Solutions – The Fork/Join Framework*. The main objective of this algorithm is to select the objects that satisfy certain conditions from a very big set of objects. You can also implement this example using the following components of the concurrency API:

- **Threads**: Each thread will process a subset of objects. If you're looking for one result, when one thread is found, it must suspend the execution of the rest. If you are looking for a list of elements, that list must be a shared data structure.
- **Executor**: The same as earlier, but executing the tasks in an executor instead of using independent threads.
- **Streams**: You can use the `filter()` method of the `Stream` class to make the search over the objects. Then, you can reduce those results to get them in the format you need.

Searching an inverted index

You have implemented this algorithm in *Chapter 7, Processing Massive Datasets with Parallel Streams – The Map and Reduce Model*. In a previous example, we discuss about how to implement the algorithm that creates the inverted index to speed up the searches of information. This is the algorithm that makes that search of information. You can also implement this example using the following components of the concurrency API:

- **Threads**: This is the list of results in a common data structure. Each thread processes a part of the inverted index. Each result is inserted in order to generate a sorted data structure. If you get a good enough list of results, you can return that list and cancel the execution of the tasks.
- **Executor**: This is similar to the previous one, but executes the concurrent tasks in an executor.
- **Fork/Join framework**: This is similar to the previous one, but each task divides the part of the inverted index to process it into smaller chunks until they are small enough.

A numeric summarization algorithm

You have implemented this example in *Chapter 7, Processing Massive Datasets with Parallel Streams – The Map and Reduce Model*. This kind of algorithm wants to obtain statistical information about a very big set of data. You can also implement this example using the following components of the concurrency API:

- **Threads**: We will have an object to store the data generated by the threads. Each thread will process a subset of the data and store the results of that data in the common object. Maybe, we will have to postprocess that object to generate the final results.
- **Executor**. This is similar to the previous one, but executes the concurrent tasks in an executor.
- **Fork/Join framework**: This is similar to the previous one, but each task divides the part of the inverted index to process into smaller chunks until they are small enough.

A search algorithm without indexing

You have implemented this example in *Chapter 8, Processing Massive Datasets with Parallel Streams – The Map and Collect Model*. This algorithm obtains the objects that meet certain conditions when you don't have an inverted index to speed up the search. In these cases, you have to process all the elements when you make the search. You can also implement this example using the following components of the concurrency API:

- **Threads**: Each thread will process a subset of objects (files in our case) to get a list of results. The list of results will be a shared data structure.
- **Executor**: This is similar to the previous one, but the concurrent tasks will be executed in an executor.
- **Fork/Join framework**: This is similar to the previous one, but the tasks divide the part of the inverted index to process into smaller chunks until they are small enough.

A recommendation system using the Map and Collect model

You have implemented this example in *Chapter 8, Processing Massive Datasets with Parallel Streams – The Map and Collect Model*. A **recommendation system** recommends a product or service to a customer based on the products/services he has bought/used and in the products/services bought/used by the users that has bought/used the same services as him. You can also implement this example using the Phaser component of the concurrency API. This algorithm has three phases:

- **First phase**: We need to convert the list of products with their reviews into a list of buyers with the products they have bought. Each task will process a subset of products, and the list of buyers will be a shared data structure.
- **Second phase**: We have to obtain a list of the users that bought the same products than the reference user. Each task will process an item of the products bought by the user and will add the users who bought that product to a common set of users.
- **Third phase**: We obtain the recommended products. Each task will process a user of the previous list and add the products he has bought to a common data structure that will generate the final list of recommended products.

Summary

In this book, you implemented a lot of real-world examples. Some of these examples can be used as a part of a bigger system. These bigger systems normally have different concurrent parts that must share information and be synchronized between them. To make that synchronization, we can use three mechanisms: the shared memory, when two or more tasks share an object or data structure, asynchronous message passing, when a task sends a message to another task and doesn't wait for its processing, and synchronous message passing, when a task sends a message to another task and waits for its processing.

In this chapter, we implemented an application to cluster documents formed by four subsystems. We used the mechanisms presented earlier to synchronize and share information between those four subsystems.

We also revised some of the examples presented in the book to discuss other alternatives to their implementation.

In the next chapter, you will learn how to obtain debug information of the components of the concurrency API and how to monitor and test a concurrent application.

11
Testing and Monitoring Concurrent Applications

Software testing is a critical task of every development process. Every application has to fulfill the end user requirements and the testing phase is the place to prove this. It has to generate valid results in an acceptable time and with the specified format. The main objective of the testing phase is to detect as many errors as possible in the software to correct them and increase the global quality of the product.

Traditionally, in the waterfall model, the testing phase begins when the development phase is very advanced but nowadays more and more development teams are using agile methodologies where the testing phase is integrated into the development phase. The main objective is to test the software as soon as possible to detect the errors earlier in the process.

In Java, there are a lot of tools such as **JUnit** or **TestNG** to automatize the execution of tests. Other tools such as **JMeter** allow you to test how many users can execute your application at the same time, and there are other tools such as **Selenium** that you can use to make integration tests in web applications.

The testing phase is more critical and more difficult in concurrent applications. You have two or more threads running at the same time, but you can't control their order of execution. You can do a lot of tests of an application, but you can't guarantee that there isn't an order of execution of the different threads that provokes a race condition or a deadlock. This circumstance also causes difficulty in the reproduction of errors. You can find an error that only occurs in certain circumstances, so it can be difficult to find its real cause. In this chapter, we will cover the following topics to help you to test concurrent applications:

- Monitoring concurrency objects
- Monitoring concurrency applications
- Testing concurrency applications

Monitoring concurrency objects

Most of the concurrency objects provided by the Java concurrency API include methods to know their status. This status can include the number of threads that are executing, the number of threads blocked waiting for a condition, the number of tasks executed, and so on. In this section, you will learn the most important methods you can use and the information you can obtain from them. This information can be very useful to detect the cause of an error, especially if it only occurs in very rare conditions.

Monitoring a thread

The thread is the most basic element in the Java concurrency API. It allows you to implement a raw task. You decide what code is going to execute (extending the Thread class or implementing the Runnable interface), when it starts its execution, and how it synchronizes with other tasks of the application. The Thread class provides some methods to obtain information about a thread. These are the most useful methods:

- getId(): This method returns the identifier of the thread. It's a long positive number and it's unique.
- getName(): This method returns the name of the thread. By default, it has the format Thread-xxx but it can be modified in the constructor or using the setName() method.
- getPriority(): This method returns the priority of the thread. By default, all the threads have a priority of five but you can change it using the setPriority() method. Threads with a higher priority may have preference over threads with a lower priority.
- getState(): This method returns the state of the thread. It returns a value of Enum Thread.State, which can take the values: NEW, RUNNABLE, BLOCKED, WAITING, TIMED_WAITING, and TERMINATED. You can check the API documentation to see the real significance of every state.
- getStackTrace(): This method returns the stack of calls of this thread as an array of StackTraceElement objects. You can print this array to know what calls have made the thread.

For example, you can use a piece of code like this to obtain all the relevant information of a thread:

```
System.out.println("**********************");
System.out.println("Id: " + thread.getId());
System.out.println("Name: " + thread.getName());
System.out.println("Priority: " + thread.getPriority());
System.out.println("Status: " + thread.getState());
System.out.println("Stack Trace");
for(StackTraceElement ste : thread.getStackTrace()) {
   System.out.println(ste);
}

System.out.println("**********************\n");
```

With this block of code, you will obtain an output as follows:

```
**********************
Id: 9
Name: Thread-0
Priority: 5
Status: TIMED_WAITING
Stack Trace
java.lang.Thread.sleep(Native Method)
java.lang.Thread.sleep(Unknown Source)
java.util.concurrent.TimeUnit.sleep(Unknown Source)
com.javferna.packtpub.book.mastering.test.common.CommonTask.run(CommonTask.java:13)
java.lang.Thread.run(Unknown Source)
**********************

**********************
Id: 9
Name: Thread-0
Priority: 5
Status: TERMINATED
Stack Trace
**********************
```

Monitoring a lock

A **lock** is one of the basic synchronization elements provided by the Java concurrency API. It's defined in the `Lock` interface and in the `ReentrantLock` class. In a basic way, a lock allows you to define a critical section in your code, but the `Lock` mechanism is more flexible than other mechanisms as the synchronized keyword (for example, you can have different locks to read and write operations or have non-linear critical sections). The `ReentrantLock` class has some methods that allow you to know the status of a `Lock` object:

- `getOwner()`: This method returns a `Thread` object with the thread that currently has the lock, that is to say, the thread that is executing the critical section.
- `hasQueuedThreads()`: This method returns a `boolean` value to indicate if there are threads waiting to acquire this lock.
- `getQueueLength()`: This method returns an `int` value with the number of threads that are waiting to acquire this lock.
- `getQueuedThreads()`: This method returns a `Collection<Thread>` object with the `Thread` objects that are waiting to acquire this lock.
- `isFair()`: This method returns a `boolean` value to indicate the status of the fairness attribute. The value of this attribute is used to determine which will be the next thread that acquires the lock. You can check the Java API information to get a detailed description of this functionality.
- `isLocked()`: This method returns a `boolean` value to indicate if this lock is owned by a thread or not.
- `getHoldCount()`: This method returns an `int` value with the number of times this thread has acquired the lock. The returned value is zero if this thread does not hold the lock. Otherwise it returns the number of times the `lock()` method was called in the current thread for which the matching `unlock()` method was not called.

The `getOwner()` and the `getQueuedThreads()` methods are protected so you don't have direct access to them. To solve this problem, you can implement your own `Lock` class and implement methods that provide you that information.

For example, you can implement a class named `MyLock` as follows:

```
public class MyLock extends ReentrantLock {

    private static final long serialVersionUID =
        8025713657321635686L;

    public String getOwnerName() {
        if (this.getOwner() == null) {
            return "None";
        }
        return this.getOwner().getName();
    }

    public Collection<Thread> getThreads() {
        return this.getQueuedThreads();
    }
}
```

So, you can use a fragment of code similar to this to obtain all the relevant information about a lock:

```
System.out.println("************************\n");
System.out.println("Owner : " + lock.getOwnerName());
System.out.println("Queued Threads: " +
  lock.hasQueuedThreads());
if (lock.hasQueuedThreads()) {
    System.out.println("Queue Length: " +
      lock.getQueueLength());
    System.out.println("Queued Threads: ");
    Collection<Thread> lockedThreads = lock.getThreads();
    for (Thread lockedThread : lockedThreads) {
        System.out.println(lockedThread.getName());
    }
}
System.out.println("Fairness: " + lock.isFair());
System.out.println("Locked: " + lock.isLocked());
System.out.println("Holds: "+lock.getHoldCount());
System.out.println("************************\n");
```

With this block of code, you will obtain an output similar to the following:

```
<terminated> MainLock [Java Application] C:\Program Files\Java\jre1.8.0_65\bin
*************************

*************************

Owner : pool-1-thread-3
Queued Threads: true
Queue Length: 9
Queued Threads:
pool-1-thread-1
pool-1-thread-2
pool-1-thread-10
pool-1-thread-8
pool-1-thread-6
pool-1-thread-4
pool-1-thread-9
pool-1-thread-7
pool-1-thread-5
Fairness: false
Locked: true
Holds: 0
*************************
```

Monitoring an executor

The **executor framework** is a mechanism that allows you to execute concurrent tasks without worrying about the creation and management of threads. You can send the tasks to the executor. It has an internal pool of threads that re-utilize to execute the tasks. The executor also provides a mechanism to control the resources consumed by your tasks so you won't overload the system. The executor framework provides the Executor and ExecutorService interfaces and some classes that implement those interfaces. The most basic class that implements them is the ThreadPoolExecutor class. It provides some methods that allow you to know the status of the executor:

- getActiveCount():This method returns the number of threads of the executor that are executing tasks.
- getCompletedTaskCount(): This method returns the number of tasks that have been executed by the executor and have finished its execution.

- `getCorePoolSize()`: This method returns the core number of threads. This number determines the minimum number of threads in the pool. Even if there are no tasks running in the executor, the pool won't have less threads than the number returned by this method.
- `getLargestPoolSize()`: This method returns the maximum number of threads that have been in the pool of the executor at the same time.
- `getMaximumPoolSize()`: This method returns the maximum number of threads that can exist in the pool at the same time.
- `getPoolSize()`: This method returns the current number of threads in the pool.
- `getTaskCount()`: This method returns the number of tasks that have been sent to the executor including waiting, running, and already completed tasks.
- `isTerminated()`: This method returns `true` if the `shutdown()` or `shutdownNow()` method has been called and the `Executor` has finished the execution of all its pending tasks. This method returns `false` otherwise.
- `isTerminating()`: This method returns `true` if the `shutdown()` or `shutdownNow()` method has been called but the executor is still executing tasks.

You can use a fragment of code similar to this to obtain the relevant information of a `ThreadPoolExecutor`:

```
System.out.println
    ("*********************************************");
System.out.println("Active Count:
    "+executor.getActiveCount());
System.out.println("Completed Task Count:
    "+executor.getCompletedTaskCount());
System.out.println("Core Pool Size:
    "+executor.getCorePoolSize());
System.out.println("Largest Pool Size:
    "+executor.getLargestPoolSize());
System.out.println("Maximum Pool Size:
    "+executor.getMaximumPoolSize());
System.out.println("Pool Size: "+executor.getPoolSize());
System.out.println("Task Count: "+executor.getTaskCount());
System.out.println("Terminated: "+executor.isTerminated());
System.out.println("Is Terminating:
    "+executor.isTerminating());
System.out.println
    ("*********************************************");
```

With this block of code, you will obtain an output similar to this:

```
**************************************************
Active Count: 9
Completed Task Count: 1
Core Pool Size: 0
Largest Pool Size: 10
Maximum Pool Size: 2147483647
Pool Size: 10
Task Count: 10
Terminated: false
Is Terminating: false
**************************************************
**************************************************
Active Count: 7
Completed Task Count: 3
Core Pool Size: 0
Largest Pool Size: 10
Maximum Pool Size: 2147483647
Pool Size: 10
Task Count: 10
Terminated: false
Is Terminating: false
**************************************************
```

Monitoring the Fork/Join framework

The **Fork/Join Framework** provides a special kind of executor for algorithms that can be implemented using the divide and conquer technique. It is based in a work-stealing algorithm. You create an initial task that has to process the whole problem. This task creates other subtasks that process smaller parts of the problem and waits for its finalization. Each task compares the size of the sub-problem it has to process with a predefined size. If the size is smaller than the predefined size, it solves the problem directly. Otherwise, it splits the problem in other subtasks and waits for the results returned by them. The work-stealing algorithm takes advantage of the threads that are executing tasks that are waiting for the results of their child tasks to execute other tasks. The `ForkJoinPool` class provides methods that allow you to obtain its status:

- `getParallelism()`: This method returns the desired level of parallelism established for the pool.
- `getPoolSize()`: This method returns the number of threads in the pool.

- `getActiveThreadCount()`: This method returns the number of threads in the pool that are currently executing tasks.
- `getRunningThreadCount()`: This method returns the number of threads that are not waiting for the finalization of their child tasks.
- `getQueuedSubmissionCount()`: This method returns the number of tasks that have been submitted to a pool that haven't started their execution yet.
- `getQueuedTaskCount()`: This method returns the number of tasks in the work-stealing queues of this pool.
- `hasQueuedSubmissions()`: This method returns `true` if there are tasks that have been submitted to the pool that haven't started their execution yet. It returns `false` otherwise.
- `getStealCount()`: This method returns the number of times the Fork/Join pool has executed the work-stealing algorithm.
- `isTerminated()`: This method returns `true` if the Fork/Join pool has finished its execution. It returns `false` otherwise.

You can use a fragment of code like this to obtain the relevant information of a `ForkJoinPool` class:

```
System.out.println("**********************");
System.out.println("Parallelism: "+pool.getParallelism());
System.out.println("Pool Size: "+pool.getPoolSize());
System.out.println("Active Thread Count:
    "+pool.getActiveThreadCount());
System.out.println("Running Thread Count:
    "+pool.getRunningThreadCount());
System.out.println("Queued Submission:
    "+pool.getQueuedSubmissionCount());
System.out.println("Queued Tasks:
    "+pool.getQueuedTaskCount());
System.out.println("Queued Submissions:
    "+pool.hasQueuedSubmissions());
System.out.println("Steal Count: "+pool.getStealCount());
System.out.println("Terminated : "+pool.isTerminated());
System.out.println("**********************");
```

Where `pool` is a `ForkJoinPool` object (for example, `ForkJoinPool.commonPool()`). With this block of code, you will obtain an output similar to this:

```
<terminated> MainFork [Java Application] C:\Program Files\Java\jre1.8.0_65\bin\javaw.exe (2 de dic. de 2
Wed Dec 02 01:16:17 CET 2015-ForkJoinPool-1-worker-0: Working 43 milliseconds
Wed Dec 02 01:16:17 CET 2015-ForkJoinPool-1-worker-0: Working 63 milliseconds
***********************
Parallelism: 2
Pool Size: 2
Active Thread Count: 2
Running Thread Count: 0
Queued Submission: 0
Queued Tasks: 15
Queued Submissions: false
Steal Count: 1
Terminated : false
***********************
Wed Dec 02 01:16:17 CET 2015-ForkJoinPool-1-worker-1: Working 22 milliseconds
Wed Dec 02 01:16:17 CET 2015-ForkJoinPool-1-worker-1: Working 50 milliseconds
Wed Dec 02 01:16:17 CET 2015-ForkJoinPool-1-worker-0: Working 37 milliseconds
```

Monitoring a Phaser

A **Phaser** is a synchronization mechanism that allows you to execute tasks that can be divided into phases. This class also includes some methods to obtain the status of the Phaser:

- `getArrivedParties()`: This method returns the number of registered parties that have finished the current phase.
- `getUnarrivedParties()`: This method returns the number of registered parties that haven't finished the current phase.
- `getPhase()`: This method returns the number of the current phase. The number of the first phase is `0`.
- `getRegisteredParties()`: This method returns the number of registered parties in the Phaser.
- `isTerminated()`: This method returns a `boolean` value to indicate if the Phaser has finished its execution.

You can use a fragment of code like this to obtain the relevant information of a Phaser:

```
System.out.println
    ("*********************************************");
```

```
System.out.println("Arrived Parties:
  "+phaser.getArrivedParties());
System.out.println("Unarrived Parties:
  "+phaser.getUnarrivedParties());
System.out.println("Phase: "+phaser.getPhase());
System.out.println("Registered Parties:
  "+phaser.getRegisteredParties());
System.out.println("Terminated: "+phaser.isTerminated());
System.out.println
  ("*********************************************");
```

With this block of code, you will obtain an output similar to this:

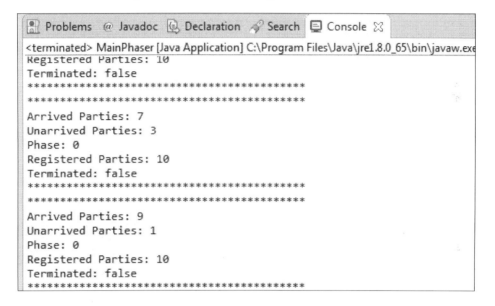

Monitoring a stream

The stream mechanism is one of the most important new features introduced in Java 8. It allows you to process big collections of data in a concurrent way, transforming that data and implementing the map and reduce programming model in an easy way. This class doesn't provide any method (except the `isParallel()` method that returns if the stream is parallel or not) to know the status of the stream, but includes a method named `peek()` that you can include in the pipeline of methods to write log information about the operations or transformations that you are executing in the stream.

For example, this code calculates the average of the square of the first 999 numbers:

```
double result=IntStream.range(0,1000)
    .parallel()
    .peek(n -> System.out.println
        (Thread.currentThread().getName()+": Number "+n))
    .map(n -> n*n)
    .peek(n -> System.out.println
        (Thread.currentThread().getName()+": Transformer "+n))
    .average()
    .getAsDouble();
```

The first `peek()` method writes the numbers the stream is processing and the second one the square of those numbers. If you execute this code, as you're executing the stream in a concurrent way, you will obtain an output similar to this:

```
<terminated> MainStream [Java Application] C:\Program Files\Java\jre1.8.0_65\bin\javaw.exe
ForkJoinPool.commonPool-worker-1: Transformer 992016
ForkJoinPool.commonPool-worker-1: Number 997
ForkJoinPool.commonPool-worker-1: Transformer 994009
ForkJoinPool.commonPool-worker-1: Number 998
ForkJoinPool.commonPool-worker-1: Transformer 996004
ForkJoinPool.commonPool-worker-1: Number 999
ForkJoinPool.commonPool-worker-1: Transformer 998001
main: Number 505
main: Transformer 255025
main: Number 506
main: Transformer 256036
main: Number 507
main: Transformer 257049
```

Monitoring concurrency applications

When you implement Java applications, you normally use an IDE such as Eclipse or NetBeans to create your projects and write your source code. But the **JDK** (short for **Java Development Kit**) includes tools you can use to compile, execute, or generate Javadoc documents. One of those tools is **Java VisualVM**, which is a graphical tool that shows you information about the applications that are executing in a JVM. You can find it in the bin directory of your JDK installation (`jvisualvm.exe`). You can also install a plugin for Eclipse (Eclipse launcher for VisualVM) to integrate its functionality on Eclipse.

If you execute it, you will see a window similar to this:

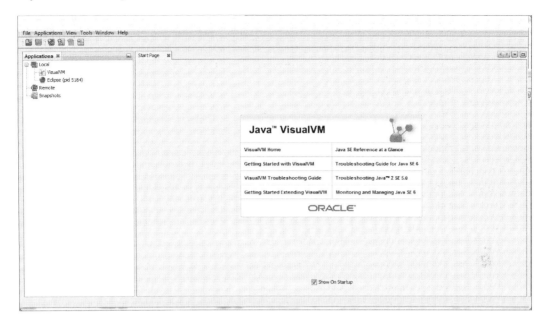

In the left side of the screen, you can see the **Applications** tab where you will see all the Java applications that are currently running by the current user in your system. If you make a double-click in one of those applications, you will see five tabs:

- **Overview**: This tab shows general information about the application.
- **Monitor**: This tab show graphical information about the CPU, memory, classes, and threads used by the application.
- **Threads**: This tab shows the evolution over time of the threads of the application.
- **Sampler**: This tab shows you information about the utilization of memory and CPU by the application. It's similar to the **Profiler** tab, but it obtains the data in a different way.
- **Profiler**: This tab shows you information about the utilization of memory and CPU by the application. It's similar to the **Sampler** tab, but it obtains the data in a different way.

In the next sections, you will learn what information you can obtain in every tab. You can consult the complete documentation about this tool at https://visualvm.java.net/docindex.html.

The Overview tab

As we mentioned before, this tab shows you general information about the application. This information includes:

- **PID**: The process ID of the application.
- **Host**: The name of the machine that is executing the application.
- **Main class**: The full name of the class that implements the `main()` method you're executing.
- **Arguments**: The list of arguments you pass to the application.
- **JVM**: The version of the JVM that is executing the application.
- **Java**: The version of Java you're running.
- **Java Home**: The location of the JDK in the system.
- **JVM Flags**: Flags used with the JVM.
- **JVM Arguments**: This tab shows you the arguments we (or the IDE) passed to the JVM to execute the application.
- **System properties**: This tab shows you the properties and the values of the properties of the system. You can get this information using the `System.getProperties()` method.

It's the default tab when you access the data of an application and has an appearance similar to the following screenshot:

The Monitor tab

As we mentioned earlier, this tab shows you graphical information about the CPU, memory, classes, and threads used by the application. You can see the evolution of these metrics over time. The appearance of this tab is similar to this:

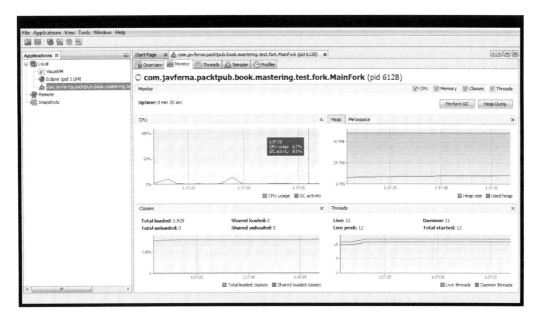

In the upper-right corner, you have some checkboxes to select the information you want to see. The **CPU** graphic shows you the percentage of CPU used by the application. The **Heap** graphic shows you the total size of the heap and the size of that heap used by the application. In this part, you can see the same information about the **Metaspace** (the memory zone used by the JVM to store the classes). The **Classes** graphic shows you the number of classes used by the application and the **Threads** graphic shows you the number of threads that are running inside the application. You can also use two buttons in this tab:

- **Perform GC**: It performs a garbage collection in the application immediately
- **Heap Dump**: It allows you to save the current status of the application to check it later

When you create a heap dump, you will have a new tab with its information. Its appearance is similar to this:

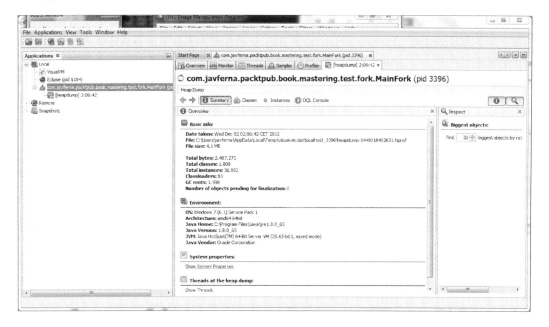

You have different sub-tabs to consult the status of the application in the moment you did the heap dump.

The Threads tab

As we mentioned earlier, in the **Threads** tab, you can see the evolution of the threads of the application over time. It shows you the following information:

- **Live threads**: Number of threads in the application.
- **Daemon threads**: Number of threads marked as daemon threads in the application.
- **Timeline**: The evolution of threads over time including the status of the threads (using a color code), the time the thread has been running, and the time the thread has existed. On the right of the column `Total`, you can see an arrow. If you click it, you can select the columns you see in this tab.

Its appearance is similar to this:

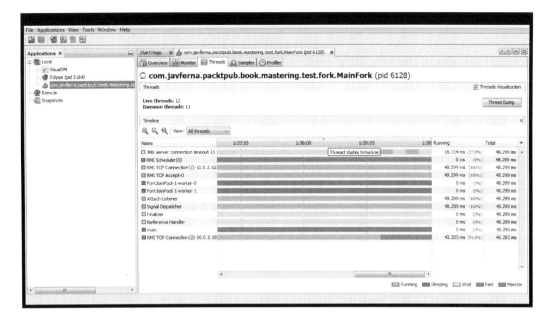

This tab also has the **Thread Dump** button. If you click this button, you will see a new tab with the stack trace of every thread running in the application. Its appearance is similar to this:

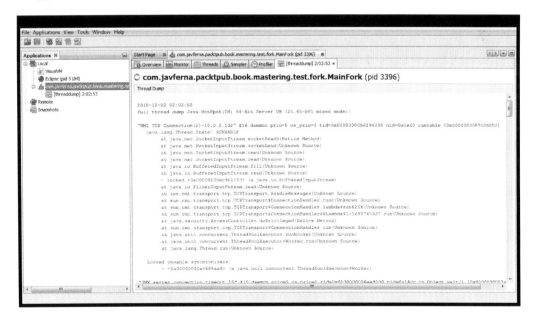

The Sampler tab

The **Sampler** tab shows you information about the utilization of CPU and memory made by your application. To obtain this information, it obtains dumps of all the threads of the application and processes that dump. This tab is similar to the **Profiler** tab but, as you will see in the next section, the difference between them is the way they are used to obtain the information.

This tab's appearance is similar to this:

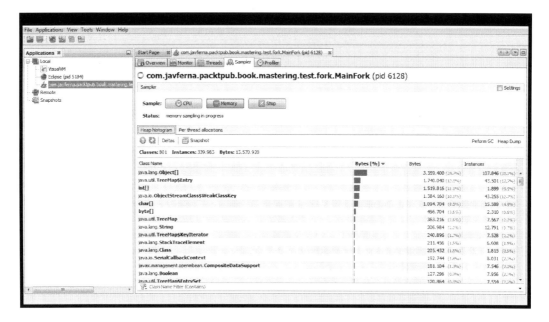

You have two buttons:

- **CPU**: This button is used to obtain information about the use of CPU. If you click this button, you will see two sub-tabs:
    - **CPU samples**: In this tab, you will see the utilization of CPU of the classes of the application
    - **Thread CPU time**: In this tab, you will see the utilization of CPU per thread

- **Memory**: This button is used to obtain information about the use of memory. If you click this button, you will see another two sub-tabs:
    - **Heap histogram**: In this tab, you will see the number of bytes allocated by data type
    - **Per thread allocations**: In this tab, you can see the amount of memory used per every thread

The Profiler tab

The **Profiler** tab shows you information about the CPU and memory utilization by the application using the instrumentation API. Basically, this API adds some bytecodes to the methods when the JVM loads them to obtain this information. This information is updated over time.

This tab's appearance is similar to this:

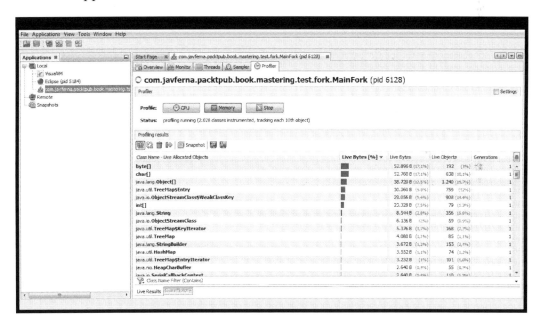

By default, this tab doesn't obtain any information. You have to start a profiling session. To make this, you can use the **CPU** button to obtain information about the CPU utilization. This includes the execution time per method and the number of invocations to those methods. You can also use the **Memory** button. In this case, you can see the amount of memory and the number of objects per data type.

You can stop the profiling session when you don't need to obtain more information using the **Stop** button.

Testing concurrency applications

Testing concurrency applications is a hard task. The threads of your application run in your computer without any guarantee of their execution order (except the synchronization mechanisms that you have included) so it's very difficult (impossible most of the time) to test all the circumstances that can occur. You can have errors impossible to reproduce because it only happens under rare or unique circumstances or errors that happen in one machine but not in others due to the number of cores within the CPU. To detect and reproduce this situation, you can use different tools:

- **Debug**: You can use the debugger to debug the application. This process will be very tedious if you have only a few threads in the application and you have to go step by step in every thread. You can configure Eclipse or NetBeans to test concurrent applications.
- **MultithreadedTC**: This is an archived project of **Google Code** that can be used to force the order of execution in a concurrent application.
- **Java PathFinder**: This is an execution environment used by NASA for verification of Java programs. It includes support for validating concurrent applications.
- **Unit testing**: You can create a bunch of unit-tests (using JUnit or TestNG) and launch every test, for example, 1,000 times. If every test succeeds then even if your application has races, their chance is not very high and probably acceptable for production. You can include assertions in your code to verify that it hasn't any race condition.

In the following sections, you will see basic examples of testing concurrent applications with the MultithreadedTC and Java PathFinder tools.

Testing concurrent applications with MultithreadedTC

MultithreadedTC is an archived project that you can download from http://code.google.com/p/multithreadedtc/. Its latest version is from 2007, but you can still use it to test small concurrent applications or parts of big applications independently. You can't use it to test real tasks or threads but you can use it to test different orders of execution to check if they provoke race conditions or deadlocks.

It's based in an internal clock that works with ticks that allows you to control the order of execution of different threads to test if that order of execution can cause any concurrency problems.

First of all, you need to associate two libraries to your project:

- **The MultithreadedTC library**: The latest version is the 1.01 version
- **The JUnit library**: We have tested this example with the 4.12 version

To implement a test using the MultithreadedTC library, you have to extend the `MultithreadedTestCase` class that extends the `Assert` class of the JUnit library. You can implement the following methods:

- `initialize()`: This method will be executed at the beginning of the test execution. You can override it if you need to execute initialization code for the creation of data objects, database connections, and so on.
- `finish()`: This method will be executed at the end of the test execution. You can override it to implement the validations of the test.
- `threadXXX()`: You have to implement a method whose name begins with the `thread` keyword per every thread you have in your test. For example, if you want to make a test with three threads, you will have three methods in your class.

The `MultithreadedTestCase` provides the `waitForTick()` method. This method receives as a parameter the number of ticks you wait for. This method sleeps the calling thread until the internal clock arrives at that tick.

The first tick is the tick number 0. The MultithreadedTC framework checks every certain time the status of the test threads. If all the running threads are waiting in the `waitForTick()` method, it increments the tick number and wakes up all the threads that are waiting for that tick.

Let's see an example of its use. Suppose you want to test a `Data` object with an internal `int` attribute. You want a thread that increments the value and a thread that decrements the value. You can create a class named `TestClassOk` extending the `MultithreadedTestCase` class. We use three attributes with the data object: the amount we will use to increment and decrement the data and the initial value of the data:

```
public class TestClassOk extends MultithreadedTestCase {

    private Data data;
    private int amount;
```

```
            private int initialData;

            public TestClassOk (Data data, int amount) {
                this.amount=amount;
                this.data=data;
                this.initialData=data.getData();
            }
```

We implement two methods to simulate the execution of two threads. The first thread is implemented in the `threadAdd()` method:

```
            public void threadAdd() {
                System.out.println("Add: Getting the data");
                int value=data.getData();
                System.out.println("Add: Increment the data");
                value+=amount;
                System.out.println("Add: Set the data");
                data.setData(value);
            }
```

It reads the value of the data, increments its value, and writes again the value of the data. The second thread is implemented in the `threadSub()` method:

```
            public void threadSub() {
                waitForTick(1);
                System.out.println("Sub: Getting the data");
                int value=data.getData();
                System.out.println("Sub: Decrement the data");
                value-=amount;
                System.out.println("Sub: Set the data");
                data.setData(value);
            }
        }
```

First, we wait for the tick 1. Then, we get the value of the data, decrement its value, and rewrite the value of the data.

To execute the test, we can use the `runOnce()` method of the `TestFramework` class:

```
            public class MainOk {

                public static void main(String[] args) {

                    Data data=new Data();
                    data.setData(10);
```

```
        TestClassOk ok=new TestClassOk(data,10);

        try {
            TestFramework.runOnce(ok);
        } catch (Throwable e) {
            e.printStackTrace();
        }

    }
}
```

When the execution of the test begins, the two threads (`threadAdd()` and `threadSub()`) are launched in a concurrent way. `threadAdd()` begins the execution of its code and `threadSub()` waits in the `waitForTick()` method. When `threadAdd()` finishes its execution, the internal clock of the MultithreadedTC detects that the only thread running is waiting in the `waitForTick()` method, so it increments the tick value to 1 and wakes up the thread that executes its code.

In the following screenshot, you can see the output of the execution of this example. In this case, everything goes well.

```
<terminated> MainOk [Java Application] C:\Program Files\Java\jre1.8.0_65\bin\javaw.exe (3
Add: Getting the data
Add: Increment the data
Add: Set the data
Sub: Getting the data
Sub: Decrement the data
Sub: Set the data
```

But you can change the order of execution of the threads to provoke an error. For example, you can implement the following order that will provoke a race condition:

```
    public void threadAdd() {
        System.out.println("Add: Getting the data");
        int value=data.getData();
        waitForTick(2);
        System.out.println("Add: Increment the data");
        value+=amount;
        System.out.println("Add: Set the data");
        data.setData(value);
    }
```

```
public void threadSub() {
    waitForTick(1);
    System.out.println("Sub: Getting the data");
    int value=data.getData();
    waitForTick(3);
    System.out.println("Sub: Decrement the data");
    value-=amount;
    System.out.println("Sub: Set the data");
    data.setData(value);
}
```

In this case, the order of execution makes sure that both threads first read the value of the data and then makes its operation so the final result won't be correct.

In the following screenshot, you can see the result of the execution of this example:

```
<terminated> MainKo [Java Application] C:\Program Files\Java\jre1.8.0_65\bin\javaw.exe (3 de dic. d
Add: Getting the data
Sub: Getting the data
Add: Increment the data
Add: Set the data
Sub: Decrement the data
Sub: Set the data
junit.framework.AssertionFailedError: expected:<10> but was:<0>
        at junit.framework.Assert.fail(Assert.java:57)
        at junit.framework.Assert.failNotEquals(Assert.java:329)
        at junit.framework.Assert.assertEquals(Assert.java:78)
        at junit.framework.Assert.assertEquals(Assert.java:234)
        at junit.framework.Assert.assertEquals(Assert.java:241)
```

In this case, the assertEquals() method throws an exception because the expected and actual values are not equal.

The main limitation of this library is that it is only useful to test basic concurrent code and, as you implement the tests, can't be used to test real Thread code.

Testing concurrent applications with Java Pathfinder

Java Pathfinder or JPF is an open source execution environment from NASA that can be used to verify Java applications. It includes its own virtual machine to execute the Java byte code. Internally, it detects the points of the code where there can be more than one execution path and executes all the possibilities. In concurrent applications, this means that it will execute all the possible execution orders between the threads that run in your application. It also includes tools that allow you to detect race conditions and deadlocks.

The main advantage of this tool is that it allow you to completely test your concurrent application to guarantee that it is free of race conditions and deadlocks. The inconvenient features of this tool are:

- You have to install it from its source code
- If your application is complex, you will have thousands of possible paths of execution and the test will be very long (maybe a lot of hours if the application is complex)

In the following sections, we will show you how to test a concurrent application using Java Pathfinder.

Installing Java Pathfinder

As we mentioned earlier, you have to install JPF from its source code. That code is in a Mercurial repository so the first step is to install Mercurial and, as we will use the Eclipse IDE, the Mercurial plugin for Eclipse.

You can download Mercurial from `https://www.mercurial-scm.org/wiki/Download`. You download the installation program that provides an assistant to install Mercurial in your computer. Maybe you will need to restart your system after the installation of Mercurial.

You can download the Mercurial plugin for Eclipse using `Help > Install new software` from the Eclipse menu and using the URL `http://mercurialeclipse.eclipselabs.org.codespot.com/hg.wiki/update_site/stable` as the URL to look for the software. Follow the same steps as with other plugins.

You can also install a JPF plugin for Eclipse. You can download from `http://babelfish.arc.nasa.gov/trac/jpf/wiki/install/eclipse-plugin`.

Now you can access the Mercurial repository explorer perspective and add the repository of Java Pathfinder. We will use only the core module that is stored in `http://babelfish.arc.nasa.gov/hg/jpf/jpf-core`. You don't need a username or password to access the repository. Once you have created the repository, you can right-click over the repository and select the **Clone repository** option to download the source code in your computer. The option will open a window to select some options, but you can leave the default values and click on the **Next** button. Then you have to choose the version you want to load. Leave the default value and click on the **Next** button. Finally, click on the **Finish** button to finish the download process. Eclipse will automatically run `ant` to compile the project. If you have any compilation problems, you have to solve them and relaunch `ant`.

If everything went well, you will have a project named `jpf-core` in your workspace as in the following screenshot:

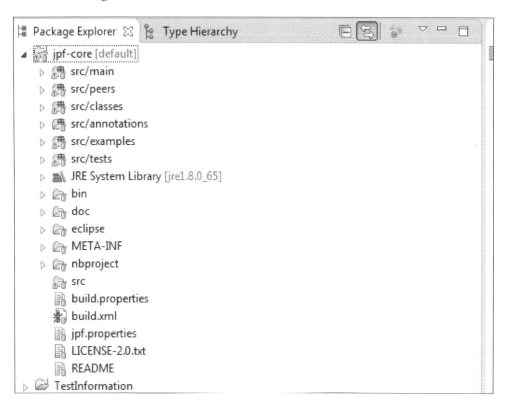

The last configuration step is to create a file named `site.properties` with the configuration of JPF. If you access the configuration window in **Window | Preferences** and select the **JPF Preferences** option, you will see the route where the JPF plugin is looking for that file. You can change that route if you want.

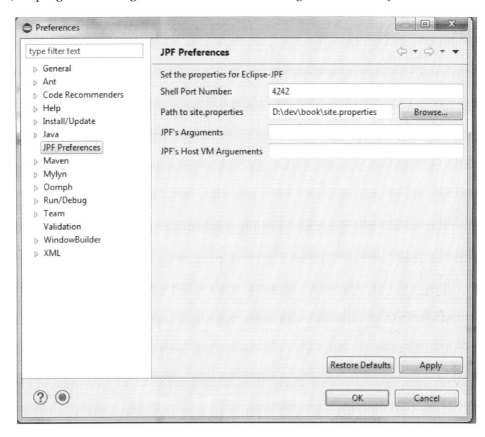

As we will only use the core module, the file will only content the route to the `jpf-core` project:

```
jpf-core = D:/dev/book/projectos/jpf-core
```

Running Java Pathfinder

Once we have installed JPF, let's see how we can use it to test a concurrent application. First, we have to implement a concurrent application. In our case, we will use a `Data` class with an internal `int` value. It will be initialized with 0 and will have an `increment()` method to increment the value.

Then, we will have a task named `NumberTask` that implements the `Runnable` interface that will increment 10 times the value of a `Data` object.

```java
public class NumberTask implements Runnable {

    private Data data;

    public NumberTask (Data data) {
        this.data=data;
    }

    @Override
    public void run() {

        for (int i=0; i<10; i++) {
            data.increment(10);
        }
    }

}
```

Finally, we have the `MainNumber` class that implements the `main()` method. We will launch two `NumberTasks` objects that will modify the same `Data` object. Finally, we will obtain the final value of the `Data` object.

```java
public class MainNumber {

    public static void main(String[] args) {
        int numTasks=2;
        Data data=new Data();

        Thread threads[]=new Thread[numTasks];
        for (int i=0; i<numTasks; i++) {
            threads[i]=new Thread(new NumberTask(data));
            threads[i].start();
        }

        for (int i=0; i<numTasks; i++) {
            try {
                threads[i].join();
            } catch (InterruptedException e) {
```

```
                e.printStackTrace();
            }
        }

        System.out.println(data.getValue());
    }

}
```

If everything goes well and no race conditions occur, the final result will be 200, but our code doesn't use any synchronization mechanism so it's possible that this circumstance occurs.

If we want to execute this application with JPF, we need to create a configuration file inside the project with the `.jpf` extension. For example, we have created the `NumberJPF.jpf` file with the most basic configuration file we can use:

```
+classpath=${config_path}/bin
target=com.javferna.packtpub.mastering.testing.main.MainNumber
```

We modify the class path of JPF adding the `bin` directory of our project and indicate the main class of our application. Now, we're ready to execute the application through JPF. To make this, we right-click over the `.jpf` file and select the **Verify** option. We will see how in the console we can see a lot of output messages. Every output message comes from a different execution path of the application.

```
Problems  Javadoc  Declaration  Search  Console
NumberJPF.jpf(run)
Executing command: java -jar D:\dev\book\proyectos\jpf-core\build\RunJPF.jar +site=D:\dev\book\site.prope
JavaPathfinder core system v8.0 (rev 29) - (C) 2005-2014 United States Government. All rights reserved.


====================================================== system under test
com.javferna.packtpub.mastering.testing.main.MainNumber.main()

====================================================== search started: 3/12/15 2:26
200
200
190
190
180
180
```

When JPF ends the execution of all the possible execution paths, it shows statistical information about the execution:

```
70
60
50
40
30
20

===================================================== results
no errors detected

===================================================== statistics
elapsed time:       00:00:16
states:             new=72199,visited=101549,backtracked=173748,end=57
search:             maxDepth=67,constraints=0
choice generators:  thread=72199 (signal=0,lock=2,sharedRef=65612,threadApi=1504,reschedule=5081), data=0
heap:               new=632,released=1301,maxLive=370,gcCycles=173619
instructions:       1721841
max memory:         353MB
loaded code:        classes=64,methods=1476

===================================================== search finished: 3/12/15 2:27
```

The JPF execution says that no errors were detected but we can see that most of the results are different from 200, so our application has race conditions as we expected.

In the introduction of this section, we said that JPF provides tools to detect race conditions and deadlocks. JPF implements this as a `Listener` mechanism that implements the `Observer` pattern to respond to certain events that occur in the execution of the code. For example, we can use the following listeners:

- `PreciseRaceDetector`: Use this listener to detect race conditions
- `DeadlockAnalyzer`: Use this listener to detect deadlock situations
- `CoverageAnalyzer`: Use this listener to write coverage information at the end of the execution of JPF

You can configure the listeners you want to use in the `.jpf` file with the configuration of an execution. For example, we have extended the previous test in the `NumberListenerJPF.jpf` file by adding the `PreciseRaceDetector` and the `CoverageAnalyzer` listeners:

```
+classpath=${config_path}/bin
target=com.javferna.packtpub.mastering.testing.main.MainNumber
listener=gov.nasa.jpf.listener.PreciseRaceDetector,gov.nasa.jpf.li
   stener.CoverageAnalyzer
```

If we execute this configuration file through JPF with the **Verify** option, you will see as the application ends when it detects the first race condition showing in the console information about this circumstance:

```
====================================================== system under test
com.javferna.packtpub.mastering.testing.main.MainNumber.main()

====================================================== search started: 3/12/15 2:43
200
200

====================================================== error 1
gov.nasa.jpf.listener.PreciseRaceDetector
race for field com.javferna.packtpub.mastering.testing.common.Data@15e.value
   Thread-1 at com.javferna.packtpub.mastering.testing.common.Data.increment(Data.java:12)
 "  WRITE: putfield com.javferna.packtpub.mastering.testing.common.Data.value
   Thread-2 at com.javferna.packtpub.mastering.testing.common.Data.increment(Data.java:12)
 "  READ:  getfield com.javferna.packtpub.mastering.testing.common.Data.value


====================================================== snapshot #1
thread java.lang.Thread:{id:0,name:main,status:WAITING,priority:5,isDaemon:false,lockCount:0,suspendCount:0}
   waiting on: java.lang.Thread@160
   call stack:
         at java.lang.Thread.join(Thread.java)
         at com.javferna.packtpub.mastering.testing.main.MainNumber.main(MainNumber.java:20)

thread java.lang.Thread:{id:1,name:Thread-1,status:RUNNING,priority:5,isDaemon:false,lockCount:0,suspendCount:0}
   call stack:
         at com.javferna.packtpub.mastering.testing.common.Data.increment(Data.java:13)
         at com.javferna.packtpub.mastering.testing.task.NumberTask.run(NumberTask.java:17)

thread java.lang.Thread:{id:2,name:Thread-2,status:RUNNING,priority:5,isDaemon:false,lockCount:0,suspendCount:0}
   call stack:
         at com.javferna.packtpub.mastering.testing.common.Data.increment(Data.java:12)
         at com.javferna.packtpub.mastering.testing.task.NumberTask.run(NumberTask.java:17)
```

You will also see how the `CoverageAnalyzer` listener also writes the information:

```
==================================================== coverage statistics
------------------------------------ class coverage ------------------------------------
bytecode       line           basic-block    branch         methods        location
-              -              -              -              -              [B
-              -              -              -              -              [C
-              -              -              -              -              [D
-              -              -              -              -              [F
-              -              -              -              -              [I
-              -              -              -              -              [J
-              -              -              -              -              [Ljava.io.ObjectStreamField;
-              -              -              -              -              [Ljava.lang.String;
-              -              -              -              -              [Ljava.lang.Thread$State;
-              -              -              -              -              [Ljava.lang.Thread;
-              -              -              -              -              [Ljava.util.Hashtable$Entry;
-              -              -              -              -              [S
-              -              -              -              -              [Z
-              -              -              -              -              boolean
-              -              -              -              -              byte
0,80 (16/20)   0,75 (6/8)     0,80 (4/5)     -              0,75 (3/4)     char
0,89 (47/53)   0,77 (10/13)   0,83 (15/18)   1,00 (2/2)     0,50 (1/2)     com.javferna.packtpub.mastering.testing.common.Data
1,00 (18/18)   1,00 (6/6)     1,00 (7/7)     1,00 (1/1)     1,00 (2/2)     com.javferna.packtpub.mastering.testing.main.MainNumber
-              -              -              -              -              com.javferna.packtpub.mastering.testing.task.NumberTask
-              -              -              -              -              double
-              -              -              -              -              float
0,00 (0/3)     0,00 (0/1)     0,00 (0/2)     -              0,00 (0/1)     gov.nasa.jpf.BoxObjectCaches
0,00 (0/31)    0,00 (0/11)    0,00 (0/17)    0,00 (0/2)     0,00 (0/6)     gov.nasa.jpf.ConsoleOutputStream
0,00 (0/36)    0,00 (0/13)    0,00 (0/19)    0,00 (0/3)     0,00 (0/5)     gov.nasa.jpf.FinalizerThread
```

JPF is a very powerful application that includes more listeners and more extension mechanisms. You can find its whole documentation at `http://babelfish.arc.nasa.gov/trac/jpf/wiki`.

Summary

Testing concurrent applications is a very hard task. There's no guarantee of the order of execution of the threads (unless the synchronization mechanisms have been introduced in your application) so you should test many more different situations than in a serial application. Sometimes, you will have errors in your application that you can reproduce because they only occur in very rare situations, and sometimes you will have errors that only occur in specific machines because of their hardware or software configurations.

In this chapter, you have learned some mechanisms that can help you to test concurrency applications more easily. First, you have learned how to obtain information about the status of the most important components of the Java concurrency API as `Thread`, `Lock`, `Executor` or `Stream`. This information can be very useful if you need to detect the cause of an error. Then, you learned how to use Java VisualVM to monitor Java applications in general and concurrent applications in particular. Finally, you learned to use two different tools to test concurrent applications.

Through the chapters of this book, you have learned how to use the most important components of the Java concurrency API as the executor framework, the `Phaser` class, the Fork/Join framework, and the new stream API included in Java 8 to support functional-style operations on streams of elements implementing real-world applications from the machine learning, data mining, or natural language processing world. You have also learned how to work with concurrency data structures and synchronization mechanisms and how to synchronize different concurrent blocks that are part of a bigger application. Finally, you learned the design principles of concurrent applications and how to test them, two critical factors to guarantee success using these kinds of applications.

Implementing concurrent applications is a difficult task but also an exciting challenge. I hope this book has been helpful for you to meet this challenge successfully.

Index

A

advanced search
  about 280, 281
  ConcurrentObjectAccumulator class 282
alternatives
  implementing, with concurrent programming 354
  k-nearest neighbors' algorithm 354
Amazon product co-purchasing network metadata
  about 275
  URL 216
Amdahl's law 10
AssignmentTask class
  attributes 196
asynchronous message passing 349
atomic operation 4
atomic variable 4
attributes, NewsBuffer class
  ConcurrentHashMap 90
  LinkedBlockingQueue 90

B

Bank Marketing dataset
  about 34
  URL 34
base classes, social network
  about 293
  DataLoader class 293
  Person class 293
basic classes
  Product class 275
  ProductLoader class 276
  Review class 276
basic concurrency classes
  about 12
  Runnable interface 12
  Thread class 12
  ThreadFactory interface 12
  ThreadLocal class 12
basic concurrency concepts
  about 1
  atomic operation 4
  atomic variable 4
  concurrency, versus parallelism 2
  immutable object 3
  message passing 4
  shared memory 4
  synchronization 2, 3
basic search
  ConcurrentStringAccumulator class 279
  defining 277, 278
best-matching algorithm
  about 105
  and word exists algorithm, comparing 120, 121
  common classes 106
  concurrent version 117
  first concurrent version 109
  for words 355
  serial version 107
  solutions, comparing 120
  Word exists algorithm 115
blocking data structure 59
blocking operations
  methods, implementing 63

C

cache system
  CacheItem class 55
  CleanCacheTask class 56
  ParallelCache class 56
Callable interface
  defining 104
Census-Income KDD dataset
  about 203
  references 203
  URL 203
char sequence 105
chromosomes 162
client part
  about 88, 89
  ConcurrentClient class 88
  MultipleConcurrentClient class 88
client/server environment
  interest methods 63, 64
client/server model 44
clustering algorithm 124
Clustering system
  elements, defining 348
coarse-grained granularity 3
Coffman's conditions
  circular waiting 5
  hold and wait condition 5
  mutual exclusion 5
  no pre-emption 5
collect() method
  about 272-274
  arguments 273
  parameters 272, 278
Collectors factory class
  methods 273, 274
command classes
  about 77
  concrete commands 79, 80
  ConcurrentCommand class 77-79
common classes, genetic algorithm
  about 164
  GeneticOperators class 165, 166
  Individual class 164, 165
common classes, inverted index
  Document class 124
  DocumentParser class 124, 125

common classes, keyword extraction algorithm
  about 146
  Document class 148
  DocumentParser class 149
  Keyword class 147
  Word class 146, 147
common classes, k-means clustering algorithm
  about 187
  DistanceMeasurer class 190
  Document class 188-190
  DocumentCluster class 191, 192
  DocumentLoader class 188-190
  VocabularyLoader class 188
  Word class 188-190
common classes, recommendation system
  about 284
  ProductRecommendation class 285
  ProductReview class 285
compare-and-swap (CAS) 3
CompletableFuture class
  main() method 339
components, concurrency API
  about 354
  defining 355-357
  Fork/Join framework 354, 355
  streams 354, 355
  thread 355
  threads 354
components, concurrent server
  cache system 55-58
  defining 53
  log system 59-61
  status command 54, 55
  two solutions, comparing 61, 62
components, document clustering application
  Clustering system 343
  Indexer system 343
  Mapper system 343
  Reader system 342
components, k-nearest neighbors algorithm
  distance metric 33
  test dataset 33
  train dataset 33

components, log system
  Logger 59
  LogTask 59
concurrency
  about 1
  versus parallelism 2
concurrency applications
  monitoring 372, 373
  Monitor tab 375, 376
  Overview tab 374
  Profiler tab 379
  Sampler tab 378, 379
  testing 380
  testing, with Java Pathfinder 385
  testing, with MultithreadedTC 380-384
  Threads tab 376, 377
concurrency design patterns
  about 15
  barrier pattern 18
  double-checked locking 18
  Multiplex design pattern 17
  mutex 17
  read-write lock 19
  rendezvous 16
  signaling 16
  thread local storage 20
  thread pool 20
concurrency objects
  executor, monitoring 366, 367
  Fork/Join framework, monitoring 368, 369
  lock, monitoring 364, 365
  monitoring 362
  Phaser, monitoring 370, 371
  stream, monitoring 371, 372
  thread, monitoring 362, 363
concurrent data structures
  about 15, 304
  AtomicBoolean 15
  AtomicInteger 15
  AtomicLong 15
  AtomicReference 15
  blocking data structures 15, 63, 304
  ConcurrentHashMap 15
  ConcurrentLinkedDeque 15
  ConcurrentLinkedQueue 15
  ConcurrentSkipListMap 15
  defining 305

  interfaces 305
  LinkedBlockingDeque 15
  LinkedBlockingQueue 15
  non-blocking data structures 15, 63, 304
  PriorityBlockingQueue 15
concurrent programming 1
ConcurrentStatistics class
  Age data, from subscribers 236, 237
  Campaign data,
    from nonsubscribers 238-240
  duration data, from nonsubscribers 242
  job information, from subscribers 235, 236
  Marital data, from subscribers 237
  multiple data filter 240-242
  people between 25 and 50 242, 243
concurrent version, data filtering algorithm
  about 207
  ConcurrentMain class 214
  ConcurrentSearch class 213
  IndividualTask class 209, 210
  ListTask class 211
  TaskManager class 207, 208
concurrent version, genetic algorithm
  about 169, 170
  ConcurrentGeneticAlgorithm class 175, 176
  ConcurrentGeneticTask class 172-174
  ConcurrentMain class 176
  GeneticPhaser class 171, 172
  SharedData class 170
concurrent version,
    keyword extraction algorithm
  about 154
  ConcurrentKeywordExtraction
    class 159-161
  KeywordExtractionTask class 154-157
concurrent version, k-means clustering
    algorithm
  about 195, 196
  AssignmentTask 196-198
  ConcurrentKMeans class 199, 200
  ConcurrentMain class 201
  UpdateTask 196-198
concurrent version, merge sort algorithm
  about 220
  ConcurrentMergeSort class 222
  ConcurrentMetaData class 223
  MergeSortTask class 220, 221

concurrent version, numerical
    summarization application
  about 234
  ConcurrentDataLoader class 234, 235
  ConcurrentMain class 243-245
  ConcurrentStatistics class 235
concurrent version, social network
  CommonPersonMapper class 294
  ConcurrentMain class 299
  ConcurrentSocialNetwork class 295-298
concurrent version, word exists algorithm
  about 117
  ExistBasicConcurrentCalculation
      class 119, 120
  ExistBasicConcurrentMain class 120
  ExistBasicTasks class 117, 118
control synchronization 2
critical section 2

D

DAO (Data Access Object) 45
data
  collecting, streams used 271, 272
  searching, without index 274
data access synchronization 2
data decomposition 8
data filtering algorithm
  about 203
  common parts 203
  concurrent version 207
  serial version 204
  two versions, comparing 214, 215
data search, without index
  advanced search 280, 281
  basic classes 275
  basic search 277, 278
  implementations, comparing 283, 284
  serial implementation, of example 283
data structures 303
design concurrent algorithms
  tips and tricks 21
design pattern 15
DF (document frequency) 145
document clustering application
  example 342, 343

main class 349-352
testing 352-354

E

Euclidean distance 34, 186
executor framework
  about 12, 13, 31
  Callable interface 13
  components 33
  Executor interface 13, 33
  Executors 13
  Executors class 33
  ExecutorService interface 13, 33
  Future interface 13
  ScheduledThreadPoolExecutor 13
  ThreadPoolExecutor class 13, 33
executors
  characteristics 32, 67, 68
  defining 31, 32, 67, 100
  executor methods, overriding 69
  initialization parameters, changing 69
  task execution, scheduling 68
  tasks, cancelling 68
Executors class
  methods 63

F

Facebook dataset
  URL 292
Factory pattern 15
filtering data algorithm 358
fine-grained granularity 3
finish criteria 163
first concurrent version,
    best-matching algorithm
  about 109
  BestMatchingBasicConcurrentCalculation
      class 111-113
  BestMatchingBasicTask class 110, 111
First-In-First-Out (FIFO) 305
fitness function 162
Fork/Join framework
  about 14
  characteristics 183

components 184
defining 182
examples 182
ForkJoinPool 14
ForkJoinTask 14
ForkJoinWorkerThread 14
limitations 184
methods 224
full document query
about 249, 250
basicMapper() method 250, 251
QueryResult class 252
Token class 251
Future interface
defining 104

G

generation 162
genetic algorithm
about 162-164, 356
common classes 164
conclusions 178
concurrent version 169, 170
serial version 166
two solutions, comparing 177
GeneticOperators class
methods 165, 166
granularity 3
Gustafson-Barsis' law 10

H

handouts
URL 356
HTML file
ContentMapper class 256
generating, with results 254, 255

I

IDF (inverse document frequency) 145
immutable object 3
information retrieval search tool
about 246, 247
average tfxidf value, obtaining in file 261
ConcurrentData class 260

ConcurrentMain class 263, 264
full document query 249, 250
HTML file, generating with results 254, 255
inverted index, preloading 257
maximum and minimum tfxidf values,
    obtaining in file 262, 263
number of words, obtaining in file 260
own executor, using 259
reduced document query 253
reduction operation 247, 248
serial version 264
solutions, comparing 265-268
URL 246
interfaces, concurrent data structures
about 305
BlockingDeque 306
BlockingQueue 305, 306
inverted index
about 123, 246
building, of collection of documents 355
common classes 124
ConcurrentFileLoader class 258
creating, for document collection 123
methods of interest 137
multiple documents per task 133
preloading 257, 258
searching 358
serial version 125, 126
solutions, comparing 136
task per document 127
InvertedIndexTask class
internal attributes 129

J

Java collections framework (JCF) 305
Java concurrency API
about 12
basic concurrency classes 12
executor framework 13
Fork/Join framework 14
synchronization mechanisms 12, 13
Java memory model 20
Java Pathfinder
concurrent applications, testing with 385
installing 385-387
running 387-391

Java Virtual Machine (JVM) 21, 159
JMH framework
 URL 42
JPF
 about 391
 URL 391
JPF plugin, for Eclipse
 references 386
 URL 386

K

keyword extraction algorithm
 about 144-146, 357
 common classes 146
 concurrent version 154
 serial version 150-153
 two solutions, comparing 161
KeywordExtractionTask class
 attributes 154
k-means clustering algorithm
 about 185, 186, 357
 common classes 187
 concurrent version 195
 limitations 186
 serial version 192
 solutions, comparing 201, 203
k-nearest neighbors algorithm
 coarse-grained concurrent version 40, 41
 defining 33, 34
 fine-grained concurrent version 36-40
 serial version 34-36
 solutions, comparing 42, 43

L

lambda expressions 227
Levenshtein distance
 about 105
 URL 105
LINQ (Language-Integrated Query) 228

M

machine-learning algorithm 32
mechanisms, for avoiding deadlocks
 avoidance 6
 detection 6
 ignore 6
 prevention 6
Mercurial
 references 385
merge sort algorithm
 about 215, 216
 concurrent version 220
 serial version 216
 shared classes 216
 two versions, comparing 223
message passing 4
message passing techniques
 asynchronous 342
 synchronous 342
methodology, design concurrent algorithms
 about 7
 analysis 8
 conclusion 11
 design 8
 implementation 9
 starting point 7
 testing 9
 tuning 9
methods
 used, for registering participant 142
 used, for synchronizing phase change 143
methods, ForkJoinTask class
 fork() method 183
 join() method 183
multiple documents per task,
   second concurrent version
 MultipleConcurrentIndexing class 135
 MultipleIndexingTask class 133
 MultipleInvertedIndexTask class 134
MultithreadedTC
 concurrent applications,
   testing with 380-384
mutual exclusion 2

N

non-blocking data structure 59
non-blocking operations
 methods, implementing 64
numerical summarization application
 about 233
 concurrent version 234

serial version 245
two versions, comparing 245
numeric summarization algorithm 359

O

operation
　used, for serial streams 245, 246
optimization and search problems
　about 162
　defining 356

P

parallel streams
　about 14
　Collectors 14
　Lambda expressions 14
　Optional interface 14
　Stream interface 14
parallel version, client/server model
　command part 53
　defining 48
　server part 49-51
periodic tasks
　advanced reader 96-99
　basic reader 92-95
　common parts 90-92
　executing 89, 90
phaser 141
Phaser class
　about 142
　characteristics 142
　methods, defining 144
　other functionalities 143, 144
　participants, deregistration 142, 143
　participants, registering 142, 143
　phase change, synchronizing 143
phases
　defining, for keywords 145
phases, generation
　Crossover 162
　Mutation 162
　Selection 162
phases, recommendation system
　first phase 360
　second phase 360

third phase 360
phenotypes 162
portability 11
problems, in concurrent applications
　about 4
　data race 4
　deadlock 5
　livelock 6
　priority inversion 7
　resource starvation 6, 7
Producer/Consumer design pattern 90

Q

queue 305

R

recommendation system
　about 284, 360
　common classes 284
　ConcurrentLoaderAccumulator class 289
　defining 284
　defining, Map and Collect model used 360
　main class 285-289
　serial version 290
　two versions, comparing 290
reduced document query
　about 253
　limitedMapper() method 253
RSS feed reader 89

S

SAX (Simple API for XML) 90
scalability 11
scheduled executor 97
search algorithm, without indexing
　defining 359
second concurrent version,
　　best-matching algorithm 114
SerialMergeSort class
　references 217
serial version, best-matching algorithm
　about 107
　BestMachingSerialMain class 108, 109
　BestMatchingSerialCalculation
　　class 107, 108

serial version, client/server model
  command part 45, 46
  DAO part 45
  defining 45
  server part 47
serial version, data filtering algorithm
  about 204
  SerialMain class 205, 206
  SerialSearch class 204
serial version, genetic algorithm
  about 166
  SerialGeneticAlgorithm class 167, 168
  SerialMain class 168
serial version, k-means clustering algorithm
  about 192
  SerialKMeans class 192-194
  SerialMain class 194, 195
serial version, merge sort algorithm
  about 216
  SerialMergeSort class 217
  SerialMetaData class 219
serial version, social network
  about 300
  two versions, comparing 300
serial version, word exists algorithm
  defining 115
  ExistSerialCalculation class 116
  ExistSerialMain class 116
server application
  client part 88
  command classes 77
  defining 70, 71
  new characteristics, implementing 70
  ServerExecutor class 71
  server part 81
ServerExecutor class
  about 71
  executor 74-76
  executor tasks 73
  rejected task controller 72
  statistics object 71
server part
  about 81
  ConcurrentServer class 81-84
  RequestTask classification 85-88
shared memory 4, 349
short-circuit operation 117

simplicity 11
Singleton pattern 15
SOA (Service-Oriented Architecture) 44
social network
  base classes 293
  common contacts 291, 292
  concurrent version 294
  references 291
  serial version 300
software testing 361
speedup 10
states, phaser
  Active 144
  Termination 144
stream
  about 227, 228, 271
  characteristics 228, 229
  elements 272, 280
  intermediate operations 231
  MapReduce, versus MapCollect 232
  sections, defining 229
  sources 229, 230
  terminal operations 232
  used, for collecting data 271, 272
stream API 227
synchronization
  about 2, 141
  control synchronization 2
  data access synchronization 2
synchronization mechanisms
  about 303
  CountDownLatch class 13
  CyclicBarrier class 13
  defining 342
  Lock interface 12
  message passing 342
  Phaser class 13
  Semaphore class 13
  shared memory 342
  synchronized keyword 12
systems, k-means clustering
  Clustering system 348, 349
  defining 343
  Indexer system 345, 346
  Mapper system 347
  Reader system 343, 344

T

task decomposition 8
task per document, first concurrent version
  ConcurrentIndexing class 130-132
  IndexingTask class 128
  InvertedIndexTask class 129, 130
tasks
  executing 104
term frequency 123
term frequency-inverse document frequency (tf-idf) 187
tips and tricks, design concurrent algorithms
  atomic variables, using instead of synchronization 27, 28
  blocking operations, avoiding in critical section 29
  concurrency, implementing at higher possible level 22
  correct independent tasks, identifying 22
  deadlocks, avoiding by ordering locks 26
  easier parallelizable version of algorithm, finding 25
  execution of tasks 24
  immutable objects, using 25
  local thread variables, preferring over static 24, 25
  locks, holding 28
  precautions, taking with lazy initialization 29
  scalability, taking into account 23
  thread-safe APIs, using 23
Travel Salesman Problem (TSP)
  about 163
  characteristics 163

U

UCI Machine Learning Repository 34, 233
UK Advanced Cryptics Dictionary (UKACD) 105

W

word exists algorithm
  and best-matching algorithm, comparing 122
word list
  URL 105
worker-threads 32
work-stealing algorithm 182
World Bank
  URL 44
World Development Indicators 44

Thank you for buying
Mastering Concurrency Programming with Java 8

About Packt Publishing

Packt, pronounced 'packed', published its first book, *Mastering phpMyAdmin for Effective MySQL Management*, in April 2004, and subsequently continued to specialize in publishing highly focused books on specific technologies and solutions.

Our books and publications share the experiences of your fellow IT professionals in adapting and customizing today's systems, applications, and frameworks. Our solution-based books give you the knowledge and power to customize the software and technologies you're using to get the job done. Packt books are more specific and less general than the IT books you have seen in the past. Our unique business model allows us to bring you more focused information, giving you more of what you need to know, and less of what you don't.

Packt is a modern yet unique publishing company that focuses on producing quality, cutting-edge books for communities of developers, administrators, and newbies alike. For more information, please visit our website at www.packtpub.com.

About Packt Open Source

In 2010, Packt launched two new brands, Packt Open Source and Packt Enterprise, in order to continue its focus on specialization. This book is part of the Packt Open Source brand, home to books published on software built around open source licenses, and offering information to anybody from advanced developers to budding web designers. The Open Source brand also runs Packt's Open Source Royalty Scheme, by which Packt gives a royalty to each open source project about whose software a book is sold.

Writing for Packt

We welcome all inquiries from people who are interested in authoring. Book proposals should be sent to author@packtpub.com. If your book idea is still at an early stage and you would like to discuss it first before writing a formal book proposal, then please contact us; one of our commissioning editors will get in touch with you.

We're not just looking for published authors; if you have strong technical skills but no writing experience, our experienced editors can help you develop a writing career, or simply get some additional reward for your expertise.

Learning Reactive Programming with Java 8

ISBN: 978-1-78528-872-2 Paperback: 182 pages

Learn how to use RxJava and its reactive Observables to build fast, concurrent, and powerful applications through detailed examples

1. Learn about Java 8's lambdas and what reactive programming is all about, and how these aspects are utilized by RxJava.

2. Build fast and concurrent applications with ease, without the complexity of Java's concurrent API and shared states.

3. Explore a wide variety of code examples to easily get used to all the features and tools provided by RxJava.

Java EE 7 First Look

ISBN: 978-1-84969-923-5 Paperback: 188 pages

Discover the new features of Java EE 7 and learn to put them together to build a large-scale application

1. Explore changes brought in by the Java EE 7 platform.

2. Master the new specifications that have been added in Java EE to develop applications without any hassle.

3. Quick guide on the new features introduced in Java EE7.

Please check **www.PacktPub.com** for information on our titles

Java EE 7 Developer Handbook

ISBN: 978-1-84968-794-2   Paperback: 634 pages

Develop professional applications in Java EE 7 with this essential reference guide

1. Learn about local and remote service endpoints, containers, architecture, synchronous and asynchronous invocations, and remote communications in a concise reference.

2. Understand the architecture of the Java EE platform and then apply the new Java EE 7 enhancements to benefit your own business-critical applications.

3. Learn about integration test development on Java EE with Arquillian Framework and the Gradle build system.

Java 7 New Features Cookbook

ISBN: 978-1-84968-562-7   Paperback: 384 pages

Over 100 comprehensive recipes to get you up-to-speed with all the exciting new features of java 7

1. Comprehensive coverage of the new features of Java 7 organized around easy-to-follow recipes.

2. Covers exciting features such as the try-with-resources block, the monitoring of directory events, asynchronous IO and new GUI enhancements, and more.

3. A learn-by-example based approach that focuses on key concepts to provide the foundation to solve real world problems.

Please check www.PacktPub.com for information on our titles

Printed in Great Britain
by Amazon